Derenne/Müller-Rappard/Kaczmarek (eds)

ENFORCEMENT OF EU STATE AID LAW AT NATIONAL LEVEL 2010

Reports from the 27 Member States

Derenne/Müller-Rappard/Kaczmarek (eds)

ENFORCEMENT OF EU STATE AID LAW AT NATIONAL LEVEL 2010

Reports from the 27 Member States

Coordinated by Hogan Lovells, Brussels

THE LEGAL PUBLISHER
lexxion
BERLIN

Jacques Derenne is partner at Hogan Lovells, Brussels and Associate Professor of State aid law at the University of Liège

Alix Müller-Rappard is counsel at Hogan Lovells, Brussels

Cédric Kaczmarek is associate at Hogan Lovells, Brussels

A catalogue record for this book is available from the German National Library, detailed bibliographical data can be found on the internet at http://dnb.d-nb.de.

ISBN-Print: 978-3-869 65-025-8
ISBN-E-Book: 978-3-869 65-026-5

www.lexxion.eu

Cover: Tozman Satz & Grafik, Berlin
Typeset: typossatz GmbH, Berlin

Table of contents

Foreword

So much ground has been covered since the adoption of the first Notice on the cooperation with national courts[1] in 1995. As the present book reveals, the European Union has experienced a surge in State aid cases in national courts, and this trend is not likely to revert, in particular in view of the current public and business interest on State aid matters in the recent years.

The European Commission has been a strong advocate of private State aid litigation throughout this time. Joaquin Almunia, Vice President of the European Commission, recently declared[2] that the increase in State aid cases brought before national courts is "one of the most important recent developments in the field of State aid, and one which I wholeheartedly welcome".

In April 2009, the European Commission adopted a new Notice on the enforcement of State aid law by national courts[3], which had two key aims: to explain the role of national courts in the State aid field as defined by the European Courts, and to offer national courts practical and user-friendly support in individual cases. The Notice is the result of a comprehensive review of the Commission's 1995 notice and takes into account recent legislative developments and case-law.

This has been accompanied by a series of advocacy actions including conferences, publications, and State aid training for national judges. Directorate General for Competition also launched dedicated pages on its website[4] containing relevant information on private enforcement, including a compilation of State aid judgments which are mentioned in this book.

I would like to commend the quality of the work of the 27 national rapporteurs under the direction of Hogan Lovells, who have produced a thorough, clear, and wide picture of private State aid-related litigation in the European Union. This book will therefore provide the reader not only with information about how State aid law is enforced 'at home', but also with useful comparisons and examples from other national jurisdictions.

In my view, it is also particularly significant that each national report includes a section on "trends, reforms and recommendations". While, as the reader will soon discover, it is obvious that some difficulties and important issues remain which may stand in the way of the successful

---

1 Notice on cooperation between national courts and the Commission in the State aid field, OJ (1995) C 312.

2 Http://ec.europa.eu/competition/publications/state_aid/national_courts_booklet_en.pdf.

3 Commission notice on the enforcement of State aid law by national courts, OJ (2009) C 85/1.

4 Http://ec.europa.eu/competition/court/state_aid.html.

protection of competitors against unlawful State aid, our common objective should be to look ahead, together with the legal community, in order to jointly promote the reinforcement of private State aids enforcement at national level in the future.

Barbara Brandtner[5]
Head of Unit, Enforcement and Procedural Reform
Directorate General for Competition
European Commission

5 The views expressed are purely those of the writer and may not in any circumstances be regarded as stating an official position of the European Commission.

Introduction

The present book includes 27 national reports as well as a brief EU report on the application of State aid rules by national courts. It is the result of a longstanding collective research project, conducted in the wider context of general legal work carried out for the European Commission.

In 2005, the European Commission signed a research contract with Lovells (now Hogan Lovells) commissioning a far-reaching study on the application of State aid rules at national level. This study ("2006 study") was completed in March 2006 under the co-directorship of Jacques Derenne (Lovells), Thomas Jestaedt (Jones Day) and Tom Ottervanger (Allen & Overy)[1]. The 2006 study examined (i) the national courts' judgments in 15 Member States (before the 2004 accessions) and (ii) the enforcement of negative Commission decisions by Member State authorities in five sample Member States.

The results of this seminal 2006 study were used extensively by the Commission for the drafting of its Recovery Notice in October 2007[2] and again when preparing its Enforcement Notice in April 2009[3]. These notices provide national courts and third parties with a comprehensive overview of the remedies that are available when a Member State infringes its obligation to notify the Commission of any draft State aid, and of its standstill obligation in this regard.

In December 2008, Lovells (now Hogan Lovells) concluded a new exclusive contract with the European Commission to update the 2006 study and to enlarge it to the 27 Member States (the "2009 update study"). On 19 October 2009, the results of this 2009 update study were presented at a conference in Brussels. Mrs Neelie Kroes, the then EU Commissioner for Competition Policy, was the keynote speaker and discussed the achievements of the 2005 State Action Plan[4] in the field of private enforcement. The purpose of the Commission was more limited than for the 2006 study in that the results of the update survey were used to select sample cases for the new pages of the Directorate General for Competition's website dedicated to private enforcement (application of EU competition law by national courts). Since 2009, a new page gives access to the EU report included in this book as well as to a number of summaries of representative State aid national cases[5]. This completes the section of the Directorate General for Competition's website which was previously limited to antitrust cases.

---

1 Http://ec.europa.eu/competition/state_aid/studies_reports/studies_reports.html#studies.

2 Notice from the Commission – Towards an effective implementation of Commission decisions ordering Member States to recover unlawful and incompatible State aid, OJ (2007) C 272/4.

3 Commission notice on the enforcement of State aid law by national courts, OJ (2009) C 85/1.

4 State aid action plan – Less and better targeted State aid: a roadmap for state aid reform 2005–2009, COM(2005) 107 final.

5 See http://ec.europa.eu/competition/court/state_aid_judgments.html.

Although we note that national courts do not always communicate all national antitrust judgments to the Commission, as required by Article 15 of Regulation (EC) No 1/2003[6], it can be inferred from the recorded cases that private enforcement before national courts in State aid cases is as developed, if not more developed, as enforcement in antitrust matters.

In the context of the background research carried out for the 2009 update study, Lovells (now Hogan Lovells) developed a State aid Thesaurus with e-Competitions (www.concurrences.com). This provides exhaustive direct on-line access to decisions of national courts in their own language, along with summaries and comments in English. Jacques Derenne, partner and head of the Antitrust, Competition and Economic Regulation practice of the Brussels Hogan Lovells office as well as of Hogan Lovells' State aid practice, and Cédric Kaczmarek, a Brussels based State aid specialist lawyer, directed the research, with the assistance of Counsel Alix Müller-Rappard, as well as Rainer Wessely and Katharine Wilson, in coordinating the work of an international consortium of 27 national rapporteurs established in every single Member State (made up of specialist lawyers from 11 Hogan Lovells offices around the European Union and local counsel from the remaining Member States). Rachel Candler, Sarah Bowyer, Heather Craig, Laura Shearing, Andin Fonyonga, Franck Avignon and Jonathan Clovin, trainee solicitors, have worked with dedication to ensure the harmonisation of the English language, style and references throughout the 27 reports.

The 27 national reports analyse the domestic legal framework within which national courts apply Article 107(1) TFEU (concept of State aid) and Article 108(3) TFEU (notification and standstill obligations of the Member States). The reports examine key national judgments in this context. The analysis is based on the analysis of more than 660 cases. The reports make particular reference to those cases which have been summarised and commented upon in the context of the Commission 2009 update study and e-Competitions State aid Thesaurus.

The present book aims at providing national judges, EU and national officials, in-house lawyers and interested parties (grantors of the aid measures, beneficiaries, third parties, investors) as well as private practitioners an extensive overview of the remedies available before national courts in relation to State aid issues. This is the first exhaustive analysis of how the EU State aid rules are applied in practice by the national courts in all the 27 Member States.

Jacques Derenne, Cédric Kaczmarek
August 2010

---

6 Council Regulation (EC) No 1/2003 of 16 December 2002 on the implementation of the rules on competition laid down in Articles 81 and 82 of the Treaty, OJ (2003) L 1/1.

NATIONAL RAPPORTEURS

The following national rapporteurs contributed to the project:

AUSTRIA
Thomas Jaeger
Max Planck Institute for IP,
Competition and Tax Law
Munich

BELGIUM
Jacques Derenne
Cédric Kaczmarek
Hogan Lovells
Brussels

Corapporteur Tony Joris
VUB University,
Centre for European Law
Brussels

BULGARIA
Plamen Vassilev
Ministry of Finance
Sofia

CYPRUS
Constantinos Lycourgos
Law Office of the Republic of Cyprus
Nicosia

CZECH REPUBLIC
Michal Nulicek
Hogan Lovells
Prague

DENMARK
Michael Honoré
Bech-Bruun
Copenhagen

ESTONIA
Vaido Põldoja
Tarmo Peterson
Advokaadibüroo Varul Vilgerts
Smaliukas AS
Tallinn

FINLAND
Mikko Eerola
Laura Koponen
Waselius & Wist
Helsinki

FRANCE
Jacques Derenne
Alix Müller-Rappard
Cédric Kaczmarek
Hogan Lovells
Brussels

GERMANY
Rainer Wessely
Alix Müller-Rappard
Hogan Lovells
Brussels

Greece

Dr. Ioannis Koimtzoglou
KGDI Law Firm
Athens

Antigoni Lykotrafiti
European University Institute
Florence

Hungary

Christopher Noblet
Partos & Noblet – associated office with Hogan Lovells
Budapest

Ireland

Damian Collins
McCann FitzGerald Solicitors
Brussels

Katharine Wilson
Hogan Lovells
Brussels

Italy

Gianluca Belotti
Hogan Lovells
Rome

Latvia

Andris Vitols
Lawyer – linguist at the European Parliament
Brussels

Martinš Tarlaps
Sandija Novicka
Raidla Lejins & Norcous
Riga

Lithuania

Irmantas Norkus
Ilona Janciauskaite
Raidla Lejins & Norcous
Vilnius

Luxembourg

Emmanuelle Ragot
Philippe & Partners
Luxembourg

Malta

Franco Vassallo
Mamo TCV Advocates
Valletta

The Netherlands

Mariëtte Swart
Anton Louwinger
Selma ter Kuile
Hogan Lovells
Amsterdam

Paul Adriaanse
Leiden University

Poland

Robert Gago
Hogan Lovells
Warsaw

Portugal

Manuel Porto
João Nogueira de Almeida
Coimbra University

Romania

Dragos Dumitru
Fruth Oprisan Si Asociatii
Bucharest

SLOVAKIA

Erika Csekes
Andrea Oršulová
Juraj Corba
Ružička Csekes s.r.o.
Bratislava

SLOVENIA

Lea Lekočevič
Head of the State aid Monitoring Department
Ljubljana

SPAIN

Casto González-Páramo
Sonia Pérez
Hogan Lovells
Madrid

SWEDEN

Ulf Öberg
Ida Otken Eriksson
Jakob Lundström
Advokatfirman Öberg & Associés AB
Stockholm

UNITED KINGDOM

Katharine Wilson
Hogan Lovells
Brussels

Abbreviations

ADA	Administrative Dispute Act
ABGB	Allgemeines Bürgerliches Gesetzbuch (Austrian Civil Code)
APC	Administrative Procedure Code
AVG	Allgemeines Verwaltungsverfahrensgesetz (Law on General Administrative Procedure)
AWR	Algemene Wet inzake Rijksbelastingen (Dutch General Tax Act)
BAO	Bundesabgabenordnung (German Law on Federal Charges)
BGB	Bürgerliches Gesetzbuch (Civil Code)
BGH	Bundesgerichtshof (German Federal Court of Justice)
BGBl	Bundesgesetzblatt (German Federal Law Gazette)
BIS	Department for Business Innovation and Skills
CCP	Code of Civil Procedure
CJEU	Court of Justice of the European Union
CFI	Court of First Instance
Commission	European Commission
CM	Council of Ministers
CNC	Comisión Nacional de la Competencia (Spanish Competition Commission)
CPC	Commission for the Protection of Competition
DCA	Danish Competition Authority
DCC	Dutch Civil Code
DG COMP	Directorate General for Competition
DG AGRI	Directorate General for Agriculture and Rural Development
DG TREN	Directorate General for Mobility and Transport
EC	European Community
ECR	Enforcement Case Review
EU	European Union
FCA	Finish Competition Authority
GALA	Dutch General Administrative Law Act
GBER	General Block exemption Regulation
LDC	Ley de Defensa de la Competencia (Spanish Competition Act)
NCA	National Competition Authority
OCCP	Office of Competition and Consumer Protection
OFT	Office of Fair Trading
OGH	Oberster Gerichtshof (Austrian Supreme Court)
OJ	Official Journal of the European Union
RSC	Rules for the Superior Court

RT	Riigi Teataja (Estonian State Gazette)
SGAE	Secrétariat Général des Affaires Européennes
SRCA	State Receivables Collection Agency
SSA	State Aid Act
TFEU	Treaty on the Functioning of the European Union
TSSPC	Tax and Social Security Procedure Code
UWG	Gesetz gegen den Unlauteren Wettbewerb (Law against Unfair Competition)
VAT	Value added tax
VfGH	Verfassungsgerichtshof (Constitutional Supreme Court)
VwGH	Verwaltungsgerichtshof (Administrative Supreme Court)
VwGO	Verwaltungsgerichtsordnung (Administrative Court Act)
ZPO	Zivilprozessordnung (Code of Civil Procedure)

European Report

I. Scope of the analysis

This report summarises the trends drawn from the national court cases and reports that were analysed in the context of the present research project and compares them to the findings of the 2006 Commission Study[1] on the enforcement of State aid law at national level.

The analysis deals with national court cases, as well as cases of other bodies (NCAs) having jurisdiction over the implementation of State aid rules at national level. Approximately 305[2] cases were selected, from the period 1 January 2006 to around mid 2009, on the basis of publicly available information.

II. Increase of national cases

The first observation that needs to be made is that, during the period concerned, there has been a reasonably large increase in the number of court cases in the field of State aid.

Increase of cases not equally shared between Member States

The main reason for this increase is not the recent enlargement of the EU, as only a few cases were identified in the "*new*" Member States that joined the EU in 2004 and 2007. Two possible explanations for why there are so few cases from "new" Member States are that: (i) national judges (and practitioners) have only limited experience in this field, which is complex and diffused in national law; and (ii) a precondition to the new Member States' accession to the EU was the existence of *ex ante* control mechanisms.

As was the case in the previous study, the largest number of cases came from France, Italy and Germany, followed by the Netherlands, Spain, Sweden and Austria. The number of cases in Belgium and the United Kingdom has decreased significantly.

Recovery actions rather than action for damages

In general, private enforcement in the area of State aid appears to be evolving positively with the number of direct actions against unlawful aid having increased globally, and a number of competitors having been successful in their claims, especially where they were seeking the suspension or the recovery of unlawful aid. Despite claims having been brought in a few cases, national courts remain reluctant to award monetary damages to competitors of the beneficiary of unlawful State aid. In some cases, however, national courts have recognised that they have jurisdiction to grant damages on the basis of Article 108(3) TFEU, without actually giving judgment in favour of the claimants.

---

1 Http://bookshop.europa.eu/eubookshop/bookmarks.action?target=EUB:NOTICE:KD7506493:EN:HTML.

2 Some cases were regrouped according to their similarities (same national court and issues concerned, but with different parties).

Tax cases

The most frequent cases dealt with tax measures. Taxpayers often rely on State aid rules to contest the payment of taxes, alleging that the taxes are being used to finance unlawful State aid. Parties also sometimes rely on these rules to claim that a tax exemption that they could not benefit from granted an unlawful selective advantage to the beneficiaries of that exemption. A large number of cases also concern the imposition of, or changes to, compulsory charges on members of a professional organisation or of a specific sector. In these cases claimants are, most of the time, unsuccessful as the case law of the CJEU on the State resources criteria, and imputation to the State, is now clear. However, several cases have provided the opportunity for national courts to clarify their jurisdiction in the field of State aid rules (see *Comité National des Interprofessions des Vins à Appellations* case[3], where the French Conseil d'État held that a refusal to notify was an act subject to judicial review).

III. Who are the national judges involved in State aid cases?

State aid cases are often appealed to appellate and supreme courts, as they raise fundamental questions of law. Supreme courts are also keen to ask for support from the CJEU on these delicate questions (see, *CELF*, *Saumon*). Many judges facing questions on State aid therefore tend to sit at the Supreme Court level.

National courts often play the role of "*juges de droit commun*" and guarantee the implementation of Court of Justice case law in cases that have been referred to the judges in Luxembourg. In some cases, it can be observed that this dialogue with the CJEU can be useful to avoid unhelpful consequences, in particular when Commission decisions are challenged before the General Court. The second *CELF* case[4] of the Conseil d'État is a case in point, in particular on the question of national courts' jurisdiction to stay national proceedings (see the clear answer of the CJEU, Case C-1/09, *CELF v. SIDE*, not yet published, confirming what it was judged in the *SFEI* case of 11.7.1996, C-39/94). The High Court of Ireland in the *Belgium v. Ryanair* case[5] was confronted with a similar issue but applied the standard rule that application for annulment does not have suspensory effect.

There are also examples showing that judges of lower instance courts play an important role in the enforcement of State aid rules, especially in public procurement cases and in the context of local public services.

---

3 France, Council of State (Administrative supreme court), "Conseil d'État", 7.11.2008, N° 282920, Comité national des interprofessions à appellations d'origine et autres.

4 France, Council of State, 19.12.2008, N° 274923 and 274967, Centre d'exportation du livre français v. Ministre de la culture et de la communication.

5 Ireland, High Court of Ireland, 30.6.2006, 2005 9985, Kingdom of Belgium v. Ryanair Limited.

IV. Dialogue with the commission

Cases where the Commission intervened as *amicus curiae* in national proceedings are still quite rare. This situation is likely to change as a result of the recent *Enforcement* notice[6], but as of yet national courts have not made full use of the possibility to ask the Commission for its opinion or for information.

One case which should be mentioned however, is the *Haren-Airport Eelde* case[7] (NL – grant of €18 million to the company operating this regional airport), where the Dutch Conseil d'État referred (under the 1995 Notice) eight detailed questions to the Commission in July 2007. The Legal Service of the Commission, in connection with DG TREN (now named DG MOVE), responded in due course, and the Conseil d'État delivered its final judgment in June 2008 (the whole procedure of referral to the Commission took no more than four months).

In other cases, the lack of communication has raised some issues, especially in cases where the Commission initiated an investigation in parallel to the national court proceedings.

In the *UPC* case (NL)[8], the court of appeal of Amsterdam refused to order the Municipality of Amsterdam to suspend an investment that was liable to constitute State aid, even though the Commission had initiated an investigation pursuant to Article 108(2) TFEU. Similarly, in the *AirOne v. Ryanair* case (IT)[9], the court of first instance in Sassari held that the opening of an Article 108(2) TFEU procedure did not constitute an obvious breach of law, which was necessary to grant an interlocutory injunction suspending the granting of the aid, pending the outcome of the Commission investigation.

In respect of the recovery procedure, national courts have recognised that a negative Commission decision constitutes an appropriate legal basis on which to grant a recovery order and that this is required under the principle of primacy of EU law over national law (see *Brandt Italia* case[10]).

V. Powers held by the national courts

State aid rules grant extensive powers to national judges in the event of an infringement of Article 108(3) TFEU. National courts' competences are not subject to discussion with the parties. The CJEU's case law has always been very clear in that respect. However, a certain

6 Commission notice on the enforcement of State aid law by national courts, OJ (2009) C85/1.

7 The Netherlands, "Raad van State", 11.6.2008, LJN BD 3589, Applicants v. State Secretary of Transport and Water Management and State Secretary Housing, Spatial Planning and Environment.

8 The Netherlands, Court of Appeal Amsterdam, "Gerechtshof Amsterdam", 18.1.2007, LJN AZ 6508, UPC Netherlands B.V. v. Municipal Amsterdam.

9 Italy, Court of First Instance of Sassari, Alghero Division Civil Division, "Tribunale di Sassari", 9.9.2008, AirOne S.p.A v. Ryanair Ltd. e Sogeal S.p.A.

10 Italy, Court of First Instance of Brescia, Labour Division, "Tribunal di Brescia", 8.7.2008, 212/08, Brandt Italia S.p.A. v. INPS, ESATRI S.p.A.

line of case law in Germany seems to be at odds with the fundamental principles enshrined in the *Costa v. Enel*, *SFEI*, and *Streekgewest* cases[11].

National courts have a duty to ensure that the *"effet utile"* of Article 108(3) TFEU is respected, especially by ensuring that State aid rules have primacy over national procedural rules (see *Scott* and *Mineralölsteuer* cases where the financial court of Hamburg ruled that Regulation (EC) No 659/1999 supersedes German tax law).

On the whole, national courts' powers of inquiry remain limited as far as State aid matters are concerned. A national court has to judge a case on the basis of the facts presented to it by the parties. State aid cases are often complex and involve economic considerations (in particular for the qualification of aid in the event of an application of the market investor test or of the *Altmark* principles) for which national courts often lack the appropriate means to establish the factual information necessary for their decision. The burden of proof, therefore, is often a hurdle that leads to the claimant being unsuccessful. Claimants are often unable to present sufficient evidence to support the view that the State aid criteria have been fulfilled. In the *AirOne* case (IT)[12], the court of first instance in Sassari rejected the applicant's request on the ground that AirOne had not proved that the alleged State aid met the criteria of selectivity and that the disputed measures constituted an undue advantage. In the *P1 Holding* case (NL)[13], the district court of Maastricht held that the claimant had failed to provide sufficient evidence to prove an effect on trade between Member States (see also *Thomas Svensson* case (SWE)[14]).

The *Boiron* case[15], however, simplified the situation for claimants, in particular in complex cases where the question involved verifying whether the *Altmark* criteria had been fulfilled. The French Civil Supreme Court applied the CJEU case law, according to which the principle of effectiveness requires national courts to set aside national requirements rendering the production of evidence impossible or excessively difficult.

In that respect, national courts have found it easier to identify elements of State aid in public procurement cases, and this has led to a number of judgments in which the national court has ruled in favour of the claimants and found the existence of unlawful State aid.

National courts are also able, and are often obliged, to assess *ex officio* whether the State aid rules have been infringed even if the argument has not been brought by the parties themselves (provided it does not change the subject matter of the litigation, see *van Schijindel*, Joined Cases C-430/93 and C-431/93). This principle has been welcomed by the national courts concerned.

---

11 Germany, Landesgericht Potsdam, 23.10.2006, Oberlandesgericht Schleswig Holstein, 20.5.2008, Landgericht Bad Kreuznach, 16.5.2007, Oberlandesgericht Koblenz, 25.2.2009.

12 Cited above.

13 The Netherlands, District Court Maastricht, "Rechtsbank Maastricht", 8.10.2008, LJN BF 7031, P1 Holdings B.V. v. Municipal of Maastricht.

14 Sweden, The Administrative Court of Appeal in Stockholm, "Kammarrätten": Stockholm, 16.2.2009, 4514-07, Thomas Svensson v. Stockholms stad.

15 France, Cour de Cassation – Chambre commerciale, 26.6.2007, N° Z-02-31.241, Société Laboratoires Boiron v. Union de recouvrement des cotisations de sécurité sociale et d'sllocations familiales (URSSAF) de Lyon, venant aux droits de l'Agence centrale des organismes de sécurité sociale (ACOSS).

In the *Residex* case (NL)[16], the district court accepted the principle that State aid rules could be applied *ex officio* (even if *in casu* the public authorities had raised the issue themselves) and ordered recovery of unlawfully granted State aid (the court of appeal of The Hague did not rule on the *ex officio* point explicitly). In liability cases in France, courts have not taken that line, rejecting arguments based on Article 107(1) TFEU whilst, further to a Commission decision (as was the case in the *Borotra* case), it was obvious that the State had infringed Article 107(3) TFEU and not only Article 103(3).

VI. The rights of competitors/third parties

There have been an increasing number of cases where competitors have claimed for the recovery of unlawfully granted State aid or for the national judge to order injunctive measures to prevent or suspend the granting of unlawful aid. National courts have ordered interim measures in several cases (see *Federchemica* case in Italy).

For third parties and competitors, however, the path to private enforcement of the State aid rules remains difficult. As was pointed out in the 1999 and 2006 Studies, *locus standi* remains an important hurdle for private enforcement. The (in)famous cases of the German courts[17], relating to aid measures granted to Ryanair from German airports, which were contested by Ryanair's competitors, are good examples of instances where the CJEU's case law (*SFEI*, *Streekgewest* and *Pape* cases) continues to be incorrectly applied by national courts.

Damages actions remain limited and there have not been any cases in which competitors have actually been awarded monetary compensation. The same conclusion was drawn from the 2006 Study. The main obstacle to damages actions brought by private parties, based on a violation of State aid law, is the lack of a clear legal basis under national law. Member States differ in their treatment of this question. Moreover, the requirement to prove causation between a breach of Article 108(3) TFEU and the economic loss sustained by the claimant remains a major problem, as this requires the claimants to show how its market share would have developed had the aid not been granted to its competitor. However, this does not appear to be different from the classic issue of the counterfactual in damages cases, which raises issues generally in antitrust matters.

---

16 The Netherlands, Court of Appeal of The Hague, "Gerechtshof Den Haag", 10.7.2007, LJN BD 6981, Residex Capital IV C.V. v. Municipal Rotterdam.

17 Cited above.

AUSTRIA

Thomas Jaeger*

* Max Planck Institute for IP, Competition and Tax Law, Munich.

I. General setup of Austrian State aid law

1. Substantive provisions

The Austrian Federal Constitution (B-VG)[18] does not contain or assign a specific competence for subsidies or State aid[19]. Accordingly, Austria does not recognise a designated field of law termed "State aid law" or assemble all of the applicable provisions on the granting of aid.

The competence to grant aid follows the general attribution of (horizontal or vertical) competences in the constitution. Importantly, however, insofar as aid is granted via recourse to civil law measures, no legal basis is required, i.e. authorities may also grant aid outside areas falling within their sole or shared administrative competence, unless the authority competent for the matter concerned has regulated aid activities for the matter in a binding and general manner. Therefore, the power to grant State aid, and aid activities in practice, are evenly distributed across all (local, regional and federal) administrative bodies. A summary of those voluntary aid activities on the federal level ("Bund") is provided in a yearly report drawn up under Article 54 Bundes-Haushaltsgesetz (Federal Budgetary Law).[20] Some provinces ("Länder")[21] and communities ("Gemeinden")[22] draw up similar reports, but a consolidated overview is not available.

The concept of aid (subsidies in Austrian legal terminology)[23] is, however, not congruent with the EU concept as laid down in Article 107(1) TFEU. The Austrian concept of aid is both broader and narrower than the EU concept. The Austrian concept is narrower than the EU concept, insofar as it only covers payments made by administrative bodies or bodies acting on behalf of such a body. In turn, the concept is broader, insofar as it also covers aid to consumers.

No provisions exist to incorporate the EU law concept of aid under Article 107(1) TFEU into Austrian law. The enforcement of Article 107(1) TFEU is therefore typically based directly on the EU law provisions.

---

18 BGBl. No. 1/1930. (Note: This as well as all following citations of the Austrian Federal Gazette BGBl. or of the former Imperial Gazette RGBl. refer to the initial version of the act and do not reflect amendments. The Gazette reference is cited only upon the first mentioning of the act in this text and omitted for subsequent citations.)

19 Article 10 to 15 B-VG.

20 Available at https://www.bmf.gv.at/Budget/.

21 E.g., a 2006 report of the Land Salzburg, available at http://www.salzburg.gv.at/subventionsbericht-2006.pdf.

22 E.g., a 2008 report of the community of Mödling, available at http://www.moedling.at/html/gemeinde/formulare/subventionsbericht08.doc.

23 Cf., e.g., OGH of 26 January 1995, 6 Ob 514/95.

2. Procedural rules

For civil law-based aid contracts concluded by the federal administration, compulsory guidelines[24] exist in the form of a ministerial regulation, which lay down a general framework for the design of federal aid contracts and a set of accompanying procedural preconditions and rules dealing with how the contracts should be concluded and supervised. At the level of the regions and communities, such rules were apparently not drawn up or, at least, not made available to the general public.

As regards aid measures based on instruments of public law, no common rules exist on any administrative level ("Bund" or "Länder/Gemeinden"). The procedure for granting the aid follows the procedures laid down specifically in the respective legal basis. There is, apparently, no coherent procedural approach in this respect.

3. Notification and *ex ante* control

The notification of intended aid measures to the Commission was brought together at the federal level for all aid measures in Austria, irrespective of their federal, regional or local origin. Unit C 1/8 of the Federal Ministry of Economy, Family and Youth (name subject to frequent change) is responsible for making notifications. That unit also provides some pre-notification advice for the design of measures, to the extent required or requested in a given case. The basis for this notification and advice procedure is apparently informal and flexible. A uniform and binding statutory rule for centralised notification or *ex ante* control does not exist. Monitoring of the implementation of the aid is, again, the responsibility of the body granting the aid – the federal reporting unit is not involved.

Unintended aid contained in public measures may be detected only in the course of the normal evaluation procedure for legislative drafts. Typically, those drafts circulate among the various ministries and the federal chancellery, and its legal service ("Verfassungsdienst") in particular, for optional comments. The federal reporting unit is involved in this circulation process as a part of the general administration, but its review capacities are very limited, due to its limited number of staff. Therefore, although State aid concerns could come up in the course of a pre-legislative review, very often they do not, unless a specific unit (typically the chancellery's legal service) is expressly requested to assess a suspected State aid problem in relation to a specific legislative project.

4. Litigation and recovery

Litigation before the EU Courts in State aid cases is done centrally by the chancellery's legal service, irrespective of the origin of the measure. In handling the factual side of a case, however, the agents of the legal service are regularly assisted – and dependant upon – the collaboration

24 Verordnung des Bundesministers für Finanzen über Allgemeine Rahmenrichtlinien für die Gewährung von Förderungen aus Bundesmitteln (ARR 2004), BGBl. II No. 51/2004.

of the respective governmental units responsible for the measure in question. Litigation on a national level in respect of contractual obligations, including in the case of recovery orders, is the responsibility of the administrative body concerned, or its legal representation (e.g. the "Finanzprokuratur"[25] as the general legal counsel and representative of the federal state).

II. State aid issues at the national level

The vast majority of cases where the State aid argument is used in Austria come from the field of public litigation. A good number of classic "shield-ligitation" cases can be found in Austria, i.e. where the standstill obligation is used as a defence in public law litigation over taxes and parafiscal charges.[26] Here, in particular, it seems that the majority of cases did not lead to the desired outcome in terms of relief from the payment obligation. Furthermore, in some cases parties to proceedings before the Austrian public courts have sought the extension of an aid granted to them by applying to the administrative authority and going to court to contest the negative decision.[27] Such litigation is a mix between a sword and a shield, but closer to the latter, given that the low cost and hurdles for bringing the application and since the loss of the illegal benefit by competitors is neither the primary objective nor the automatic effect of such actions. Finally, public litigation has been brought in Austria over disagreements as to the conditions and entitlement to aid granted on a legislative basis between the recipient and the administration where the latter harbours a suspicion that illegal aid may be involved.[28]

Austria has seen a few instances of competitor actions before civil courts against illegal aid for competitors ("sword litigation").[29] While none of these actions has, thus far, been ultimately successful, the final decision in the Bank Burgenland case[30] is still pending and seems to be leaning towards the full outcome for the competitor. It also appears that there is an ever increasing awareness and willingness among competitors to act against illegal aid. The civil law-based sword-cases are all relatively recent and do not yet form a solid line of respective case law. Rather, such case law is currently being established by applying and adapting the rules of the Austrian Law against Unfair Competition (UWG)[31] to cover civil law-based sword-cases in State aid. Civil law shield litigation, in particular use of the standstill obligation in contractual relationships, has not, thus far, come up before the Austrian civil courts.

---

25 See http://finanzprokuratur.bmf.gv.at/.

26 VwGH of 20 March 2006 et al., 2005/17/0230 et al. (AMA-Marketingbeiträge); VwGH of 18 April 2008 et al., 2008/17/0035 et al. (AMA-Weinmarketing); VwGH of 29 May 2006, 2002/17/0337 et al. (Kosten der Bankenaufsicht); VwGH of 11 December 2009, 2006/17/0103.

27 VwGH of 20 November 2006 et al., 2006/17/0157 et al. (Energieabgabenvergütung); VwGH of 11 December 2009, 2006/17/0118.

28 VfGH of 26 June 2008, G 263/07 (Ökostromgesetz).

29 OGH of 15 December 2008, 4 Ob 133/08z (Bank Burgenland); OGH of 10 June 2008, 4 Ob 41/08w (Die Presse).

30 OGH of 15 December 2008, 4 Ob 133/08z (Bank Burgenland).

31 BGBl. No. 448/1984.

According to official information in response to an enquiry by the author, Austria has not yet had any recovery actions by the public authorities. Similarly, neither have there been any recovery orders by the Commission for intentionally granted aid. As far as unintentionally granted aid is concerned, the first major case where recovery was ordered still awaiting execution at the national level is the negative Commission decision in Bank Burgenland.[32]

During the reporting period between January 2006 and September 2009, the following State aid issues were dealt with by national courts:

- interpretation of the State aid prohibition[33] and the question of new or existing aid;[34]
- binding effect of a final Commission decision for the national court;[35]
- retroactive effect of the standstill obligation;[36]
- scope of the standstill obligation;[37]
- hypothecation for parafiscal charges;[38]
- recovery and limitation of legitimate expectations for breaches of the standstill obligation;[39]
- competitor standing before civil courts in sword-litigation;[40]
- the right of competitors to seek recovery of unlawful aid.[41]

III. Powers of the Austrian courts to adjudicate claims based on Article 108(3) TFEU

The procedural powers of Austrian courts to remedy the unlawful granting of aid responds to the claims brought by the parties, so that the scope of court powers in the procedure depends on the scope of the claim. These claims, which are either of a civil or public law nature, must, be adjudicated before either the civil courts or before one of Austria's two public supreme courts. The availability and scope of claims before Austrian courts is discussed in detail in

32 Decision 2008/719/EC, [2009] OJ L 239/32.

33 OGH of 10 June 2008, 4 Ob 41/08w (Die Presse).

34 OGH of 10 June 2008, 4 Ob 41/08w (Die Presse).

35 OGH of 15 December 2008, 4 Ob 133/08z (Bank Burgenland).

36 Cf. VwGH of 8 January 2007 et al., 2002/17/0356 et al. (Energieabgabenvergütung); cf. also the decision no. 2006/17/0118 (cited in fn. 16 above), rendered after submission of this report and thus not discussed here in substance.

37 Cf. VwGH of 20 March 2006 et al., 2005/170230 et al. (AMA-Marketingbeiträge); VwGH of 20 November 2006 et al., 2006/17/0157 et al. (Energieabgabenvergütung).

38 Cf. VwGH of 20 March 2006 et al., 2005/17/0230 et al.; VwGH of 30 June 2006 et al., 2006/17/0092 et al.; VwGH of 21 December 2006 et al., 2006/17/0092 et al. (all: AMA-Marketingbeiträge); cf. also the decision no. 2006/17/0103 (cited in fn. 15 above), rendered after the submission of this report and thus not discussed here in substance.

39 Cf. VfGH of 26 June 2008, G 263/07 (Ökostromesetz).

40 OGH of 15 December 2008, 4 Ob 133/08z (Bank Burgenland).

41 OGH of 15 December 2008, 4 Ob 133/08z (Bank Burgenland).

sections IV (public recovery) and V (private actions) below.[42] First, however, this section gives a brief outline of the general framework that governs the procedure before the Austrian civil and public courts in litigation relating to the standstill obligation for State aid. This is followed by a more detailed discussion of two important procedural issues: namely, the provisions governing the availability of interim measures; and the extent of the courts' powers to determine the scope of a case.

1. General framework of procedure before the courts

The procedural powers of the court competent to adjudicate claims brought by parties under Article 108(3) TFEU and Austrian substantive laws are laid down in the Code of Civil Procedure (ZPO)[43] and the Execution Act (EO),[44] as well as in the rules of procedure for the Constitutional (VfGH)[45] and Administrative (VwGH)[46] supreme courts. The procedure before the VfGH is complemented by a partial reliance on the provisions of the ZPO and the EO (VfGH), which apply before the VwGH by reason of a limited reliance on the Law on General Administrative Procedure (AVG).[47]

In civil as well as in public procedures under the aforementioned laws, courts may:

- issue desist orders to parties (civil procedure) or suspend the execution of the act at issue (public procedure), as discussed in more detail in the next subsection;
- annul (public procedure) or declare void (civil procedure) any act (contract, law, administrative order or other) by which aid is granted;
- award damages (in public law cases damages can only be sought before the VfGH), as discussed in detail in section V below;
- award costs depending on the outcome of the case.

In addition, civil courts may order recovery of the illegal aid, as discussed in section IV below.

The public procedure, by contrast, does not recognise this type of claim or court competence. The public courts only have the competence to annul the administrative act in question, at which point the administrative procedure reverts back to the stage before the act was issued. Recovery is therefore a consequence of annulment and the public courts rely on the admin-

42 For avoidance of a separation of connected problems and of duplication of remarks, sections III.2 to III.7 of the questionnaire to national rapporteurs where merged into sections IV and V of that questionnaire, since all of those sections concern the availability and scope of claims before the Austrian courts. Section III.1 is understood as concerning not claims but procedural powers of the courts and is, therefore, answered separately.

43 RGBl. No. 113/1895.

44 RGBl. No. 79/1896.

45 Arts. 137, 139, 140, 144 and 148 B-VG; §§ 15 to 93 VfGG (Law on the Constitutional Supreme Court), BGBl. No. 85/1953.

46 Arts. 130 to 132 B-VG; Arts. 21 to 70 VwGG (Law on the Administrative Supreme Court), BGBl. No. 10/1985.

47 BGBl. No. 51/1991.

istrative authorities to effect recovery in a separate administrative procedure or via recovery litigation, as discussed in detail in section IV below.

2. Procedural bases for interim measures

Interim measures in the strict sense, i.e. understood as active court orders to safeguard parties' rights relating to litigation, are only available under civil procedure. In public procedures relating to illegal aid granted by a public law act, the rights of the applicant are safeguarded by suspending execution of the act.[48] That suspension is, however, not automatic, it must be applied for by the applicant.

As regards civil procedure, the Austrian Execution Act (EO) provides for several kinds of interim measures, for which a party can apply. In terms of State aid litigation, two types of measures provided for in the EO are particularly relevant. Firstly, an interim measure to secure a right to payment if a certain sum of money (Einstweilige Verfügung zur Sicherung von Geldleistungen) is available under Article 379 EO. This accords the court ample discretion to, in particular, freeze assets or funds by way of interim measure. For this measure to apply, the party merely needs to demonstrate the existence of a monetary claim as well as a subjective risk to its interests (e.g. that the defendant might proceed with the illegal granting of aid). This level of proof lies well below the standard level of proof for civil claims. Secondly, to secure rights other than debts, a separate interim measure is available under Article 381 EO (Einstweilige Verfügung zur Sicherung anderer Ansprüche). Here, a more stringent level of proof applies, as the applicant needs to demonstrate the existence of an immediate threat that irrevocable damage will occur in relation to its rights or protected interests.

3. Party disposition vs. court disposition in the procedure

As regards the determination of the scope of the case and, therefore, the question of whether courts are competent to raise the issue of unlawful aid (or any other pertinent issue, like respect for a decision of the Commission that is relevant to the case) in a case before them on their own motion, a distinction needs to be made between the civil and public procedures.

a. Civil procedure

Austrian civil procedure, as laid down in the Code of Civil Procedure (ZPO) applies a form of party/court-cooperation or weak *ex officio* approach rather than the fully fledged, rigid party disposition approach (Dispositionsmaxime) that is typically associated with civil procedure. In addition, court powers lean more towards the principle of party disposition or towards the *ex officio* approach, depending on the type of litigation.[49]

48 For the VwGH, cf. Art. 30 VwGG; for the VfGH cf. Arts. 44 and 85 VfGG.

49 I.e. notwithstanding special areas of litigation not relevant for State aid, such as annulment of marriage, guardianship, insolvency, where more extensive powers are accorded to the court. Cf., e.g., Art. 460(4) ZPO.

For litigation relating to State aid, thus the approach in Austrian civil procedure can be described as a softened principle of party disposition. This means that civil courts are bound by the claims adduced by the parties and by the delineation of the scope of the litigation resulting from those claims. As regards the collection of evidence, however, civil courts of first instance may decide to complement any evidence offered by the parties by evidence collected *ex officio*.[50] This power, however, is not accorded to the civil courts of appeal, as the scope of the appeals procedure is determined by the scope and substance of the appeals[51] and as (unlike in Germany, for example) no new evidence may be introduced upon appeal (Neuerungsverbot).[52]

In line with the Peterbroeck-van Schijndel-Kraaijeveld line of case-law of the CJEU in respect of EU law for the passive role accorded to civil courts in certain legal systems, Austrian civil courts of first instance are obliged to consider infringements of the standstill obligation and any other relevant issues of EU law on their own motion. The discretion accorded to those courts in Austrian civil procedure on the collection of evidence has the effect of creating a respective obligation from the point of view of EU law. Nonetheless, to the knowledge of the author, there are no Austrian cases to date, where the civil court of first instance has exercised its respective power and obligation to examine a State aid issue on its own account.

Before the civil courts of appeal, however, State aid arguments introduced there for the first time must be dismissed as new evidence. Because the appeals courts do not enjoy discretion as regards the admissibility of such new evidence, EU law neither obliges nor empowers them to consider new State aid arguments on their own motion.

b. *Public procedure*

The Austrian rules governing public procedure do not (unlike, for example, in Germany) explicitly lay down a principle of *ex officio* court disposition over the case. However, the applicability principle of *ex officio* disposition flows implicitly from the applicable procedural provisions.

As regards procedure before the VfGH, the merits of an application for infringement of constitutional rights are to be examined by that Court on its own account[53] and any evidence necessary is to be collected *ex officio*.[54] Procedure before the VwGH dictates that the principle of *ex officio* disposition flows from the applicability of the Law on General Administrative Procedure (AVG), which lays down the same principle vis-à-vis administrative authorities.[55] Before courts, therefore, the claim that such infringement of the standstill obligation has occurred is sufficient basis to bring a case. The merits of that claim, as well as its neces-

50 Art. 276(1) ZPO.

51 Art. 462(1) ZPO.

52 Art. 482 ZPO.

53 Art. 144(1) B-VG.

54 Art. 20 VfGG.

55 Art. 6(2) VwGG and Art. 39(2) AVG.

sity, are examined *ex officio*. This includes, in particular, arguments and facts that were not considered by the administrative authority that issued the contested act.[56]

In relation to the Austrian public courts, therefore, the Peterbroeck-van Schijndel-Kraaijeveld case-law of the CJEU is understood as requiring a consideration and examination *ex officio* of possible infringements of the standstill obligation or of any other relevant points of Community law.

In practice, the assessment of the scope and implications of the standstill obligation, beyond that which is pleaded by the applicant, is in fact a commonplace exercise undertaken in most of the cases reported.[57] Usually, the exercise relates to details, as the State aid issue has already been raised before the administrative authority, i.e. before the case reaches a public court. There are also, however, precedents where a public court has detected and examined a possible State aid problem of its own volition. This was, for example, the reason behind the VwGH's application for a preliminary ruling in the Transalpine case[58] (dating from before the applicable reporting period), where the Court detected a State aid problem in VfGH case law interpreting the scope of the standstill obligation following the CJEU's judgment in Adria-Wien.[59]

IV. Control of recovery procedure

This section deals with recovery claims and procedures following a negative Commission decision. Recovery based on the autonomous competence of the national courts under Article 108(3) TFEU is dealt with in section V, below. According to information provided by the federal notification unit, there is no record of a case of recovery in Austria in relation to aid granted intentionally through the unit. As concerns aid granted unintentionally, the first major example where recovery was ordered, and will now have to be carried out, followed the negative Commission decision in Bank Burgenland.[60] This case, which is quite complex in terms of the federal and regional levels of administration involved, and of the economic transaction at its base, will, therefore, be a test for the workability and effectiveness of recovery under Austrian civil law.

1. Rules applicable to recovery by the Member State

Austrian law does not provide for any specific rules applicable to the recovery of unlawful aid. Rather, recovery must be based on the general provisions of civil and public law. The proce-

56 Art. 41(1) VwGG.

57 For just one example, the consideration of the relevance of the Alcan line of case-law of the CJEU by the VfGH in its judgment of 26 June 2008, G 263/07.

58 Case C-368/04, Transalpine; VwGH of 12 August 2004, 2003/17/0001 et al.; similarly already VwGH of 30 January 2003, 2003/17/0001 et al.

59 Case C-143/99, Adria-Wien, and the follow-up decisions by the VfGH of v. 13 December 2001, B 2251/97 et al., and of 12 December 2002, B 1348/02 et al.

60 Commission Decision 2008/719/EC, OJ 2009 L 239/32.

dures for the recovery of aid in Austria differ, therefore, according to two major parameters: firstly, whether the aid instrument includes rules on the possibility and modalities of recovery; and secondly, on the public or private law basis of the aid instrument.

a. *The aid instrument provides for recovery*

The aid instrument typically provides for rules on recovery where the aid is granted knowingly.

Civil law-based aid

In practice, State aid in Austria is mostly granted by means of civil law contracts. These contracts lay down the mutual rights and obligations between the public authority and the aid recipient.

For civil law-based aid contracts concluded by the federal administration ("Bund"), compulsory guidelines,[61] in the form of a ministerial regulation, determine what clauses are to be included in federal aid contracts. Regarding recovery, Article 22 of those guidelines stipulates that the aid recipient must be contractually obliged to effect immediate repayment of the aid upon an order of the public authority, that authority's agent or an EU organ, in the event of any one eleven specifically enumerated circumstances. These circumstances extend mostly to default in performance of the contract (e.g. false information by the recipient, misuse of the aid, obstruction of public control measures, insolvency of the recipient, etc.). One of the circumstances which must be contractually agreed as a reason for repayment is, however, the issuing of a suspension or recovery order by an EU organ, without any conditions applying.[62] According to the guidelines, the agreed basis for that repayment is unjust enrichment (as discussed further below).[63] Furthermore, the guidelines state that the contracts must also provide for repayment of interest, irrespective of whether the reason for repayment is the responsibility of the recipient.[64] Depending on the recipient's fault, however, different interest rates apply.[65] Another safeguard included in contracts, with a view to ensuring full and effective recovery, is that third parties benefiting from aid must agree in a separate legal instrument to joint liability for any repayment, before the aid is granted.[66]

The regional governments ("Länder") can act on behalf of the Federation and are then regarded as organs of the Federation, who must apply federal guidelines when granting aid.[67] For aid contracts concluded by the regions under an autonomous capacity, however, the federal guidelines do not apply. It appears that none of the regions has comparable guidelines in force.

61 Verordnung des Bundesministers für Finanzen über Allgemeine Rahmenrichtlinien für die Gewährung von Förderungen aus Bundesmitteln (ARR 2004), BGBl. II Nr. 51/2004.

62 Art. 22(1)(11) ARR 2004 (fn. 50).

63 Mainly Art. 877 Austrian Civil Code (ABGB).

64 Art. 22(2) ARR 2004 (fn. 50).

65 Art. 22(2) ARR 2004 (fn. 50).

66 Art. 22(5) ARR 2004 (fn. 50).

67 Art. 4 ARR 2004 (fn. 50) and Art. 5(2) Bundeshaushaltsgesetz, BGBl. Nr. 213/1986.

It is unclear, therefore, to what extent recovery clauses are included in those contracts and what conditions are applied.

Public law-based aid

Where aid is granted by an instrument of public law, the principle of legal basis for all public acts ("Legalitätsprinzip")[68] requires that any subsequent decision affecting or reversing the decision to grant the aid, such as suspension or recovery, is in itself made on a legal basis with the requisite authority for such an act. This means that recovery by way of a subsequent, individual recovery decision ("Bescheid") of a public authority presupposes that the public law instrument (law, regulation ("Verordnung") or individual administrative decision) granting the aid has already provided for the possibility of recovery.

For public law-based aid, no general[69] guidelines for the format of aid measures exist.[70] Consequently, no uniform legal basis for public law-based recovery exists either. The conditions and procedures for recovery therefore differ depending on the legal basis. In fact, several laws and regulations deal with the question of recovery insofar as they mention a respective obligation.[71] In particular, in the important field of EU-financed or co-financed aid, Austrian lawmakers and granting authorities are already required under EU law to provide for the possibility of recovery,[72] so that the corresponding provisions of Austrian law set out recovery in more detail.[73]

However, the quality of the recovery provisions contained in these texts varies in terms of their ability to be used as a legal basis for immediate recovery. Only some laws contain an express legal basis for a recovery decision in cases where conditions mentioned (which again vary as to the degree of detail) are fulfilled.[74]

Similarly, where sector-specific guidelines for the format of public law aid measures exist, and insofar as they stipulate a principle of recovery,[75] individual decisions of a public authority which is based on those guidelines will also include the possibility of a subsequent act for

68 Art. 18(1) Bundes-Verfassungsgesetz.

69 However, some sector-specific guidelines for the design of public law aid instruments exist. Cf., e.g., Art. 3 KMU-Förderungsgesetz, BGBl. Nr. 432/1996 (SME); Art. 9c KommAustria-Gesetz, BGBl. I Nr. 32/2001 (media sector); Art. 13d Ökostromgesetz, BGBl. I Nr. 149/2002 (green energy); Art. 13 Umweltförderungsgesetz, BGBl. Nr. 185/1993 (environmental aid).

70 In particular and as was mentioned, the federal guidelines apply only to civil law measures, cf. Art. 1(1) ARR 2004 (fn. 50).

71 Cf., e.g, Art. 5 Ausfuhrerstattungsgesetz, BGBl. Nr. 660/1994; Art. 3 KMU-Förderungsgesetz (fn. 58); Art. 9c KommAustria-Gesetz (fn. 58); Art. 4 Publizistikförderungsgesetz, BGBl. Nr. 369/1984; Art. 10 Umweltfondsgesetz, BGBl. Nr. 561/1983; Art. 13d Ökostromgesetz, (fn. 58); Art. 13 Umweltförderungsgesetz (fn. 58); Art. 13 MMP-IntervV 2008, BGBl. II Nr. 439/2008; Art. 18 Produktionserstattungsverordnung Stärke 2008, BGBl. II Nr. 231/2008.

72 Cf., e.g., Art. 73 Regulation 769/2004, OJ [2004] L 414/18; Arts. 44 and 47 Regulation 1974/2006, OJ [2006] L 368/15.

73 Cf. Art. 5 Ausfuhrerstattungsgesetz (fn. 60); Art. 13 MMP-IntervV 2008, BGBl. II Nr. 439/2008; Art. 18 Produktionserstattungsverordnung Stärke 2008, BGBl. II Nr. 231/2008.

74 Cf., e.g., Art. 5(1) Ausfuhrerstattungsgesetz (fn. 60).

75 Cf. fn. 58.

recovery, so that no other legal basis will be necessary. In these cases, it will often not be necessary to annul the preceding decision, since the recovery decision is still compatible with the conditions contained in the initial decision. Where it is necessary to replace the initial decision, annulment and recovery can be achieved by one act, based on the pre-existing authorisations.

In those situations where the laws are less detailed, in that they state the principle of recovery but do not also spell out the means,[76] the procedure for recovery is likely to be based on the alternative, general provisions discussed below.

b. The aid instrument does not provide for recovery

The problem of missing recovery rules in the aid instrument typically arises where the aid is not granted knowingly, i.e. where the public authority was not aware of the State aid character of the measure. Exceptionally, however, as has been shown, some Austrian laws do not provide a basis for recovery even though their aim is to grant aid.

General tool: Condictio sine causa

For aid granted by the federal authorities ("Bund"), a general recovery obligation is contained in Article 60 of the Federal Budgetary Law ("Bundeshaushaltsgesetz"),[77] which stipulates that payments granted erroneously must be recovered as soon as the error becomes apparent to the authority.

This provision includes several characteristics: first, it is subject, insofar as its practical relevance, to situations where the authority is not already bound by more specific recovery obligations and procedures (i.e. the federal guidelines or the provisions of the legal basis for the aid). Secondly, it does not by itself provide the legal basis for a public law recovery decision ("Bescheid") by the competent authority. Instead, it expressly looks to civil law ("ABGB")[78] for the conditions and remedies for recovery. Finally, the provision cited in Article 60 is exclusively designed for cases of error (*condictio indebiti*)[79], whereas recovery in the case of State aid will typically be a question of conflict of the contract (or decision) with the overriding legal prohibition of Article 108(3) TFEU. For such cases, however, the Austrian Civil Code provides a different legal basis (*condictio sine causa*)[80] to that set out in Article 60. In short, therefore, it is unclear how far that provision, either directly or via interpretation in conformity with EU law, is capable of being applied to cases of recovery of State aid. For aid granted by regional governments ("Länder") in their autonomous capacity, no general recovery obligations like Article 60 exist.

---

76 Cf., e.g., Art. 4 Publizistikförderungsgesetz (fn. 60); Art. 11(3) Presseförderungsgesetz, BGBl. I Nr. 136/2003.

77 Cf. fn. 56.

78 Cf. fn. 52.

79 Arts. 1431 et seq. Austrian Civil Code.

80 Art. 877 Austrian Civil Code.

The general tools for recovery in cases of aid instruments based on civil and public law alike, where the instrument does not specifically provide for the modalities of recovery, therefore derive from civil law. For public law, subject to the exceptions discussed below, this follows not only from the shaky legal basis of Article 60, but also from the aforementioned principle that there must be a legal basis for all public acts ("Legalitätsprinzip"). Where there is no basis for a public law-based action, the public authorities must place themselves on an equal footing with individuals and revert to the civil law in order to defend their interest.[81]

As mentioned, the Austrian Civil Code's main tool for recovery of payments made in contravention of a legal prohibition, such as the standstill obligation contained in Article 108(3) TFEU, is the *condictio sine causa* provided for in Article 877 ABGB. By contrast, the specific provisions of Articles 1431 et seq. ABGB, providing for recovery due to error over the existence of the legal obligation to pay (*condictio indebiti*), will probably not be applicable to recovery of State aid, as the infringement of a legal prohibition is not a case of error. In the case of insolvency of the recipient, provisions of the Austrian Insolvency Act govern the method of recovery.[82]

Public law-based acts: Annulment and substitution

Recovery on the basis of *condictio sine causa* in Article 877 ABGB is only possible where recovery is not obstructed by the continuing legal force of the initial act. As regards contracts and other acts of civil law, this does not constitute a problem. Acts of civil law in contravention of the standstill obligation of Article 108(3) TFEU are considered null and void ("absolut nichtig") under Austrian civil law doctrine.[83] The recovery claim does not, therefore, encounter the problem of residual legal force of the illegal contract.

As regards public law acts, however, contravention of the standstill obligation of Article 108(3) TFEU only entails the relative nullity ("relative Nichtigkeit") of that act, owing to the principle of legal certainty. This means that the act remains in force and legally binding until it is formally declared invalid by the competent authority or a court. Until that formal declaration is made, the *condictio sine causa* encounters the problem of the continuing legal force of the act granting the aid. That act must, therefore, be removed before the recovery procedure under civil law can succeed.

The general legal basis in Austrian administrative law for the annulment of legally binding administrative decisions is Article 68 Allgemeines Verwaltungsverfahrensgesetz (law on general administrative procedure; AVG). This provides that an annulment *ex officio* of binding administrative decisions ("Bescheide") is only possible in certain limited cases, one of which is the breach of a statutory prohibition, sanctioned by the nullity of the decision in question. Academics in Austria have long debated whether Article 108(3) TFEU can be seen as such a statutory prohibition and, if not, whether EU law requires that a change of doctrine is adopted,

81 Cf., in this regard, also Art. 5 Publizistikförderungsgesetz (fn. 60).

82 Cf. Arts. 44 and 46(1)(6) Austian Insolvency Act (Konkursordnung).

83 Cf., only recently, the decision of the appeals court in the BankBurgenland-case discussed here, OLG Wien of 5 February 2007, 2 R 150/06b.

shifting from the current theory of relative nullity to a concept of absolute nullity for public law acts. This question is essentially still unsolved. However, its practical relevance is probably limited. In view of the fact that most aid in Austria is, as has been mentioned, granted in the form of contracts and, where public law is concerned, either taxes will be concerned (where another norm applies, as is discussed below) or a more specific legal basis is available, very few aid cases will require recovery on the basis of the AVG. Given, however, that it cannot be excluded that such cases could nonetheless arise, and, furthermore, in view of the fact that beyond the field of State aid this problem arises vis-à-vis other breaches of EU law by Austrian administrative decisions, a clarification of the law is necessary.

In the case of State aid contained in decisions in the field of taxation, where, in practice, a lot of (typically accidentally granted) unlawful aid occurs, the more specific provisions of the law on federal charges (Bundesabgabenordnung; BAO) apply. Article 299(1) BAO is significantly more flexible in relation to tax decisions than the aforementioned Article 68 AVG is for general administrative decisions, insofar as it allows for *ex officio*-corrections of a decision ("Bescheid") at first instance, where the decision turns out to be incorrect ("nicht richtig"). The BAO also makes it clear that the term "incorrectness" is meant to include infringements of EU law in particular.[84] This corrective power at first instance is coupled with an obligation to replace the old decision with a new, corrected one. In this case there is, therefore, neither need nor room for recovery of undue tax benefits from the recipient before the civil courts. A similar rule applies under Article 300(1)(a) BAO to decisions at higher instances, which can also be annulled using a flexible standard of illegality ("Rechtswidrigkeit") against the previous decision. Here again, the annulment has the effect of reopening the administrative procedure,[85] so that typically a new decision will follow and there is no room for civil action.

In conclusion, therefore, the *condictio since causa* is in theory applicable to public law-based acts, on the condition that these acts are formally annulled before civil court action is taken. In the case of general administrative decisions, the applicability of the AVG's provision for *ex officio* annulment to State aid cases is unclear. At the same time, however, in the areas where voluntary or involuntary State aid is most likely to occur (taxes and specific aid legislation) there is typically a specific legal basis allowing for annulment of the initial decision as well as, very often, for a replacement decision to be taken. In the areas of taxes and most[86] specific aid legislation, therefore, recovery can take place immediately within the (continued or reopened) administrative procedure and by public law means. The *condictio since causa* is therefore only a means for recovery for civil law-based aid or exceptional[87] (very rare) cases of public law-based measures.

84 Cf. Art. 302(2)(c) BAO.

85 Cf. Art. 300(3) BAO.

86 Cf. already fn. 63 and 64.

87 For such a case, cf. Art. 5 Publizistikförderungsgesetz (fn. 60).

c. *Time limitations to recovery*

Under civil law, a claim or counterclaim that a contract infringing the standstill obligation is nul and void ("absolut nichtig") can be brought without any time limitation. The ensuing claim for a recovery of payments made on the basis of the invalid contract (i.e. the *condictio sine causa* under Article 877 ABGB as well as any related recovery condictions), is limited to thirty years.[88]

In public law, the annulment of general administrative decisions is not limited in time.[89] Subsequent recovery under civil law encounters the same time limit of thirty years. In tax cases, decisions at first instance can be annulled and replaced within a limit of three to five years, depending on the type of tax.[90] Decisions at higher tax instances can always be annulled within a five year period.[91] Recovery of unlawful State aid in tax cases may be ordered by a replacement decision within a period of five years.[92]

2. Actions for recovery by the State brought by a competitor

Actions for recovery brought by competitors on the basis of the standstill obligation is dealt with in section V below. This section deals with the possibility to coerce the Member State to act to execute a Commission decision.

In general, in civil law, as enshrined in the Austrian Civil Code, third parties have, as a matter of principle, no right or remedy vis-à-vis invalid contracts to demand that any of the parties to the contract exercise their rights for restitution or recovery. In other words, competitors cannot rely on any right or remedy to bring about a decision whereby the public administration is compelled to plead the invalidity of the contract or initiate a *condictio sine causa.* Competitors may, however, initiate recovery (and other) actions before the civil courts by relying on their own rights flowing from the standstill obligation, i.e. the right to have the effects of illegal aid neutralised. This point is discussed further in section V below.

Furthermore, under Austrian public law, competitors do not enjoy a subjective right to coerce the administration to act to effect recovery. Parties may approach an authority responsible for recovering aid and suggest that a Commission decision should be complied with and that aid should be recovered,[93] whether any action is taken, however, is at the discretion of that authority.[94] Unlike under EU law, the discretion of the authority is not subject to review. Although Article 73(2) AVG entitles individuals to bring an administrative (and subsequently: court)[95]

---

88 Art. 1478 ABGB.

89 Art. 68 AVG.

90 Arts. 207(2) and 302(2)(c) BAO. This limit is a special extension for infringements of EU law of the usually applicable time limit of one year.

91 Art. 302(2)(d) BAO.

92 Art. 207(4) BAO.

93 Particularly Arts. 13(1) and 17(1) AVG.

94 Particularly Arts. 8, 13(6) and 73(1) AVG.

95 Art. 132 Bundes-Verfassungsgesetz.

complaint for failure to act ("Devolutionsantrag", "Säumnisbeschwerde"), that remedy is only open to parties within the scope of that law.[96] Competitors do not enjoy that status as far as a request to the public authority to recover unlawful aid is concerned, because the AVG does not foresee such a remedy. Consequently, an action for a failure to act to recover State aid is not open to competitors. In addition, it is, as discussed in section V below, also disputed in Austrian literature to what extent competitors can rely on available remedies to exercise their own right to recovery accorded by Article 108(3) TFEU.

Given these insufficiencies, the only realistic possibility of complaint open to competitors, without initiating court action of their own, is a complaint to the Commission that the Member State has failed to recover the aid. Clearly, this legal situation in Austria is not satisfactory from the point of view of protecting EU rights.

3. Challenging to the validity of the Commission decision or the recovery order

There is no specific procedure in place in Austria to challenge the validity of recovery orders resulting from Commission decisions. Consequently, the general procedural remedies for defending claims of the opposing party or of the public authority will apply. Where, however, the national recovery action is based on a Commission decision, the validity of that decision can only be contested within the narrow margins permitted by EU law.[97] As long as the Commission decision is not declared invalid, however, Austrian authorities and courts are bound by it as a matter of primacy. Attempts by the recipient to challenge the recovery order on the basis of national civil or public law remedies, therefore, are unlikely to succeed. This may explain why, apparently, no such cases have yet come before the Austrian courts.

There are, therefore, only two perceptible bars to recovery orders based on valid Commission decisions. One of those bars is time limits, as discussed above. The second possible bar to recovery is the protection of legitimate expectations of the recipient. Academics argue that Austrian law enshrines this principle at constitutional level[98] and restates it in specific areas of legislation (e.g. tax law etc.). If the principle of legitimate expectations has the quality of a constitutional principle, however, pleas of infringement of legitimate expectations will be successful not only in public recovery proceedings but also before civil courts. It is further argued that the concept of what constitutes legitimate expectations is not necessarily congruent with the concept in EU law, but that the "effet utile" of the Commission's recovery order serves to correct the allegedly rather generous standard in Austria.

---

96 Paras. cf. Art. 8 AVG.

97 Cf. in particular the *Foto-Frost* (doubts of the court over the validity of the decision), *Atlanta* (interim invalidity) and *TWD* (bar against the invalidity claim by the defendant before the national court) doctrines.

98 Via Art. 18(1) B-VG.

V. Rules applicable to competitor action (standing of third parties)

1. Legal bases of standing of third parties before Austrian courts

The standstill obligation, as interpreted by the CJEU, requires Austrian law to accord standing to all persons with an interest in erasing the negative effects of the distortion of competition created by the grant of unlawful aid, or in obtaining a refund of a tax levied in breach of that provision.[99] This concept is closely modelled on the conditions of direct and individual concern under Article 263 TFEU. The persons directly and individually concerned by an aid are typically competitors and the persons to whom a decision breaching the standstill obligation is addressed. These persons must at least therefore be accorded standing before the Austrian courts to claim the rights accorded to them under the standstill obligation.

a. Civil law-based aid

Contracts containing illegal aid elements are nul and void ("absolut nichtig") under Austrian civil law.[100] The nullity of the contract can be invoked by any third party with a respective legal interest. Depending on the type of legal interest that the third party has, the legal bases available to bring the nullity claim before a court differ. Thus, the nullity may, for example, be invoked as a shield by the third party in the context of contractual litigation or litigation over torts under general civil law, i.e. the provisions of the Austrian Civil Code (ABGB).

The extent to which third parties may use the ABGB to successfully construct claims based on breaches of the standstill obligation (sword-cases), e.g. for damages or "cease and desist" claims, is untested in practice and little discussed in literature.

The reason is that, in such cases, typically the Austrian Law on Unfair Competition (UWG) will apply. The UWG applies to unfair acts in the course of business, capable of affecting competition and to breaches of professional care affecting consumption patterns.[101] The UWG offers a comprehensive set of remedies to third parties to tackle illegal aid, as discussed below.

Entitlement to claims under the UWG presupposes the existence of a competitive relationship between the parties.[102] However, the Austrian Supreme Court (OGH) has recently clarified that this also includes ad hoc competition and competition over market entry, which may be distorted by unlawful aid.[103] Furthermore, the OGH has (albeit not in the context of State aid) acknowledged that consumers may base certain claims on the UWG, in particular for

99 Cf., e.g., Case C-174/02, SWNB, para. 19.

100 Cf. OLG Wien of 5 February 2007, 2 R 150/06b.

101 Art. 1 UWG.

102 Art. 14(1) UWG.

103 Cf. OGH of 15 December 2008, 4 Ob 133/08z.

damages.[104] Beyond the scope of application of the UWG and thus beyond competitors (in a broad sense) and consumers, no other texts allow for an effective construction of third-party civil law claims in relation to illegal aid. As has been shown, this is, however, in line with EU law.

b. *Public law-based aid*

Third-party court action against unlawful aid granted by public law acts encounters the aforementioned problem of the relative nullity of administrative decisions ("Bescheid") in breach of the standstill obligation. Therefore, the invalidity of the decision can in principle only be claimed by the parties to whom it is addressed. Third parties do not have standing to attack that decision. In addition, even a decision declaring the previous decision invalid would not necessarily have the effect of safeguarding all third-party interests, such as a right of the third party to demand recovery. This problem occurs not only under general administrative law (AVG), but also, and more importantly, in the area of taxation (BAO). It should be noted, however, that there are, to date, no examples of competitors bringing actions against illegal aid on the basis of public law (sword-cases) in Austria, thus the provisions discussed here as possible bases for legal standing so far only figure in academic discussion.

Under general administrative law, without a reopening of the procedure, decisions can only be invalidated *ex officio*.[105] However, a reopening of procedure may be applied for by a party to the initial procedure.[106] This possibility, however, suffers from two uncertainties. First, none of the reasons for reopening enumerated in the respective provision (fraud, new facts, new line of case law) is unambiguously fit to apply to breaches of the standstill obligation: Furthermore, although solutions to this problem have been discussed in the literature, competitors and third parties cannot easily be brought under the definition of "parties"[107] – as the group of persons entitled to reopen proceedings under the wording of that provision. Where there is no possibility to do so at the stage of the administrative proceedings, there is, accordingly, also no possibility for subsequent court review.

Similarly in the area of tax law, decisions can be invalidated for a wide range of reasons, possibly including unlawful State aid, but only upon the application of a party to the initial proceedings.[108] Also, as regards a reopening of the procedure, parties are only entitled to rely on one of the three grounds (fraud, new facts, and new line of case law) enumerated in that provision.[109] Here again, competitors and third parties encounter the problem that they lack

104 Cf. OGH of 24 February 1998, 4 Ob 53/98t.

105 Art. 68 AVG.

106 Art. 69 AVG.

107 Art. 8 AVG.

108 Art. 299 BAO.

109 Art. 303 BAO.

standing before the tax authorities to attack decisions granting unlawful aid.[110] Furthermore, lack of standing before the administration entails lack of access to the courts.

In this area, therefore, Austrian public law remains far behind the requirements of EU law. With a view to bringing enforcement rights in line with EU law, some academics have contemplated the possibility for third parties to apply for declaratory decisions under general administrative law[111] and tax law[112] as a way to open the possibility of court review. It is, however, highly uncertain how declaratory decisions should be framed to serve as a means of legal protection for third parties and how they could possibly affect the (separate) decision by which the aid was actually granted. Others have argued that where public law does not provide any means for third parties to challenge decisions granting aid, the "effet utile" of the standstill obligation requires that those decisions should, exceptionally, be regarded as null and void ("absolut nichtig") in public law. Alternatively, some academics argue that the aforementioned provisions of the Austrian Law against Unfair Competition (UWG) could also be interpreted as applying to aid granted by public law measures. The problem again is, of course, that as a precondition for any such claims to be brought before the civil courts, the public decision's State aid quality would have to be ascertained, i.e. review by the competent authorities must have taken place (which, for the aforementioned reasons, cannot easily be initiated by the third party). In the absence of such preliminary review by the public authorities, it is not easy to see how the civil courts could decide an UWG-based case in favour of the applicant while ignoring a formally valid public decision entitling the applicant, to the respective benefit, without reviewing that measure themselves (for which they are not competent). One way to avoid this dilemma might, however, be the combination of a declaratory decision that aid has been granted illegally and a subsequent UWG-based action before a civil court relying on that declaratory decision. Again, this has yet been tested in practice. As far as damages for infringements of the standstill obligation are concerned, there is no problem of standing in relation to public law aid measures. Damages claimed on the basis of the Austrian Law on Administrative Liability (Amtshaftungsgesetz, AHG) can be brought by anyone who has suffered loss.[113]

2. Claims available

The standstill obligation, as interpreted by the CJEU, foresees the following claims, which must be made available under Austrian law to ensure effective enforcement: suspension, restrictive injunctions and (full or limited[114] for retroactively authorised aid) recovery,[115] interim

110 Art. 78 BAO.

111 Cf. Arts. 56 and 59 AVG.

112 Cf. Arts. 78(2) and 185 et seq. BAO.

113 Art. 1(1) AHG.

114 Case C-199/06, CELF, paras. 45 et seq.

115 E.g., Case C-39/94, SFEI, para. 71.

measures,[116] (sometimes)[117] repayment of unduly levied charges and, finally, damages against the Member State for infringement of EU law.[118]

a. Civil law-based aid

The claims open to competitors as required by EU law, are fully available under the Law against Unfair Competition (UWG). Suspension and restrictive injunctions can be claimed on the basis of Article 108(3) TFEU and Articles 1 and 14 UWG, redress and recovery on the basis of Article 108(3) TFEU and Articles 1 and 15 UWG. Interim measures are available under paragraph 24 UWG. Damages, which include lost profits, are available under Article 108(3) TFEU and Articles 1 and 16 UWG.

These claims can be directed against the aid recipient as well as against the Member State, which is also an addressee of the prohibition.[119] Infringement of the standstill obligation conveys an unfair competitive advantage through the breach of a statutory prohibition ("Vorsprung durch Rechtsbruch").[120] The recipient and the Member State are jointly liable for damages.[121]

However, where a competitor applies for interim measures, such as suspension of the aid, freezing of assets, prevention of execution of a contract or the like, he is liable for any damages to the other party if the application is unfounded.[122] In other words, the application for interim measures may give rise to a counter-claim for damages by the aid recipient or the State. Given that State aid cases involve particular uncertainties about the outcome of the case following an assessment of the characteristics and/or compatibility of the measure by the court seized, the CJEU and/or the Commission, interim measures to safeguard rights flowing from the standstill obligation carry a significant economic risk. Accordingly, unlike in public procedure, where suspension of the execution of an act is typically applied for, applications for interim measures in civil law cases are rarer.[123]

Finally, the group of persons enjoying standing under the UWG (competitors and consumers) is even broader than the group for which EU law requires standing (competitors only). There is, accordingly, no need to examine the possibility of constructing civil law claims on the basis of other provisions of Austrian law, e.g. under the general Civil Code (ABGB).

116 E.g., Case C-39/94, SFEI, paras. 52 et seq.

117 Hypothecation, e.g., Case C-1740/2, SWNB, para. 25; Joined Cases C-266/04 et al., Nazairdis, para. 44.

118 E.g., Case C-390/98, Banks, para. 80.

119 E.g., OGH of 16 July 2002, 4 Ob 72/02w.

120 Cf., e.g., OGH of 11 March 2008, 4 Ob 225/07b.

121 Cf. Art. 17 UWG.

122 Cf. Art. 394 EO.

123 To state one example, interim measures directed against the closing of the sale of the undertaking were applied for (but dismissed) before the lower instances (Landesgericht Eisenstadt and Oberlandesgericht Wien) in the Bank Burgenland case.

b. *Public law-based aid*

Actions brought by competitors against public law-based aid encounter the problem of a lack of clear legal basis for standing, as discussed in the previous section. Furthermore, public law does not, as a matter of principle, recognise the civil law concept of claims, but instead aims at ensuring legality in terms of the correct application of norms and individual protection vis-à-vis the State. Leaving the problem of the construction of standing aside, therefore, where a legal basis for annulment of an administrative decision exists, the replacement decision ensures the correct application of the law. Ideally, such a decision would incorporate those rights accorded to the applicant by the standstill obligation which are pertinent in the given case, i.e. to ensure redress and recovery.

Claims for damages for infringement of the standstill obligation by public authorities of any level (federal, regional or local) can be based on the Austrian Law on Administrative Liability (Amtshaftungsgesetz, AHG). This claim must be brought before the civil courts[124] within three years of discovery of the damage.[125]

VI. Cooperation with EU authorities

1. Administrative level

The notification of intended aid measures to the Commission was centralised at the federal level for all aid measures in Austria, irrespective of their federal, regional or local origin. Unit C 1/8 of the Federal Ministry of Economy, Family and Youth (name subject to frequent change) is responsible for notifying the Commission. The basis for that unit's functions appears to be informal and flexible. A uniform and binding statutory rule for centralised notification does not exist. Beyond this unit, no centralised body or uniform procedures for interaction with the Commission exist.

As regards interaction with the EU courts, the conduct of litigation and related communication is the responsibility of the chancellery's legal service ("Verfassungsdienst"), irrespective of the origin of the measure. Cooperation differs depending on the requirements at hand. There is no standardised cooperation procedure.

2. Courts

There are no instances of cooperation between the national courts and the Commission, in terms of Austrian courts requesting access to information held by the Commission, or of counsel in the form of an amicus curiae brief.

---

124 Cf. Art. 9 AHG.

125 Cf. Art. 6(1) AHG.

Cooperation of the Austrian courts with the CJEU under the preliminary rulings procedure is generally quite well developed. The court before which most State aid cases have been pleaded is the VwGH (administration court). The VfGH (constitutional court) and the OGH (civil supreme court) are, by contrast, only occasionally hear State aid problems and have therefore only rarely (the OGH; never) requested preliminary rulings on a State aid problem. The VwGH, as the court most affected, shows a high degree of State aid awareness and knowledge and accordingly makes frequent use of the preliminary rulings procedure.[126] At the same time, the relative sophistication of the VwGH in terms of State aid also enables it to refrain from seeking preliminary rulings in application of the "acte claire"[127] doctrine.[128] The assessment undertaken on that basis is generally solid, although the reporting period shows a case where retroactively, following the CJEU's later judgment in CELF,[129] a different outcome may have been warranted.[130] By contrast, the "acte claire"[131] doctrine, i.e. an independent solution to a State aid problem in the absence of guiding CJEU case law, has not yet been attempted by the VwGH or any other Austrian court.

VII. Trends – reforms – recommendations

On the basis of the scrutiny of court practice and academic discussion on State aid enforcement in Austria undertaken in this report, the following systemic improvements are called for:

- clarification of the legal basis and conditions applicable to an annulment of public law acts in breach of the standstill obligation under both general administrative law (AVG) and for taxes (BAO);
- creation or, alternatively, clarification of legal bases for the standing of competitors before administrative authorities in public law under both the AVG and the BAO;
- creation of a legal basis for recovery of public-law based by administrative authorities in general terms (in the AVG) and for taxes (in the BAO);
- creation of a legal basis or right of third parties in general administrative law (AVG) and for taxes (BAO) to demand public action for recovery and/or an administrative or court claim for review of failure of the authority to act upon a complaint;
- finally, the creation of a national "State aid Authority" to pre-assess and consequently clear or notify to the Commission all State aid measures envisaged by the public authorities.

126 Cf. in the reporting period e.g. VwGH of 31 July 2007 et al., 2004/05/0274 (Wienstrom).

127 Cf. Case 28/62 et al., Da Costa, 81; Case 283/81, CILFIT, para. 14.

128 Cf. VwGH of 20 March 2006 et al., 2005/17/0230 et al. (AMA-Marketingbeiträge); VwGH of 30 June 2006 et al., 2006/17/0092 et al. (AMA-Marketingbeiträge).

129 Case C-199/06, CELF; reaffirmed and sophisticated in Case C-1/09, CELF II.

130 Cf. VwGH of 8 January 2007 et al., 2002/17/0356 et al. (Energieabgabenvergütung).

131 Case 283/81, CILFIT, para. 15.

In terms of trends, an area in which there could be significant changes as regards court enforcement of the standstill obligation and of relief to competitors is the question of a possible abandonment of the nullity doctrine for civil law breaches of the standstill obligation. The nullity sanction has long been propagated by Austrian authors and was recently explicitly confirmed by the court of appeal in the Bank Burgenland case.[132] However, following the CJEU's obiter dictum on the scope of the standstill obligation and the interests protected by it in the CELF judgment of 2008,[133] Austrian case law may again shift away from the application of a fully-fledged nullity sanction. Under the current doctrine, nullity is considered imperative to safeguard the "effet utile" of a standstill obligation and is understood as being concerned with both the protection of competitors against distortions resulting from the premature granting of aid and with safeguarding the effectiveness of the obligation for Member States to notify new aid. Where the latter consideration is no longer relevant following the CELF judgment and where, therefore, the payment of interest by the recipient for the period of illegality may suffice to remedy the distortive effect of the illegal aid, nullity of the legal basis of the aid may be deemed an excessive sanction. Depending on the standpoint taken, this may apply not only to aid authorised by the Commission *ex post* facto, but for any point in time before a definitive assessment of a measure by the Commission is available. A similar argument was recently made in German literature and there is reason to assume that the assessment by the Austrian courts in future State aid cases may also move away from a stringent nullity sanction. For competitors, the nullity sanction is important for the prospect of invalidating contracts at an early stage of the granting of illegal aid. Where the threat of that sanction is removed, the incentives for taking court action at any time before a negative Commission decision is available are virtually nil.

---

132 Cf. OLG Wien of 5 February 2007, 2 R 150/06b.

133 Cf. Case C-199/06, CELF, paras. 47 et seq. in particular; Case C-1/09, CELF II para. 29.

BELGIUM

Jacques Derenne, Cédric Kaczmarek*
Corapporteur Tony Joris**

* Hogan Lovells, Brussels. The rapporteurs would like to thank Tony Joris who assisted them in identifying and analysing some of the Dutch speaking cases which were used to draft this report.

** VUB University, Centre for European Law, Brussels.

I. General principles of Member State's State aid law

1. National authorities that are competent to grant aid and to be involved in the notification procedure

Belgium is a federal State divided into both Regions and Communities. The constitutional organisation of the country is complex. There are three Regions, Flanders, Wallonia and Brussels-Capital and three Communities based on the language spoken, the Flemish Community (merged with the Flemish Region), the French Community and the German Community.

The Regions enjoy executive and legislative authority in economic matters relating to their territory, such as employment, economic development, transport, agriculture, housing and also in international trade and cooperation related to matters with respect to which they have been granted autonomy. The Communities have executive and legislative authority with respect to other matters, such as cultural affairs, education, tourism, health and social affairs.

The transfer of powers to the Regions and Communities includes the grant of State aid competence in areas where the Regions and Communities enjoy authority. Thus, broadly speaking, authority for granting aid is split as follows within Belgium:

- federal government and agencies are responsible for aid of a federal nature, and in particular, fiscal (tax reductions or exemptions) or social measures (social contributions reductions and exemptions);
- regional government and agencies are responsible for investment, R&D aid, social aid, export aid and some forms of fiscal aid;
- Community government and agencies are responsible for training aid and aid to promote culture.

The legal basis needed to grant an aid depends on the origin of the aid.

2. National authorities that are competent to recover aid and an overview of the procedure

With respect to the recovery of unlawful aid, the Belgian authorities generally send the beneficiary a letter of formal notice requesting repayment of the aid. If the beneficiary does not comply with such a request, the authorities must bring a debt action against the aid beneficiary before the Commercial Court in order to recover the money.

Certain legislative and regulatory measures contain recovery provisions for administrative reasons (non compliance with the conditions of the aid), which could be extended to a recovery procedure for unlawfulness of the aid.

II. Identification of State aid issues at national level

1. State aid compliance by the national legislator and/or the executive power

Currently there is no system for surveying State aid in Belgium in order to ensure that Article 108(3) TFEU and Article 14 of Regulation (EC) No 659/1999 (notification requirement) are complied with.

There is no obligation to publish the intention to grant aid measures at national level. There is no specific procedure, nor any recommendations relating to the notification of aid projects, either at Federal or Regional level.

To verify the compliance of the received aid with Block exemptions Regulations, the beneficiaries are supposed to be surrounded by proficient advisors on Community law. In addition, "the Federal Public Service for Economy, SMEs, self-employed and Energy" and the relevant ministries for economy in the regions can advise them.

2. State aid compliance by national judges and/or the national competition authority (NCA)

Three different types of court in Belgium are generally competent in respect of State aid litigation:

- the supreme (and unique) administrative court: the Council of State ("Council of State"/"Raad van State");
- the judicial courts (commercial and civil courts: courts of first instance and commercial courts, and their relevant courts of appeal – "tribunal de première instance"/"rechtbank van eerste aanleg", "tribunal de commerce"/"rechtbank van koophandel", "cours d'appel"/"hoven van beroep"– and the Supreme Court – "Cour de cassation"/"Hof van cassatie");
- the constitutional court, the Court of Arbitration ("Cour d'arbitrage"/"Arbitragehof"), which has the power to review legislative acts on limited points of constitutional law (constitutional disputes and the principle of non-discrimination between Belgian citizens).

III. Unlawful aid and judicial review

1. General powers of the national courts concerning the direct effect of Article 108(3) TFEU

Proceedings before the Council of State

Any administrative act of a non-legislative nature can be reviewed by the Council of State (action for annulment – "recours en annulation" or "recours pour excès de pouvoir"). This type of action largely originates from the judicial mechanisms of the French and Dutch Councils of State.

The action can be lodged by any party demonstrating an interest (such interest must be personal, present, certain, direct and legitimate). The time limit for submitting the action is two months from the notification, publication or full knowledge of the act.

Until now, State aid cases before the Council of State have involved challenges by beneficiaries against a recovery decision, and against a decision rejecting a tender on State aid grounds. So far, no actions have been brought by competitors before the Council of State against a decision granting State aid in breach of Article 108(3) TFEU.

It may be that the procedure before the Council of State, which is quite lengthy, is not convenient for a claimant who is a competitor of a beneficiary of unlawfully granted State aid. More interesting is the possibility of requesting, in parallel with the action for annulment, the suspension of the challenged act (decision granting State aid, for instance). A decision by the Belgium Council of State is then delivered within 45 days. The pleas invoked in a request for suspension must be "serious and likely to justify the annulment" and there must be a risk of serious and irreparable harm (the latter condition is very difficult to fulfil since pecuniary damage is only deemed to be irreparable if it leads a claimant to bankruptcy).

If it is not possible for the claimant to wait 45 days, it can make use of the extreme urgency procedure ("procédure d'extrême urgence"). The risk of damage from an immediate implementation of the challenged act must be imminent or, at least, likely before the expiry of the 45 days; in addition, the claimant must have taken all steps to prevent the damage and must have lodged the request with the Court as soon as possible.

The case may then be registered immediately (within one or a few hours). A decision can be delivered on the day of the request. It should be noted that, to the best of our knowledge, neither the suspension procedure nor the extreme urgency procedure have been used in State aid matters.

Proceedings before civil courts

Actions may be brought before the civil courts (and the commercial courts) regarding litigation between private parties, or between the latter and the State, when there is no intention to request the annulment of a particular State measure (the sole administrative court in Belgium is the Council of State described above).

Civil courts have jurisdiction to rule on the State's liability. The commercial courts have jurisdiction over litigation between professionals in the course of their business, and over any litigation concerning business acts.

Actions for damages brought against a competitor should be brought before the commercial courts. Where the claimant is not a commercial operator, such an action can also be brought before the civil courts.

Judgments of the commercial courts can be appealed to the commercial division of the court of appeal and further appealed, on points of law only, to the Supreme Court.

Procedure before the Court of Arbitration (Constitutional Court)
The Court of Arbitration is competent to review the constitutionality of certain legislative acts. It can review the compatibility of laws ("lois"/"wetten" from the federal parliament), decrees ("décrets"/"decreten": legislative acts of the Flemish region, of the Walloon region and of the French and German speaking Communities) and ordinances ("ordonnances"/"ordonnanties": legislative acts of the Brussels region) with:

- the rules establishing the division of powers between the State, the Communities and the Regions found in the Constitution and in special laws;
- the fundamental rights and liberties guaranteed in Section II of the Constitution (Articles 8 to 32 of the Constitution);
- the principle of legality of taxation as laid down in Article 170 of the Constitution;
- the principle of non-discrimination in fiscal matters as laid down in Article 172 of the Constitution; and
- the protection for non-citizens as expressed in Article 191 of the Constitution.

A violation of EC State aid rules constitutes a violation of such fundamental rights. Thus, in some State aid cases, the Court of Arbitration has found that the relevant laws breached Articles 10 and 11 of the Constitution (principle of non-discrimination) in parallel with State aid rules.

Prior to the extension of the Court of Arbitration's competences in 2004, only the violation of the principle of non-discrimination (and not the other fundamental rights mentioned in Section II of the Constitution) could be directly invoked before the Court of Arbitration. Before 2004, claimants invoked the violation of this principle read in conjunction with the State aid rules. It should be noted that, following the extension of the Court's competences, these rules remain an indirect ground of review. Regulations having the force of law, which are subject to constitutional control, include both substantive and formal rules adopted as "lois"/"wetten", "décrets"/"decreten" and "ordonnances/ordonnanties" mentioned above.

All other regulations, such as royal decrees, decisions by governments, Communities and Regions, ministerial decrees, regulations, and decisions of provinces and municipalities, as well as court judgments, fall outside the jurisdiction of the Court of Arbitration. A case may be brought before the Court of Arbitration by virtue of a direct action or through a preliminary reference by another court. The claimants in such actions are not necessarily competitors of the beneficiary.

In two cases, the claimants were municipalities seeking to withdraw the tax exemption granted to a beneficiary of aid. In other cases, the claimants have been parties unwilling to pay taxes under a regime which may constitute State aid.

In one case, the claimant was a professional association representing insurance companies against a measure which would benefit a competitor of the members of that association.

2. Prevention of the granting of unlawful aid

As before the Council of State, suspension of the implementation of the decision granting unlawful aid can be requested by competing undertakings before the relevant civil court (in fact, the president of the civil or commercial court, acting "en référé"/"kort geding" – interim relief). However, suspension can only be requested when the administrative decision to grant the aid creates personal rights ("droits subjectifs") for the person seeking the interim relief (see also section concerning judicial review of administrative acts by the Council of State).

The conditions for this type of interim measure are urgency, a *prima facie* case and serious and immediate harm. It should be noted that a judge may consider, according to the circumstances, that it is not competent to grant interim relief and may ultimately decide that it is up to the Council of State to deal with such an action.

3. Recovery of unlawful aid and interests

Competitors can bring an action before a commercial court and request it to order the beneficiary to repay the aid to the relevant administration. Such an action would be based upon the principle of the supremacy of EU law over national law.

A complainant who wishes to obtain such an order must show sufficient interest. The enforcement of the law (in this case, Article 108(3) TFEU) is not in itself a sufficient interest. Therefore, a competitor would have to show how the grant of aid directly affected it by putting it at a competitive disadvantage.

However, it should be noted that when the claimant contests the payment of an illegal tax, for instance, by relying upon Article 108(3) TFEU, it does not have to show that this tax puts it at a competitive disadvantage (as compared to the beneficiaries of the aid financed by the tax, for instance) but only that it is affected by the tax being illegal.

There is also a specific procedure based on unfair competition law principles. A competitor may sue a beneficiary before the President of the Commercial Court with a view to obtaining a "cease and desist" order (in an accelerated procedure, similar to the interim relief procedure, but this is an action on the merits of the case leading to a definitive decision) for any unfair competitive behaviour (see the *Breda* case below).

This action is based on liability principles since an unfair trade practice constitutes a fault. The action is provided for by Article 93 of the Law of 14 July 1991 on Trade Practices and Consumer Information. Article 93 of the Law grants the right to order the cessation of an action contrary to fair trade practices by which a seller damages or could damage the professional interests of one or more other sellers.

According to this provision, a seller can require the cessation of any action it deems contrary to fair trade practices, even if that action has not been penalised or prohibited by a legal text. Within a State aid context, the unfair behaviour of the beneficiary which could be targeted from a competition perspective is the fact that the beneficiary would benefit from an unlawful aid when any diligent economic operator is expected to verify the procedural compliance of such grant.

The fact that the beneficiary will act on the market and take advantage of this unlawfully received/granted aid (for instance, in order to offer a lower price in a tender) may also be relevant. The President of the Commercial Court can only deliver "cease and desist" orders under this procedure. Any action for damages (see below) in relation to such a decision will have to be lodged before the Commercial Court in a separate action.

4. Damages claims by competitors/third parties against the granting authority before the national courts

Damages can be sought from the Belgian State for non compliance with Community law in the following two ways.

First, under national liability law, a person has to make good in full any damage caused by his fault (Article 1382 of the Belgian Civil Code) or by his negligence (Article 1383 of the Belgian Civil Code). The Belgian State and its organs can also be held liable for fault or negligence under these provisions.

Unlike French law, therefore, Belgian law allows in principle the grant of damages in cases of State liability according to the same conditions which apply to individuals. It is necessary to prove a fault, the resulting damage and a causal link. These provisions can therefore be used to engage the State's responsibility (including the legislator and even the judiciary in certain circumstances) for adopting an act which breaches Community law. Harm can include the breach of a legitimate interest.

Secondly, damages can also be sought from the Belgian State under European law liability principles, in line with the principles set out in Court of Justice cases (Joined Cases C-6/90 and C-9/90, *Francovich and Bonifaci* [1991] ECR I-5357 and Joined Cases C-46/93 and C-48/93 *Brasserie du Pêcheur-Factortame* III [1996] ECR I-1090).

Under this case law, the liability of the State will be engaged where: (i) the rule of law infringed is intended to confer rights on individuals; (ii) the breach is sufficiently serious; and (iii) there is a direct causal link between the breach of the obligation resting on the State and the damage sustained by the injured parties. As regards the second condition, where the State has a large margin of discretion in implementing a policy, the CJEU has considered that the State's liability can only be engaged where the State has manifestly and gravely disregarded the limits on its discretion.

This second condition can therefore be much harder to satisfy than the test under civil liability, where a simple breach is sufficient evidence of damage. However, this is not the case in the field of State aid, as no margin of discretion is left to the Member States on the application of Article 108(3) TFEU. By definition therefore, a violation of Article 108(3) TFEU should always be regarded as a serious breach, likely to engage the State's liability within the meaning of the case law mentioned above. Concerning State aid rules, the Court of Justice's case law may therefore seem more favourable (or at least equivalent to, since any breach of the law by the State is regarded as a fault on behalf of the State) than the traditional national liability system based on "fault, damage and causal link" (Article 1382 of the Civil Code).

5. Damages claims by the beneficiary (against the granting authority) before the national courts

There are no examples of such an action under Belgian law (however, actions for unfair competition, described above, are based on liability principles). The question of the liability of the beneficiary of unlawful aid must be brought before the civil courts under Article 1382 of the Civil Code. The relevant courts will have to determine whether the beneficiary benefited from the aid in full knowledge of its unlawful character, or whether the beneficiary ought to have been aware of this illegality, as well as the amount of damages to be granted to the competitors. This would appear to be a difficult test to satisfy.

6. Damages claims by competitors/third parties against the beneficiary before the national courts

There has, in fact, only been one case in which a Belgian court has had to rule on an action brought by a competitor against a recipient of State aid (the *Breda-Fucine* case, where the claimant successfully obtained a "cease and desist" order against an Italian company regarding its participation in a tender process. Another action, brought by Hays against La Poste in 2000, was finally not ruled upon by the Court).

The *Breda* case (President of Brussels Commercial Court, 13 February 1995, Breda Fucine Meridionali v. Manoir Industries, JTDE, 1995, p. 72) merits some discussion, as it constitutes an exemplary decision which refers to all the consequences, vis-à-vis the beneficiary of unlawful aid, of the violation of Article 108(3) TFEU. The Belgian national railways (SNCB-NMBS) launched a tender process for the provision of railways materials. Breda, an Italian company, and Manoir Industries, a French company, submitted competing offers. It appeared that Breda's offer was priced at 40 % lower than Manoir's offer.

Manoir filed a complaint with the Commission, alleging that Breda benefited from State aid granted by the Italian State. Manoir also lodged an action for a cease and desist order before the President of the Brussels Commercial Court alleging that Breda's offer was abnormally low due to this State aid, which had not been notified to the Commission. An order was rendered by default in favour of Manoir.

Breda filed an opposing claim with the same judge, requesting a contradictory judgment. The President of the Brussels Commercial Court first recalled, rejecting Breda's pleas, that the national court has powers to interpret and apply the concept of aid with a view to determining whether a State measure had to comply with Article 108(3) TFEU.

The President of the court explicitly referred to *Steinike & Weinlig* (Case 78/76, Steinike & Weinlig [1977] ECR 595). The President of the court further rejected the argument that the definitive and non-provisional nature of the powers of the court, in the context of the "cease and desist" order procedure, would be incompatible with a possible Commission decision on the compatibility of the aid with the Internal Market.

The Court also referred to *Saumon – FNCE* (Case C-354/90, Fédération nationale du commerce extérieur des produits alimentaires and Syndicat national des négociants et transformateurs de Saumon [1991] ECR I-550) in order to confirm that any Commission decision could not have the effect of *a posteriori* regularising a violation of Article 108(3) TFEU. The national court may not therefore be requested to stay the proceedings while waiting for such a Commission decision.

Finally, the President of the court ruled that Breda could not exonerate itself by arguing that the notification obligation is imposed on the Italian State and not on itself, the State aid being *"incompatible with the Internal Market, and therefore unacceptable on this market [sic]. Breda committed an abuse in intervening as it did with its offer to the SNCB, with the help of such State aid; this abuse constitutes an act of unfair competition prohibited by Article 93 of the Law on the Protection of Commerce and Consumers, since it infringes or may infringe a subjective right of Manoir to an "undistorted competition, inherent to its professional interests."*

Under Court of Justice case law, the beneficiary by claiming any benefit from the violation of Article 108(3) TFEU, commits an act of unfair competition under national legislation (Case C-39/94, SFEI a.o. v. La Poste a.o. [1996] ECR I-3547). The competitor of such a beneficiary has the right to stop this act of unfair competition by having recourse to an efficient litigation procedure which leads to a definitive decision, even though the latter is adopted by virtue of an interim relief procedure (specific procedure for a "cease and desist" order).

There is, however, one confusing point in the judgment. Rejecting Breda's argument, the President of the court rightly stated that the question of the eventual compatibility of the State aid was not at stake. However, in its concluding decision, the President of the court wrongly qualified the State aid in question as being "incompatible with the Internal Market".

This was perhaps an error of wording, but it should nevertheless not be repeated in order to avoid confusing the important distinction between the legality/lawfulness of the aid, on the one hand, and its compatibility with the Internal Market, on the other hand (the only scope of intervention of the judge under Article 108(3) TFEU read in conjunction with Article 107(1) TFEU).

This is quite an isolated case and it is not really clear what discourages competitors from bringing proceedings against beneficiaries of State aid. Another attempt was made in the *Hays* case (President of Commercial Court of Brussels, 15 September 2000 and Court of Appeal of Brussels of 7 December 2001, Hays v. La Poste (Assurmail service) and Key Mail, unreported). Hays brought an action for a cease and desist order against the conditions adopted by La Poste for setting up a division (Assurmail) which would compete with Hays' Document Exchange service (DX) in the insurance sector. Hays claimed that Assurmail benefited from cross-subsidies constituting not notified State aid in breach of Article 108(3) TFEU. Hays also claimed that La Poste's action breached Article 102 TFEU abusing its dominant position. The President of Commercial Court decided to question the Commission but on the day of the re-opening of the oral hearing, its decision was appealed; the Court of Appeal did not come to a ruling on this matter as the Commission issued a decision (on 5 December 2001) declaring that the service was in breach of Article 102 TFEU. This was sufficient for La Poste to discontinue Assurmail (the Court of Appeal decided on 7 December 2001 to stay the proceedings until the adoption of a Commission decision, which was adopted two days before the delivery of this judgment). There are no specific procedural or legal obstacles, except the difficulty encountered in some cases with qualifying the measure as State aid, or the usual length of the procedure before the courts in Belgium (however, the "cease and desist" order procedure may lead to a quite satisfactory result in that respect).

7. Interim measures taken by national judges

To the best of our knowledge, the interim relief procedure has not been used in State aid matters. A request for interim measures can be made before the Council of State (in parallel with a request for suspension, which in turn will require a request for annulment). It is technically possible for the Belgian State to seek interim measures from the civil judge requiring the beneficiary of unlawful aid to pay a bank guarantee for the aid in question before the final judgment.

The conditions for this type of interim measures are urgency, the existence of a *prima facie* case and the risk of a serious and immediate harm. However, it is apparent from the sole recovery case in which such an interim measure action was brought that the "urgency" criterion is a very difficult one to satisfy. Indeed, in the *Ter Lembeek* case (Commercial Court of Kortrijk, 26.2.2004, Wallon Region v. Ter Lembeek International NV, Case 088/03) an action for interim measures brought by the Walloon Region was rejected by the Commercial Court for lack of urgency.

Indeed, the court considered that there was no evidence that the beneficiary of the aid, Ter Lembeek, would become insolvent in the near future, and that the Walloon Region would therefore suffer any irreparable damage. From this sole example, it would therefore appear that a Belgian court would only grant interim measures where there is a possibility that the beneficiary of the unlawful aid would be unable to repay the aid in question at the end of the main recovery proceedings.

However, in the *Fortis* case (Brussels Court of Appeal, 12.12.2008, Fortis, Case n° 2008/KR 350), the Brussels Court of Appeal rejected the claimants' arguments seeking the suspension of operations in favour of Fortis Bank in the context of the financial crisis. They claimed that there was strong evidence that the measures of the Belgian government constituted unlawful State aid in favour of the financial institution.

The Brussels Court of Appeal dismissed the plea, judging that the violation of the standstill obligation of Article 108(3) TFEU by a Member State does not necessarily lead to the annulment of the disputed conventions.

IV. Control of recovery procedure

1. Rules applicable to recovery

In Belgium, a variety of national and regional bodies may be responsible for the recovery of aid, either of their own initiative or following a negative Commission decision. Indeed, in recovery cases, the Belgian Federal Government, the Walloon region, the Flemish region, the Brussels region, the various Communities, the Belgian Social Security office, as well as other public bodies responsible for granting financial assistance, have all taken measures to recover aid.

The Belgian Permanent Representation to the EU is generally the intermediary for correspondence between the Commission and the relevant authorities responsible for recovering the aid. Sometimes, the relevant authorities communicate directly with the Commission.

Where the Federal State is not concerned, the relevant Region or Community will be closely associated during the procedure with the Commission. In fact, in such a case, the regional or community entity manages the case, with the Federal State (Ministry for Foreign Affairs and the Permanent Representation) merely liaising with the Commission for formal correspondence on the basis of the decisions at the regional or community level.

The addressees of negative Commission decisions can only be Member States – and not the regional or local powers of a State. Such a decision cannot therefore be directly used as an enforceable instrument ("titre exécutoire"), requiring the beneficiary of the unlawful aid to repay this aid.

In the Belgian recovery cases examined, it is apparent that, in order to recover unlawful aid, the Belgian authorities follow the general Belgian civil rules relating to the recovery of a debt, the legal basis thereof being the Commission decision. The first step of the debt recovery procedure requires the creditor (the relevant Belgian authority responsible for the recovery of the unlawful aid) to send a formal letter of notice to the debtor (beneficiary of the aid) requesting payment of its debt (the aid).

In the event that the beneficiary of the aid refuses to comply with the letter of formal notice, the relevant Belgian authority can bring an action before the civil courts in order to obtain a jugdment ordering the beneficiary to pay the debt (unlawful aid). The first instance judgment, generally rendered by a Commercial Court, can be appealed to the Court of Appeal and then to the Supreme Court (on points of law only).

2. Action for recovery

a. By the State

In Belgium, there is one example of a case whereby the Belgian State adopted a law so as to ensure the recovery of unlawfully paid aid (*Maribel* case). The Belgian Government increased the reduction of the social security contributions due from companies which were active in some specifically designated business sectors (the so-called "Maribel-bis" and "Maribel-ter" schemes).

All of these sectors were exposed to very high international competition. The Commission found that these schemes were unlawful and constituted incompatible aid and ordered the Belgian State on 4 December 1996 to recover from all of the beneficiaries the total amount of the aid (Decision 97/239/EC of 4 December 1996, OJ (1997) L 97/25).

On 19 February 1997, the Belgian State lodged an action for annulment against that decision (Case C-75/97, Belgium v. Commission [1999] ECR I-3671). This action was dismissed by the CJEU on 17 June 1999. In parallel, the Commission brought, on 21 October 1998, an action against the Belgian State for failing to comply with its decision (Case C-378/98, Commission v. Belgium [2001] ECR I-5107).

The CJEU held on 3 July 2001 that Belgium had failed to comply with the decision. By virtue of the Law of 24 December 1999, the Belgian State had laid down the arrangements for the recovery of the aid. In the Commission's view, this law still did not enable all of the aid in question to be recovered.

In fact, it allowed firms which had repaid the aid to deduct the amount repaid once more for tax purposes, which was tantamount to granting them fresh unlawful aid. Moreover, the application by the Belgian authorities of the *de minimis* rule appeared to the Commission to be incorrect in that it permitted firms in the excluded sectors (transport, agriculture, coal and steel) to benefit from the rule.

Following this disagreement, the Belgian Government and the Commission concluded a Protocol Agreement which laid down the arrangements for repayment of the unlawful aid. Shortly afterwards, the agreement was implemented in Belgian law by the Law of 30 December 2001.

The *de minimis* rule was abolished and the tax deduction was limited to amounts which had been reimbursed before 31 December 2001 and compensated by a new tax imposed on the sums paid. The Law of 30 December 2001 was subsequently modified by the Law of 2 August 2002, on the basis of which a Royal Decree was passed. This Royal Decree of 3 October 2002 provided that the sums would be recovered by the Ministry of Finance and indicated that in the case of non-payment within the required time frame, the sums owed would be increased by ten per cent.

The relevant Belgian law further prescribed that those companies which did not benefit financially from the decrease in the corporate tax rate because of the burden caused by the payment of the reimbursements made in implementation of the provisions of the Law of 24 December 1999, were not required to pay the reimbursements.

The main beneficiaries of this new regime were companies which at the time of the original reimbursement had suffered fiscal losses.

In the *Blondiau* case (Commercial Court of Mons, 21.1.2002, SRIW (Wallon Region) v. Mrs Blondiau, RG 03630/01), a Commission decision found that capital injected into Verlipack, by the Walloon Region in 1997 and two loans granted by the region's investment company in 1997 to Heye to finance Heye's capital contribution to Verlipack constituted unlawful and incompatible aid and ordered recovery of the aid.

The Walloon Region sought an order from the Commercial Court allowing it to lodge its claim regarding the loans against the bankrupt's estate (the normal limitation period open to creditors under Belgian law to lodge their claims with the bankrupt's trustee had already passed). The Commercial Court issued two orders allowing the claim by the Walloon Region concerning the loans to the bankrupt's estate.

Thus, without expressly saying so, the Commercial Court accepted the Commission's decision in which recovery of aid was ordered as an autonomous cause of action, thus justifying admittance of the State as a creditor of the bankrupt's estate. Incidentally, the Commission's decision was upheld by the Court of Justice on 3 July 2003.

In the *Idealspun* case, after an Court of Justice judgment finding that Belgium had failed to recover aid granted to Idealspun in the form of a capital increase (Case 5/86, Commission v. Belgium [1987] ECR I-1773), the Flemish Government (successor in title to the Belgian Government in the area of economic expansion policy) sued Idealspun and its other shareholders to recover the aid on the basis that the subscription was void (Commercial Cort Kortrijk, 20.9.1994, Gimvindus and Flemish Region v. Idealspun, De Clerck o. a., Case no. 130/90). The Commercial Court rejected the arguments raised by the aid recipient (legitimate expectation and possibility to challenge the Commission decision) and ruled that the decision could be provisionally enforced pending any appeal, on the grounds that it was in the Community's interest that the aid be recovered as soon as possible.

Despite the possibility of provisional enforcement afforded to the authorities, it is interesting to note that it took more than four years for the Commercial Court to come to a decision on the matter after the State introduced its action for recovery, and that it took another six years for the Court of Appeal to handle the appeal. All in all, the Belgian State's action for recovery took more than ten years.

This is obviously not in line with the principles provided by Article 14(3) of Regulation (EC) No 659/1999.

In the *Beaulieu* case, the Belgian Government filed an action for recovery before the Commercial Court to recover aid declared incompatible by the Commission in 1983. The Belgian government was found to have failed to implement the State aid decision by a 1989 ruling by the Court of Justice (Case C-74/89, Commission v. Belgium [1990] ECR I-491).

The Commercial Court, in a judgment of 25 February 1994, ordered Beaulieu to reimburse the aid (Commercial Court of Ghent, 25 February 1994, Socobesom, Flemish Region, Belgian State v. Beaulieu and others, extract published in J.T.D.E. 1994, p. 141). The case was upheld by the Ghent Court of Appeal on 5 October 2000 (Court of Appeal of Ghent, Case no. 1994/AR/1609, 5 October 2000, NV Imcopack, Beaulieu and others v. NV Socobesom, Flemish Region and Belgian State (recovery capital investment), unreported).

Again, this is an example of where the national court proceedings took excessively long and delayed a rapid recovery of the aid, in a manner inconsistent with Article 14(3) of Regulation (EC) No 659/1999.

In the *Tubemeuse* case, the Belgian State granted aid to the company Tubemeuse in the form of a subscription for shares in the capital of the company. In its decision of 4 February 1987, the Commission declared the aid incompatible and ordered the Belgian State to recover it.

Tubemeuse, the beneficiary of unlawful and incompatible aid, was subject to insolvency proceedings. The Belgian State requested that it should be registered as a creditor in order to recover the unlawful aid in accordance with a Commission decision. The first instance judge and the Court of Appeal rejected this request on the grounds that the Commission decision did not transform the Belgian State's participation in the capital of Tubemeuse into a simple debt for the receiver.

In an exemplary decision, however, the Supreme Court set aside the Court of Appeal's ruling and thus the application of national law, in order to ensure the full effectiveness of EU law (Supreme Court, Case no. 9152, 18 June 1992, Belgian State v. NV Tubemeuse). The Supreme Court considered that the Court of Appeal's refusal to register the Belgian State as a creditor did not recognise the effect of the absolute nullity of the capital injection (as a consequence of the violation of Article 108(3) TFEU) and violated EU law.

The *Ryanair* case should also be mentioned here in that it represents a specific aid recovery case sought before foreign jurisdictions. On 12 February 2004, the Commission decided to order recovery of the unlawful and incompatible aid granted by the Walloon Region and Brussels South Charleroi Airport to the airline Ryanair in connection with its establishment at Charleroi. Ryanair has challenged this decision before the General Court (Case T-196/04, Ryanair Ltd. v. Commission [2008] ECR II-3643).

Ryanair has been requested by the Walloon Region to repay all unlawful State aid. Ryanair has apparently written to the Walloon authorities and agreed to repay €4 million to an escrow account until Ryanair's action is heard and the General Court renders a definitive decision on this matter. The Walloon Region has also initiated proceedings before the Irish courts in order to seek the recovery of the aid in question.

In June 2006, the High Court decided to reject a request by Ryanair for a stay of the proceedings until the ruling of the General Court was handed down. This is the first example of a case in which a public authority has gone before another Member State jurisdiction in order to recover State aid. It should be noted that, in the *Verlipack* case (see Commercial Court of Mons, 21.1.2002, SRIW (Walloon Region) v. Mrs Blonidan (Curator of the bankrupt estate of Verlipack); Commercial Court of Kortrijk, 7.10.2003, Walloon Region v. NV Ter Lembeek International, unreported; Commercial Court of Kortrijk, 26.2.2004, Walloon Region v. Ter Lembeek International NV (interim action), unreported; and Case C-457/00 Belgium v. Commission [2003] ECR I-6931), a debt recovery action was brought by the Walloon region against Heye in Germany before the Court of Bückelburg on 25 April 2000, in order to recover aid paid out to this company.

This action was brought on the grounds that Heye had not met its contractual obligations. This was technically not an action seeking to enforce a negative Commission decision. Indeed, in the *Verlipack* case, a Commission decision was only issued in October 2000.

b. By competitors

We are not aware of any case where a competitor has sought to obtain the recovery of unlawful aid.

c. By beneficiaries

There have been few actions brought by beneficiaries opposing a recovery order. This can be explained by the fact that a recovery order only becomes enforceable after a judgment of the relevant court. The beneficiary of the aid can contest the recovery order by bringing an action for annulment of the decision ordering the recovery before the Council of State.

Recipients of incompatible aid have thus preferred challenge the grounds for recovery before national courts, in actions for debt recovery brought by the authorities. In the cases identified, beneficiaries of the aid have usually resisted returning the aid after the initial request from the Member State.

The beneficiary has usually appealed against the court orders for repayment of the unlawful aid. Such actions by the beneficiary, albeit logical, delay the date by which the aid can be fully recovered. In the *Dufrasne* case (Council of State, 16.3.2001, SA Dufrasne Métaux v. the Walloon Region, Case no. 94.080 – action for annulment of decision withdrawing grant of investment aid), Dufrasne brought before the Council of State an action for annulment of a decision of the Walloon Region, requesting the reimbursement of an aid which the Walloon Region had granted to Dufrasne.

Unfortunately, the Council of State annulled the recovery order on the grounds that there was in fact no Commission decision declaring the aid in question incompatible and ordering its recovery, and thus did not consider all the normal consequences of the direct effect of Article 108(3) TFEU. Indeed, given that the measure in question did not fall within the scope of the Community Framework of Aid to Steel Industry (Walloon Region), any implementation of the aid measure in question would breach the notification requirement to the Commission under Article 108 TFEU.

3. Challenging the validity of national recovery order

In Belgium, the administrative act ordering recovery (which may simply be a letter to the beneficiary, or court proceedings) can be based directly on the negative Commission decision. As mentioned above, the beneficiary of the aid can contest the recovery order by bringing an action for annulment before the Council of State.

The beneficiary can also contest the recovery order before the Commercial Court in its defence of a recovery action brought by the relevant Belgian authority. There have only been a few direct actions brought by beneficiaries of State aid. Two of these cases were actions for annulment, brought before the Council of State against administrative measures taken by a relevant national authority or public body which had negatively affected the beneficiary of the State aid.

One case was brought by a beneficiary before an Employment Tribunal challenging a recovery order of the Social Security service (see the *Dufrasne* case).

In the first case before the Council of State, a company successfully challenged a decision of the national authority to suspend further payment of aid to this company and ordering reimbursement of aid already paid, on the grounds that this constituted unlawful aid which had not been notified to the Commission. The Council of State annulled the national authority's decision on the grounds that there was no decision by the Commission prohibiting the aid in question.

In the other case before the Council of State, a company was prevented from submitting a tender offer because it had benefited from unlawful State aid. The company's action for annulment of that decision was dismissed.

If, following a Commission decision, the State does not order the recovery of the aid from the recipient, competitors may request the State to take action and, in case of a refusal, bring an action for annulment of this refusal (or initiate an action for damages for not having recovered the aid).

The *Dufrasne* case (Council of State, 16.3.2001, SA Dufrasne Métaux v. the Walloon Region, Case no. 94.080 – action for annulment of decision to withdrawing decision granting investment aid) can be also mentioned. In 1995, an investment aid was granted by the Walloon region to the company Dufrasne Métaux SA in order to purchase a specific piece of machinery.

In June 1996, the Walloon region discovered that the aid did not fall within the scope of the Community Framework of Aid to Steel Industry. On this basis, it decided to withdraw the aid granted to Dufrasne, to request that Dufrasne refund the aid already paid out, and to not provide the final instalments of the aid. Dufrasne brought an action seeking the annulment of this decision.

The Region considered that the action was deprived of any purpose since, if annulled, the new act could only be identical. Indeed, the sum granted to Dufrasne would constitute an unlawful aid contrary to Article 108(3) TFEU. By virtue of the *Alcan* case law of the CJEU (Case C-24/95, Land Rheinland Pfalz v. Alcan Deutschland GmbH [1997] ECR I-1591), this would require the Walloon Region to seek reimbursement of that aid. The Council of State did not accept this argument. According to the Council of State, it was unclear whether the measure in question would be prohibited by Commission decision 3855/91/ECSC, establishing Community rules for aid to the steel industry.

Moreover, the *Alcan* case was not directly relevant since the present case did not concern an obligation to withdraw an aid declared incompatible by a definitive Commission decision. Indeed, in the present case there was no Commission decision declaring the aid incompatible.

The Council of State further considered that there was no reason to disapply the case law stating that an act "creating rights", even if irregular, cannot be withdrawn after the expiry of the time period for challenging it (60 days). On this basis, the contested decision was annulled.

The judgment contains no reference to Article 108(3) TFEU, the violation of which would seem to justify a solution similar to *Alcan* (obligation to withdraw an illegal act even if not allowed under national law).

Indeed, given that the measure in question did not fall within the scope of the Community Framework of Aid to Steel Industry (Walloon Region), any implementation of the aid would breach the notification requirement to the Commission under Article 108 TFEU.

4. Action contesting the validity of the Commission decision

National courts have no jurisdiction under EU law to declare acts of the Community institutions void. Even though they might consider the Commission's negative decision to be illegal, a national court may not prevent the ensuing recovery procedure. Should they disagree with a Commission decision, the courts should refer a preliminary question as to its validity to the CJEU under Article 267 TFEU.

Such requests (by the beneficiaries of aid or competitors of the beneficiaries) are, however, inadmissible if a direct of the Commission decision before the General Court under Article 263 TFEU would have been manifestly admissible (the Commercial Court of Ghent anticipated this rule a few days before the General Court in the *TWD* case (Case C-355/95 P, TWD v. Commission [1997] ECR I-2549). In a recent example (*Ter Lembeek*), the national court suspended the proceedings of the Belgian State seeking recovery of aid from a beneficiary until the General Court came to a decision on the action for annulment against the Commission decision ordering the recovery of the unlawful aid.

The Commission decided, as a result, to lodge an action against Belgium under Article 108(2) TFEU before the CJEU for failure to comply with the principle enshrined in Article 14 of Regulation (EC) No 659/99 which provides for an immediate and efficient recovery (Case C-187/06, Commission v. Belgium). However, the Comission withdraw its action following the recovery of the aid by the Belgian authorities.

In a number of cases in which the relevant Belgian authorities have sought to recover aid from the beneficiaries of the aid, those beneficiaries have argued that the Commission decision was unlawful.

Thus, in the *Idealspun* and *Beaulieu* cases, those beneficiaries of the aid considered that the national court should refer questions to the CJEU in order to ascertain the validity of the Commission decisions in question and relied upon the principle of protection of legitimate expectations. In the recent decision of the Commercial Court in the *Ter Lembeek* case (Commercial Court of Kortrijk, 26.2.2004, Wallon Region v. Ter Lembeek International NV, Case 088/03), the court suspended proceedings pending the General Court's judgment on the action for annulment brought by Ter Lembeek against the Commission decision ordering the recovery of the unlawful aid.

Although the Commercial Court did require the beneficiary to set up a bank guarantee, the court's failure to impose any penalty payment on the beneficiary for failing to set up such a bank guarantee basically prevented the Walloon region from immediately recovering the unlawful aid, following the General court's judgment.

5. Damages for failure to implement a recovery decision and infringement of EU law

We are not aware of any case in which the liability of the Belgian State for failure to implement a recovery decision has been invoked. Failure to implement a recovery decision is an infringement of the EU law principles of direct effect and primacy. In such situations, the CJEU has ruled that State liability could be engaged and damages granted, provided the conditions in the *Francovich* and *Brasserie du Pêcheur* cases are fulfilled. Therefore a claimant can directly rely on the Commission decision to claim that it suffered from the lack of or from ineffective recovery of the unlawful aid.

V. Standing of third parties before national court

The issue of *locus standi* of third parties has not been specifically discussed before the Belgian General courts. Generally speaking, the position of third parties in Belgium is comparable to the situation found in the French and Dutch judicial systems.

An action against any administrative act of a non-legislative nature (action for annulment – "recours en annulation" or "recours pour excès de pouvoir") can be lodged by any party demonstrating an interest, such interest being personal, present, certain, direct and legitimate. The time limit for submitting an action is two months from the notification, publication or full knowledge of the act.

VI. Cooperation with EU authorities

1. Cooperation with the CJEU

Belgian courts have, in a number of cases, not hesitated to refer questions to the CJEU in order to obtain clarification on various points of law (see reference made by the Court of Appeal of Antwerp in the Joined Cases C-261 and C-262/01 Van Calster and Cleeren [2003] ECR I-12249 and the reference of the Court of Appeal of Brussels of 5 February which led to the C-49/93, Namur-Les Assurances de Crédit SA v. Office National du Ducroire [1994] ECR I-3829), although it is interesting to note that neither the Court of Arbitration (the Constitutional Court) nor the Council of State has ever made such reference in relation to a State aid matter.

VII. Trends – reforms – recommendations

Over the last few years there has been a steady increase in the number of State aid cases handled by the Belgian courts. There have been remarkably few actions brought by competitors. In particular, no party has ever brought an action for damages in relation to a State aid measure.

There is no clear explanation for this, as Belgian law provides adequate opportunities for competitors to bring actions. There are also few examples of actions brought by beneficiaries. This may be more understandable given that beneficiaries are generally the defendants in recovery proceedings initiated by the State.

On the other hand, national authorities have been more wiling to bring State aid actions. Although there have been no actions for damages, there have been a number of cases brought by parties seeking the reimbursement of certain contributions made to the State to set up a fund which was later considered to be an unlawful aid scheme.

The length of judicial proceedings, especially in the civil courts, is probably the main obstacle to the effective application of EU State aid rules in Belgium. Indeed, a case can last up to ten years when it has to run through all of the various levels of court (including references for a preliminary ruling to the CJEU). Concerning the implementation of Article 14(3) of Council Regulation (EC) No 659/99, the Belgian courts appear to have a good overall grasp of the EU State aid rules.

However, in the *Ter Lembeek* case, the national court suspended recovery proceedings, pending judgment of the CFI. Such an order goes against the obligation of the Member States to seek immediate recovery of the aid (and against the principle that an action for annulment does not have suspensory effect (see Case Commission v. France (Scott) – suspension of proceedings only being allowed in specific circumstances defined by the CJEU's case law under Article 278 TFEU).

Another problem is that recovery proceedings can be lengthy and if an appeal is made by the beneficiary against the first instance judgment, the State only has a right to recover the aid in question after the ruling of the Court of Appeal. This does not appear to be in line with Article 14 of Regulation (EC) No 659/1999, which provides that the judicial review under national law has to be sufficiently limited in order to "allow the immediate and effective execution of the Commission's decision".

There is presently no system of surveillance of State aid in Belgium to ensure that Article 108(3) TFEU and Article 14 of Regulation (EC) No 659/1999 (notification requirement) are complied with. A general proposal for improving State aid procedures would be to create a national, independent authority in charge of controlling the granting and recovery of State aid in Belgium.

The surveillance authority could, at a preliminary stage, be in charge of advising beneficiaries of public subsidies in order to determine what constitutes State aid and to question the Belgian (federal and regional) authorities on notification to the Commission. This independent authority could also review notifications, in order to ensure that all the necessary information has been provided.

It could also monitor all actions of the six governments and the six Parliaments in Belgium, including lower local authorities, which are likely to contain elements of aid and alert them against this situation, whilst informing the Commission and the public, thereby discouraging the executive powers or the federal, regional and local legislators from engaging in actions contrary to the EU Treaty and encouraging strict compliance with EU State aid procedure.

The difficulty with this type of surveillance authority would be, in light of its links with the authorities granting the aid and the State, guaranteeing its independence vis-à-vis the State. In order to be credible for all parties concerned (beneficiaries, competitors, national authorities and the Commission), the surveillance authority would have to have the status of an independent regulatory authority, with all the privileges and organisational characteristics that are usually granted to such an authority.

Bulgaria

Plamen Vassilev*

* Ministry of Finance, Sofia.

I. General principles of member state's state aid law

1. National authorities competent to grant aid and to be involved in the notification procedure

Bulgaria has had a State Aid Act ("**SAA**") since 2002. It was amended in 2006 and was effective as from the date of entry into force of the Treaty concerning the accession of the Republic of Bulgaria to the EU. This Act sets out the conditions, order and procedures for notification in accordance with Article 108(3) TFEU, categories of State aid, compatibility with the Internal Market, the obligation to report, collect and save information, as well as the assessment of the State aid, for which it is not obligatory to notify the Commission.

It consists of four chapters (1. General Provisions, 2. Powers of The Minister of Finance and The Minister of Agriculture and Forestry, 3. Procedures and 4. Administrative Penalty Provisions), plus additional provisions and transitional and concluding provisions.

The Minister of Finance is the national authority responsible for the supervision, transparency and coordination of State aid at central, regional and municipal level, with the exception of the aid schemes and individual aid in agriculture and fisheries.

In Bulgaria the competent authority for State aid and the only contact point in that regard is the Ministry of Finance. The SAA is designed to exist in parallel with this contact and coordination point.

All donors (administrators) of aid are obliged to apply the SAA and EU State aid legislation in close cooperation with the Ministry of Finance. Officially it is the Ministry who sends all notifications to the Commission. It also approves State aid cases exempted under Block exemption Regulations.

The Minister of Finance shall:

- carry out monitoring and coordination and cooperate with the Commission in the field of State aid;
- receive, examine and assess State aid notifications for their compatibility with the legislation on State aid; observe the drafts of new aid and the amendments to existing aid as regards their compatibility with EU and Bulgarian State aid policy;
- submit State aid notifications to the Commission;
- deliver opinions on State aid within the scope of block exemption Regulations, as well as on *de minimis* aid;
- assess the maximum aid intensity of regional aid and the specific local coverage in the regions of the Republic of Bulgaria eligible for regional aid and submit a notification for the State aid regional map, coordinated in advance with the Minister of Regional Development and Public Works, to the Commission;
- require, collect and process the information from all aid-granting authorities, including the information on *de minimis* aid, and keep a summary of this information;

- prepare an annual consolidated report on State aid and submit it to the Commission;
- deliver opinions and assist the aid granting authorities in order to fulfil the obligations arising out of the EU legislation and Bulgarian law on State aid;
- deliver opinions on the proposals for new legislation or amendments to the existing legislation in the field of State aid; and
- participate in the activity of the working bodies of the Commission on State aid issues.

Each aid-granting authority shall submit to the Minister of Finance the necessary information concerning State aid administered by it, in conformity with EU law and the SAA and is obliged to inform the Minister of Finance in advance of any intention to provide a new State aid.

The Minister of Finance shall assist the granting authority, if necessary, and observe the State aid policy. Should the Commission decide to suspend the aid, the Minister of Finance shall request the granting authority take all necessary measures to execute this decision within a seven-day period and publish the decision for suspension of the aid on the relevant Internet site of the granting authority as part of the requirements under Article 12, paragraph 2.

Any granting authority which does not fulfil any of its obligations under the SAA shall be punished pursuant to Chapter 4 – Administrative Penalty Provisions.

II. Identification of State Aid Issues at National Level

1. State aid compliance by the national legislator and/or by the executive power

Ex ante control organised at constitutional or legislative level: The *ex ante* control organised at constitutional or legislative level is based on the procedural rules for preparing (for example) drafts of the legislative acts by the Council of Ministers (“**CM**”) and approving them by the Parliament. Acts of the CM are coordinated in advance with all the respective institutions before a decision is taken. The drafts of the new Parliamentary legislative acts are preliminarily discussed in the different commissions and sub-commissions of the Parliament in relation to *inter alia* compatibility with EU legislation.

Special legislative procedure
As stated above, Articles 5, 6, 7 and 8 of the SAA deal with the procedures of *ex ante* control at national level. In practice at a preliminary stage the administrators of aid deal with *ex ante* control when preparing State aid schemes. At the second and final stage the State aid Department, authorized by the Minister of Finance also exercises *ex ante* control in relation to State aid in Bulgaria.

Control by the Council of Ministers
The CM in Bulgaria regularly implements sessions on the basis of a daily order endorsed by the Prime minister. These implementing daily orders are differentiated in three parts:

- project of deeds, which are accompanied by positive responses, which do not need to be discussed;
- positions for participating in conferences of the European Council and in the Council of European Union, reports and other documents concerning the European Union;
- bills, project of deeds of the CM and reports, requiring discussion.

The CM adopts acts on its sessions after discussing them with all the relevant authorities and harmonizing all legislative procedures with the institutions concerned.

Acts of the CM are coordinated with all respective institutions in advance before taking decision. The drafts of the new legislative acts in the Parliament are first discussed in the different commissions and sub-commissions of the Parliament in relation to, *inter alia*, compatibility with EU legislation.

Ex post non judicial control to the same end

The *ex post* control is accomplished by the Public Financial Inspection Agency under supervision of the Minister of Finance. The main purpose of public financial inspection is to protect public financial interests and to obtain the necessary information for the implementation of the *ex post* financial inspections, on the observance of the statutory acts, regulating the budget, economic or accounting activities of the organizations and entities, and detecting fraud and irregularities affecting the financial interests of the EU. The Public Financial Inspection Act shall define the objectives, the tasks, the principles and the scope of the public financial inspection activity, as well as the role and functions of the Public Financial Inspection Agency (the "**Agency**"). Public financial inspection shall be performed on State aid beneficiaries, entities financed with funds from the central government budget or municipal budgets, extra-budgetary accounts or funds, under international agreements or under EU programs, as well as the entities funded by State-owned enterprises (under Article 62, Paragraph 3 of the Commerce Act – as regards the spending of such funds). Financial inspections shall be conducted to verify the use of State aid and the spending of target subsidies, provided under the State Budget of the Republic of Bulgaria Act for the respective year and Decrees issued by the Council of Ministers.

Procedure and effectiveness

Financial inspections shall be conducted:

- upon any requests, complaints or alerts received in relation to violations of the budget, financial, economic or accounting activities of the organisations and entities, as submitted by State authorities, natural persons or legal entities;
- for checking procedures carried out on the assigning and execution of public procurement based on information from the Public Procurement Register, the Public Procurement Agency and the National Audit Office;
- for checking the use of State aid and the spending of target subsidies, provided under the State Budget of the Republic of Bulgaria Act for the respective year and Decrees issued by the Council of Ministers;

- upon request of the Council of Ministers or the Minister of Finance;
- upon assignment by the Prosecutor's Office under the procedure set out in Article 145, Paragraph 1, item 3 of the Judiciary System Act;
- upon alerts for irregularities, affecting the financial interests of the EU, established by the AFCOS Central Unit with the Ministry of Interior; and
- for observation of the instructions and time limits.

On receiving the results of the financial inspection, the respective financial inspector shall draw up a report, which shall contain the findings supported by evidence. Depending on the results of the inspection activities performed, the Director of the Agency or his authorised officials shall: make proposals to the competent authorities to stop the actions which lead to irregularities and cause damage to the organizations and entities inspected; make proposals to the competent authorities to repeal any illegal administrative instruments of the managers of the organizations and entities inspected; propose that the competent authorities seek property and/or disciplinary liability under the relevant procedures; propose to the Minister of Finance to discontinue the transfer of the subsidies provided for in the State Budget of the Republic of Bulgaria Act for the relevant year; or freeze the accounts of budget organizations pending the elimination of the irregularities.

Where there is evidence of the infringement committed, the opinions shall be sent within seven days to the authorities of the Prosecutor's office. The amount of damage under this Act shall be determined as of the date on which it was caused, and if that date cannot be identified, as of the date it was discovered. The amount of the damage shall be calculated to market or book value, whichever is higher.

Damage caused in a foreign currency shall be recovered in the same foreign currency or in Bulgarian levs, using the highest exchange rate of the Bulgarian National Bank as at the date of the occurrence, discovery or recovery. Those responsible for the damage shall be charged the amount of interest stipulated by law as from the date of occurrence of the damage and, if such a date cannot be identified, as of the date of discovery, until the date of recovery. Property liability, including interest, shall expire with the expiry of a statute of limitation of five years as from the date the damage was caused, and if this day cannot be identified, as from the date of discovery of such damage.

The fines and property sanctions imposed under this Act shall be collected pursuant to the procedure set out in the Tax and Social Insurance Procedure Code. State aid compliance by the executive power applies as above *mutatis mutandis.*

Centralised administration in charge of State aid compliance

The Ministry of Finance is the central administration charged with maintaining compliance in the field of State aid. Its competences are explained in Chapter 4 of SAA. As stated above, the Minister of Finance shall carry any monitoring and coordination tasks and shall cooperate with the Commission in the field of State aid. He is also responsible for submitting State aid notifications to the Commission, requiring, collecting and processing information from all aid granting authorities, (including the information on *de minimis* aid) and keeping summarized information, delivering opinions and assisting the aid granting authorities in order to fulfil the obligations arising out of EU and Bulgarian law on State aid.

2. State aid compliance by national judges and/or the national competition authority (NCA)

From 2002 until 2007 the Commission for Protection of Competition (CPC) was the national competition authority responsible for the State aid assessment for Bulgaria. However, since Bulgaria's acceptance as a Member State of the EU, the Commission for Protection of Competition is no longer competent in the field of State aid. Until 1 January 2007, before Bulgaria was accepted as a Member State, State aid authorisation and control was handled by the CPC. The CPC had to be notified in advance of any intention to grant State aid or modify aid already granted. The CPC then investigated the relevant circumstances and took a substantiated decision. By 31 March of the current year the CPC was obliged to publish and provide the Parliament with an annual report of such activities carried out in the previous year. The responsibility for the monitoring of State aid rested with the Ministry of Finance. It prepared and published a consolidated annual report and submitted it to the Council of Ministers, the Parliament and the Commission and provided a copy to the CPC. After 1.1.2007, the ultimate decision-making power was transferred to the Commission and the Ministry of Finance. They became the authorities responsible for supervision, transparency and coordination of State aid at central, regional and municipal level and must carry out any monitoring, coordination and cooperation with the Commission. Nowadays CPC is responsible in the fields of antitrust policy, concentrations, unfair competition, sector analyses, competition policy and European integration.

a. Competence of the Bulgarian courts in State aid litigation

In accordance with "The Commission notice on the enforcement of State aid law by national courts (2009/C 85/01)"[134], the national courts can offer claimants very effective remedies in the event of a breach of the State aid rules.

It is within the national courts' competence to deal with the applicability of the General Block exemption Regulation or an existing or approved aid scheme, or both. However, the national courts can only assess whether all the conditions of the Regulation or scheme are met. It cannot assess the compatibility of an aid measure where this is not the case, since that assessment is the exclusive responsibility of the Commission.

If the national court needs to determine whether the measure falls under an approved aid scheme, it can only verify whether all the conditions of the approval decision are met. Where the issues arising at national level concern the validity of a Commission decision, the national court has no jurisdiction to declare acts of Community institutions invalid.

In Bulgaria the national courts do not yet have experience in the field of State aid litigation.

---

134 OJ (2009) C85/1.

b. Assessment of the existence of aid within the meaning of Article 107(1) TFEU

Third parties
Third parties can lodge a complaint against allegedly unlawful State aid. They may either submit a complaint to the Commission or pursue the matter before the national courts. Proceedings before national courts give third parties an opportunity to address and resolve many State aid-related concerns directly at national level. The interests of third parties (other competitors) are taken into account only to the extent that competition has not been violated. However, third parties do not have the ability to intervene in the procedure.

Application of EU regulations and guidelines
National courts have the ability to verify that an aid benefiting from one of the exemption Regulations has been granted with respect to the rules on cumulation provided therein whenever they need such information. The Ministry of Finance is obliged by Article 11 of the State Aid Act to maintain the "*De Minimis* Register" on the application of Article 3.3 of the Regulation (EC) No 1998/2006.

III. Unlawful aid and judicial review

1. General powers of national courts concerning the application of Article 108(3) TFEU

Bulgaria has no experience in this field as yet. However, when such cases arise, Bulgaria is obliged to act in accordance with the Commission notice on the enforcement of the State aid law by national courts cited above.

2. Prevention of the granting of unlawful aid

Bulgaria does not differentiate between unlawful acts of a private or public law nature. Each authority granting aid is obliged to communicate with the Minister of Finance in advance with regard to any intention to provide a new State aid. Where the Minister of Finance deems that the notification of State aid or the proposed aid is not in conformity with the rules and policy in the field of State aid, the granting authority shall be notified and appropriate measures for bringing the aid into compliance shall be proposed.

A granting authority which does not bring the aid into compliance following a proposal by the Minister of Finance, shall be obliged to prepare and submit a written declaration and reasons for non-compliance to the Minister of Finance. The Minister of Finance shall forward the notification to the Commission in the form stated in the declaration. Communications with the Commission on all issues related to State aid shall be carried out by the Minister of Finance, and the Minister of Agriculture and Forestry respectively and through the Permanent Representation of the Republic of Bulgaria to the EU.

The Commission shall assess the compatibility of the planned State aid. After receiving a positive decision from the Commission, the Minister of Finance shall inform the granting authority that the aid may be granted. The granting authority shall not put the aid into effect until the adoption of the positive decision. The granting authority shall be entirely responsible for the lawfulness of the notified granted aid, as well as for the execution of the Commission decisions taken in relation to them. Where the aid is within the scope of a Block exemption Regulation, the granting authority shall coordinate the planned State aid with the Minister of Finance in advance.

As stated above, the State Aid Act is the legal act applied in Bulgaria at a national level. The Rules for Implementation of the State Aid Act arrange the conditions and the order for the implementation of the State Aid Act.

Ordinance № H-16 dated 23 November 2006 on the procedure for ensuring the transparency of financial relations between the public authorities and local self-governing bodies, the State and municipal undertakings as well as financial transparency within certain undertakings, approved by the Minister of Finance, aims to ensure the transparency of financial relations at national level.

After Bulgaria was accepted as a Member State of the EU, it was obliged to implement the European Regulations on State Aid. The Tax and Social Security Procedure Code shall set out the procedures for the establishment of obligations related to taxes and insurance payments as well as providing security and collecting public funds, as assigned to the authorities on receipts and from public executors.

The Public Financial Inspection Act shall define the objectives, the tasks, the principles and the scope of the public financial inspection activity, as well as the role and functions of the Public Financial Inspection Agency.

The Administrative Violations and Sanctions Act shall lay down the general rules in relation to administrative violations and sanctions, the order for the establishment of administrative violations and for the imposition and application of sanctions, and shall provide the necessary limits for the protection of rights and legal interests of both citizens and organisations.

3. Recovery of unlawful aid and interest

Where a national court is confronted with unlawfully granted aid, it must consider all legal consequences of this unlawfulness under national law. The national court must therefore order the full recovery of unlawful State aid from the beneficiary. Ordering the full recovery of unlawful aid is part of the national court's obligation to protect the individual rights of the claimant (such as the competitor) under Article 108(3) TFEU. The national court's recovery obligation is thus not dependent on the compatibility of the aid measure with Article 107(2) or (3) TFEU.

Any State aid defined as unlawful on the basis of an EU decision falls within the scope of public receivables under Article 162 of the Tax and Social Security Procedure Code ("**TSSPC**") – receivables under Article 162, paragraph 2, sub-paragraph 6, etc. of TSSPC. As such it is subject to voluntary payment or enforcement under the procedures of TSSPC.

For this purpose, following receipt of the European Commission's decision for recovery of unlawful State aid, pursuant to Article 14, paragraph 2 of the SAA the Minister of Finance requests the granting authority take measures to execute the decision within a seven-day period whilst informing the latter about the decision and sending a copy to the National Revenue Agency (NRA).

Where the decision of the Commission specifies the beneficiaries and the amount of the recoverable unlawful State aid, on the grounds of Article 209, paragraph 2, sub-paragraph 6 of TSSPC it represents a power of direct enforcement and is subject to enforcement under the procedures of the same Code and no further act needs to be issued assessing the grounds and size of the public liability.

If the act of the Commission for recovery of unlawful State aid does not specify the persons or the amount recoverable, the grounds and amount of the public liability are to be assessed under the procedure laid down in Article 166, paragraph 2 of TSSPC. The act is issued by the granting authority against the beneficiary of the aid in accordance with the procedure for issuance of administrative acts under the Administrative Procedure Code (APC) – Chapter 5 of APC.

As far as the act is issued under the procedure for issuance of administrative acts under APC, on the grounds of Article 59, paragraph 2 of APC, the said act states:

- name of the issuing authority;
- title of the act (Act for assessment of public state receivable);
- addressee of the act;
- grounds of fact and law on which the act is issued (the specific decision of the Commission is indicated);
- operative part, wherein the amount of the principal and interest, the manner and time limit for enforcement are specified;
- direction regarding costs;
- identification of the authority and time limit for appeal of the act; and
- the date of issue and signature of the person who issued the act, indicating the position thereof (where the authority is collective, the act shall be signed by the chairperson or by a deputy chairperson).

It should be taken into account that, based on the EU decision, the granting authority states in the act the total amount of the public liability (principal and interest set by the EU and accrued from the date on which the aid was granted until the date of the final payment of the liability).

The granting authority issues the act for the assessment of the public liability to the aid beneficiary under the procedure of Article 61 of APC. The administrative act is communicated within three days after the issuance thereof to all persons concerned, including to those who did not participate in the proceedings. Communication may be effected through oral notification of the content of the act, which is certified by a signature of the notifying official, or through dispatch of a written communication, *inter alia* via e-mail or fax, if the party has indicated such address or number.

Where the address of some of the persons concerned is unknown or the said person has not been reached at the address indicated thereby, the communication is posted on the notice board on the Internet site of the relevant authority, or is announced in another customary manner.

Pursuant to Article 23 of the SAA any granting authority that fails to take measures to implement a Commission's decision for recovery of unlawful State aid is liable to a fine in the range of BGN 4,000 to BGN 10,000.

Should it be that, within the time limit for voluntary payment set in the act for assessment of the public liability, the aid is not recovered, then the granting authority, in his capacity as public claimant, issues and sends (in a manner similar to the described above) an invitation for voluntary payment to the debtor. The granting authority, on the grounds of Article 182(1) of the TSSPC must then provide him with a seven-day period to pay his/her liability. The invitation is served under the rules of Chapter Six, Section I, of TSSPC. If the liability is not paid within a seven-day period from the receipt of the invitation under Article 182(1), the granting authority must send the enforcement title or effective decision of the EU, the effective act for assessment of the public liability issued by the granting authority and the invitation according to Article 181, together with due evidence of its regular communication under the above procedure, to the public enforcement agent at the SRCA and request that enforcement proceedings for collection of the unlawful aid be instituted under the rules of TSSPC.

In the case of an aid scheme, to what extent have national courts the possibility to identify the beneficiaries of an aid? Is the granting authority responsible for identifying the beneficiaries under judicial review?

It is entirely within the competence of the granting authorities to identify the beneficiaries of an aid. This is possible since the granting authorities keep registers containing all the requisite information on beneficiaries. As set out in Chapter 3 of the SAA each aid granting authority shall submit to the Minister of Finance the necessary information concerning the State aid, administered by it in conformity with EU law and the SAA. The central State administration bodies and the local self-administration authorities, as well as any other body, administering State aid, shall submit to the Minister of Finance a report for all granted aid on the basis of the reporting data from the previous year by 31 March of the current year. The granting authority shall be entirely responsible for the lawfulness of the notified granted aid, as well as for the execution of the Commission decisions taken in relation to them. All reports by the aid-granting authorities to the Minister of Finance shall be published on the Internet site of the relevant aid granting authority.

How does a national court normally quantify the amount to be recovered? What is the methodology used? To what extent do national courts use the EU guidance and the Commission's decision making practice? Are there any cases in which the determination of the amount was at stake?

The Bulgarian courts have no experience in this field as yet. When such cases occur, the national courts will act in accordance with European Regulations. Taking into account the role of the Ministry of Finance as a coordination unit between Bulgaria and the EU, he will provide assistance when it is necessary. The decisions of violations, and the issuing, appeal and execution of penal ordinances shall be carried out under the Administrative Violations and Penalties Act. The administrative penalty provisions are contained in the SAA. When the Commission takes a decision for recovery of unlawful aid, the Minister of Finance shall request the granting authority take all necessary measures for recovery. The aid shall be recovered pursuant to the decision of the Commission. The unlawful aid will have been at disposal of the beneficiary until the date of its recovery. The interest rate shall be fixed by the Commission. Once the national court has decided that unlawful aid has been disbursed in violation of Article 108(3) TFEU, it must quantify the aid in order to determine the amount to be recovered.

IV. Recovery of interest

Bulgaria has no such cases in this field yet. However, if recovery is ordered by the Commission, it requires not only the recovery of the nominal aid amount, but also the recovery of interest from the day the unlawful aid was put at the disposal of the beneficiary to the date on which it is effectively recovered. The interest rate to be applied in this context is defined in Article 9 of Commission Regulation (EC) No 794/2004 of 21 April 2004 implementing Council Regulation (EC) No 659/1999 laying down detailed rules for the application of Article [93] of the Treaty ("the Implementing Regulation").

Direct damage actions

The procedure at a national level is arranged by The Tax and Social Security Procedure Code, The Public Financial Inspection Act and The Administrative Violations and Sanctions Act. The enforcement is implemented by a public enforcement agent at NRA under the procedure set out in Chapter 25, Section IV, of TSSPC.

According to Article 220 of TSSPC, when the liability is not paid within the seven-day period set out in the invitation the public enforcement agent proceeds to enforcement by sending a notice to the beneficiary of the aid providing the latter with another seven-day period for voluntary payment.

In cases where no security measures have been imposed, the enforcement in respect of a debtor's receivables from third parties as well as on his movables or estates starts with the imposition of an attachment and issuing an injunction by decree of the public enforcement agent. The next stages of enforcement include an inventory and evaluation and sale of the property subject to attachment or injunction. The proceeds from the public sale of the debtor's property are used for the payment of the costs of enforcement and the principal and interest related to unlawful State aid.

Cyprus

Constantinos Lycourgos*

* Law Office of the Republic of Cyprus, Nicosia.

I. General principles of member state's state aid law

1. National authorities that are competent to grant aid and to be involved in the notification procedure

Cyprus developed a State aid control system in 2001, as a result of the requirement imposed by the European Union ("**EU**") on the ten countries that were, at the time, candidates for accession, to establish such a system and prove its effectiveness before the Chapter on Competition in the accession negotiations could be closed. On 16 March 2001, the Public Aid Control Law of 2001 (Law No. 30(I)/2001) was published. This law introduced into the national legislation provisions equivalent to those of Articles 107 and 108 TFEU and established an independent authority competent for the control of State aid, the Commissioner for Public Aid (hereinafter the "**Commissioner**").

During the pre-accession period, the Commissioner performed, by and large, the role that is now performed by the European Commission (the "**Commission**") as far as State aid control was concerned. The Commissioner was competent to investigate, assess and approve the granting of State aid, to monitor the implementation and final impact of the public aid provided, and to prepare and keep an up-to-date electronic register of public aid. The Commissioner had to assess the compatibility with State aid rules of all existing and new aid measures.

After Cyprus's accession to the EU on 1 May 2004, EU State aid rules became directly applicable, thus shifting the substantive control of State aid to the Commission. However, the Commissioner, whose title has changed to Commissioner for State Aid Control, continues to play an important role regarding State aid control at national level, acting as the national focal point and coordinator for State aid matters in Cyprus and as the authority controlling aid which falls within the ambit of the Block exemption Regulations.

State aid can be granted in Cyprus by the State, local authorities (municipalities and communities) and public bodies. The necessary funds must be included in the relevant budget, which means that for most State aid schemes, the approval of the House of Representatives (i.e. the Parliament) has to be obtained. However, the House of Representatives cannot take the initiative to include in the budget, or in any other legislative act, a provision which directly or indirectly increases the budgetary expenditure.[135] Thus, with the exception of fiscal aid[136], the initiative for the granting of State aid must necessarily come from the executive, even though the approval of the House of Representatives is generally required as part of the budgetary procedure.

There is no legal requirement that aid be granted only on the basis of a law enacted by the House of Representatives. Even though laws sometimes form the legal basis for the granting

135 Article 80.2 of the Constitution.

136 The Supreme Court has recently held that the Houses of Representatives can, without infringing Article 80.2 of the Constitution, enact a law on the basis of a draft tabled by one of its members, which can reduce taxes imposed on undertakings (Supreme Court ("Ανώτατο Δικαστήριο"), 1 December 2009, President of the Republic v. House of Representatives, Referral 1/2009).

of aid (fiscal aid is the obvious example), in most cases the existence of budgetary provisions is sufficient, the detailed conditions being determined by a decision of the Council of Ministers.

Notification of aid to the Commission is made on the initiative of the relevant local authority or public body or, where the aid is granted by the State, of the ministry or department which is competent for the specific aid scheme or individual aid. The notification is made through the Commissioner for State Aid Control.

2. National authorities competent to recover aid and an overview of the procedure

According to the legislation currently in force, namely the State Aid Control Laws of 2001 to 2009 (hereinafter the "**State Aid Control Law**"), the Commissioner is competent for the implementation of Regulation (EC) No 659/1999[137]. Furthermore, until October 2009, the Commissioner had, under section 18(b) of the State Aid Control Law, the power to order the recovery of aid where the provisions of the Law had been infringed. Under a wide construction of section 18, it could be argued that the provisions of the said section could allow the Commissioner to order the recovery of State aid found to be unlawful by the Commission. However, in the absence of any specific case which could confirm such wide construction and in order to eliminate any uncertainty, section 18 was amended through Law 108(I)/2009, which entered into force on 30.10.2009. Under its new wording, section 18 explicitly gives the power to the Commissioner to order the recovery of aid which was granted without having been notified to the Commission. By adding a new section 18B, the said law also empowers the Commissioner to oversee that all possible measures are taken for the purpose of securing the implementation of the Commission's decisions, where these decisions order the recovery of aid.

If the Commissioner were to act for the recovery of aid by making use of these powers, he could:

(a) issue a reasoned decision ordering the recovery. Then, the procedure to be followed would vary depending on the way in which the unlawful aid was granted. If aid was granted through an administrative act, the granting authority would have to withdraw the act with retrospective effect. If the unlawful aid was granted through a law, the Government and the Parliament would have to take the necessary steps for the abolition or amendment of the law in question. If, finally, the unlawful aid was granted through a contract, the authority or body having signed the contract would have to take steps in order to terminate the contract or to eliminate all aid elements contained therein; or
(b) apply to the District Court for an order for the return of the sums received as unlawful aid.

137 Section 9A(c) of the State Aid Control Law.

Another possible option for the recovery of aid, following a decision of the Commission, is that the granting authority or body takes the steps described above, without the Commissioner having to intervene in the matter.

To date, two cases can be mentioned where the recovery of aid was achieved, even though no decision was issued finding that unlawful aid had been granted. Furthermore, the formal powers of the Commissioner did not have to be used, given the spirit of cooperation existing between the Commissioner and the granting authorities.

In Commissioner's decision No. 284, published in the Official Gazette on the 7 of December 2007, concerning the scheme entitled "Indemnity/aid to farmers because of foot and mouth disease", the Commissioner observed that in certain cases, due to shortcomings of the competent authority, certain farmers had been overcompensated and thus these amounts had to be recovered. The competent authority gradually recovered the aid (totalling €17,171) by reducing other subsidies due to these farmers.

In another case, a company belonging to the State had been granted a number of loans by the Government, but was not keeping up with the repayments. The government was showing tolerance and not taking any action to demand payment of the installments and thus the Commissioner intervened. Under the direction of the Commissioner, the loans were rearranged into a single loan and repayment recommenced.

II. Identification of State aid issues at national level

1. State aid compliance by the national legislator and/or by the executive

Ex ante control

Under the provisions of the State Aid Control Law, a national system of *ex ante* control of State aid has been put in place which, *inter alia*, secures a high level of compliance with the obligation imposed on the Member States, under Article 108(3) TFEU, to notify draft State aid measures to the Commission.

According to the provisions of this law, authorities and public bodies intending to grant any types of State aid are under an obligation to notify all draft measures to the Commissioner, before such measures can be put into effect.[138]

No distinction is made in that respect according to the means used for the granting of aid. All draft aid measures have to be notified to the Commissioner, irrespective of whether the aid is to be granted under the provisions of a law or as a result of an administrative act, or on the basis of a contract. In the case of an aid measure which has its legal basis in a law, the notiication to the Commissioner, as a matter of practice, is not made by the House of Representatives, but by the public authority which has prepared the relevant draft law. Therefore, the developments that follow apply irrespective of the legal basis of the aid measure.

138 Sections 10(1) and (3) and 11(1) and (4) of the State Aid Control Law.

When a draft aid measure is notified to the Commissioner, two cases have to be distinguished according to whether the aid to be granted falls within a block exemption or not.

Aid falling within a block exemption

In the case of draft aid measures which fall within the provisions of Regulation (EC) No 800/2008 (the General Block exemption Regulation), Regulation (EC) No 1857/2006 (aid to small and medium-sized enterprises active in the production of agricultural products) and Regulation (EC) No 736/2008 (aid to small and medium-sized enterprises active in the production, processing and marketing of fisheries products), the Commissioner issues a binding decision regarding the compatibility of the draft measure with these provisions.

According to section 9A(a) of the State Aid Control Law, the Commissioner is competent to assess and issue legally binding decisions on compatibility with the relevant rules of State aid measures granted on the basis of regulations issued by the European Commission, exempting certain categories of aid from the notification requirement of Article 108(3) TFEU (the currently applicable regulations are Regulation (EC) No 800/2008, Regulation (EC) No 1857/2006 and Regulation (EC) No 736/2008). Once he has issued a positive decision regarding a given aid measure, the Commissioner forwards to the Commission summary information on the measure in question.

Whenever State aid is to be granted by a granting authority or body on the basis of the Block exemption Regulations, the following procedure must be adhered to:

(a) as provided by section 10(1) of the State Aid Control Law, the draft measure must be notified to the Commissioner; and
(b) within two months of notification, the Commissioner must, by virtue of section 10(2), assess the draft measure and either approve it or declare it to be incompatible with the relevant block exemption provisions. The reasoned decision of the Commissioner is published in the Official Gazette of the Republic.

No State aid measure can be considered compatible with the provisions of the Block exemption Regulations and be implemented in Cyprus without having been previously approved by the Commissioner.[139] If such an aid measure is put into effect without having been previously notified to, and approved by, the Commissioner, all the provisions described below relating to un-notified/unlawful aid, apply.

In practice, experience has shown that the existence of a single independent competent authority responsible for the application of the Block exemption Regulations has minimised the risk of a public authority or body operating an unlawful aid scheme in Cyprus.

139 Section 10(3) of the State Aid Control Law.

Aid which must be notified to the Commission

For all aid measures which need to be notified to the European Commission, i.e. those which do not fall within a block exemption and do not constitute *de minimis* aid,[140] the Commissioner issues a non-binding opinion on the compatibility of the notified draft measure with EU State aid rules[141]. This presents the advantage of avoiding notifying to the Commission draft measures which do not have a good chance of being found compatible with the Internal Market.

According to section 9A(c) of the State Aid Control Law, the Commissioner is the competent authority in Cyprus for the implementation of Council Regulation (EC) No 659/1999 of 22 March 1999, which sets out detailed rules for the application of Article 108 TFEU. The Commissioner being, as a result of this provision, the authority which, on behalf of the Republic of Cyprus, notifies all draft aid measures to the Commission, the granting authorities and bodies have good reason to seriously take into account the opinion issued by the Commissioner. They should co-operate with the Commissioner before notification to the Commission, so as to adapt the draft measures in a way that the Commissioner considers to be compatible with the Internal Market. This is what generally happens in practice, even though political considerations lead certain authorities or bodies to insist, from time to time, that draft measures be notified, despite the Commissioner's opinion finding the measures to be incompatible with EU State aid rules.

Under the system described above, the procedure of notification of measures to the European Commission under Article 108(3) TFEU comprises the following steps: the State aid measure is notified to the Commissioner in a draft form, before its formal approval by the relevant authority or body; after the Commissioner's opinion is issued and, often, after minor or more substantial changes are made by the competent authority or body in close consultation with the Commissioner, the Council of Ministers or other competent authority or body takes the final decision on whether to proceed with the proposed measure; if the decision to proceed is taken, the final measure is notified to the Commissioner who subsequently formally notifies the measure to the Commission.

This *ex ante* control system aims to avoid unlawful or incompatible aid being granted in Cyprus and is effective, as non compliance with its provisions has legal consequences. No aid measure may be lawfully granted in the Republic of Cyprus without having been notified to the Commissioner and the latter having approved it or having issued an opinion in relation thereto[142]. Failure to comply with this requirement may result in an order being made by the Commissioner, under section 18 of the State Aid Control Law, for the recovery of such aid. Furthermore, if such unlawful aid is granted through an administrative act, the act is subject to annulment by the Supreme Court following a possible application by a competitor, under Article 146 of the Constitution.

---

140 The Commissioner is also competent for monitoring the application of rules on *de minimis* aid (section 9A(h) of the State Aid Control Law). The aid granting authorities and bodies are obliged to submit to the Commissioner all information regarding de minimis aid to enable him to keep an up-to-date central de minimis aid electronic register, which constitutes an efficient tool for controlling cumulation of de minimis aid.

141 Sections 9A(b) and 11(2) of the State Aid Control Law.

142 Sections 10(3) and 11(4) of the State Aid Control Law.

Ex post control

The Commissioner has powers allowing him to secure, *ex post*, transparency with regard to all aid granted.[143] He is responsible for collecting progress reports from all granting authorities and bodies, for compiling and monitoring information on the implementation and impact of all aid granted, for keeping an up-to-date inventory of all State aid schemes and *ad hoc* measures, and for submitting to the Commission all information required with regard to State aid granted in Cyprus.

Section 17(2) of the State Aid Control Law provides that all granting authorities and bodies, including local authorities, must submit an annual report to the Commissioner which must include, *inter alia*, the total amount of aid granted and the total number of beneficiaries of such aid. By virtue of section 17(3), the same authorities and bodies are under the obligation to keep, for a period of 10 years, information on all the amounts of aid granted to each beneficiary. On the basis of the information gathered from the authorities and bodies, the Commissioner prepares and submits to the President of the Republic, pursuant to section 9A(j) of the State Aid Control Law, an annual statistical survey of all State aid granted in the country. The Commissioner also presents to the President of the Republic an annual report on his activities. These two reports are published on the Commissioner's web site and, at the time of their presentation to the President, always get media coverage.

In specific cases, where the Commissioner detects a State aid measure which, in the case of a measure covered by a block exemption, has been implemented without having previously been approved by him or, in the case of a measure not covered by such exemption, has been implemented without the Commissioner having issued a relevant opinion and/or without the measure having been notified to the Commission, the Commissioner has the power to issue a decision suspending the application of the measure in question and ordering the recovery of all aid received under the measure.[144] The authority which adopted the State aid measure is then under an obligation to take all the necessary measures for the implementation of the Commissioner's decision.[145]

Finally, where the European Commission issues a decision ordering the recovery of aid, the new section 18B of the State Aid Control Law imposes on the aid granting authority an obligation to take all necessary measures for the implementation of the Commission's decision and on the Commissioner an obligation to oversee such implementation.

In practice, the above system works smoothly, given that, since Cyprus' accession to the EU, only one case in which aid was granted without having been previously notified has been detected.

143 Sections 9A and 17 of the State Aid Control Law.

144 Section 18 of the State Aid Control Law as amended by Law 108(I)/2009.

145 Section 18A of the State Aid Control Law (new article inserted by Law 108(I)/2009).

2. State aid compliance by national judges and/or the national competition authority (NCA)

All decisions issued to date by the Cypriot courts on State aid issues concern the judicial review of decisions of the Commissioner, which were adopted before the accession of Cyprus to the EU.

The court which is likely to hear the most State aid cases in the future is the Supreme Court, as a result of its exclusive jurisdiction for the judicial review of administrative acts[146]. However, cases regarding aid granted through contracts (e.g. public land sold or leased under preferential terms) could, at some stage, be brought before the District Courts. The same applies for cases where an undertaking demands damages as a result of aid granted unlawfully to a competitor. One such case is now pending, where the plaintiff is an undertaking seeking to obtain damages because, according to its submissions, its competitor has obtained incompatible/unlawful aid.

Application of EU regulations and guidelines

In the absence of court decisions that can be analysed here, it is useful to stress that the Commissioner regularly applies EU regulations and guidelines, with legally binding effect. He has issued, from the date of accession to the end of June 2009, a total of 77 decisions on the compatibility of State aid measures with the EU Block exemption Regulations. These decisions,[147] which include all those summarised for the purposes of this State aid project, were adopted both prior to and after the entry into force of Regulation (EC) No 800/2008.

On the issue of cumulation, the Commissioner does not have the capacity to carry out *ex post* checks regarding compliance with cumulation rules contained in the Block exemption Regulations. However, as part of the *ex ante* control of all aid measures prior to their enforcement, the Commissioner verifies that aid measures based on a Block exemption Regulation, as well as any *de minimis* measures, contain provisions regarding the cumulation rules. All granting authorities and bodies, prior to approving the granting of an aid, require the submission of a signed declaration from the beneficiary that he has not received any other aid from other competent authorities for the same eligible expenses. This practice is a direct consequence of the fact that, in the overwhelming majority of Cypriot State aid schemes, the aid which can be obtained under the scheme reaches the maximum allowable intensity, thus leaving no scope for any cumulation with aid from another source.

Beside the implementation of Block exemption Regulations, the Commissioner regularly refers in his decisions to "soft-law" produced by the Commission, in the form of guidelines

---

146 Article 146 of the Constitution.

147 The Commissioner's decisions are published in the Official Gazette and are also available (only in Greek) on the web site of the Commissioner's Office: http://www.publicaid.gov.cy/publicaid/publicaid.nsf/dmldecisions_gre/dmldecisions_gre?OpenDocument.

or recommendations. By way of example, in decisions No. 251 and 254,[148] the Commissioner applied the definitions of micro, small and medium-sized enterprises as contained in Commission Recommendation 2003/361/EC. Also interesting is decision No. 247,[149] where the Commissioner applied the Community Framework for State aid for Research and Development of 1996, for the purpose of establishing that certain measures did not constitute State aid.

III. Unlawful aid and judicial review

The absence, for the time being, of court decisions in this area renders any lengthy analysis very difficult and of little practical interest, given that it could not be substantiated by references to existing case law and that future case law could easily reverse conclusions based on a purely theoretical construction. Some remarks can, however, be made on the existing means which allow the prevention of the granting of unlawful aid and the recovery of such aid when it is granted, as well as on the possibility for the beneficiary of aid and for his competitors to claim damages before national courts.

1. Prevention of the granting of unlawful aid

As explained in detail under point II.1 above, national State aid rules in Cyprus have, as one of their main objectives, the establishment of an efficient system which, through the competences and powers granted to the Commissioner, achieves compliance with the obligations of Article 108(3) TFEU and prevents the granting of unlawful/non-notified aid. This system, which covers all decisions to grant aid, irrespective of the legal basis of that measure (law, administrative act or contract), has already proved its effectiveness and, therefore, renders unnecessary the intervention of the courts.

If, nevertheless, an individual were to apply to a court for the purpose of stopping an unlawful aid from being granted, the most likely procedure would be a recourse to the Supreme Court, under Article 146 of the Constitution, against the decision to grant the aid in question and, at the same time, an application for an order to suspend the implementation of the decision for the reason that its non-notification renders it obviously unlawful. It should be noted, however, that this procedure could only be effective if the decision to grant the aid has not already, by the time of the application to the Supreme Court, been followed by the enactment of a law, or the signature of a contract, which provides for the granting of the aid in question.

148 Decision No. 251 of 31.8.2006. Aid scheme for the Holstein-Friesian cattle breeder Association; decision No. 254 of 30.11.2006, Single-company continuing training programmes in Cyprus.

149 Decision No. 247 of 27.4.2006, Joint Cooperation Programme between Cyprus and Greece.

2. Recovery of unlawful aid and interest

The possibility to recover unlawful aid with the assistance of the courts varies according to the legal form used for the granting of aid: a law, an administrative act or a private law contract.

Where aid is granted directly by law (fiscal aid) the termination of such aid is relatively simple, given that no one can invoke the right to continue benefiting from a positive legal provision[150] in a way which would prevent the Parliament from abolishing the said provision at any time. The recovery of such aid may be problematic, given that under Article 24.3 of the Constitution, "no tax, duty or rate of any kind whatsoever may be imposed with retrospective effect".

However, even though no case law exists on that matter, one may consider likely that, if aid granted directly by a law were to be found unlawful, within the meaning of Article 1 of Regulation (EC) No 659/1999, the Supreme Court[151] could find that the recovery of aid would not entail the retrospective imposition of a tax, duty or rate as the relevant provisions would have been unlawful from the very beginning, being contrary to Article 108 TFEU and the aforementioned Regulation. This procedure, which would entail an action before the civil courts (District Courts) if the beneficiary of the aid were to resist the recovery, is open only to the State or the body which granted the aid.

The second, and most commonly used, legal form for the granting of aid is by an administrative act. As already mentioned, individual administrative acts are subject to judicial review by the Supreme Court, under Article 146 of the Constitution, upon an application being made by any person whose existing legitimate interest is adversely and directly affected by such act. The recovery of unlawful aid granted through an administrative act may be obtained as a result of the initiative either of a competitor, or of the authority or body which granted the aid.

A competitor of the beneficiary could apply to the Supreme Court in order to obtain the annulment of the relevant act, arguing that the non-notified aid is contrary to both Community State Aid rules and the State Aid Control Law, given that the latter imposes an obligation of notification to the Commissioner in addition to the obligation imposed by Article 108(3) TFEU to notify aid measures to the Commission. Following the annulment of the relevant act by the Supreme Court, it would be up to the authority or body which granted the aid to oblige the beneficiary to return the aid received, if necessary through an action before the civil courts, under general rules of civil law.

The alternative and probably most frequent procedure for recovery of aid granted through an administrative act would be the retrospective withdrawal of the act by the authority or body which granted the aid, followed by an action before the civil courts for recovery. It should be

150 Supreme Court ("Ανώτατο Δικαστήριο"), 25 September 2000, Dimitris Karadjas et al. v. the Republic and the Central Bank, Appeal No. 1008/94, (2000) 3 C.L.R. 480.

151 Even though proceedings for the recovery of such aid would have to be brought before a District Court, if the beneficiary of the unlawful aid measure were to invoke Article 24.3 of the Constitution in order to resist paying retrospectively a higher rate of tax, the matter would probably be referred to the Supreme Court under Article 144 of the Constitution. The Supreme Court would decide on the issue of the alleged unconstitutionality, following what the case would return to the District Court which would give its judgment on the substance of the case.

noted that, according to the case law of the Supreme Court and to section 7 of the Law on the General Principles of Administrative Law, it is possible for an illegal act of the administration to be withdrawn with retrospective effect.

The third possible legal form for granting aid is that of a private law contract. This form is used mainly when public land is leased at preferential terms. According to the case law of the Supreme Court, acts and contracts through which the State or a public body manage their property, constitute acts of private law.[152] In Cyprus Tourism Organisation v. Charilaou[153], the Supreme Court held that the decision to lease public land for reasons of public interest constitutes an administrative act which is subject to judicial review under Article 146 of the Constitution. However, once a contract is signed as a result of such decision, relations between the State or the relevant public body and the tenant are governed by the provisions of the contract. In a similar way, in public procurement procedures, the choice of the successful bidder falls within the sphere of public law, while the contract which, as a result of such decision, is signed between the bidders in question and the state or the relevant public body is governed by private law.[154]

Given this case law, if the State or a public body were found to be granting unlawful aid through a contract signed with an undertaking, initiatives for obtaining restitution of the aid in question would have to follow normal civil law rules and procedures. The State or public body, as the case may be, could try to have the contract declared illegal as having an illegal consideration, and demand that possession of the land be returned to it. As for the recovery of aid illegally received under the contract, if the beneficiary refused to comply, the State or public body would have to bring an action in the District Court, founded on its obligation under EU law and under section 18B of the State Aid Control Law to obtain recovery of the aid in question, such obligation emanating from the Commission's decision which finds the said aid to be unlawful.

Finally, beside the aforementioned procedures which may allow the recovery of aid with the assistance of the courts, it is noted that the Commissioner has powers additional to those of the granting authorities and bodies, which allow him to secure the recovery of unlawful aid. These are described under points I.2 and II.1 above.

3. Damages claims by competitors/third parties or the beneficiary before the national courts

No decision has yet been issued by a court following a claim for damages being filed, either by the beneficiary of unlawful aid, or by a competitor. However, a case is now pending before

152 See *inter alia* Supreme Court ("Ανώτατο Δικαστήριο"), 23 April 2003, Mintikis farm v. Republic, Case no. 750/2002, and the cases referred to therein.

153 (1998) 1 C.L.R. 607, 613.

154 See *inter alia* Supreme Court ("Ανώτατο Δικαστήριο"), Medcon Construction and Others v. the Republic (1968) 3 C.L.R. 535, 544 and Dr. Georgiou v. Cyprus Electricity Authority (1995) 3 C.L.R. 424, 439.

the District Court of Nicosia[155] which may provide interesting elements in that respect. In that case, the claimant seeks to obtain damages both from the State and from the beneficiary of the aid, for the reason that, according to the claimant, the aid was incompatible and unlawful and/or that, the beneficiary of the aid, a public undertaking, has not respected the obligation to keep separate accounts for the activities benefiting from that aid. For the time being, all that can be said is that the claimant's *locus standi* was not contested.

IV. Control of recovery procedure

1. Challenging the validity of national recovery order

When national recovery orders take the form of an administrative act (e.g. an order made by the Commissioner under section 18 of the Public Aid Control Law), they could be subject to judicial review before the Supreme Court on the basis of Article 146 of the Constitution. In accordance with this Article, recourse to the Supreme Court may be made by a person whose existing legitimate interest is directly affected by the decision or act under review. The Supreme Court can only order the suspension of the contested act or decision if the applicant can show that the act or decision is blatantly illegal or that, if the suspension were not ordered, the applicant would be in serious danger of sustaining irreparable damage[156]. Thus, it does not appear that the procedure of judicial review would be likely to prevent the immediate and effective execution of orders for recovery of aid.

The average duration of a judicial review procedure is approximately 18 months to two years.

Even though no case of judicial review of a recovery order has occurred to date, the limitation that can be foreseen in such cases is that the Supreme Court cannot address injunctions to an administrative authority which would oblige the latter to exercise its powers. Therefore, while a recourse under Article 146 could potentially be useful for a beneficiary of aid who would challenge the form or the substance of an order of recovery issued against him, and it could also potentially allow a competitor to argue that the amount ordered to be recovered (either the unlawful aid itself or the interest thereon) is insufficient, but it would not allow a competitor to require that a recovery order be issued immediately or without delay. However, if the competent authorities (including the Commissioner) were to fail to act effectively and in time for the recovery of unlawful aid, the procedure of judicial review could provide the basis for a claim for damages on behalf of an aggrieved competitor (see point IV.2 below).

When national recovery orders take the form of a court order (order issued by a District Court upon an application by the aid granting authority), an appeal before the Supreme Court is open to the parties involved. Such an appeal has no suspensive effect.

155 Nicosia District Court ("Επαρχιακό Δικαστήριο Λευκωσίας"), Sigma Radio TV Public Ltd et al. v. the Attorney General of the Republic and Cyprus Broadcasting Corporation, Case 1929/08, pending.

156 See *inter alia* Supreme Court ("Ανώτατο Δικαστήριο"), 29 May 1990, Kronidou et al. v. the Republic, Case no. 741/89 and Dogan v. the Republic, Case no. 167/95, 10.4.1995.

2. Damages for failure to implement a recovery decision and infringement of EU law

Where the beneficiary of unlawful aid resists a recovery order, the State can oblige him to comply by using the means available under civil law for the recovery of debts. In particular, execution measures can target the movable and immovable assets of the person in question.

As for the possibility of engaging State liability, Article 146.6 of the Constitution provides that "*[a]ny person aggrieved by any decision or act declared to be void under paragraph 4 of this Article or by an omission declared thereunder that it ought not to have been made shall be entitled (...) to institute legal proceedings in a court for the recovery of damages*". Therefore, if the aid granting authority, or the Commissioner, fail to act effectively and in time for the recovery of unlawful aid, an aggrieved party could potentially file an action before the Supreme Court challenging this failure to act and, having won before the Supreme Court, could apply for damages before a District Court, provided, however, that the party could show that it had sustained loss as a result of the public authority's omission.

V. Standing of third parties before national courts

As mentioned under point III.3 above, no case law exists as yet concerning a competitor's claim in a State aid case, besides a pending civil case in which the competitor's *locus standi* has not been contested. It is, therefore, useful to refer to the wider case law regarding *locus standi* in competition cases.

As already mentioned, under Article 146.2 of the Constitution, recourse to the Supreme Court for judicial review of an administrative act or decision "*may be made by a person whose any existing legitimate interest, which he has either as a person or by virtue of being a member of a Community, is adversely and directly affected*" by the challenged act or decision.

Interpreting the notion of "existing legitimate interest", the Supreme Court held[157] that owners of vehicles of public transport had a legitimate interest in challenging a decision of the national competition authority (the Commission for the Protection of Competition) granting an individual exemption to a consortium formed by all insurance companies active in Cyprus, for the purpose of providing insurance to vehicles of public transport. The Supreme Court held that the owners of such vehicles had an interest in trying to maintain competition, instead of having a monopoly on the insurance market as regards the type of vehicles they owned.

In 2002[158], the Supreme Court, in rejecting the application of an undertaking against a decision of the Commission for the Protection of Competition relating to the merger of Exxon Corp. and Mobile Corp., held that the applicant was not, at the time of the merger, active on the market of distribution of oil products and, therefore, could not argue that any interest existing at that

---

157 Supreme Court ("Ανώτατο Δικαστήριο"), 23 November 2003, G.Y.L. Wheels (Rent A Car) Ltd. et al. v. the Commission for the Protection of Competition, Case no. 1166/02.

158 Supreme Court ("Ανώτατο Δικαστήριο"), 23 October 2002, Lefkoniko Investment Group of Cooperative Companies v. the Commission for the Protection of Competition, Case no. 499/01.

time was affected by the decision under review. The fact that his future prospects to become active on that market could have been affected was insufficient, as the interest he invoked was a future and purely hypothetical one. In this judgment, the Supreme Court implied that it would have been ready to consider the recourse of the applicant, if he had been a competitor of the merged undertakings at the time of the merger.

From this case law, it appears likely that the Supreme Court will recognise that an undertaking has a legitimate interest in filing recourse for judicial review of a decision granting aid to one of its competitors.

VI. Cooperation with EU authorities

There does not appear to have been any direct cooperation between the Cyprus courts or the Commissioner and the EU institutions (Commission and Court of Justice) for the handling of specific State aid cases. However, the Commissioner's opinions and decisions make frequent references to the case law of the CJEU and the General Court, to the decisions of the Commission, and to the various texts that the Commission publishes on State aid issues.

VII. Trends – reforms – recommendations

Cyprus, through the institution of the Commissioner for State Aid Control, offers an example of good practice as regards expert advice provided to aid granting authorities, prevention of the non-notification of aid, transparency of all aid provided, control of *de minimis* aid and of aid falling under a Block exemption Regulation and ease of recovery of unlawful aid.

Certain shortcomings which had been detected prior to 2009 as regards the procedures applied and the powers of the Commissioner, particularly in relation to the recovery of aid, were corrected through the State Aid Control (Amending) Law of 2009 (Law 108(I)/2009).

Amongst others, the new provisions introduced by Law 108(I)/2009 clarify that, if an aid measure is subject to the notification requirement of Article 108(3) TFEU, this requirement is not made redundant by the issuing of any opinion by the Commissioner, or by the approval of the Council of Ministers or any other governmental authority. Such an aid measure cannot be put into effect unless it has been notified and approved by the Commission.

Most importantly the amending law introduced more detailed and clearer provisions, which have already been presented above, regarding the powers of the Commissioner and the obligations of the aid granting authorities as to the termination of the granting of unlawful aid and the recovery of the aid unlawfully granted.

Finally, new provisions were introduced concerning the evidentiary value of decisions of the Commissioner and of the European Commission in the framework of actions for compensation before the national courts.

All these amendments appear to reinforce the state aid control system in Cyprus. It is, however, too early to assess their efficiency in practice.

Czech Republic

Michal Nulicek*

* Hogan Lovells, Prague.

I. General principles of member state's state aid law

There are two competent authorities concerned with State aid, the Ministry of Agriculture (the "Ministry") and the Office for the Protection of Competition which is the National Competition Authority (referred to hereinafter as the "NCA"). While the NCA is an authority with general State aid competence in almost all areas of the economy, the Ministry is a competent authority only in relation to agriculture and fishery.

The NCA is the central coordination, advisory, consulting and monitoring authority (further described below) in relation to State aid. It has an important role in the notification procedure as it cooperates with both the grantor of the aid and the Commission and sends the State aid notification forms to the Commission. However, the NCA has no decision-making powers.

The national regulation of State aid-related procedures is set out in Act No. 215/2004 Coll., on Certain Relations in the Area of State aid, as amended (the "Act"), which became effective upon the accession of the Czech Republic to the EU. The Act governs the role of the NCA (and the Ministry) in relation to State aid, the rights and duties of providers and beneficiaries of State aid towards the NCA, as well as some ancillary issues relating to the provision of State aid.

II. Identification of state aid issues at national level

1. State aid compliance by the national legislator and/or the executive

The compliance of new legislation with State aid rules is controlled *ex ante* during the legislative process. Before a piece of legislation raising State aid issues is passed, the NCA is asked to provide a statement as to whether the legislation complies with State aid law. The statement of the NCA is then taken into account during preparation of the legislation in question.

Ex post control consists mainly of reporting and related obligations on the part of both the providers and the beneficiaries of State aid. The Act sets out a special procedure for notification of State aid to the NCA:

(a) The grantor of State aid is obliged to provide to the NCA:
   (i) until 30 April of each calendar year, information about all State aid it has granted in the previous year and information about its State aid schemes;
   (ii) duplicates of all documents submitted to the Commission within the framework of formal procedures (procedures concerning notified aid, unlawful aid, misuse of aid, existing aid and aid schemes, on-site monitoring regarding the notified aid); and
   (iii) upon request by the NCA, any other documents and information within a fixed time limit.

(b) Beneficiaries of State aid are obliged to cooperate with the NCA in relation to Commission′ investigations and to provide the NCA, upon its written request, within the set deadline, with all documents and information concerning a certain State aid.

If the above-mentioned obligations are breached, the NCA can impose on the grantor and the beneficiary of the aid a penalty up to 1 % of the amount of State aid provided. There is no other authority concerned with State aid compliance besides the NCA and the Ministry.

2. State aid compliance by national judges and/or the national competition authority (NCA)

The NCA has wide powers in relation to State aid, as it operates as a central coordination, advisory, consulting and monitoring authority. However, the NCA has no decision-making powers besides the power to impose fines for breaches of the reporting and related obligations of the providers and beneficiaries of State aid.

Besides the power to impose fines, the individual powers of the NCA laid down by the Act include:

(a) liaising with the grantor prior to the notification of the aid to the Commission, and liaising with the Commission and with the grantor during the Commission's investigations; and
(b) maintaining a register of all State aid granted in the Czech Republic and submission of a report to the Commission.

Since the accession of the Czech Republic to the EU, there has been no case law involving State aid (except a very specific case involving the possible grant of state aid due to a change in legislation). There are, therefore, no indications as to how Czech judges would interpret and apply State aid rules in individual cases and any difficulties they might have in doing so.

Theoretically speaking, and conditioned to the *locus standi* of complainants (please see section V below), both civil and administrative courts might have jurisdiction to decide cases involving State aid.

Whether a civil or administrative court would have jurisdiction depends on the nature of the act through which State aid were granted. If State aid is granted solely on the basis of a contract, the civil courts should have jurisdiction. Where State aid is granted by means of an administrative act, the administrative courts would be competent for any actions challenging the act. Even if the State aid was granted by way of an administrative act, civil courts would have jurisdiction for actions for damages against the State based on the Act No. 82/1998 Coll., On Liability For Damage Caused In The Course Of Public Powers Execution Due To An Unlawful Decision Or Incorrect Official Procedure, as amended (the "State Liability Act").

The courts do not have any special powers of investigation for State aid cases and would have to rely on the general powers provided by the Acts on civil and administrative procedure. If a case is brought before a court, the court generally has the ability to summon witnesses, appoint experts, and request third parties to deliver any documentary evidence and information they have in their possession. Where the third party fails to deliver the documentary evidence or provide information, the court may impose a fine and obtain the evidence itself, or from another court or State authority.

The court also may, either upon motion before the commencement of the proceedings, or even *ex officio* after such commencement, order that evidence be secured if there is a danger that such evidence might not be available at a later stage, or if the evidence could later be obtained only with great difficulty. The security may cover any type of evidence and must be conducted in a manner prescribed for by law for the relevant form of evidence.

Due to the lack of case law since the accession of the Czech Republic to the EU it is impossible to state (predict) whether there is (will be) any reluctance to make a preliminary reference.

Third parties

It is, in the absence of case law, impossible to predict whether the courts will take into account the interests of third parties in an assessment of the existence of a State aid. Generally, third parties are able to enjoin proceedings before a civil court, on the part of the plaintiff or the defendant, where third parties have (and are able to prove) legal interest in the outcome of the dispute. The enjoining party then has the same procedural rights and obligations as the plaintiff or defendant, whichever is relevant. In proceedings before administrative courts, third parties may act directly as intervening parties (ie as participants) to the proceedings or can apply their (limited) rights as persons involved in the proceedings (persons who are not direct participants but decide to protect their rights, which were affected by the relevant decision, or which could be affected by its annulment).

Application of EU regulations and guidelines

As there is no relevant case-law, it is impossible to predict whether and how national courts would apply any of the exemption Regulations adopted by the Commission (prior to or after Regulation (EC) No 800/2008). The same applies regarding the court's potential reference to one of the Commission's communications and notice/guidelines-framework (soft-law) issued by the Commission to assess the existence of an aid.

III. Unlawful aid and judicial review

1. General powers of national courts concerning the application of Article 108(3) TFEU

As stated above, the Czech courts do not have any specific powers concerning the application of Article 108(3) TFEU. However, Czech civil and administrative courts generally do have the powers to decide disputes on the basis of a legal action brought by an individual (especially for invalidity of the measure, whether public or private or for damages). Czech courts will therefore have all the powers granted to them by Act 99/1963, Act 99/1963 (the "Act on Civil Procedure"), as amended, and by Act 150/2002, on Judicial Administrative Procedure, as amended. These include the power to issue preliminary injunction, order security of evidence and to declare the State aid measure invalid (or quash the unlawful administrative act in proceedings before administrative courts).

As there is no relevant case law available, it is difficult to estimate which types of litigation will prevail.

2. Prevention of the granting of unlawful aid

As described above, where the State aid is granted by an act of private law, third parties are able to challenge the validity of such unlawful act based on a private law legal action before civil courts. It should however be pointed out that (besides the general *locus standi* issues described in section V below) the Act on Civil Procedure requires that a party seeking a court declaration that a legal act is void must show "urgent legal interest". It remains to be seen whether the courts will be prepared to consider this condition to be met in case of legal actions brought by third parties in relation to State aid.

Where the unlawful act is one of public law carried out by a public authority, third parties are able to claim damages against the State authority that has carried out that act. Theoretically, third parties are also entitled to bring a legal action requesting that the administrative court quashes the decision or other act of public law granting the unlawful aid.

The grant of unlawful aid may also be prevented temporarily by a preliminary injunction. Even though both the civil and administrative courts do generally have jurisdiction to grant preliminary injunctions, it remains to be seen whether the courts are prepared to grant such injunctions in State aid cases.

On a related note, it should be pointed out that the jurisdiction of the administrative courts covers a wide range of measures (individual administrative acts, measures of public authorities and measures of general application). However, the administrative courts do not have competence over legal acts and cannot decide on invalidity of a legal act whereby unlawful State aid has been granted.

There are no specific national law provisions on which individuals could rely before national courts in order to ensure that the obligation to notify is respected.

3. Recovery of unlawful aid and interest

a. "Vertical litigations": Member State v. beneficiary resisting the recovery

The mechanism for vertical recovery of unlawful aid is laid down by the Act, which expressly states that if the Commission decides that the State aid is to be recovered or provisionally recovered, the beneficiary is obliged to repay the State aid (including interest calculated by the Commission) to its provider or its legal successor.

The grantor of the State aid is obliged by the Act to take "any measures necessary to ensure fulfilment of this obligation by the beneficiary". To this end, the provider will immediately request the beneficiary to recover the State aid, if no deadline for recovery has been set by the Commission, the provider of the State aid will set a deadline for recovery in its request. If the

State aid is not recovered within the set deadline, the provider has an obligation to bring legal action against the beneficiary, unless the aid can be recovered in accordance with specific legislation.

b. *"Horizontal litigations": competitors v. beneficiaries – third parties v. beneficiaries*

Czech law does not grant third parties (including competitors) the possibility of enforcing an obligation to recover the State aid. Such third parties may, of course, petition the granting public authority to initiate the recovery proceedings as per the previous paragraph and request that they be informed of the outcome.

According to the Act, the grantor of an aid is obliged to report any grants of State aid and schemes to the NCA and the beneficiary is obliged to provide it with information in respect of individual aid – the form of this information is set out in a decree of the NCA. Although the decree does not oblige the provider to identify the beneficiaries of an aid scheme, the NCA may request further information regarding the aid scheme from the grantor and provide the same to the court upon its request. The court is also entitled to directly request information on the identity of the beneficiaries of State aid from any individual that may possess such information (including the grantor of State aid).

There is no case law available regarding the ability of the court to grant the provider any specific alternative remedies in lieu of recovery, nor does national law confer such power. However, the option to claim additional remedies such as unjust enrichment should be unaffected.

4. Recovery of interest

Claims for recovery of illegality interests can be based directly on Article 108(3) TFEU, what are the procedures in national law available to competitors to introduce such a claim?

The Act imposes an obligation on (and grants the right to) the provider of the State aid to take all possible steps to recover the aid with the interests, as calculated by the Commission. However, as there is no procedure for enforcement of this obligation by the competitors, they may therefore only claim damages against the provider (arising under private or public law, depending on the status of the provider) for a failure to fulfil the obligation to recover the aid including interests.

5. Damages claims by competitors/third parties before national courts against the granting authority

Damages claims against the granting public authority may be claimed pursuant to the previously defined State Liability Act, which provides for a division of competence between the executive and the courts. Such division of competence means that third parties must first assert their right before a relevant public authority (Ministry of Justice, Ministry of Finance or other relevant public authority) and only if the claim for damages has not been fully satisfied by such public authority, can third parties apply to court.

In order to raise a successful claim for damages, the claimant must prove: (i) that an unlawful decision has been made or incorrect official procedure has been followed, (ii) the damage it has suffered and (iii) a causal link between the breach of law and the damage. The claimant may claim both actual damages (*damnum emergens*) and lost profit (*lucrum cessans*).

The State Liability Act obviously does not cover all possible types of damages that can arise as a consequence of a breach of the State aid. In particular, this Act does not cover the liability of the State for a statute passed in contravention of the State aid rules. The existence of this type of liability has been questioned by some academics.

In addition, the State Liability Act does not expressly state whether it applies with respect to *Francovich*-type liability for breach of EU law. As the State Liability Act does not contain any provisions specific to that liability (such as conditions under which such liability may arise), it appears that it does not apply to such liability (even though in the absence of case law, it cannot be excluded that the courts will take another approach).

If a court held that the State Liability Act does not apply to *Francovich*-type liability, this type of liability would likely be enforceable on the basis of general liability principles, in addition to the liability based on the State Liability Act. However, it must be pointed out that the conditions of the State Liability Act will in most cases be easier to fulfil, as they do not require the existence (and proof) of a "sufficiently serious breach".

Explain the differences if any between the liability by the legislator or the executive (government) for violation of Article 108(3) TFEU?

As stated above, the very concept of liability of the legislator is being questioned under Czech law. The liability of the executive will be governed by the State Liability Act.

Concerning the assessment of the damage caused, does national law distinguish between situations where the breach caused the claimant the loss of an asset or whether it prevented the claimant from improving its asset position?

The claimant generally has the right to claim damage, consisting of the actual damage (*damnum emergens*) and loss of profit (*lucrum cessans*). These claims may arise cumulatively or alternatively, depending on the facts. In any case, the claimant can only claim damage that was foreseeable and that has a causal relation to the breach of the statutory obligation.

As to the assessment of the damage, it will be up to the claimant to prove the amount of actual damage and/or loss of profit. Besides damages, the claimant may also claim compensation for immaterial harm; the amount of such immaterial harm will be assessed by the court taking into account, in particular, the seriousness of the immaterial damage and the circumstances of the case.

Are there specific provisions under national law dealing with situations where the claimant is forced out of business, for example through insolvency or bankruptcy, as the direct consequence of the granting of an unlawful aid? Are there any cases in which such a situation has arisen?

There are no specific provisions dealing with situations where the claimant is forced out of business, for example through insolvency or bankruptcy, as the direct consequence of the granting of an unlawful aid. However, as stated above, the claimant may claim immaterial damages which could theoretically include damages that are normally not recoverable as monetary damages.

Is there any distinction in terms of liability when the unlawful aid is granted by an authority which is not the central State? If so, to what extent is the State responsible for the unlawfulness of the measure? If there is any disagreement between the levels of powers, what is the competent jurisdiction to settle the dispute?

To the extent that the liability of the authority granting aid is covered by the State Liability Act (see above), it is immaterial whether such authority is a central State. According to the State Liability Act, the State is liable for damage caused by State institutions, natural or legal persons conducting State administration, or by the regional self-governing units conducting State administration. Where the regional self-governing units (municipalities and regions) do not conduct state administration (i.e. they are conducting self-administration), the State Liability Act imposes liability directly on these self-governing units.

Even though it is the State or the self-governing units that are ultimately liable, the State Liability Act provides for limited recourse against the individuals and self-governing units (in case they are liable for unlawful state administration) actually responsible for the breach of law.

6. Damages claims by the beneficiary before national courts against the granting authority

How are damages split between the beneficiary and the State in case of shared liability?

There is no relevant case law. However, as a general principle, if the damage also arises as a result of the negligence of the party that has suffered harm, that party's claim for damages will be proportionately decreased. In other words, the court will assess the extent to which the conduct of the party that has suffered the harm has contributed to the damage and will decrease the amount of damage it awards accordingly.

7. Damages claims by competitors/third parties before national courts against the beneficiary

a. Direct damage actions

There is no relevant case law available, nor is there any specific procedure for bringing a damages action against the beneficiary for accepting an aid. Theoretically, such action could be based on non-contractual (tort) liability, arising from a breach of (EU) law. However, the courts might find it difficult to assess whether a breach has indeed occurred (and, therefore, whether the basic condition for granting damage based on tort has been satisfied), as Article 108(3) TFEU expressly imposes an obligation on the Member States, rather than on the beneficiary.

Theoretically, wilful acceptance of an unlawful aid could be considered unfair competition as defined by the Act No. 513/1991, the Commercial Code, as amended (the "Commercial Code"). Unfair competition generally consists of an act of economic competition against the good faith of competition, which is capable of causing harm to other competitors or consumers. Even though the Commercial Code lists types of conduct that are considered to constitute unfair competition and this list does not expressly include acceptance of an unlawful aid or other violations of the State aid rules, the list is not exhaustive.

Should the courts accept the applicability of the unfair competition regulation to breaches of State aid rules, third parties would have all claims prescribed by the commercial code including action to cease the unlawful conduct, restitution, claim for damages, unjust enrichment, and for reasonable compensation (which can be granted in money).

Does the regime of liability allow for suing the beneficiary, in the event that it opposes and delays the process of recovery? Which procedures can be relied on in case of incomplete restitution?

As stated above, only the grantor of the State aid can sue the beneficiary to enforce recovery. This also includes cases where the beneficiary opposes and delays the process of recovery. The same procedure (i.e. civil legal action) would be available to the provider of the State aid if it is unable to get full recovery from the beneficiary.

The liability regime does not allow private enforcement of recovery in the event that the beneficiary opposes and delays the process of recovery, or does not make full repayment (any such claim would likely be refused due to an absence of *locus standi*). Third parties may theoretically sue the beneficiary for damages based on tort (non-contractual) liability or based on unfair competition. However, it may be rather difficult to prove the damage (both the existence and amount) on the part of the claimant, and/or prove causation.

Can competitors/third parties sue the beneficiary of an unlawful aid for damages before a national court? Is there a distinction of locus standi to be made between competitors/third parties (please refer to Case C-174/02, Streekgewest)? If yes, which procedures are applicable (e.g. unfair competition)? Are there any example cases?

As stated above, third parties may theoretically sue the beneficiary of State aid for damages arising from its failure to repay the aid as required by the Act. However, the courts might find it difficult to make a finding that a breach of law has occurred (and, therefore, that the basic condition for granting damage based on tort has been satisfied) as Article 108(3) TFEU imposes an obligation on the Member States, rather than on the beneficiary.

Any third party that is able to prove the fulfilment of the three basic conditions (for a damage claim) on its part – breach of law, damage and causal link – can claim damages, irrespective of whether it is a competitor or not.

As there is no case law available yet, it is rather hard to predict whether the courts will allow an action against the beneficiary at all and if so, what types of mitigating circumstances would be considered.

b. Recovery of undue advantages enjoyed by the beneficiary

Upon motion of the provider of the State aid, the courts can decide on the recovery of unjust enrichment by the beneficiary.

IV. Control of recovery procedure

1. Challenging the validity of national recovery order

There is no specific procedure for challenging a recovery order. As the recovery will in most cases be ordered by a court based on an action by the provider of the aid, the methods for challenging the court recovery order will correspond to the appellate instruments available against any other decision of a civil court. These appellate instruments include an ordinary appeal against decisions that are not yet legally effective and extraordinary appeals (based on specific grounds only), aiming against decisions that are already legally effective.

The beneficiary has the option to appeal (with suspensive effect) the decision to make a recovery order. If the appellate court upholds the order, it becomes binding and enforceable. The beneficiary could subsequently also bring an extraordinary appeal if the specific conditions for such an application to appeal are met. These extraordinary appeals do not have an *ex lege* suspensive effect, this may however be granted an application by a party/parties.

There is no specific procedure on which a third party could rely if an aid has not been recovered effectively, immediately and "without delay". Such a third party could only theoretically claim damages against the provider and the beneficiary.

There is no relevant case law available. However, there are currently no specific methods of challenging the course (time necessary, etc.) and the outcome (amount recovered, beneficiaries concerned, etc.) of the recovery procedure before the court. As stated above, it is theoretically possible to claim damages against the provider and the beneficiary for breach of their obligations relating to recovery, as set out in the Act.

2. Damages for failure to implement a recovery decision and infringement of EU law

The principles of State liability as described above apply *mutatis mutandis* to the State liability for a failure to implement a Commission recovery decision.

V. Standing of third parties before national courts

As indicated above, *locus standi* is an issue relating to the above-described proceedings before the national civil and administrative courts.

As regards a civil law action for a declaration of invalidity of the private law legal act pursuant to which the State aid has been granted, the claimant (third party, competitor) must demonstrate it has an "urgent legal interest". This means that the claimant must prove that without the court declaration as regards validity, the rights of the claimant would be threatened or its legal position would remain uncertain. It remains to be seen whether the Czech courts will be prepared to consider this condition fulfilled in the event that a declaration is sought by a third party, who will not be party to the agreement between the grantor and beneficiary.

In relation to an action brought before the administrative courts, the situation can be even more complicated. In proceedings for the annulment of the administrative act, the claimant must prove that it has been deprived of its rights directly, or as a consequence of violation of its rights in proceedings before the administrative body. In either case it must be as a result of an act that creates amends or terminates its right or obligations. The claimant may alternatively prove that it has been deprived of its rights by the proceedings before the administrative body in such a way that this could lead to an unlawful decision. It is evident that in order to be successful, the claimant must always prove that it has been deprived of its own rights. It remains to be seen whether the Czech administrative courts will be prepared to consider this condition satisfied in case legal action is brought by a third party, which is not involved in the administrative act to be quashed.

Generally, both with respect to the civil and administrative proceedings relating to State aid, the claimants should, in order to raise the chance that *locus standi* will be granted to them, refer to the relevant State aid legislation, EU principles of equivalence and effectiveness, and to the softlaw issued by the "Commission notice on the enforcement of State aid law by national courts" (2009/C 85/01).

What is the burden of proof which lies on the claimant?

Generally, the claimant must provide evidence of the factual statements it makes. It is then up to the court to decide which evidence will be considered. The court may also decide that other evidence than that presented by the claimant is to be adduced, if the necessity to conduct such evidence arises in course of the proceedings.

Instead of using this evidence, the court can accept a consistent statement from the parties involved. It is also not generally necessary to prove facts that are publicly known or known to the court.

As regards types of evidence, anything that can contribute to establishing the facts of the case can be used as evidence. Each piece of evidence is evaluated solely by the court according to its own internal opinion, individually and in connection with other types of evidence, while taking into account anything that has been revealed in course of the proceedings.

VI. Trends – reforms – recommendations

Unfortunately, there is not yet any case law relating to enforcement of State aid legislation. It is therefore difficult to state how not only the Commission's guidelines, but the basic principles of EU State aid regulation, will be applied by the Czech courts. We are not aware of any pending reform of the Act or the Act on Civil Procedure relating to State aid.

With no available case law, it is very hard to predict what areas will require additional legislation or amendment of the existing legislation. However, taking into account the principles and requirements laid down by the recent "Commission notice on the enforcement of State aid law by national courts" (cited above), it is obvious that at least some will be needed. Such legislation should focus mainly on issues relating to private enforcement of State aid rules, such as *locus standi*, access to evidence by third parties, prevention of grant/payment of the aid, enforcement of the recovery obligation, etc.

Based on our experience from other areas such as intellectual property law, we believe the Czech government might consider proposing a single act on enforcement of all claims based on competition law (including those arising under State aid rules), which would expressly grant certain rights to third parties (including competitors) and would amend the Act on Civil Procedure in order to ensure effective enforcement of such claims.

DENMARK

Michael Honoré*

* Bech-Bruun, Copenhagen.

I. General principles of Member State's State aid law

1. National authorities competent for granting aid and involved in the notification procedure

The ministry granting the aid measure is responsible for the notification to the Commission. The notification, as with most correspondence with the Commission, is sent through the Danish government's permanent representation in Brussels.

On 1 January 2007, a State aid Committee was set up to assist the central administration *inter alia* in the notification procedure under Article 108(3) TFEU (see below, section II).

2. National authorities competent for recovery and brief description of the procedure

The obligation to recover an unlawful aid rests with the public authority that granted the aid. If the aid beneficiary does not comply with a direct request for recovery issued by the ministry, the latter must instigate court proceedings in order to compel the beneficiary to repay the State aid. Proceedings can be brought before the local City Court ("Byretten") and, possibly, before the Maritime and Commercial Court ("Sø- og Handelsretten").

See section III.3 below for a more detailed description of the procedures for the recovery of unlawful aid.

II. Identification of State aid issues at national level

1. State aid compliance by the national legislator and/or the executive power

On 1 January 2007 the Danish Government created a State aid Committee to carry out *inter alia* an *ex ante* scrutiny ("pre-assessment") of new regulatory initiatives in the light of State aid rules.

The State aid Committee is an inter-ministerial committee composed of permanent representatives (senior civil servants) from four ministries, these being the Ministry of Economic and Business Affairs (chair), the Ministry of Justice, the Ministry of Foreign Affairs and the Ministry of Finance. When it meets, the Committee is joined by the ministry responsible for the aid measure under scrutiny.

The State aid Committee is assisted by a State aid Secretariat, composed of civil servants of the Danish Competition Authority (the "Competition Committee").

All new regulatory initiatives that might constitute State aid have to be presented to the Committee which issues a recommendation on the draft legislation.

The first State aid pre-assessment is carried out by the relevant ministry before it tables a formal legislative draft. Based on a questionnaire ("screening-list") issued by the Prime Minister's cabinet, the individual ministry must first consider whether the draft legislation (1) includes State aid (2) is covered by a State aid Block exemption Regulation or (3) must be notified to and approved by the Commission. If the proposal is found to include State aid, it must identify: (1) the objective of the aid; (2) the volume and intensity of the aid; (3) expected beneficiaries; (4) selection procedure; (5) impact on markets, competition and internal community trade; (6) EU Regulation that may indicate approval of the scheme.

If it is found that the draft legislation may constitute State aid, the relevant ministry must involve the State aid Committee (via the Secretariat) and present its observations on the above questions. The Secretariat then carries out its own assessment of the measure, which it presents to the State aid Committee. Following this, the State aid Committee issues its opinion on the measures and on the procedural aspects. The Committee and the Secretariat stress that their recommendations are advisory only.

The clear aim of this *ex ante* scrutiny is to identify and to clarify any potential State aid issues linked to a legislative draft before it is formally submitted.

In addition to the formal screening of regulatory drafts as described above, the State aid Committee and Secretariat offer:

(a) general advice on State aid matters;
(b) advice on and assistance in early contact with the relevant services at the European Commission;
(c) advice on and assistance in the preparation of State aid notifications and the handling of the State aid procedure.

The aim is that measures that comply with the recommendation of the State aid Committee should be approved by the Commission within six months of being notified. No succesful infringement actions should be brought by the Commission against the Danish State in cases where the Committee or the Secretariat provided advice and where such advice has been followed.

In 2007 and 2008, the Committee reportedly issued recommendations in 17 cases of substantial importance and impact. In addition, the Secretariat reportedly assisted the Ministries in 139 cases.

2. State aid compliance by national judges and/or the national competition authority (NCA)

a. State aid compliance by the NCA

Under the Danish Competition Act, the Danish Competition Authority has competence in the field of State aid.

Section 11a of the Act provides that:

> *"(1) The Competition Council may issue orders for the termination or repayment of aid granted from public funds to support certain forms of commercial activity.*
> *An order under subsection (1) may be issued in case:*
> *– the direct or indirect object or effect of the aid is distortion of competition; and*
> *– the aid is not lawful according to public regulation.*
>
> *The decision of whether granted aid is lawful according to public regulation shall be made by the relevant minister or the relevant municipal supervisory authority unless otherwise provided by other legislation. Decisions as to the lawfulness of granted aid according to public regulation shall be made not later than 4 (four) weeks after receipt of a request from the Competition Council. The Competition Council may extend this time limit.*
>
> *An order for repayment of aid under subsection (1) may be issued to private undertakings, self governing institutions and corporate undertakings owned fully or partly by public authorities. The Minister for Economic and Business Affairs may lay down specific rules to the effect that orders under subsection (1) for repayment of aid may also be issued to certain quasi-corporate undertakings owned fully or partly by public authorities.*
>
> *The Competition Council's powers to order repayment of public aid under subsection (1) above shall be barred by limitation five years after the aid was paid out. The Competition Council shall, in accordance with the rules of the Interest Act, fix the amount of interest accrued in connection with a repayment order issued under subsection (1) and may allow interest to be charged from the time when the distortive aid was paid out.*
>
> *The Competition Council may, upon notification, declare that based on the conditions known to it certain grants of public aid are not covered by subsection (2), paragraph i and that, accordingly, it has no grounds for issuing an order under subsection (1). The Council may lay down specific rules on notification, including rules on the use of special notification forms.*
>
> *The Competition Council may refrain from dealing with a case under subsections (1) – (6) if the aid scheme at issue may affect trade between the member states of the European Union."*

The following observations may be made in relation to Section 11a:

The concept of "aid" is the same as under Article 107 TFEU. As regards the effect on competition, the Danish Competition Act provides for no *de minimis* threshold. As regards the geographic scope of Section 11a, its wording (see paragraph 7) suggests that the Competition Council may be competent to deal with State aid measures that affect trade between Member

States. The question is therefore whether this provision may be reconciled with the fact that the Commission assumes exclusive competence in the field of Article 107 TFEU.

As regards the issue of lawfulness, the Competition Council may only condemn a State aid measure if it is "not lawful according to public regulation" (see Section 11a, paragraph 2). The decision on lawfulness is taken by the public authorities who are responsible for the particular area (normally the relevant Ministries or the municipal supervisory authorities). The Competition Council, being a national authority on the same level as other authorities, has no power to veto the decision on lawfulness taken by other public authorities. Accordingly, the decision on lawfulness may be entirely unrelated to competition law concerns. In this way the assessment of lawfulness under Section 11a may deviate considerably from the compatibility assessment carried out by the European Commission under Article 107 TFEU.

Moreover, it is noteworthy that under Section 11a, paragraph 4, the Competition Council is not obliged to order the recovery of the unlawful State aid. Instead, the Competition Council has a large discretion as to the appropriate remedy and may for instance limit itself to ordering the termination of the unlawful conduct. In only one reported case has the Competition Council ordered the recovery of unlawful aid (Decision of 27.9.2006, Case no. 4/0120-0100-0002SEK/DRP, "Portal Fyn.dk").

Private parties cannot rely directly on Section 11a in civil courts. However, a complaint can be made to the Competition Council, whose decisions can be appealed to the Danish Competition Appeals Tribunal. Appeals may be brought by the party to whom the decision is addressed and by other parties who have an individual and substantial interest in the case. Decisions by the Competition Council must be appealed to the Appeals Tribunal before being brought before the ordinary courts. The time limit for lodging an appeal to the Appeals Tribunal is four weeks, whilst there is an eight week time limit for appealing to the ordinary courts.

On 1 July 2007, Section 11a was supplemented by Section 11b. Section 11b is relevant only in areas where the Danish citizens have a "free choice" between a public service provider and a private service provider (the field of residential care services). In this area, the central question is usually whether the price paid by the municipality to the private service provider (the "settlement price") is correctly calculated. Section 11b improves the ability of the Danish Competition Authority to examine and rule upon the calculation of the settlement prices. In particular Section 11b widens the DCA's discretion in deciding on the costs to be taken into account for the calculation of the settlement price.

Section 11b is worded as follows:

> *"11b.-(1) The Competition Council may investigate the extent to which a public authority offers private providers of services covered by the Free Choice programme a settlement price fixed in accordance with the rules established in other legislation on the Free Choice programme, cf. subsection (5).*
>
> *If the settlement price referred to in subsection (1) is lower or estimated to be lower than the price which the public authority should have used according to the relevant provisions on*

Free Choice, the Competition Council may issue an order addressed to the public authority to the effect that the public authority shall

- *stop calculating and stipulating settlement prices that are contrary to the Free Choice rules,*
- *use specified bases of calculation, calculation methods or settlement prices in respect of private providers of Free Choice services and*
- *ensure post-payment of an amount to private suppliers of Free Choice services corresponding to the difference between the settlement price that the authority has used and the settlement price that the authority should have used in accordance with paragraph i.*

Unless otherwise specified in the provisions on the Free Choice programme in question, the order to ensure post-payment may not relate to payments that were made more than one year prior to the date on which the Competition Authority launched an investigation into the conditions of the public authority in question.

The Competition Council may refrain from dealing with a case under subsections (1)–(3) if the programme in question may affect trade between the Member States of the European Union.

The Minister for Economic and Business Affairs shall, after negotiation with the relevant minister, lay down rules to specify the Free Choice programmes that fall within the Competition Council's field of competence."

A significant number of State aid decisions have been adopted by the Competition Authority in the field of residential care services, mainly on the basis of Article 11a (prior to the introduction of Section 11b on 1 July 2007). In several cases, the Competition Council found that the municipality should make a post-payment to the complainant (the private supplier of Free Choice services).

b. State aid compliance by national judges

As at 1 September 2009 there have been no published Danish court cases in which Articles 107 and/or 108 TFEU have been applied. The experience of the Danish judiciary in handling State aid cases and the State aid criteria is therefore highly limited. For the same reason, no preliminary references have been made pursuant to Article 267 TFEU.

As regards the courts' powers of investigation, the courts must generally decide a case based on the facts presented before it by the parties. Accordingly, the courts have limited inquiry powers for the purpose of establishing factual information necessary for their decisions. Besides putting questions to the parties, the courts have no general rights or duties under Danish procedural rules to order parties to produce evidence. If a party refuses to produce requested evidence, the courts may resort to sanctions of procedural nature, i.e. decide that the refusal to produce evidence will have a prejudicial effect on the party.

As regards the right to intervene, a third party may intervene independently (main intervention) or in support of a party (supportive intervention). Under the Administration of Justice Act:

(a) main intervention requires that:
    (i) Denmark is the jurisdiction for the intervening claim;
    (ii) the claim can be tried under the same procedural rules as the original claims; and
    (iii) the intervening claim constitutes an independent claim with regard to the subject-matter of the case or the claim has such connection to the original claims that the intervening claim should be heard during the main proceedings, if this does not cause substantial inconvenience to the initial parties;
(b) supportive intervention requires a legal interest in the outcome of a case.

III. Unlawful aid and judicial review

1. General powers of national courts concerning the direct effect of Article 108(3) TFEU

Under Danish law, there are specific procedural provisions relating to State aid, but these only apply to State aid covered by the Danish Competition Act (see above). Danish law contains no procedural provisions specifically dealing with Articles 107 or 108 TFEU. The legal basis for any procedure concerning the direct effect of Article 108(3) TFEU therefore must be founded on Articles 107 and 108 TFEU.

2. Prevention of the granting of unlawful aid

There are no specific procedures in national law preventing the payment of unlawful aid. Nor are there any provisions on which individuals can rely before the national courts in order to ensure the obligation to notify is respected.

3. Recovery of unlawful aid and interest

There are no specific procedures under national law enabling the recovery of unlawful aid. Both in the case of "vertical litigation" (a Member State versus a beneficiary resisting the recovery), and in the case of "horizontal litigation" (competitors or third parties v. beneficiaries), proceedings can be brought before the local City Court ("Byretten"). Decisions by the local city court may be appealed to the High Court ("Landsretten"). Since 1 January 2007, proceedings may also be brought before the Maritime and Commercial Court ("Sø- og Handelsretten") in cases where the Danish Competition Act is of significant importance.

The Danish Competition Act contains provisions (Sections 11a and 11b) in relation to State aid with a predominately national dimension (see above, section IV). It remains to be seen whether court proceedings founded on the Treaty (Articles 107 and 108 TFEU) may be assimilated with a national competition case and may, therefore, be brought before the Maritime and Commercial Court. In the light of the EU principle of equivalence the answer would seem to be in the affirmative.

Judgments of the Maritime and Commercial Court may be appealed to the Supreme Court ("Højesteret"). Judgments of the High Court (as the court of second instance) may only be appealed to the Supreme Court if the Supreme Court so authorises.

If the beneficiary refuses to comply with a court judgment ordering the repayment of State aid, the appropriate remedy is an injunction from the Bailiff's Court ("Fogedretten"), which is a subdivision of the City Court.

4. Damages claims by competitors/third parties before national courts against the granting authority

Under Danish law, a public authority may incur non-contractual liability for damages caused by that authority's failure to observe obligations placed on it, provided that: (i) the authority has acted wrongfully, (ii) actual and quantifiable damage was suffered; (iii) there is a causal link between the damage and the wrongful behaviour, and (iv) the damage was foreseeable.

It seems obvious that there is wrongful behaviour if a public authority were to grant unlawful (i.e. non-notified) State aid. It would also be the case if a public authority were to violate the notification obligation under Article 108(3) TFEU, even if the measure were later approved by the Commission (as compatible with the Internal Market).

In the case of non-notified aid, the greatest obstacle to a successful action would seem to be establishing a causal link between, on the one hand, the failure to notify a State aid measure and, on the other hand, the damage suffered by the competitor/third party.

A claim for damages may also be based directly on the rules on State liability developed by the CJEU. As of 1 July 2010, there are no reported court judgments on damages in a State aid context. The same remark can be made concerning damages claims cases introduced by the beneficiary before national courts against the granting authority.

5. Damages claims by competitors/third parties before national courts against the beneficiary

It is assumed that a claim for damages by a competitor or a third party against the beneficiary would be based on the general principles of non-contractual liability.

In order to obtain damages in such cases, the applicant would have to demonstrate that: (i) the defendant acted wrongfully; (ii) an actual and quantifiable damage was suffered; (iii) there is a causal link between the damage and the wrongful behaviour; and (iv) the damage was foreseeable.

As of 1 July 2010, there are no reported court judgments on damages in a State aid context.

IV. Control of recovery procedure

1. Challenging the validity of the national recovery order

There is no specific State aid procedure under which a beneficiary can challenge the validity of a national recovery order. As mentioned above, in section I.2, if the aid beneficiary does not comply with a direct request for recovery issued by the public authority, the latter must instigate court proceedings in order to oblige the beneficiary to repay the State aid. Such proceedings can be brought before the local City Court ("Byretten") and, possibly, before the Maritime and Commercial Court ("Sø- og Handelsretten"), cf. section III.3 above.

If the beneficiary refuses to comply with a court judgment ordering the repayment of State aid, the appropriate remedy is an injunction from the Bailiff's Court ("Fogedretten"). There is no specific procedure on which a third party can rely if an aid has not been recovered effectively, immediately and without delay. It is believed that a third party would have to commence ordinary court proceedings in such case.

As at 1 July 2010 there are no reported judgments in which Articles 107 and/or 108 TFEU have been applied.

2. Damages for failure to implement a recovery decision and infringement of EU law

Under Danish law, a public authority may incur non-contractual liability for damages caused by that authority's failure to observe obligations placed on it, provided that: (i) the authority has acted wrongfully, (ii) actual and quantifiable damage was suffered; (iii) there is a causal link between the damage and the wrongful behaviour; and (iv) the damage was foreseeable.

It seems obvious that a public authority may incur liability if it fails to implement a recovery decision of the Commission.

V. Standing of third parties before national court

Under general principles of Danish law, a third party may challenge public acts in court provided that they have a sufficient legal interest. This principle will apply to public acts granting State aid covered by Article 107 TFEU. Equally, a third party with a sufficient legal interest can claim that the effects of a public act (i.e. the grant of State aid) should cease or request the recovery of an aid. It is likely that a competitor would have *locus standi* to challenge a public measure granted in breach of Articles 108(3) TFEU.

As stated above, in section III, there are no procedural rules under Danish law specifically governing State aid matters. Therefore, it would be the general principles of Danish procedural law that apply in a State aid context, combined with EU principles of effectiveness and equivalence.

VI. Cooperation with EU authorities

1. Cooperation with the CJEU

As of 1 July 2010, there are no reported judgments in which Articles 107 and/or 108 TFEU have been applied.

2. Cooperation with the Commission

As of 1 July 2010, there are no reported judgments in which Articles 107 and/or 108 TFEU have been applied.

VII. Trends – reforms – recommendations

As of 1 July 2010, there are no reported judgments in which Articles 107 and/or 108 TFEU have been applied. It is therefore difficult to reach any conclusions as to the development of State aid enforcement at court level. However, in relation to legislation, a State aid Committee and a State aid Secretariat were established in 2007. These provide valuable assistance to the ministries both prior to the adoption of formal legislative drafts and during the notification procedure with the Commission. Judging by the cases handled during the first two years (more than 150 cases handled by either the Committee or the Secretariat), it would seem that the system has been a success.

ESTONIA

Vaido Põldoja, Tarmo Peterson*

---

* Advokaadibüroo Varul Vilgerts, Smaliukas AS, Tallinn.

I. General principles of Member State's State aid law

1. National authorities competent for granting aid and involved in the notification procedure

According to Article 301(1) of the Competition Act 2001[159] the grantor of State aid is the State, local government or other body such as a foundation, non-profit association, legal person in public law, or public undertaking specified in Article 31(1) of the Competition Act, which directly or indirectly use the resources of the State or a local government for granting State aid. According to Article 31(1) of the Competition Act, a public undertaking is an undertaking over which the State or a local government exercises a dominant influence, either directly or indirectly, by virtue of right of ownership or financial participation, on the basis of the legislation applicable to the person or in any other manner.

The authority responsible for preliminary review of State aid notices, cooperation with the grantors of State aid and the Commission, reporting obligations vis-à-vis the Commission and assisting the Commission with supervision of State aid and on-the-spot checks is the Ministry of Finance ("Ministry").

State aid notices are sent to the Commission by the Permanent Representation of the Republic of Estonia to the European Union ("Permanent Representation"). The Permanent Representation also acts as a contact point for additional information requested by the Commission.

2. National authorities competent for recovery and brief description of the procedure

According to Article 42(3) of the Competition Act, if the Commission or the CJEU has forwarded a decision that unlawful State aid or misused State aid has to be recovered by the beneficiary of the State aid, this decision shall be forwarded to the grantor of unlawful or misused State aid. The grantor of State aid is required to demand recovery of the State aid with interest pursuant to the decision of the Commission or the CJEU.

There are no detailed national provisions for recovery procedures nor has recovery occurred in practice. Although it is not proven in practice and it remains to be clarified by future court practice, in our opinion recovery orders are likely to be implemented via civil law actions by the grantors of aid as long as there are no specific provisions on recovery procedures.

Civil law actions are likely to be used in the absence of specific rules even if State aid were granted under administrative law provisions. That is because although Article 42(3) of the Competition Act provides for the obligation of a grantor of aid to demand recovery from the beneficiary, the Competition Act does not provide for an obligation for the beneficiary to return the aid together with interest to the grantor of aid nor for the procedure to be used for recovery of aid. According to Article 7(4) of the code of Administrative Court Procedure[160] a

159 Competition Act ("Konkurentsiseadus"), 27 June 2001, RTI, 27.6.2001, 56, 332.

160 Administrative Court Procedure Act ("Halduskohtumenetluse seadustik"), 22 March 1999, RTI, 22.3.1999, 31, 425.

public authority may file an action against an individual or against a legal person in private law only in the cases provided by law.

No such basis is provided for by national law for State aid matters. Procedure for recovering any benefits transferred in a public law relationship is also regulated in Article 69(1) of the Administrative Procedure Act[161] and Article 22(3) of the State Liability Act[162]. According to Article 69(1) of the Administrative Procedure Act things, money and other benefits transferred to a person on the basis of an administrative act which is repealed retroactively has to be returned or compensated according to the private law provisions concerning unjust enrichment.

The Administrative Procedure Act therefore enacts that private law provisions are used for recovery of benefits given in a public law relationship. The provision does clarify which procedural rules should be used and the provision does not, in our opinion, allow the grantor of aid to issue an administrative act to obligate the beneficiary to return the benefit. Article 22(3) of the State Liability Act on the other hand provides that a public authority may request from a person the return of a thing or money transferred without legal basis in a public law relationship on the bases of, and pursuant to the procedure provided by private law. Therefore, recovery decisions are likely to be implemented via actions on the basis of civil law, even if aid was granted under administrative law provisions.

We also refer to the practice of the Supreme Court according to which benefits transferred in a public law relationship have to be recovered, in the absence of specific provisions, by filing an action with a civil court. In a dispute concerning repayment of support measures in the field of agriculture, the Supreme Court concluded that in the absence of legislative provisions that would allow the relevant State authority to file an administrative action against the receiver of support, the dispute is in the jurisdiction of civil court[163]. The Supreme Court also referred to Article 22(3) of the State Liability Act.

II. Identification of State aid issues at national level

1. State aid compliance by the national legislator and/or the executive power

State aid compliance is organised by establishing *ex ante* control carried out by the Ministry of Finance. According to Article 34(1) of the Competition Act, the grantor of State aid has to submit the notice on State aid together with all necessary information in writing and by electronic means through the web-application prescribed by the Commission to the Ministry of Finance for review. If the grantor of State aid fails to submit the required information in the notice on State aid, the notice does not comply with the requirements, or there are deficiencies in the notice or information submitted together with it, the Ministry has the right to request

161 Administrative Procedure Act ("Haldusmenetluse seadus"), 7 July 2001, RTI, 2.7.2001, 58, 354.

162 State Liability Act ("Riigivastutuse seadus"), 22 May 2001, RTI, 22.5.2001, 47, 260.

163 Supreme Court ("Riigikohus"), 19 February 2009, AS Andressel v. PRIA, administrative proceedings no. 3-3-4-1-09, RTIII, 10.3.2009, 9, 61.

the submission of additional information from the grantor of State aid or to make a proposal to supplement the notice within 20 working days as of the receipt of the notice.

Upon the grant of State aid covered by group exemption the grantor of State aid has to submit, not later than 20 working days before granting the individual State aid or implementation of the aid scheme, a summary information sheet concerning the grant of State aid covered by group exemption ("notice on group exemption") complying with the requirements set by the Commission in writing and by electronic means through the web-application prescribed by the Commission to the Ministry for review. The legislation or the draft legislation on the basis of which individual State aid is granted or an aid scheme is implemented and, if necessary, description of the aid proving the compliance of the planned State aid with the conditions laid down in the relevant group exemption regulation of the Commission has to be submitted to the Ministry together with the notice on group exemption. If the grantor of State aid fails to submit the required information in the notice on group exemption, the notice on group exemption does not comply with the requirements or there are deficiencies in the notice or information submitted together with it, the Ministry has the right to request the submission of additional information from the grantor of State aid or to make a proposal to supplement the notice on group exemption within 10 working days as of the receipt of the notice.

The above system seems to be rather effective and it has not received criticism.

As explained above, the main national institutions responsible for granting State aid are the Ministry and the Representation. Whereas the former is the main point of contact for the grantors of State aid, the Representation is in charge of communicating with the services of the Commission.

2. State aid compliance by national judges and/or the national competition authority (NCA)

The Estonian court system consists of three levels. County courts (maakohus) and administrative courts (halduskohus) are the courts of first instance. County courts hear matters pertaining to civil and criminal law. Appeals against decisions of courts of first instance are heard by circuit courts (ringkonnakohus) that are courts of second instance. The highest court is the Supreme Court (Riigikohus) that hears appeals in cassation after having passed through all other courts.

Due to lack of practice, jurisdictional issues concerning State aid are still to be clarified by future practice. Although it is debatable, we anticipate that jurisdiction for litigation with grantors of aid would take place in administrative courts and litigation with beneficiaries would take place in civil courts.

Adjudication of disputes in public law is within the jurisdiction of administrative courts (Article 3(1)1) of the Administrative Procedure Act). An action could be filed in administrative courts against administrative acts (acts that regulate individual cases in public law relationships, issued by agencies, officials or other persons who perform administrative functions in public law) and administrative measures (measures in public law relationships by agencies, officials or other persons who perform administrative functions in public law).

Articles 51(1) and 106(1) of the Administrative Procedure Act provide for additional definitions of administrative act and measure. According to the Administrative Procedure Act an administrative act is an act which is issued by an administrative authority upon performance of administrative functions in order to regulate individual cases in public law relationships and which is directed at the creation, alteration or extinguishment of the rights and obligation of persons. An administrative measure is a factual activity performed by an administrative authority that is not the issue of an administrative act and that is not performed in civil law relationships.

It could be claimed that State aid is always granted in a public law relationship, even if the form in which the aid is provided is of private law. Therefore, disputes between grantors of aid and competitors/third parties are likely to fall within the jurisdiction of administrative courts.

As explained above, recovery orders are likely to be implemented via civil law actions on the basis of civil law, even if aid was granted under administrative law provisions. The civil court is also likely to have jurisdiction in litigation concerning recovery orders where the plaintiff is a competitor/ third party and the defendant is the beneficiary. Such a relationship would not be that of public law and there are no specific provisions that would give jurisdiction to administrative court.

Therefore, depending on the issues involved, State aid litigation can take place in county (e.g., disputes concerning claiming recovery of State aid granted under civil law provisions) or administrative courts as courts of first instance (e.g., disputes concerning validity of a measure granting State aid). Appeals and appeals in cassation are heard by circuit courts and the Supreme Court.

Since there are no national decisions concerning State aid, it is not possible to estimate what would be the most difficult criteria to assess existence of State aid by the courts. Taking account of the lack of experience in applying EU State aid rules and practice, it could be presumed that all criteria could create difficulties.

The extent to which a national court can and has to use powers of investigation depends on whether the court in question is a county or administrative court.

Administrative courts

In accordance with the principle of investigation, administrative courts are under a legal obligation to clarify all facts necessary for adjudicating over a matter. A participant in the proceeding has to prove the facts on which the allegations of the participant in the proceeding are based. According to Article 16(2) of the Code of Administrative Court Procedure, a court makes a proposal to the participants in the proceedings to submit the necessary evidence or, if necessary, has to collect evidence on its own initiative. In using its powers to collect evidence on its own initiative, the court may use all procedural possibilities provided for in the Code of Civil Procedure[164]: to summon a witness to a court session for hearing; to require a party to be heard under oath if previously collected and presented evidence does not allow

164 Code of Civil Procedure ("Tsiviilkohtumenetluse seadustik"), 19 May 2005, RTI, 19.5.2005, 26, 197.

assessing the truthfulness of the facts to be proven by a party; to require a person in possession of documentary evidence and physical evidence to submit the document or physical evidence to the court; to organise an inspection and obtain the opinion of experts. According to Article 16(6) of the Code of Administrative Court Procedure, the court may require information necessary for the adjudication of a matter from the participants in the proceedings and an administrative authority not participating in the proceedings. A participant in a proceeding and an administrative authority is obliged to provide information within the term set by the court.

Civil court procedure

Differently from administrative court procedure, in civil court procedure the principle of investigation is not used and the court does not collect evidence on its own initiative. The court can perform all the procedural activities discussed under administrative court proceedings at the request of the participants to proceedings: to summon a witness to a court session for hearing; to require a party to be heard under oath if previously collected and presented evidence does not allow assessing the truthfulness of the facts to be proven by a party; to require a person in possession of documentary evidence and physical evidence to submit the document or physical evidence to the court; to organise an inspection and obtain the opinion of experts. Each party has to prove the facts on which the claims and objections of the party are based (Article 230(1) of the Code of Civil Procedure) and evidence is submitted by the participants in the proceedings (Article 230(2) of the Code of Civil Procedure). The court may, however, make a proposal to parties to submit additional evidence proceedings (Article 230(2) of the Code of Civil Procedure). A party may also request the court to collect evidence if the party wishing to provide evidence is unable to do so.

Since there are no national decisions concerning State aid, it is not possible to estimate if there is any reluctance to make preliminary references to the CJEU.

Third party intervention is regulated in the Code of Administrative Court Procedure and Code of Civil Procedure.

Administrative court procedure

In administrative court procedure, participants in proceedings are the parties and the persons involved by the court (Article 14(1) of the Code of Administrative Court Procedure). According to Article 14(3)(1) a person involved is a third person if that person's rights or freedoms which are protected by law may be adjudicated in the hearing of the matter.

It is in the discretion of the court to involve or refuse to involve a person as a third party. There is no national practice concerning State aid and therefore it remains for the future court practice to clarify under what conditions a person may be involved as a third party in an administrative court procedure. We note that in a dispute concerning potentially a very large number of interested persons (an administrative decree that regulated the use of land in a nature reserve) the Supreme Court concluded that only these persons have to be involved as third parties whose interests or rights could be more widely or intensively concerned by the court ruling than other possibly interested persons, for instance persons who own land in the area[165]. On the basis of the latter case-law, it would not be surprising if the courts do not involve any interested person as a third party but only the ones that can show a concrete impact of a court ruling concerning a State aid case on its interests.

Civil court procedure
In civil court procedure there are third parties with an independent claim and third parties without an independent claim (Articles 212 and 213 of the Code of Civil Procedure).

A third party with an independent claim is a person who may file an independent claim concerning the object of the dispute between the plaintiff and defendant. The third party may file an action against both parties in the proceeding before the hearing of the merits of the matter at a county court ends. A third party with an independent claim has the rights and obligations of the plaintiff.

A third party with an independent claim can enter the court procedure on its own initiative that is adjudicated upon with a court ruling. A third party without an independent claim is a person who does not have an independent claim concerning the object of the proceeding but has legal interest in having the dispute resolved in favour of one of the parties. A third party without independent claim may enter the proceeding in support of either the plaintiff or the defendant. Requests of a party for involving a third party without an independent claim and applications of a third party without an independent claim to enter to court procedure are adjudicated upon with a court ruling. The parties or a third party may file an appeal against a ruling whereby the court involves or refuses to involve a third party in the proceeding, or removes such party from the proceeding. A ruling of a circuit court concerning an appeal against a ruling of a county court is not subject to appeal to the Supreme Court (Article 216(6) of the Code of Civil Procedure).

III. Unlawful aid and judicial review

1. General powers of national courts concerning the direct effect of Article 108(3) TFEU

As explained above, jurisdictional issues concerning State aid remain to be clarified in future due to lack of practice to date. Although it is debatable, we anticipate that jurisdiction for litigation with grantors of aid would take place in administrative courts and litigation with beneficiaries would take place in civil courts. Recovery orders are also likely to be implemented via civil law actions on the basis of civil law, even if aid was granted under administrative law provisions.

165 Supreme Court ("Riigikohus"), 8 April 2004, Jaak Vaher, Luule Velleste ja Hillar Taamal vs Vabariigi Valitsus, administrative proceedings no. 3-3-1-13-04, not published.

Therefore, cases of infringement could potentially be claimed in both administrative and civil courts.

Administrative court

According to Article 121(2) of the Code of Administrative Court Procedure, an administrative court may issue a ruling on the provisional protection of the rights of a person filing an action in all stages of proceedings at the reasoned request of the person filing the action or on its own initiative, if otherwise execution of a court judgment is impracticable or impossible.

Article 121(3) of the Code of Administrative Court Procedure empowers the court to apply the following measures of provisional protection:

- suspend the validity or execution of a contested administrative act;
- prohibit the issue of a contested administrative act or taking of a contested measure;
- require an administrative authority to issue an administrative act being applied for or take a measure being applied for or terminate a continuing measure;
- apply the measures for securing an action enacted in the Code of Civil Procedure;
- seize property, as well as make a notation in the register concerning a prohibition on disposal of property and make a notation in the register concerning the court action.

According to Article 12(5) of the Code of Administrative Court Procedure, a right, obligation and prohibition arising from a ruling on provisional legal protection, and an administrative act issued on the basis of such a ruling is valid until a court judgment or a ruling on return of an action or on termination of the proceedings enters into force, unless the court designates a shorter term.

Civil court

According to Article 377(1) of the Code of Civil Procedure, a court may secure an action at the request of the plaintiff if there is reason to believe that failure to secure the action may render compliance with the judgment difficult or impossible. Among other measures, the court may use the following for securing an action:

- establishment of a judicial mortgage on an immovable, ship or aircraft belonging to the defendant;
- seizure of the defendant's property which is in the possession of the defendant or another person, including making a notation in a property register concerning a prohibition on disposal of property;
- prohibition on the defendant from entering into certain transactions or performing certain acts;
- prohibition on other persons from transferring property to the defendant or performing other obligations with regard to the defendant;
- other measures considered necessary by the court.

Since there is currently no national practice concerning State aid, it remains for future court practice to clarify which securing measures could be used in a State aid context.

For applying measures securing an action, a court would issue a ruling.

Since there are no national decisions concerning State aid, it is not possible to identify what is the most current type of litigation on a national level in Estonia.

2. Prevention of the granting of unlawful aid

As explained above, jurisdictional issues concerning State aid remain to be clarified in future due to lack of practice to date. Although it is debatable, we anticipate that that jurisdiction for litigation with grantors of aid would in connection with unlawful acts that are basis for granting aid take place in administrative courts.

Civil and administrative court procedures are regulated by different set of rules (Code of Administrative Court Procedure and the Code of Civil Procedure) and principles. As a major difference from civil court procedure, administrative courts are bound by the duty of investigation and assisting the complainant rather than the strict obligation on each party to prove the facts on which its claim is based on. State fees are also considerably smaller for actions filed with the administrative court.

In preventing the granting of unlawful aid, there is a difference between the acts on which the State aid regime is based and acts that permit the aid to be granted individually (e.g., law v. administrative act). The Code of Administrative Court Procedure only allows filing an action against an administrative act or measure. Under national law, it is therefore not possible to file a claim against a legal act that an individual aid measure is based on. It remains for future court practice to clarify whether, as an exception in State aid cases, actions other than actions for damages against legal acts on which the State aid regime is based, could be filed with a court.

Due to lack of precedents, jurisdictional issues concerning State aid remain to be clarified by future court practice. Although it is debatable, we anticipate that jurisdiction for litigation with grantors of aid would take place in administrative courts. The two main possibilities under national law to prevent the granting or payment of unlawful aid would therefore be administrative challenge procedures and administrative court procedures.

Challenge procedure

According to Article 71(1) of the Administrative Procedure Act, a person who finds that his or her rights are violated or his or her freedoms are restricted by an administrative act or in the course of administrative proceedings may file a challenge. It is to be noted that filing a challenge is not a mandatory requirement and a person could also file an action with the administrative court.

A challenge must be filed within thirty days from the day on which a person becomes or should become aware of the relevant administrative act or measure (Article 75 of the Administrative Procedure Act).

According to Article 72 of the Administrative Procedure Act, the following may be requested under the challenge procedure:

- repealing an administrative act; or
- issuing a precept for the issue of an administrative act, new resolution of a matter or taking a measure.

It is also possible to challenge a delay or omission separately from an administrative act. According to the general rules enacted in Article 73(1) of the Administrative Procedure Act, a challenge is filed through the administrative authority which issued the challenged administrative act or took the challenged measure with an administrative authority which exercises supervisory control over the administrative authority which issued the challenged administrative act or took the challenged measure.

According to Article 81 of the Administrative Procedure Act, an administrative authority adjudicating a challenge may suspend execution of an administrative act if this is necessary for the protection of public interest or for the protection of the rights of the addressee of the administrative act or of a third party.

According to Article 85 of the Administrative Procedure Act, an administrative authority deciding over a challenge may by its decision:

- satisfy the challenge and repeal an administrative act either wholly or partially and eliminate the factual consequences of the administrative act;
- issue a precept for issue of an administrative act, for taking a measure or for new resolution of a matter;
- issue a precept for reversal of a measure; or
- dismiss the challenge.

A person whose challenge is dismissed or whose rights are violated in challenge proceedings has the right to file an action with an administrative court (Article 107(1) of the Administrative Procedure Act).

Administrative court procedure
Article 7(1) of the Code of Administrative Court Procedure entitles a person who finds that his or her rights have been violated or his or her freedoms have been restricted by an administrative act or measure to file an action with an administrative court.

A general term for filing an administrative action is 30 days (Articles 9(1)-(3) of the Code of Administrative Court Procedure). An action for compensation for damage caused in a public law relationship may be filed within three years after the person filing the action became aware or should have become aware of the damage and of the person who caused it, but not later than within ten years after the act or omission of the public authority who caused the damage (Article 9(4) of the Code of Administrative Court Procedure). An action for declaration of an administrative act or unlawful measure may be filed within three years after the administrative act was issued or the unlawful measure was taken (Article 9(5) of the Code of Administrative Court Procedure).

As explained above, Article 121(2) of the Code of Administrative Court Procedure allows an administrative court to issue a ruling on the provisional protection of the rights of a person filing an action.

In deciding on an action, Article 26(1) of the Code of Administrative Court Procedure the court may:

- annul an unlawful administrative act wholly or partially and, if possible, issue a precept for the reversal of the administrative act, indicating the method of reversal;
- issue a precept for execution of an unlawfully suspended administrative act, for the issue of an unissued administrative act or for an untaken measure to be taken;
- declare an administrative act or measure unlawful if the legitimate interest of the person who filed the action or protest in such finding is expressed in the action or protest;
- order the payment of compensation for damage caused in public law relationships; or
- establish the existence or absence of a relationship in public law.

According to Article 30(2) of the Competition Act the grantor of State aid has no right to start granting State aid before the European Commission has made or is deemed to have made a permitting decision with respect to the notice on State aid. The prohibition does not apply if State aid covered by group exemption is granted according to procedures provided for in Article 34 of the Competition Act.

It is to be noted that the meaning of the above provision has not been tested in practice, since there is no national case-law.

3. Recovery of unlawful aid and interest

As explained above, there are no detailed national provisions for recovery procedure nor has recovery occurred in practice. Although it is not proven in practice, recovery decisions are in our opinion likely to be implemented via civil law actions on the basis of civil law and civil court procedure, even if aid was granted under administrative law provisions.

Since there is no national case-law on State aid, it is currently not entirely certain what procedure would apply to horizontal litigation. However, in our opinion horizontal litigation would have to take place in the civil court as the relationship between competitors/third parties and beneficiaries is that of civil law rather than public law. Furthermore, an action may be filed with an administrative court against administrative acts or measures of agencies, officials or other persons who perform administrative functions in public law (Article 4(1) and (2) of the Code of Administrative Court Procedure). It nevertheless remains for future court practice to clarify whether and under what conditions competitors and third parties have standing in an administrative or civil court.

In the absence of any court practice regarding State aid, the issue of whether and to what extent the courts have the possibility to identify beneficiaries of aid remains unclear. However, administrative and civil courts have the powers of investigation as explained above that could *inter alia* be used for identifying beneficiaries of aid.

As explained above, administrative courts may require information necessary for adjudication upon the matter from the participants in the proceedings and an administrative authority not participating in the proceedings. Both participants in proceedings and administrative authorities are obliged to provide information within the term set by the court. Hence, the administrative court could require a participant in a court procedure and any administrative authority not participating in the court procedure *inter alia* to submit information regarding the beneficiaries.

In civil court procedures, proceedings are conducted in an action on the basis of the facts and petitions submitted by the parties, based on the claim (Article 5(1) of the Code of Civil Procedure). Each party has to prove the facts on which the claims and objections of the party are based and evidence shall be submitted by the participants in the proceedings (Article 230(1) and (2) of the Code of Civil Procedure). Although the court may propose that a party provides additional evidence, the court would not gather evidence itself. Therefore, a civil court is not in a position to identify the beneficiaries of an aid on its own initiative. If the participant in a proceeding wishing to provide evidence is unable to do so, the participant may request the court to gather evidence if the evidence is relevant for proving a fact that is material for the case. If the court allows the request for collecting evidence on identity of the beneficiaries, it is also possible in civil court procedure to identify the beneficiaries.

Since there are no national decisions concerning State aid, it is not possible to identify how a court normally quantifies the amount to be recovered and it is not possible to identify how enforcement before national courts would differ depending on the Commission's decisions.

Also, for the same reason, the issue of alternative remedies has never occurred in practice. We note that in administrative court procedure, when a court annuls an unlawful administrative act, the court can, if possible, issue a precept for the reversal of the administrative act, indicating the method of reversal. Thus, the administrative court could in principle propose a remedy other than recovery if such a remedy would serve the purpose of reversing the effects of an illegal administrative act that was basis for State aid. Please also note that administrative courts are likely to have jurisdiction over disputes between competitors/third parties and grantors of aid. Disputes concerning recovery between grantors of aid and beneficiaries and competitors/third parties and beneficiaries are likely adjudicated upon in civil courts, though there is no practice regarding State aid.

In civil court procedure, the plaintiff has to express its claim clearly (object of action) and the proceedings are conducted in an action on the basis of the facts and petitions submitted by the parties, based on the claim (Articles 5(1) and 363(1)1) of the Code of Civil Procedure). Upon making a judgment, the court has to decide whether the action should be satisfied. If several claims are filed in a matter, the court shall make a judgment concerning all of the claims (Article 438(1) of the Code of Civil Procedure). Thus, in civil court procedure the court is bound by the claim of the plaintiff and cannot propose remedies not requested by the plaintiff in its claim.

Since there are no national decisions concerning State aid, it is not possible to identify how legitimate expectation would be applied in a State aid context and the issue of jurisdiction remains questionable. However, in our opinion disputes between grantors of aid and competitors/third parties should be adjudicated upon in administrative courts and disputes between competitors and beneficiaries should be adjudicated upon in civil courts.

In disputes with grantors of aid, the complainant may file an administrative challenge or an action with the administrative court.

In civil court procedure, the plaintiff has to file an action against the defendant. A Statement of Claim shall set out the clearly expressed claim of the plaintiff (object of action), facts which constitute the basis of the action (cause of action), evidence in proof of the facts which are the cause of the action, and a specific reference to the facts which the plaintiff wants to prove with each piece of evidence; whether or not the plaintiff agrees to the conduct of written proceedings in the matter or wishes the matter to be heard in a court session and the value of the action unless the action is directed at payment of a certain sum of money. State fees also have to be paid on a Statement of Claim, though in practice it is not clear what the value of the State fee for claims concerning recovery of illegality interest would be.

Since there are no national decisions concerning State aid, it is not possible to identify how courts would determine the illegality interest.

4. Damages claims by competitors/third parties before national courts against the granting authority

There are no national decisions concerning State aid. There are also no cases where courts would have applied the *Francovich/Brasserie du Pêcheur* case law principles.

In our opinion, the *Francovich/Brasserie du Pêcheur* conditions seem to be more difficult to fulfil in case of damage caused by administrative act or measure and less difficult than national liability principles in case of damage caused by general legislation (depending on interpretation of national law by courts). Under Estonian law a public authority becomes liable for damage if damage could not be prevented and cannot be eliminated by the protection or restoration of rights in the manner provided for in the State Liability Act. It is not necessary that the public authority concerned "manifestly and gravely disregarded the limits on its discretion". Under national rules, the intent of the public authority is not relevant (except for in claims concerning loss of income, Article 13(2) of the State Liability Act).

As regards damage caused by the legislator, Article 14(1) of the State Liability Act allows compensation of damage caused by legislation or by not adopting legislation if damage resulted from material breach of obligations of the State, the provision from which such an obligation is derived is directly applicable and the injured person belongs to a group of persons that are particularly injured. It remains to be seen how the courts interpret the condition "a group of persons that are particularly injured" and whether the conditions for claiming damages caused by legislation would therefore be more stringent than State liability under the *Francovich/Brasserie du Pêcheur* conditions.

State liability is regulated in the State Liability Act. The general basis for claiming damages is provided for in Article 7(1) of the State Liability Act. According to the latter Article a person whose rights are violated by unlawful activities of a public authority in a public law relationship may claim compensation for damage caused to the person if:

- damage could not be prevented; and
- damage could not have been eliminated by claiming for annulment of administrative act, termination of measure or issuing an administrative act or taking a measure.

It is to be noted that, in contrast with the general principles of tort law, culpability is not a necessary element for State liability. As an exception, loss of income is not compensated if the person liable to compensate the damage proves that the person is not culpable for causing the damage (Article 13(2) of the State Liability Act).

With regard to the legislator, the State Liability Act contains special provisions that restrict State liability in comparison with the liability of the executive authorities. According to Article 14(1) of the State Liability Act, a person may claim compensation for damage caused by legislation (or by not adopting legislation) if the damage resulted from material breach of obligations of the State, the provision from which such an obligation derives is directly applicable and the injured person belongs to a group of person that are particularly injured.

We do not think that the courts are tempted to condemn the executive and not the legislator. If there is a difference in treatment, it is explained by the more stringent conditions for State liability caused by legislation.

Since there are no national decisions concerning State aid, it is not possible to identify what elements would be taken into account to assess and calculate the amount of the damage and loss for the competitors. However, the principles of general tort law shall be applicable, including elements normally taken into account to assess and calculate the amount of the damage and loss. These elements include the comparison between a real situation and a hypothetical one, the purpose of the obligation or provision breached and causality, but also any gain received by the injured party as a result of the damage caused and complicity of injured party. We do not see any reasonable obstacle to the court taking overall loss of market share into account within the framework of general tort law. We would like to point out that according to Article 127(6) of the Law of Obligations Act[166], the national court is authorised to determine the amount of compensation by its discretional decision if damage is established but the exact extent of the damage cannot be established, including in the event of future damage.

By making a clear distinction between direct patrimonial damage and loss of profit, national law distinguishes between situations where the breach caused the claimant the loss of an asset or whether it prevented the claimant from improving its asset position. According to Article 128(3) of the Law of Obligations, direct patrimonial damage includes, primarily, the value of the lost or destroyed property or the decrease in the value of property due to deterioration even if such decrease occurs in the future, and reasonable expenses which have been incurred or will be incurred in the future due to the damage, including reasonable expenses relating to prevention or reduction of damage and receipt of compensation, including expenses relating

166 Law of Obligations Act ("Võlaõigusseadus"), 16 October 2001, RTI, 16.10.2001, 81, 487.

to establishment of the damage and submission of claims relating to compensation for the damage. Article 128(4) of the Law of Obligations Act on the other hand gives the definition of loss of profit: it is loss of the gain which a person would have been likely to receive in the circumstances, in particular as a result of the preparations made by the person, if the circumstances on which compensation for damage is based would not have occurred. Loss of profit may also include the loss of an opportunity to receive gain.

In addition to the provisions referred to from the Law of Obligations Act, the legal theory and practice clearly distinguishes between negative damage (reliance interest) and positive damage (expectation interest which also includes loss of profit). As a general rule, in cases concerning non-contractual liability the claimant can only rely on negative damage and cannot claim for loss of profit. However, this general rule is not entirely applicable if the prevention of this kind of damage (e.g., loss of profit) was the purpose of the obligation or provision due to the non-performance of which the compensation obligation arose. We are of the opinion that the State aid provisions are likely to come under this category of provisions. However, this question remains unclear and needs further clarification by national courts.

There are no specific provisions that would deal with situations where the claimant is forced out of business as the direct consequence of the granting of an unlawful aid. There are also no national decisions concerning State aid.

General provisions on State liability do not differentiate between liabilities according to whether or not the tortfeasor is the State or any other public authority. Specific provisions concern causing damage by legislation, in the course of judicial proceedings and by lawful administrative act or measure. Furthermore, if damage is caused by a public authority which is a natural person or private law legal person, the State, local government or other public law legal person who authorised the natural person or private law legal person to perform public duties is liable for the damage. If authorisation to perform public duties arises directly from law, the application for compensation of damage has to be submitted to the administrative authority exercising State supervision over the natural person or private law legal person.

5. Damages claims by the beneficiary before national courts against the granting authority

According to State liability rules, if several public authorities are obligated to compensate for damage, the public authorities are jointly liable to the injured party. However, joint liability of a public authority is not extended to a person who is liable to the injured party under private law (Article 12(4) of the State Liability Act). Thus, an injured party has to file an action with a civil court against a person who is liable to the injured party under private law. Civil court may reduce the compensation if compensation in full would be grossly unfair with regard to the obligated person or not reasonably acceptable for any other reason. In such case, all circumstances, in particular the nature of the liability, relationships between the persons and their economic situations, including insurance coverage, shall be taken into account (Article 140(1) of the Law of Obligations Act). These grounds could also be taken into account in State liability (Article 13(1) of the State Liability Act).

6. Damages claims by competitors/third parties before national courts against the beneficiary

To the best of our knowledge, there are no national decisions concerning State aid.

Though there is no practice, in our opinion it is likely that the procedure used would be civil court procedure using civil law rules on non-contractual liability. We note that current national rules could prove to be inadequate for filing a direct damages action against a beneficiary by competitors/third parties.

The legal basis for rewarding damages under the concept of non-contractual liability is enacted in the Law of Obligations Act. According to Article 1043 of the Law of Obligations Act, a person (tortfeasor) who unlawfully causes damage to another person (victim) shall compensate for the damage if the tortfeasor is culpable of causing the damage or is liable for causing the damage pursuant to law. A major problem in the context of unlawful State aid is that an act causing damage has to be unlawful. Article 1045(1) enacts an open list of unlawful damage. In the context of State aid, the following legal bases could be relevant:

- behaviour which violates a duty arising from law; and
- intentional behaviour contrary to good morals.

It is not clear that receiving State aid would mean that the beneficiary would be acting contrary to good morals, although we cannot entirely exclude such an interpretation.

It is also arguable whether there is basis in national law that would prohibit receiving unlawful aid. Article 50(2) of the Competition Act (unfair competition) is prohibited. According to Article 50(2) of the Competition Act, (unfair competition) is dishonest trading practices and acts which are contrary to good morals and practices, including:

- publication of misleading information, presentation or ordering of misleading information for publication, or disparagement of a competitor or the goods of the competitor;
- misuse of confidential information or of an employee or representative of a competitor.

It remains for court practice to clarify whether receiving unlawful State aid could qualify as unfair competition (dishonest trading practices and acts which are contrary to good morals and practices) in the meaning of Article 50(1) of the Competition Act.

It is therefore currently debatable whether by receiving unlawful aid the beneficiary would violate a duty arising from law and could be held liable for damage under Article 1043 of Law of Obligations Act.

The tortfeasor could also prove that the tortfeasor is not culpable for causing the damage (Article 1050(1) of Law of Obligations Act). According to Article 1050(2) of the Law of Obligations Act, the situation, age, education, knowledge, abilities and other personal characteristics of a person shall be taken into consideration upon assessment of the culpability of the person.

Conclusively, the issue of possibility of direct actions for damages remains questionable and needs court practice for clarification.

Under current national rules, it is likely that recovery will be implemented by civil action and consequently civil court judgment. Enforcement of court judgments is regulated in the Code of Enforcement Procedure[167]. To enforce a judgment, the claimant may apply for enforcement of the court decision by bailiff. A judgment is enforceable if it has entered into force or is subject to immediate enforcement. A bailiff is required to take all measures permitted by law in order to enforce an enforcement instrument (e.g. a judgment).

In case of monetary claims, the bailiff may record, arrest and sell movable and immovable property of the debtor, make a claim for payment and seize proprietary rights, claims and debtor's accounts, securities, author's proprietary rights and seize payment for wages or another similar claim for the payment of income.

If a debtor or a third person does not submit information and a debtor does not present a document or other thing necessary for enforcement proceedings or a third person does not comply with an instrument of seizure, the bailiff may warn the debtor or third person that it could be fined. If the respective obligations are still left unfulfilled, the bailiff may make a proposal to the court to fine the person. The fine is 50–200 fine units (up to 500 units repeating the fine) and could be repeated. A fine unit is 60 Estonian kroons (ca €3.8).

A participant in enforcement proceedings (claimant, debtor and other persons whose rights are affected by enforcement proceedings) may file a complaint to a bailiff against a decision or the activities of a bailiff upon execution of an enforcement instrument or refusal to perform an enforcement action, within ten days as of the day on which the complainant becomes or should have become aware of the decision or action, unless otherwise provided by law. A decision of the bailiff regarding the complaint may be appealed to the county court, circuit court and ultimately to the Supreme Court.

In civil court procedures, the average length of proceedings is up to 24 months.

The issue of *locus standi* in the State aid context remains to be clarified by court practice. However, a possible (although questionable) basis for damages between competitors/third parties and the beneficiary of unlawful aid could be the provisions of the Competition Act that prohibit unfair competition. The Supreme Court has explained in connection with the provisions of unfair competition that the aim of the prohibition is to protect competition as an independent value of the market economy, from unfair competition. Unfair competition could be carried out by a person who is active in the same or similar fields of business as the undertaking claiming damage or a person who is acting in the interests of such a person[168]. Hence, the judgment of the Supreme Court could be understood as if the protective area of the prohibition of unfair competition concerned only persons who are active in the same or similar fields of business as the undertaking in breach of the prohibition. If that is the case, damage could only be claimed by persons who are active in the same or similar fields of business as the undertaking.

---

167 Code of Enforcement Procedure ("Täitemenetluse seadustik"), 19 May 2005, RTI, 19.5.2005, 27, 198.

168 Supreme Court ("Riigikohus"), 9 December 2008, OÜ LabelPrint v. AS ESTOPRESS and Eero Lattu, civil proceedings no. 3-2-1-103-08, RTIII, 23.12.2008, 51, 353.

According to Article 423(2)(1) of the Code of Civil Procedure the court may refuse to hear an action if, based on the facts presented as the cause of the action, violation of the plaintiff's rights is not possible, presuming that the facts presented by the plaintiff are correct. Thus, if the court comes to an understanding that a plaintiff is not in the protective area of the prohibition of unfair competition, the court could refuse to hear an action of a third party against the beneficiary of aid.

If damage is partly caused by circumstances dependent on the injured party or due to a risk borne by the injured party, the amount of compensation for the damage would be reduced by the court to the extent that such circumstances or risk contributed to the damage (Article 139(1) of the Law of Obligations Act). The court may also reduce the amount of compensation for damage if compensation in full would be grossly unfair with regard to the obligated person or not reasonably acceptable for any other reason. In such case, all circumstances, in particular the nature of the liability, relationships between the persons and their economic situations, including insurance coverage, shall be taken into account (Article 140(1) of the Law of Obligations Act).

In case of claims of competitors/third parties against the beneficiary, we anticipate that such disputes would be in the jurisdiction of civil courts. National material law does not contain a legal basis for recovery of undue benefits or clearing undue economic benefits.

7. Interim measures taken by national judges

There are currently no national decisions concerning State aid in Estonia.

With regard to injunctions to cease the payment of the aid we are nevertheless of the opinion that such claims would be in the jurisdiction of administrative courts. An administrative court may issue a ruling on the provisional protection of the rights of a person filing an action in all stages of proceedings at the reasoned request of the person filing the action or on its own initiative, if execution of a court judgment is otherwise impracticable or impossible.

As explained, recovery disputes between competitors/third parties and beneficiaries are likely in the jurisdiction of civil courts. According to Article 377(1) of the Code of Civil Procedure, a court may secure an action at the request of the plaintiff if there is reason to believe that failure to secure the action may render compliance with the judgment difficult or impossible. For applying measures securing an action, a court would issue a ruling.

IV. Control of recovery procedure

1. Rules applicable to recovery

There are currently no national decisions concerning State aid in Estonia.

As explained above, in the current legal situation we anticipate that recovery of State aid by the grantors of aid is implemented via civil court procedure on the basis of civil material law provisions. Hence, the grantor of aid files an action as a plaintiff against the beneficiary as a defendant with a civil court and the court would thereafter give its judgment regarding recovery.

If the beneficiary would like to challenge a civil court decision, the beneficiary may file an appeal within 30 days after the service of the judgment on the appellant but not later than within five months as of the date the judgment of the court of first instance was made public (Article 632(1) of the Code of Civil Procedure). For obligating the grantor of aid to recover aid from the beneficiary, we are of the opinion that a third party can rely on the administrative court procedure. For actions against the beneficiary for recovery of aid, the third party may file an action with civil court.

As explained above, we are of the opinion that a third party can file an action with the administrative court against the grantor of aid and with the civil court against the beneficiary. Whereas the administrative court may issue a ruling on the provisional protection of the rights of a person filing an action, the civil court may secure an action at the request of the plaintiff. Under the administrative court procedure and civil court procedure a party may also become a participant in a court procedure as a third person and acquire procedural rights that enable influence the court procedure. There is also the right to file an appeal to the circuit court and ultimately to the Supreme Court.

The normal time frame for reviewing an action in the court of first instance in civil courts is up to 24 months.

There is no construction similar to "exceptional circumstances" under national law. As explained above, recovery is implemented via the civil court procedure and civil court judgment where the court can rely on directly applicable EU law provisions. Enforcement of court judgments is regulated by the Code of Enforcement Procedure. On the basis of Article 221 of the Code of Enforcement Procedure, a debtor may file an action against a claimant for the declaration of compulsory enforcement to be inadmissible, in particular for the reason that a claim has been satisfied, postponed or set off. Satisfaction of the action does not affect the validity or legal force of the enforcement instrument (of the Code of Enforcement Procedure).

2. Action for recovery

The procedure enabling a party to engage State liability for failure to implement a Commission recovery decision is enacted in the State Liability Act. According to Article 17(1) of the State Liability Act an application for compensation for damages may be submitted to the administrative authority that caused the damage or an action may be filed with an administrative court.

If damage is caused by a public authority who is a natural person or private law legal person, the State, local government or other public law legal person who authorised the natural person or private law legal person to perform public duties is liable for the damage. Also the application has to be submitted to the administrative authority that authorised the natural person or private law legal person to perform public duties.

An application to the authority or action with the court can be filed within three years as of the date on which the injured party became aware or should have become aware of the damage and of the person who caused it, but not later than within ten years as of the causing of damage or the event which caused the damage regardless of whether the injured party became aware of the damage and of the person who caused it (Article 17(3) of the State Liability Act).

An administrative authority is required to decide upon an application within two months from receiving it. If an administrative authority denies an application for compensation for damage or fails to decide upon an application during the latter term or if the injured party does not agree to the amount or manner of compensation, the injured party can file an action with an administrative court within thirty days for the order of payment of compensation.

Ways of actions for State

As explained above, in the current legal situation it is likely that recovery of State aid by the grantors of aid is implemented by civil court procedure. Hence, the grantor of aid could file an action against the beneficiary with a civil court and the court would thereafter give its judgment regarding recovery. If the beneficiary does not comply with the judgment, the grantor of aid can use measures enacted in the Code of Enforcement Procedure for enforcing the judgment.

Ways of actions for competitors

As explained above, we are of the opinion that civil courts are likely to have jurisdiction in litigation concerning recovery orders between competitor/third party and beneficiary. A competitor/third party could commence an action against the beneficiary with a civil court and the court would thereafter give its judgment regarding recovery. If the beneficiary does not comply with the judgment, the grantor of aid can use the measures enacted in the Code of Enforcement Procedure for enforcing the judgment.

V. Standing of third parties before national court

There is no case-law regarding *locus standi* and burden of proof in the context of State aid. However, there are general rules regarding *locus standi* and burden of proof enacted in the Code of Administrative Court Procedure and Civil Court Procedure.

Administrative court procedure

In administrative court procedure, there is no clear division regarding *locus standi* between a competitor and a third party. Any person who finds that his or her rights have been violated or his or her freedoms have been restricted by an administrative act or measure has the right to file an action with an administrative court (Article 7(1) of the Code of Administrative Court Procedure). The Supreme Court has ruled that there is no *locus standi* in the administrative court only if it is completely obvious that the respective administrative act or measure cannot violate the rights or restrict the freedoms of the person filing the action. If the court admits that an administrative act or measure could violate the complainant's rights, the court has to start court procedure[169].

With regard to burden of proof, in administrative court procedure all participants in the court procedure have to prove the facts on which their allegations are based (Article 16(3) of the Code of Administrative Court Procedure). However, due to the principle of investigation, the court has the duty to collect evidence on its own initiative if it is necessary for adjudicating over a matter. The Supreme Court has declared that if different parties present inconsistent facts in a court procedure, the court has to facilitate achieving equality of the parties and collect evidence itself if necessary. Important facts cannot be left aside simply because a participant to a procedure could not have foreseen the need for submitting particular evidence. The scope of the court's obligations in collection of evidence depends on the presumptive ability of a party to bring out important facts and present relevant evidence. In case of a weaker party, the court has to be more active[170].

Civil court procedure

According to Article 3(1) of the Code of Civil Procedure, the court shall conduct proceedings in a civil matter if a person files a claim with the court pursuant to the procedure provided by law for the protection of the person's alleged right or interest protected by law.

Thus, in order to have the right for *locus standi*, a person needs to have the alleged right or interest that is protected by law. Such a right or interest could be based on national, international or EU material law provisions. The court may refuse to hear an action if, based on the facts presented as the cause of the action, violation of the plaintiff's rights is not possible, presuming that the facts presented by the plaintiff are correct (Article 423(2)1) of the Code of Civil Procedure).

In the civil court procedure, proceedings are conducted in an action on the basis of the facts and petitions submitted by the parties, based on the claim (Article 5(1) of the Code of Civil Procedure). Each party has to prove the facts on which the claims and objections of the party are based and evidence has to be submitted by the participants in the proceedings (Article 230(1) and (2) of the Code of Civil Procedure). A party may choose the facts submitted in order to substantiate the claim thereof as well as the evidence intended for proof of such facts (Article 5(1) of the Code of Civil Procedure).

VI. Cooperation with EU authorities

There are no national decisions concerning State aid. In other fields of activity that are regulated at the EU level, courts usually rely on and do not oppose the use of EU legislation and

169 Supreme Court ("Riigikohus"), 15 May 2008, AS Esmar v. Viimsi Vallavalitsus, administrative proceedings no. 3-3-1-9-08, RTIII, 30.5.2008, 24, 163.

170 Supreme Court ("Riigikohus"), 16 January 2007, J.K. v. Tartu Vangla, administrative proceedings no. 3-3-1-91-06, RTIII, 6.2.2007, 4, 35.

case-law (in particular in competition law, telecommunications, electricity & gas and taxation). We therefore presume that if there were a dispute in a national court concerning State aid, the court would indeed use EU Regulation and case-law in its decision.

VII. Trends – reforms – recommendations

Currently, there are no major developments in the enforcement of State aid. General knowledge concerning State aid rules seems to be rather low.

A way to improve national level enforcement would be to arrange study days and seminars for market participants to disseminate knowledge about State aid rules and procedural possibilities. Currently, there seems to be a lack of knowledge on the part of both the authorities and the private sector.

Finland

Mikko Eerola, Laura Koponen*

* Waselius & Wist, Helsinki.

I. General principles of Member State's State aid law

Competent authorities for granting aid and involved in the notification and recovery procedures are the State of Finland, Ministries, State agencies, municipalities and other local and regional authorities, government institutions, public entities and private entities under the control of the State of Finland.

In Finland, a large number of organizations granting aid to undertakings, such as the Employment and Economic Development Centres and certain particular institutions established by the State of Finland in order to promote economy and finance, are governed by the Ministry of Employment and the Economy (hereinafter the "Ministry").

The notification referred to in Article 108(3) TFEU shall first be lodged with the Ministry, which then notifies the Commission of the planned aid measure. The Ministry also submits annual reports to the Commission.

In Finland, there is no material regulation relating to the EU State aid rules, as the same have not been implemented in any national law. However, the Act on Application of Certain European Community Law Provisions Relating to State aid (Laki eräiden valtion tukea koskevien Euroopan Yhteisön säännösten soveltamisesta, statute number 300/2001, as amended) (hereinafter the "Application Act") and the Government Decree concerning procedures to be complied with when notifying State aid to the Commission (Valtioneuvoston asetus valtiontukien ilmoittamisessa komissiolle noudatettavista menettelyistä, statute number 86/2004) provide for enforcement of the EU State aid rules as regards notification and recovery procedures.

In addition, the Act on Discretionary Government Aid (Valtionavustuslaki, statute number 688/2001, as amended), which is not based on EU State aid rules but has been created on a purely national basis, regulates certain forms of national subsidies. The Act on Discretionary Government Aid is generally applied to subsidies other than those governed by the EU rules, such as loans and interest subsidies granted from State resources, State suretyships, guarantees and exemptions from the payment of taxes or social allowances. The recovery provisions were clarified by an amendment of the Application Act in 2008 in order to facilitate the recovery procedure. Under the Application Act, a recovery must be made by the authority that granted the aid. Where the aid has not been granted by an authority, the recovery shall be implemented by the authority that controls the undertaking which granted the aid. In situations, where it is not possible to identify the responsible authority, the Ministry shall be responsible for the recovery.

The Commission's recovery decision shall be effected by a decision by the authority having granted the aid. The amount of the aid including the interests, the undertakings ordered to repay the aid as well as other related matters must be specified in the national decision, as defined in the Commission's recovery decision. The national authority's decision may be appealed against, but it must, notwithstanding any appeal, be immediately complied with.

Prior to the above amendment, there was no actual regulation on the authority liable for the recovery, but solely a provision providing that the aid could be recovered from its recipient, either wholly or in part, in accordance with the Commission's decision to that effect.

However, it should be noted that to date, no final and enforceable recovery decisions have been addressed to Finland.

II. Identification of State aid issues at national level

1. State aid compliance by the national legislator and/or by the executive power

With respect to both the legislator and to the executive power, there is neither *ex ante* nor *ex post* control organised at constitutional or legislative level with a view to avoiding the granting of State aid in violation of Article 108(3) TFEU. The authority granting the aid shall be liable for assessing whether the aid measure fulfils the criteria laid down in Article 107(1) TFEU and for notifying the planned measure if necessary.

The Ministry coordinates communication between the national authorities and the Commission. It also submits notifications in accordance with Article 108(3) TFEU as well as other communications to DG COMP and asks the national authorities to submit information on existing aid schemes when so required by the Commission.

2. State aid compliance by national judges and/or the national competition authority (NCA)

The supervision of State aid matters does not fall within the competence of the Finnish Competition Authority (hereinafter the "FCA"), but it may take the initiative in order to eliminate harmful effects resulting from public competition restrictions. Whilst the national competition legislation does not apply to State aid matters, the FCA pays attention to the effect that an aid would have on the line of business as a whole.

a. State aid compliance by national judges

Depending on the public body which made the decision on the aid, such a decision may generally be challenged pursuant to the Administrative Judicial Procedure Act (Hallintolainkäyttölaki, statute number 586/1996, as amended) or the Municipality Act (Kuntalaki, statute number 365/1995, as amended).

Based on the direct effect of Article 108(3) TFEU, the national courts' main obligation is to safeguard third parties' rights in the event of aid having been granted in violation of EU law. Even though national courts do not have competence to assess the compatibility of aid with the Internal Market, they may examine whether the aid should have been notified by virtue of Article 108(3) TFEU.

The national courts are competent to grant interim measures to suspend the enforcement of an aid measure until the Commission has made its final decision in the matter. They shall also ensure efficient recovery of unlawfully disbursed aid and must always guarantee reasonable legal remedies for the parties adversely affected by breaches of the EU State aid rules.

b. *Assessment of the existence of aid within the meaning of Article 107(1) TFEU*

Since national courts may examine whether an aid should have been notified in accordance with Article 108(3) TFEU, they must also be able to assess whether the aid constitutes State aid within the meaning of Article 107(1) TFEU and is thus subject to the notification obligation.

As the number of cases relating to State aid matters has increased in recent years, the Finnish courts have become more familiar and experienced with the EU State aid rules. In particular, the Finnish Supreme Administrative Court has recently been seen to have taken an increased role in claims relating to breaches of EU State aid rules, in particular by ordering interim measures in the event of State aid being possibly involved in an aid measure.

State aid criteria

Due to the relatively scarce domestic decision-making practice in State aid matters, most of the difficulties in applying the criteria appear to stem from the lack of sufficient precedents relating to State aid issues. It would appear that this mainly concerns the courts of first instance, which have been seen not to have taken into account the relevant EU rules to a sufficient extent.

Powers of investigation

In order to safeguard the rights of third parties in the event of an aid having been granted in breach of Article 108(3) TFEU, the national courts shall, in principle, use all appropriate means and remedies to implement the direct effect of Article 108(3) TFEU. This requires assessment and verification of the State aid criteria. However, there are no detailed provisions regulating such verification in national law.

Article 267 TFEU

To date, no references for a preliminary ruling under Article 267 TFEU have been made in relation to State aid matters.

Third parties

As a part of the national courts' obligation to safeguard the rights of third parties, the national courts are generally required to use all appropriate means and remedies to implement the direct effect of Article 108(3) TFEU.

More generally, the right to intervene is limited to those having standing to appeal in an individual case. The appeal may, depending on which authority decided on the aid in question, be made either under the Administrative Judicial Procedure Act or the Municipality Act.

Under the Administrative Judicial Procedure Act, parties having standing to appeal include the addressees of the decision on the aid and those whose right, obligation or benefit has been directly affected by the decision on the aid, as evidenced by the appealing party in question.

Under the Municipality Act, in addition to addressees and those whose right, obligation or benefit has been directly affected by the decision, certain third parties, such as residents of a municipality, have a general standing to appeal against decisions of the municipality or its organs, as stipulated in more detail therein.

In principle, third parties may make statements at their own initiative during the process, but it is fully at the national court's discretion whether such statements are taken into account when examining the case.

Application of EU regulations and guidelines

In Case KHO 2006:68 the Supreme Administrative Court applied Commission Regulation (EC) N° 70/2001 of 12 January 2001 on the application of Articles [87] and [88] of the EC Treaty to State aid to small and medium-sized enterprises (OJ (2001) L 10), and Commission Regulation (EC) N° 2204/2002 of 12 December 2002 on the application of Articles [87] and [88] of the EC Treaty to State aid for employment (OJ (2002) L 337).

We are not aware of any limitations in this respect stemming from the national procedural rules.

In Case 08/0735/1 La Perttu Oy and Ravintola Hummeripoika Ky v. Haukivuori Municipal Council/The State of Finland, the Supreme Administrative Court has, when returning the case to the Administrative Court in order for the Administrative Court to rule on the question whether the arrangement constitutes State aid, referred to the Commission communication on State aid elements in sales of land and buildings by public authorities (OJ C 209/3 of 10.7.1997).

III. Unlawful aid and judicial review

1. General powers of national courts concerning the application of Article 108(3) TFEU

When a decision on an aid measure is challenged before a national court, it may suspend the enforcement of an aid measure breaching Article 108(3) TFEU by granting an interim measure. In addition, national courts may order the recovery of unlawfully disbursed aid.

From the very limited amount of litigation to date, it appears that the most common used types of litigation relate to actions for annulment of aid decisions against the State and actions for interim measures.

2. Prevention of the granting of unlawful aid

It makes no difference whether the unlawful act is of private or of public law. In addition, provided that the authority permitting the aid to be granted complies individually with the notified and approved scheme, there is no difference between the act on which the aid regime is based and the individual administrative act.

A national court may prohibit the granting and payment of unlawful aid using an interim measure until the Commission reaches a decision in the matter. Furthermore, in order to recover the unlawfully disbursed aid, the payer of the aid shall normally bring a civil action against the aid recipient, and the national court may then order the recovery. Obviously, the payer and the recipient may also privately agree on the refunding of the unlawful aid.

In general terms, the legality of an aid decision may be challenged pursuant to the Administrative Judicial Procedure Act or the Municipality Act. Deriving also from the direct effect of Article 108(3) TFEU, individuals have, in principle, the right to bring an infringement of State aid provision before a national court and thereby ensure that the notification obligation is complied with.

In the Case 09/0718/3 *Liikenne Rajala Ky v. The State of Finland/Municipal Council of Tammela* (Dno. 01229/08/2299), the Administrative Court of Hämeenlinna examined whether State aid had been involved in the Municipal Council's decision on supporting the operations of a private bus transport company by granting financial support for the bus tickets of the company in order for the company to be able to operate in sparsely populated areas. After the claim was introduced by one of the competitors of the beneficiary of the aid, the Administrative Court considered that the support measure did not meet the requirements set for a service of general economic interest as laid down in Regulation 1191/69/EEC of the Council of 26 June 1969 on action by Member States concerning the obligations inherent in the concept of a public service in transport by rail, road and inland waterway and in the *Altmark* case. Therefore, the Administrative Court revoked the decision of the Municipal Council.

The Application Act and the Government Decree on procedures to be complied with when notifying State aid to the Commission, which provide for enforcement of the EU State aid rules, do not contain any provisions upon which individuals can rely.

Recovery of unlawful aid and interest

With respect to "vertical litigation", the current usual means of recovering the unlawful aid is to bring a civil action before a national court demanding repayment of the disbursed aid. It is also possible that the State and the aid recipient may agree on voluntary refunding of the unlawfully paid sum.

In the event that an aid recipient is found insolvent or otherwise unable to refund the received aid, the State may be able to recover the aid ultimately through bankruptcy or similar proceedings.

As regards "horizontal litigation", competitors and third parties who have standing to appeal could claim repayment by lodging a civil action before a national court.

Apart from recovery of the unlawful aid, there are certain cases in which the authority recovers aid and undue benefits through civil action due to breach of individual terms of an aid scheme agreed between the authority and the aid recipient. These cases do not, however, concern breaches of Articles 107(1) TFEU and 108(3) TFEU but normally relate to abuse of properly granted aid or aid granted under purely national law, such as under the Act on Discretionary Government Aid (Valtionavustuslaki, statute number 688/2001) which is not connected to EU State aid rules but has been created on a purely national basis in order to provide for certain forms of national subsidies. The Act on Discretionary Government Aid may not obviously be applied contrary to the relevant EU State aid rules.

There should be no problem in identifying the beneficiaries, since in case of recovery of the unlawful aid, the granting authority shall make a decision thereof and specify, amongst other things, the undertakings ordered to repay the aid. The principle is that national courts should order all of the unlawfully paid aid to be recovered. The national courts should use the guidance of the Commission when deciding on the amount to be recovered. However, as the number of State aid matters is still limited in Finland, no cases concerning determination of the amount have been heard to date.

A beneficiary claimed legitimate expectation in the matter KHO 2006:68 Ministry of Employment v. City of Hämeenlinna and The State of Finland. The Court noted that a beneficiary may only rely on legitimate expectations when the aid has been granted in accordance with Article 108(3) TFEU, since a diligent businessman is presumed to be able to confirm whether the aid has been notified to the Commission. The Court concluded that if an aid is granted in breach of Article 108(3) TFEU, the recipient cannot fairly assume that the aid is lawful and, therefore, the principle of legitimate expectations could not prevent an unlawful grant from being repealed in this case.

3. Recovery of interest

To date, no illegality interest has been recovered at national level. Should a national court be required to determine the amount of the interest, it would use the relevant guidance provided in the EU rules. The Implementing Regulation has not yet been applied at national level in this respect.

4. Damages claims by competitors/third parties against the granting authority before the national courts

The way in which the criteria developed by the European Courts for assessing a Member State's liability to compensate damage, would, in a particular case, affect the application of the criteria under the Finnish Act on Damages (Vahingonkorvauslaki, statute number 412/1974, as amended) has not yet been tested before the Finnish courts.

Under the Act on Damages, a third party who is able to show that it has incurred loss due to an unlawful aid decision may be entitled to damages under the Act on Damages from the authority who granted the unlawful aid. If unclear, the competent court may also be required to decide whether the aid at issue should have been notified to the Commission.

Under the Act on Damages, an authority is liable to compensate loss incurred by a third party should such damage have been caused by the authority through fault or negligence in the course of its public duties. This liability has, however, been limited in so far as it will be triggered only in the event that the authority has not performed that duty to a reasonable standard.

In addition, a party seeking damages would need to prove a causal link between the authority's decision to grant the unlawful aid and the damage incurred. Basically, the Community principles stemming from the *Francovich/Brasserie du Pêcheur* precedent have not introduced any substantially new elements into the Finnish legislation on compensation of damages, since the Act on Damages also contains provisions on State liability. However, the national provisions on the requirements of fault or negligence relating to the authorities' liability may only have a limited significance in light of the *Francovich/Brasserie du Pêcheur* jurisprudence.

An action for damages may be initiated, in the first instance, in a competent District Court, whose decision may be appealed before a competent Court of Appeal and, in some cases, before the Supreme Court. According to the principle of full compensation enshrined in the national law, the compensation is usually intended to put the claimant in the position that they would have been in had the unlawful aid never been granted.

There are no differences between the liability of the legislator and the executive for violation of Article 108(3) TFEU. According to the principle of full compensation found in national law, the compensation is usually intended to restore the situation prevailing prior to the damage.

Concerning the assessment of the damage suffered, the Act on Damages provides for three different categories of damage. Both loss of an asset and prevention from improving asset position are classified as damages not relating to personal or material damage, and are treated accordingly.

In the end, the State is indirectly liable for the aid measures granted by regional or local authorities.

5. Damages claims by competitors/third parties against the beneficiary before the national courts

a. Direct damage actions

The national law does not impose any specific obligation on the recipient of aid resulting in liability for damages. The beneficiary is not usually liable for damages caused by the granting of unlawful aid.

Generally, should a damages action be introduced against the beneficiary of an unlawful aid, the correct procedure would be the one provided for by the Act on Damages. Neither the Act on Damages, nor other relevant domestic legislation prevent a damages action against the beneficiary.

The average length usually varies depending on the nature of the proceeding. Currently, the average length of proceedings initiated under the Administrative Judicial Procedure Act relating to general administrative matters is approximately 4 months.

As the beneficiary is not usually liable for damages, competitors and third parties may not sue the beneficiary before the national court, but should sue the authority which granted the aid.

The Act on Damages acknowledges that a damages action may be subject to adjustment.

b. Recovery of undue advantages enjoyed by the beneficiary

There is a general presumption in national law that unduly granted benefits shall be recovered. Under the Administrative Judicial Procedure Act, the aid decision made by the authority may be annulled if it is based on a manifestly erroneous application of law. In principle, granting aid in violation of Articles 107(1) TFEU and 108(3) TFEU could be considered to amount to such an erroneous application of law.

In addition, the authority which granted the undue benefit may, of its own initiative, recover the undue benefit from the recipient without the national court intervening in the matter.

In respect of cases where the authority recovers undue benefits through civil action due to breach of individual terms of an aid scheme agreed between the authority and the aid recipient, please see above concerning the procedures enabling the recovery of unlawful aid.

6. Interim measures taken by national judges

In the case of *Dalbo Affärsfastigheter Ab v. The State of Finland/The Province Government of Åland* (Dno. 3170/2/06), the Supreme Administrative Court granted an interim measure to suspend the enforcement of an aid decision made by the local authorities.

In connection with this case, the Supreme Administrative Court has in cases *Dalbo Affärsfastigheter Ab v. The State of Finland/The Province Government of Åland* (Dno. 0545/1/07) and *Dalbo Affärsfastigheter Ab and Marcus Måtar v. Ålands Industrihus Ab* (Dno. 2206/1/07) granted interim measures to suspend the enforcement of an aid decision made by the local authorities regarding subscription of shares.

Regarding the whole matter of substance in the issue, the Supreme Administrative Court has in cases *Dalbo Affärsfastigheter Ab v. The State of Finland/The Province Government of Åland* (Dno. 0545/1/07) *Dalbo Affärsfastigheter Ab and Marcus Måtar v. Ålands Industrihus Ab* (Dno. 2206 and /1/07) dismissed the applicants' claims whereby they requested the Supreme Administrative Court to order repayment of the aid sums granted to the aid recipient by local authorities. The Supreme Administrative Court, referring, *inter alia*, to the CJEU Case C-1/09 *CELF and Ministre de la Culture et de la Communication v. Société internationale de diffusion et d'édition (SIDE)*, ruled that due to the pending investigation procedure by the Commission, and taking into account that the Supreme Administrative Court has already granted interim measures regarding the enforcement of the aid decisions, the Supreme Administrative Court has no competence to order such enforcement measures that would entail obligations going further than those possible entailed in the forthcoming ruling in the main issue. The Supreme Administrative Court therefore refused to order repayment of the aid sums until the Commission has taken its final decision in the matter.

In the case of 09/0104/1 *Kalle Mattila v. Mikkeli City Council/The State of Finland* (Dno. 02413/08/2299), the Administrative Court of Kuopio ordered an interim measure to suspend the enforcement of an aid decision made by the local authorities.

In the case of 08/0735/1 *La Perttu Oy and Ravintola Hummeripoika Ky v. Haukivuori Municipal Council/The State of Finland* (Dno. 02142/08/2299), due to the fact that the decision by the Administrative Court was appealed, the Supreme Administrative Court granted an interim measure to suspend the enforcement of an aid decision made by the local authorities. The Administrative Court of Kuopio later revoked the interim measure as it considered that there was no State aid present.

The applicants then again appealed to the Supreme Administrative Court, which revoked the decision of the Administrative Court of Kuopio ruling that the possibility of State aid could not be excluded in the case.

An injunction to cease the payment of the aid is usually an interim measure ordered by the competent court. An order to recover the aid is usually an appealable judgment by the competent court.

IV. Control of recovery procedure

1. Challenging the validity of a national recovery order

The validity of a national recovery order must be challenged by an administrative action under the Administrative Judicial Procedure Act. The applicable rules of *locus standi* depend on which authority granted the aid, namely whether the third party may rely on the provisions of the Administrative Judicial Procedure Act or the Municipality Act.

The notion of effectivity has not yet been recognised at national level. Obviously, the national courts always have to comply with the requirement of effectivity as construed in EU law. The course or outcome of the recovery procedure would have to be challenged by an administrative action brought before the competent administrative court. Generally, such an action has a suspensive effect.

The usual time frame for an appeal is thirty days from the date of receipt or publication of the judgment.

2. Damages for failure to implement a recovery decision and infringement of EU law

Under the Act on Damages, the State shall be liable to compensate damage caused by the State through intentional misconduct or negligence in the course of its duties providing that the authority has not complied with the reasonable requirements placed on it considering the quality and purpose of the authority's duty in question.

Under the Act on Damages, a third party who is able to show that it has incurred damage due to a failure to implement a recovery decision may be entitled to damages under the Act on Damage from the authority who granted the unlawful aid. In addition, a party seeking damages would need to be able to prove a causal link between the authority's decision to grant the unlawful aid and the damage incurred. In the end, the State is indirectly liable for aid measures granted by regional or local authorities.

An action for damages may be initiated, at first instance, before a competent District Court, whose decision may be appealed before a competent Court of Appeal and, in some cases, to the Supreme Court.

Where the State and/or competitors against the beneficiaries wished to bring an action to enforce compliance with obligations where recovery is resisted, they would have to apply for an interim measure ordering the beneficiary to comply with the obligation to repay the aid.

V. Standing of third parties before national courts

Depending on the authority which granted the aid in question, the rules of *locus standi* are generally determined under the Administrative Judicial Procedure Act or the Municipality Act.

Under the Administrative Judicial Procedure Act, parties which have the right to appeal include the addressees of the aid decision and those whose rights, obligations or benefits have been directly affected by the decision, as evidenced by the appellant.

Under the Municipality Act, in addition to addressees and those whose rights, obligations or benefits have been directly affected by the decision, certain third parties, such as residents of a municipality, have a general right to appeal against decisions of the municipality or its subsidiaries as detailed in the Municipality Act.

There is no reversed burden of proof on the claimant. The claimant has to prove that unlawful aid has been granted to the beneficiary.

VI. Cooperation with EU authorities

1. Cooperation with the CJEU

To date, Finnish courts have not referred any matters concerning State aid for a preliminary ruling.

2. Cooperation with the Commission

To date, there are no matters in which a national Finnish court has asked the Commission for information of a procedural nature or for documents in its possession. There are also no matters where national Finnish courts have asked for an opinion from the Commission concerning the application of State aid rules.

Taking into consideration the relatively scarce decision-making in State aid matters at national level, a limited amount of observations can be made with respect to the national courts applying case-law, Commission decisions and other sources of law within the EU legal order. However, the national courts use case-law and other related sources of EU law when they are found to be applicable to the matter in question.

VII. Trends – reforms – recommendations

Due to the increasing number of State aid issues ruled on by the national courts during the past few years, the Finnish authorities are developing a growing awareness and understanding of the State aid provisions. Whilst the number of State aid cases has been lower than in many other Member States, it would appear that the local and regional authorities and, in certain instances, the judiciary, may not always take the relevant State aid regulation into account to a sufficient extent. One of the main challenges at national level, therefore, is to increase the awareness and understanding of the authorities, particularly at municipal, local and regional levels.

Finland has taken advantage of the Temporary Framework for State aid measures adopted by the Commission in order to help Member States tackle the effects of the financial crisis at a national level. In this respect, the Commission has approved a scheme under which the Finnish State Agency Finnvera plc provides short-term export-credit insurance coverage to undertakings established in Finland, which are confronted with a temporary unavailability of cover in the private market, for financially sound transactions.

In addition, a working group appointed by the Ministry of Employment and Economy (formerly Ministry of Trade and Industry) has examined competition neutrality problems that are potentially related to public sector business activity, and proposed recommendations for policy definitions and some amendments to relevant legislation. Even though competition neutrality does not directly concern State aid rules, it may bear some relevance to the application of State aid provisions. For example, the fact that the State agencies' risk of bankruptcy is considerably limited in relation to that of private undertakings is a contradiction per se of the State aid provisions, since the State agencies gain an advantage in this respect compared to their competitors. The focus of the working group has been on hiving off the public utilities' operations, which requires certain amendments to, for example, the municipal legislation.

Furthermore, a working group appointed by the Ministry of Finance has prepared its proposal for the Government proposal for amendment of the Municipality Act (Kuntalaki, statute number 365/1995, as amended). The working group proposes amendments in relation to converting of State agencies into private companies, as well as in relation to requirements providing for the pricing by municipalities to be carried out on a commercial basis. The working group has proposed that the amendments would enter into force as of the beginning of 2011.

As shown above, the provisions regarding which authority is liable for the recovery of unlawful aid were clarified in 2008. There are currently no reforms pending in relation to State aid regulation at national level.

On a general level, and admittedly this is similar to most Member States, in order to decrease the grant of aid measures and to improve efficiency during the grant procedure, awareness of State aid regulation and its correct application could be increased by educating, in particular, the local and regional authorities and by providing them with concrete advice on how to test for the possible existence of State aid in individual cases.

France

Jacques Derenne, Alix Müller-Rappard, Cédric Kaczmarek*

---

* Hogan Lovells, Brussels.

I. General principles of member state's state aid law

Under French law, national decisions to grant State aid are subject to specific rules in order to make them transparent for the purpose of the national budget. In establishing the national requirements for the granting of aid, three types of aid are distinguished: fiscal aid, budgetary aid and banking aid.

1. National authorities which are competent for the purpose of granting aid and which may be involved in the notification procedure

Concerning those authorities which are competent to grant aid, a distinction must be drawn between the types of aid concerned. Under French law, a fundamental distinction is made between whether the aid is governed by public or civil law.

Fiscal aid includes all kinds of tax relief, tax exemption or tax cuts which are not precluded by law ("Code général des impôts") and which are granted in accordance with a general economic policy. Article 34 of the French Constitution states that fiscal aid must be provided for by a legislative act. Therefore a parliamentary act ("agrément fiscal") is necessary to approve the grant of fiscal aid by a public authority. However the law can provide that a ministerial decree will specify the conditions of the application of such fiscal aid. The grant of fiscal aid is governed by the "Code général des impôts" which sets out the procedural conditions. However, the application rules and the final decision to grant the aid are provided for under administrative law.

Budgetary aid includes grants, loans, capital contributions and guarantees from the State which are financed through the State budget. Pursuant to Article 34 of the French Constitution, the granting of budgetary aid should be provided for by a parliamentary law, "autorisation budgétaire". A regulation of 2 January 1959 states that the general content of the budget must be drawn up by statute, with the credits divided into sections and provided for by ministerial decree.

When budgetary aid is directly granted by the State in the form of subsidies, it must be shown in the "Expenditure" section of the general budget. This also applies to aid granted by public bodies which are legally separate from the State, but which are financed by its budget. However, aid financed by special funds (e. g. "le Fonds de développement économique et social", "le Fonds forestier national", "le Soutien financier de l'industrie cinématographique"etc.) does not need to be provided for by statute.

The types of aid granted directly from the State budget or by public bodies are governed by administrative law as well. The decision to grant budgetary aid is usually an administrative decision, although it can also be granted by an administrative contract. Where loans are granted directly by the State or by public bodies, they will be governed by administrative law and budgetary law. Where the aid is granted by a private body, however, private law must be applied.

Banking aid which is granted by private funds does not need to be based on statute and is generally governed by private law. However, when the aid is granted by a private body controlled by the State ("Caisse des dépôts et consignations", "Oséo", etc.), the decision as to whether to grant the aid is an administrative one, whilst the contract between the private body and the beneficiary will be concluded under private, and more specifically, credit law. The State usually exercises its power over the private bodies which grant banking aid by giving instructions in the form of a ministerial decree or a letter of instruction. Nevertheless, when the aid is granted directly by a private body that is only marginally under the control of the State, only private law (banking law) will apply.

The State can also grant aid by the way of a capital contribution, governed by company law. However, when the beneficiary of this kind of aid is a public undertaking, the capital contribution is called a capital endowment ("dotation en capital") and public law should be applied.

2. National authorities that are competent to recover unlawful aid and an overview of the procedure

When the Commission gives a negative decision, it orders the recovery of the unlawful aid. In France, the authority responsible for enforcing negative Commission decisions is usually the Ministry of Finance ("Ministère de l'Économie, de l'Industrie et de Emploi" or "Trésor"). Other ministries, such as the Ministry of Agriculture, may also be responsible in some cases depending on the type of aid. Recovery orders issued by the Commission are addressed to the ministerial department concerned, which centralises and coordinates all the information necessary to comply with the recovery obligation (amount granted, identity of the beneficiaries).

In cases where the aid is granted by local bodies ("collectivités locales", such as regions or other State's departments) or other public bodies (such as the social security institutions), the Ministry of Finance must liaise with the local authorities in order to issue claims or acts requesting the recovery of the aid. The local authorities may be prefects, regional social security units or others, depending on which local authority granted the aid.

When the aid is granted by a local public authority, it takes on the responsibility to recover the aid pursuant Article L.1511-1-1 of the General Code for Local Authorities. If the aid is not recovered, the local authority receives an injunction to recover the aid. If recovery has not been carried out within one month of notification of the injunction, the local State representative with the necessary competent authority must act immediately to recover the aid by any means possible.

II. Identification of State aid issues at national level

Under French law, there is no specific authority tasked with ensuring compliance with State aid rules, and in particular with the Block exemptions Regulations. Furthermore, since the Commission's powers under Article 107(1) TFEU are exclusive, the national court cannot assess the compatibility of State aid. Article 107(1) TFEU has no direct effect. However, the elaboration of aid projects is coordinated by a unique administrative entity, whose role it is to ensure that State aid rules are complied with.

1. State aid compliance by the national legislator and/or the executive

As with every EU policy, the State (central State) is responsible for implementing State aid rules at national level. The State is in charge of notifying aid measures to the Commission, namely aid schemes and individual aid, and every modification of these measures, including projects designed by local authorities. The State is also the competent authority to produce annual reports on the implementation of authorised schemes and to respond to the questions or information requests made by the Commission.

The notification procedure is centralised and involves specialist bodies within the central administration. The procedure is led by the General Secretariat for European Affairs (SGAE, Secrétariat Général des Affaires Européennes) which coordinates, under the authority of the Prime Minister, the ministerial departments responsible for the elaboration and implementation of aid projects. The SGAE, in cooperation with the competent Ministry, ensures that aid projects comply with national rules. Moreover, all formal notifications to the Commission are exclusively made by the French Permanent Representation (Représentation Permanente) in Brussels.

When developing aid projects, local authorities are subject to general principles that ensure State aid rules are respected. These rules are set out in a circular issued by the Prime Minister and dated 26 January 2006 ("Circulaire du 26 Janvier 2006 relative à l'application au plan local des règles communautaires de concurrence relatives aux aides publiques aux entreprises"). The interministerial delegation for regional development and competitiveness ("Délégation interministérielle à l'aménagement et à la compétitivité des territoires") publishes a regularly updated *vademecum* summarising State aid rules for use by central State services and local authorities.

Before adopting a decision to grant aid, the local authority concerned must address a request for notification to the State representative. This request is submitted by the prefect of the region ("Préfet de région"), together with its own opinion, to the Ministry for Home Affairs and for Regional Development ("Ministère de l'Intérieur de l'Outre-Mer et des Collectivités territoriales"). The demand is then forwarded on to the SGAE, which is in charge of coordinating all notification requests at local and ministerial level.

When responding to information requests formulated by the Commission, answers are prepared by the competent ministerial departments under the SGAE. They can request information from the prefect of the department or region ("Préfet de département" or "Préfet de région") in order to answer the request fully. For that purpose, the prefect can use all the services it has under its control and can request, if necessary, the opinion of the general paymaster ("trésorier-général payeur").

The State is also responsible for respecting the provisions of the EU Block exemption Regulations and is therefore in charge of providing the Commission with the necessary information to ensure that rules on cumulation are complied with. Pursuant to Article L.15511-1-1 of the General code for local authorities, local authorities are bound by the same obligations.

2. State aid compliance by national judges and/or the national competition authority (NCA)

In actions brought before the administrative courts, the competent courts at first instance are the administrative courts ("tribunaux administratifs"), the administrative courts of appeal ("cours administratives d'appel") and the Conseil d'État ("Conseil d'État"). The Conseil d'État is competent at first and last resort for actions concerning the validity of decrees or for actions concerning decisions which fall within the scope of its exclusive competence. It is also competent to hear actions concerning administrative decisions applicable throughout the French territory. Actions before the Conseil d'État are generally dealt with within two to three years. Some actions against decrees or tax measures can be decided within a year. However, where a case first has to go through the lower administrative courts, a judgment by the Conseil d'État (as the court of last instance) can take up to seven years after the actual facts of the case.

Actions may be brought before the civil courts (including the commercial courts and labour court – see, for example, civil Supreme Court, 28.2.2006, Mme Goic, mandataire liquidateur de la société Tricotage de l'AA v. CGEA de Rennes, N°M-04-41.380) regarding litigation between private parties, including claims against a State owned company and its subsidiaries, governed by private law (this raises cross-subsidy issues). Moreover, the civil courts have exclusive jurisdiction for some specific areas, e.g., indirect taxes (see civil Supreme Court, 4.7.2006, Galerie de Lisieux v. caisse Organic de recouvrement, N°V-03-12.565). In this instance, the competent courts are the courts of first instance, ("tribunaux d'instance" and "tribunaux de grande instance"), the courts of appeal ("cours d'appel") and the Supreme Court ("Cour de Cassation").

The commercial courts have jurisdiction over litigation between professionals acting in the course of their business and over any litigation between businesses. Therefore, commercial courts are often the relevant courts in which to bring actions for damages against a competitor receiving alleged unlawful aid (see, civil Supreme Court – Commercial chamber, 15.6.1999, Etablissements J. Richard Ducros v. Société Métallique Finsider Sud, N°B 97-15.684). Where the applicant is not an undertaking, an action can also be brought before the civil courts. Judgments of the commercial courts ("tribunaux de commerce") can be appealed to the commercial division of the courts of appeal ("cours d'appel") and can be further appealed on a point of law only to the Cour de Cassation. Depending on whether there is an appeal on a point of law ("pourvoi"), a case can take between five to six years (around six months before a commercial court, two years before a court of appeal and two years before the Cour de Cassation).

The French NCA (Autorité de la Concurrence) is not competent for the application of Article 107 and 108 TFEU. Article R.462-3 of the Commercial code provides that it is competent to apply Articles 101 and 102 TFEU and their equivalent provisions at national level (L.420-1, L.420-2 and L.420-5 of the Commercial Code).

III. Unlawful aid and judicial review

The infringement of Article 108(3) TFEU can be contested by means of a private action before both the administrative and civil courts. The action to be used is dependent on the nature of the act enabling the aid to be granted.

1. General powers of the national courts concerning the direct effect of Article 108(3) TFEU

a. *Actions brought before the administrative courts*

Most actions are brought before the administrative courts because State aid measures are usually granted through acts governed by public law. This concerns applicants bringing an action for annulment of a State decision or State measure involving State aid (for example tax regulations – see, for example, Administrative appeal court of Paris, 5.11.2007 and 1.10.2007, Boucherie du marché – SAS Vitry Distribution and Société SAS P et A – SA Boucherie Bordet, N°07PA00256 – N°06PA04277 and N°07PA00118 – N°06PA03997 – and tenders – see Administrative appeal court of Bordeaux, 15.7.2008, Société Merceron TP, N°07BX00373), or an action engaging the liability of the State in order to obtain damages (in principle, the State can only be sued before administrative courts).

French administrative law distinguishes between two main types of actions. Depending on the object of the dispute, the claimant can either contest the legality of a decision of the Administration ("contentieux de l'annulation" or "contentieux de l'excès de pouvoir") or bring an action for damages for the harm caused by the decision of the Administration ("plein contentieux" or "contentieux de pleine juridiction"), whereby the Administration's decision or act can also, incidentally, be declared illegal.

For both types of actions, it is mandatory that the claimant submit a preliminary request to the Administration ("recours administratif préalable") before bringing an action in the competent administrative court. This requirement, which may take the form of an administrative action or a recours hiérarchique, obviously lengthens the procedure in the event that the Administration refuses to act, in which case the claimant would be required to challenge the decision of the Administration in court.

The object of the first action, the "contentieux de l'excès de pouvoir", is to hold the Administration liable and obtain the annulment of an administrative decision. The action is subject to strict deadlines. Usually, the claimant has two months from the date of notification or publication of the decision to bring the action. In those cases where a legislative or regulatory act provides for it, it is necessary to submit a preliminary request to the Administration ("recours administratif préalable"). In all other cases, the claimant must bring an action before the competent administrative court within the deadlines mentioned above.

The claimant must show that it has an interest in challenging the decision ("décision faisant grief, i.e. the challenged act must produce legal effects"). Various interests have been held to justify the bringing of an action by the claimant, including a purely financial interest. The conditions for admissibility are less strict than those of the second action.

The object of the second action, the "contentieux de pleine jurisdiction", is to protect the rights of the natural or legal person subject to the Administration in the context of State liability or contracts with the State. The claimant must demonstrate that it has a personal interest in the action. This requirement is not difficult to meet when the claimant requests damages from the State.

The claimant must bring the action within a two-month deadline, running from the date of publication or notification of the contested decision. In most cases, the claimant must, within these two months, first bring a preliminary administrative action ("recours préalable"), requesting that the Administration take a decision (for example, to withdraw a previous decision and/or to award damages). If the Administration refuses to withdraw its decision and to award damages, the claimant can challenge this refusal before the competent administrative court. This action should be brought within two months of the notification of the refusal.

If the Administration fails to respond to the claimant's request, the Administration is deemed to have adopted an implicit decision rejecting the request ("décision implicite de rejet" – see Conseil d'État, 7.11.2008, Comité national des interprofessions à appelations d'origine et autres, N°282920) once the two-month time limit has lapsed. Thereafter, the claimant has a further two months (from the end of the first two months running from the publication or notification of the contested decision) to bring this action in the competent administrative court.

French administrative law provides a specific regime for cases of State liability. If the claimant challenges the State's liability, it has between five and ten years (depending on the State liability regime) to bring an action, starting from the date of notification of the Administration's refusal to award damages to the claimant. It is not compulsory to submit a preliminary request save where this is expressly required by a legislative or regulatory provision.

b. *Actions brought before the civil courts*

The only actions brought before the civil courts to date have been actions for liability brought by competitors against the beneficiary of State aid (Civil Supreme Court – Commercial chamber, 15.6.1999, Etablissements J. Richard Ducros v. Société Métallique Finsider Sud, N°B 97-15.684).

2. Prevention of the granting of unlawful aid

There is no specific national authority tasked with ensuring that Article 108(3) TFEU and Article 14 of Regulation (EC) No 659/1999 are complied with (no *ex ante* control – for an *ex ante* control, see report for Cyprus). The prevention of the granting of unlawful aid can be sought before the administrative courts through actions for annulment or by contesting the legality of the act on which the aid measure is based.

The legality of the administrative decision implementing the measure can be challenged before an administrative court ("contentieux de l'annulation" or "contentieux de l'excès de pouvoir").

In order to obtain the annulment of the administrative act granting aid without clearance by the Commission or to obtain a declaration of illegality, either of these administrative actions can be used, depending on the specific circumstances.

In the context of taxes, for example, decrees establishing a tax regime can be contested (within the prescribed time limit) by means of an "*ultra vires*" action ("excès de pouvoir"). However, claimants contesting an act that imposes certain tax payments on them should bring an action requesting that they not be subject to the tax by contesting the legality of the act ("plein contentieux"). In this regard, cases concerning tax levied on the disposal of animal carcasses are a good example, since, in some cases, the claimant's right to reimbursement of the illegal tax was recognised, whereas, in other cases, it was the claimant's right not to pay the illegal tax.

Regarding contracts with the State, the decision to enter into the contract can be challenged by way of an "*ultra vires*" action ("excès de pouvoir"). The annulment of such a decision can result in the contract being declared null and void. Decisions relating to the execution of the contract can only be challenged by third parties (by bringing an "*ultra vires*" action). The parties to the contract must file an action for damages ("plein contentieux"). The *Ryanair* case provides an example of a contract involving State aid concluded between the State (Chamber of Commerce) and an airline (Conseil d'État, 27.2.2006, Companies Ryanair Limited v. Chambre de Commerce et d'Industrie du Bas-Rhin, N°264406 and 264545).

The Conseil d'État held that the refusal to notify an aid measure constitutes a contestable act (Administrative Supreme Court/Conseil d'État, 7.11.2008, N°282920, Comité national des interprofessions à appellations d'origine et autres). However the decision to notify a measure is not contestable, as the Conseil d'État has held that the relevance of such decision is intrinsically linked to the assessment of the compatibility of the aid measure, which is an exclusive competence of the Commission.

3. Recovery of unlawful aid and illegality interest

National courts are obliged to recover the nominal amount of aid granted, together with any financial advantages resulting from the premature implementation of the aid.

The fundamental principles governing national courts' obligations to recover illegality interests were defined by the CJEU in response to a question for preliminary ruling raised by the Conseil d'État in the *CELF* case (Conseil d'État (Administrative supreme court)), Conseil d'État, 29.3.2006, N°274923 and 274967, Centre d'exportation du livre Français c/Ministre de la culture et de la communication; Case C-199/06, CELF and Ministre de la Culture et de la Communication [2008] ECR I-469). It is possible for a national court to order the payment of illegality interests if the unlawful aid is later declared compatible.

However, these principles have never been fully applied and raised some major issues when the Conseil d'État gave its final judgment. When the CJEU case was referred back to the

Conseil d'État, it was confronted with the specific situation where a positive decision by the Commission had been annulled by the General Court and was therefore inexistent. Having to rule on the points of law, the Conseil d'État judged that, in such "exceptional circumstances", it was unable to apply the case law of the CJEU and therefore stayed the recovery proceeding and referred a second question to the CJEU for preliminary ruling (Conseil d'État (Administrative supreme court), Conseil d'État, 19.12.2008, N°274923 and 274967, Centre d'exportation du livre Français c/ Ministre de la culture et de la communication). This is a good example of an abnormal recovery proceeding. The unlawful aid had been granted between 1980 and 2002 and, nearly 30 years later, the aid has still not been recovered.

The CJEU, however, clarified in a second CELF case (C-1/09) the obligations of the national judges in such "*exceptional circumstances*". The Court judged that "*the adoption by the Commission of the European Communities of three successive decisions declaring aid to be compatible with the common market, which were subsequently annulled by the Community judicature, is not, in itself, capable of constituting an exceptional circumstance such as to justify a limitation of the recipient's obligation to repay that aid, in the case where that aid was implemented contrary to Article [108](3) [TFEU]*". Therefore, "*a national court before which an application has been brought, on the basis of Article [108](3) [TFEU], for repayment of unlawful State aid may not stay the adoption of its decision on that application until the Commission of the European Communities has ruled on the compatibility of the aid with the common market following the annulment of a previous positive decision*".

4. Damages claims by competitors/third parties before national courts against the granting authority

In an action engaging State liability, the claimant must request that the Administration adopt a decision permitting the award of damages from the State, prior to bringing an action before the administrative courts (rule of the "prior decision" or "décision préalable").

In principle, the Administration has two months to react to this request before the claimant can turn to the administrative courts to engage the liability of the granting authority. When the Administration fails to adopt a decision ("décision implicite de rejet"), the claimant has five years from the date of notification of the Administration's refusal (if there is one) to file an action before the administrative courts. The action before the administrative courts actually consists of a request to annul the administrative decision refusing to award damages or compensation.

It must be borne in mind that the conditions for awarding damages in cases of State liability are very strict under French law. Moreover, the court will not automatically award damages, even if it finds that the State is liable (on State liability and the award of damages for violation of secondary EU law, see M. Deguergue, "La responsabilité en matière de police sanitaire" on Case *Sté Gillot*, Conseil d'État, 12 May 2004, Case n°236834, in AJDA of 19 July 2004, p. 1487).

Damages can be awarded only if (i) the rule breached intended to confer rights on individuals; and (ii) there is a direct causal link between the damage sustained and the breach of the relevant rule. The main liability regime is liability for fault ("responsabilité pour faute"), although, in specific areas, liability of the State can be triggered without proof of fault by the Administration ("responsabilité sans faute"). Administrative courts have shown a certain reluctance to engage the liability of the legislator for infringement of a provision of EU law. It has been held that the illegality enabling State liability to be engaged should be found at the level of the administrative act implementing the law, even if it was adopted in violation of EU law. The proof of the existence of fault is hard to demonstrate, as the courts have recognised a certain margin of appreciation for the legislator (Administrative tribunal of Clermont-Ferrand, 23 September 2004, SA Fontanille, Case N°0101282).

The liability of the State under EU law was relied on, for the first time, in a State aid case brought by a beneficiary of unlawful aid before the Administrative Court of Grenoble in 2003 (Administrative Court of Grenoble, 15 October 2003, Société Stéphane Kélian). The claimant argued that the liability of the State for breach of EU law, namely Article 108(3) TFEU, could be raised without proof of fault on the part of the State, and that it concerned all "emanations" of the State, including the legislator. It was alleged that liability arose both under principles of French liability law and those principles of EU law derived from the CJEU's *Francovich* case law. The action was dismissed for reasons relating to the conditions of causation.

The liability of the State can also be based on EU law, according to the conditions laid down in the *Francovich – Brasserie du Pêcheur* cases (Joined Cases C-6/90 and C-9/90, Francovich and Bonifaci v. Italy [1991] ECR I-5357, para. 35 and 41; Joined Cases C-46/93 and C-48/93, Brasserie du Pêcheur and Factortame [1996] ECR I-1029).

Competitors of the beneficiary of unlawful State aid, as well as the beneficiary itself, can request damages from the State before the administrative courts, regardless of the final decision of the Commission (See the *Saumon* case, (i) Case C-354/90, National Federation for Foreign Trade of Food Products (Fenacomex) v. France [1990] ECR I-5505, paragraph 14; and (ii) Conseil d'État, 2 June 1993).

5. Damages claims by the beneficiary before national courts against the granting authority

This issue was dealt with in France in the context of the "Borotra plan" cases (see M. Disant, *Le juge administratif et l'obligation communautaire de récupération d'un aide incompatible: réflexions autour de la responsabilité de l'Etat du fait de l'attribution des aides publiques illégales dans les affaires "Borotra"*, RFDA, mai-juin 2007, p. 547). The administrative courts recognised the possibility that the beneficiaries of an unlawful aid Scheme may receive damages from the granting authority.

A Law of 12 April 1996 reference gave the State the ability to conclude framework agreements with professional bodies in the textile, clothing, leather and shoes sector in order to maintain or develop employment in these industries (the "Borotra plan"). The agreements enabled those undertakings to benefit from social security contributions exemption for a certain tranche of salaries. The measure had been notified to the Commission but implemented before the Commission's final approval. The French government, while granting the aid, had not informed the beneficiaries that the Commission had initiated a formal investigation procedure, pursuant to Article 108(2) TFEU. Several similar cases brought before the administrative courts in relation to this aid measure (see Administrative tribunal of Grenoble, 15.10.2003, Stéphane Kélian, Administrative tribunal Clermont-Ferrand, 23.9.2004, Fontanille, N°0101282; Administrative appeal court of Paris, 21.1.2006, Société Groupe Salmon Arc-en-Ciel, N°04PA01092; Administrative court of Douai, 29.3.2008, Blanchisserie industrielle du marais, N°07DA00071).

In the *Kélian* case, the administrative appeal court dismissed the claim based on State liability, as the claimant failed to prove the existence of a causal link between the alleged damage (delayed delocalisation planned by the beneficiary) and the failure to notify the aid. State liability was first engaged in the *Fontanille* judgment. The tribunal held the government responsible for a fault committed by the Prime Minister, who did not suspend the adoption of the decree implementing the law after the initiation of the formal investigation proceeding. The tribunal judged that the State and the beneficiary shared responsibility as the latter should have acted as a diligent businessman and verified that the measures in question were lawfully adopted. State liability was therefore mitigated and reduced to 25 %. Similarly to the present case, the tribunal judged that the damages would not cover the perceived amount of unlawful aid which had to be recovered. The tribunal ordered an external evaluation of the harm caused.

The Court of Appeal of Paris, in the *Salmon Arc-en-ciel* case, recognised the same principles. Concerning the evaluation of the harm, the Court relied on a principle founded by the CJEU in the *Asteris* case. A distinction should be drawn between claims for compensation for damage resulting from unlawfulness. *In that case, the CJEU held "that damages which the national authorities may be ordered to pay to individuals in compensation for damage they have caused to those individuals do not constitute aid within the meaning of Articles [87] and [88] of the EEC Treaty" (Case 106/87, Asteris v. Greece [1988] ECR Rec. p. 5515, paragraph 24).* Therefore beneficiaries can only claim for damages which do not constitute the sole recovery of the unlawful aid.

The question of whether damages can be claimed before the civil courts has been left open, as the civil Supreme Court has shown a certain reluctance to deal with that issue. In the *Ecomax-La Boéite* cases (civil Supreme Court, commercial chamber, 23.9.2008, Société Ecomax, n°06-20.945; civil Supreme Court, commercial chamber, 23.9.2008, Société immobilière et de services Boétie, n°06-20.947), the Cour de Cassation, qualifying a fiscal measure as unlawful aid, did not deal with the plea invoked by the appellant to claim compensation from the administration. The case has, however, been referred back to the Court of Appeal, which will have to assess whether it is possible to grant such compensation.

6. Damages claims by competitors/third parties before national courts against the beneficiary

The existence of an action for liability and damages against the beneficiary can be seen as an incentive in national law for private parties to be more cautious when they received State aid. However, these "horizontal" litigations are still rare.

Actions engaging the liability of the beneficiary of unlawful aid have to be brought before the civil courts. The court first determines whether the beneficiary benefited from the unlawful State aid and whether he knew or could have known that the aid received was unlawful, i.e. granted in violation of Article 108(3) TFEU, and secondly, evaluates the amount of damages to be granted to its competitors.

In several cases, the Cour de Cassation has confirmed the principle of extra-contractual liability of the beneficiary of the aid. Since the CJEU has ruled that the principle of liability of the beneficiary cannot be derived from EU law alone, it will have to be based upon unfair competition pursuant to Article 1382 of the French Civil Code (civil liability) as well. The claimant has to demonstrate the existence of fault, damage and a causal link between the fault and the damage. Where the Commission has already adopted a negative decision, there is a presumption that a fault has been committed.

Claims of unfair competition are often invoked in the context of public procurement cases. The beneficiary of unlawful aid can be sued for damages for unfair competition by unsuccessful bidders, arguing that the selected bidder was able to make the best offer because of aid previously granted. Civil liability of the beneficiary for accepting illegal State aid has been claimed (*SFEI* case, C-39/94, SFEI a.o. v. La Poste a.o. [1996] ECR I-3547; civil Supreme Court – Commercial chamber, 15.6.1999, Etablissements J. Richard Ducros v. Société Métallique Finsider Sud, N°B 97-15.684) but the French civil Court, rejecting the appeal on other grounds, did not explicitly recognise this principle.

Rules on unfair competition can also be invoked against a public body (local authority) participating in a public tender procedure. Under State aid rules, public bodies are not *per se* forbidden to participate in such procedures, as long as, the financing of the activity is sufficiently transparent in the State budget. The activity of the public body must be subject to fiscal and accountancy obligations which are similar to those imposed upon private undertakings. The claimant will have to show, based on the accounts of the public body, that the costs of the services provided were underestimated (for an unsuccessful action in that sense, see France, Administrative court of Bordeaux (Administrative appeal court), Cour administrative d'appel de Bordeaux, 15.7.2008 Société Merceron TP N°07BX00373).

In addition, contractual liability (Article 1116 of the French Civil Code) could also be invoked by third parties against the beneficiary, on the condition that they are bound by contractual links. Unjust enrichment cannot be invoked in State aid cases, as it can only be claimed in situations where there is no legal basis for the enrichment (absence of an administrative act or absence of a contract). Unjust enrichment is only a subsidiary means of action, to be used when no other means is available to the claimant.

7. Interim measures taken by national judges

Competing undertakings can request the suspension of a decision granting unlawful State aid ("référé-suspension"). In theory, this type of action could be based on the principle of supremacy of EU law but that principle has never been invoked in State aid cases (Case C-39/94, SFEI a.o. v. La Poste a.o. [1996] ECR I-3547).

The "référé-suspension" was introduced into French law in 2000 (Law n°2000-597 of 30 June 2000, Official Journal of 1 July 2000, in force on 1 January 2001; L.521-1 of the Code of Administrative justice). The judge can order suspension of a contested decision in the context of an action for annulment. Suspension can only be requested when the administrative decision granting the aid has not yet been fully implemented (see various cases where, however, all actions were dismissed: Conseil d'État, 11.2.2004, Syndicat national de l'industrie des viandes a.o.; Conseil d'État, 28.9.2001, AFORM a.o.; Conseil d'État, 28.7.1999, SA Bouygues a.o.: Conseil d'État, 14.3.2010, Air France e.a., n°336405).

The conditions that must be satisfied for this type of interim measure to be granted are (i) urgency; (ii) the establishment of a *prima facie* case; and (iii) harm to the claimant, if the contested measure comes into effect. Under French law, the interpretation of these criteria is generally less strict than under EU law. For example, urgency may be established on the basis of purely financial consequences resulting from the implementation of the contested measure (On the differences between French and EU law regarding interim measures, see P. Cassia *"La contribution du juge administrative français des référés au caractère complet des voies de droit communautaire"* on the Order of the Conseil d'État, 29.10.2003, Sté Techna a.o., n°260768, 261033 and 261034 in Europe, éditions du Juris-Classeur, January 2004, p. 5–11). The Council of State requires that the implementation of the administrative act must affect; o. a. sufficiently serious and immediate manner, a public interest, the legal situation of the claimants or the interest the latter wants to defend (Conseil d'État, 30.7.2003, Commune de Paulhac).

IV. Control of recovery procedure

1. Rules applicable to recovery

Actions concerning the recovery of aid will normally be brought before the administrative courts. However, the civil courts can also be competent if (i) the aid was not granted by way of an administrative act and was instead granted in practice; or (ii) when recovery is sought by competitors, which is rare in France. There are only very few civil cases which deal with recovery, mainly because most contracts, transactions and acts in which the State is involved will be governed by administrative law.

In principle, when an aid is declared unlawful following a negative Commission decision, the Administration will first inform the beneficiary of the obligation to repay the aid. When an aid is declared unlawful following the judgment of a national court, the granting authorities are enjoined to recover the aid from the beneficiary. Judgments of appeal courts are referred to the court before which the litigation was initiated. Specific departments of the Supreme Court are in charge of implementing the judgments ("Cellule d'exécution des décisions de justice"). The recovery procedure will then be initiated by the Administration, in the same way as the State would proceed to obtain reimbursement of a debt owed to the State, i.e. at central or local level.

Recovery by the State

Unlawful aid is recovered in France by means of an executory act ("acte exécutoire"), which is issued by the Judicial Officer of the Treasury ("agent judiciaire du Trésor"). This act is governed by public law.

It is possible to request that the Administration make an order for reimbursement of public monies. These "arrêtés de débet" ("état exécutoire") are orders delivered to the beneficiary of unlawful State aid, requiring it to repay the unlawful State aid to the relevant public authority (see Decree of 29 December 1962, Décret portant règlement général sur la comptabilité publique, consolidated version of 24 January 2009, Article 84). In addition, the Minister of Finance can delegate the authority to the Judicial Officer of the Treasury ("agent judiciaire du Trésor") to deliver such orders and render them mandatory.

If the undertaking concerned does not repay the aid, the State can turn to a third party that holds the undertaking's funds ("avis à tiers détenteur") to recover the aid directly by seizing the funds deposited in a bank account ("saisie administrative"). Once insolvency proceedings have been opened, the State must register its claim with the creditors' representative (see below for more details on insolvency proceedings).

Recovery by local authorities

The State generally requests that prefects ("préfets") execute recovery at local level, but recovery could also be pursued by any other local authority, namely a municipality ("commune"), the General Council ("Conseil general") of the French departments, the Regional Council ("Conseil regional") of the French Régions, or a local public undertaking.

Article L.1511-1-1 of the General Code for Local Authorities provides that "*any local authority [...] having granted aid to an undertaking is to proceed without delay to its recovery if so requested by a Commission decision or a judgment of the CJEU, whether provisional or definitive. In the absence of such recovery, after a notice has remained without effect for a month from notification, the State representative will proceed to the recovery of its own motion and by any means. The local authorities [...] will bear the financial consequences that could result for the State from a condemnation for late or incomplete implementation of recovery decisions. This is compulsory expenditure [...]*".

The provision establishes local authority liability for failing to recover State aid declared unlawful following a Commission decision or a court judgment. Local authorities are obliged to enforce recovery of the aid, even if the beneficiary has, for example, challenged the Commission's decision. The recovery act adopted by the local authority can be subject to specific performance by the representative of the State in the local authority.

2. Action for recovery

a. By the State

As mentioned above, the procedure for recovery of unlawful aid is initiated on the issuance of an executory act ("acte exécutoire") by the State requesting reimbursement. This act can be contested before the administrative courts.

In general, several cases have come before the Commission where beneficiaries resisting recovery have put forward the argument that reimbursing the aid would give rise to financial difficulties, and possibly bankruptcy. Sometimes the principle of legitimate expectations is also referred to, i.e. that they would have expected the public administration to have duly notified the aid measure to the Commission before implementing it.

Although the principle of legitimate expectations is a general principle of EU law, it is not part of the French "public policy" ("ordre public"). Moreover, the Conseil d'État has ruled that the principle can only be applied in the French legal system if EU law applied to the case before the national court, or if the contested decision was taken in order to implement EU law. The General Court has held, however, that the Administration could be liable if the principle of legitimate expectations is not respected in legal rules and administrative actions that are clear and foreseeable.

In the CELF case, the Court rejected arguments based on the principle of legitimate expectations (with regard to the size of the organisation, its activities and the fact that the system had been in place since 1980). The Court also rejected the argument that recovery would threaten the public service mission of the organisation and considered that there was no obstacle to recovery.

b. By competitors

Competitors can try to obtain a court order to enforce a Commission recovery decision against the State. If the State does not order recovery of the aid from the beneficiary following a Commission decision, then the competitors can bring an action for annulment of the State's decision in the administrative courts, and apply for an injunction (with a daily fine for non-compliance) to stop the Administration from recovering the aid. An action based on a claim for abuse of powers does not allow the national judge to order recovery.

From a purely procedural point of view, under French administrative law, a competitor can request that the administration adopt orders to reimburse public monies. These "acte exécutoire" are credit orders that have been rendered mandatory by the Minister of Finance and order the beneficiaries to repay the aid to the relevant public authority. The competitor of the beneficiary of an aid could therefore request that the administration adopt an "acte exécutoire". In case of refusal by the administration, or if the administration does not respond for a period of two months (implicit decision of rejection) the competitor could challenge this decision before an administrative court. The administrative judge can order the Administration to act by means of an injunction. The "acte exécutoire" is executory by retainer ("exécutoire par provision"), the executory force is not suspended by a judicial action. An "acte exécutoire" cannot be contested before the civil courts.

In the judicial context, once the aid has been declared unlawful by an administrative court by means of an action for indemnity ("plein contentieux"), by a civil court, or even by a Commission decision, competitors of the beneficiary can also obtain from the administrative court a ruling expressly requesting that the Administration order recovery of the unlawful aid ("exécution de jugement"). This type of request was introduced in 1995 and its aim is to ensure that court decisions are properly executed by the Administration. An injunction against the Administration executing a judgment can be requested by an applicant prior to the judgment. In the absence of a request before the judgment, the applicant can lodge an application for such an injunction if the administration has failed to comply with a judgment that has become definitive.

An action before the commercial courts, requesting that the beneficiary repay the aid to the relevant administration, can be brought by the competitors in parallel and concurrently with an action before the administrative courts. Such an action would be based on unfair competition. Applicants can also request that the judge order interim measures. These measures would be based upon the principle of primacy of EU law over national law, so that the judge would have to set aside any national legislation or regulatory act that is contrary to Article 107 TFEU (when there is a negative Commission decision) or to Article 108 (3)TFEU.

Competitors claimed the recovery of an alleged unlawful State aid in the following cases: *Ryanair* case (Administrative tribunal of Strasbourg, tribunal administratif de Strasbourg, 24.7.2003, [...], Conseil d'État (Administrative supreme court) 27.2.2006, N°264406 and 264545, Companie Ryanair Limited – Chambre de commerce et d'industrie de Strasbourg Bas-Rhin), competitors brought an action before the administrative court of Strasbourg to order the recovery of State aid. *CELF* cases (Conseil d'État (Administrative supreme court), Conseil d'État, 19.12.2008, N°274923 and 274967, Centre d'exportation du livre Français v. Ministre de la culture et de la communication; Conseil d'État (Administrative supreme court), Conseil d'État, 29.3.2006, N°274923 and 274967, Centre d'exportation du livre Français v. Ministre de la culture et de la communication), a competitor requested the Minister to suspend and recover the subsidies. Laboratoires Boiron case (France, Civil court of Appeal of Versailles – 5th chamber A, Cour d'appel de Versailles (CA) – 5ème chambre A, 13.5.2006, N°05/05183, Laboratoires Bristol Myers Squibb v. Agence centrale des affaires sanitaires et sociales de Paris; Civil Supreme Court – 2nd civil chamber, Cour de Cassation – Chambre civile 2, 14.3.2007, N°Z-04-30.043, Société Laboratoire Glaxosmithkline v. Agence centrale des organismes de sécurité sociale (ACOSS)).

c. *By beneficiaries*

The recovery of unlawful State aid is often claimed in the context of tax litigations. Taxpayers try to contest the validity of a tax measure, claiming that it constitutes unlawful State aid. However, such claims are often dismissed by the courts.

This argument was put forward in some cases where members of professional organisations contested provisions requiring compulsory contributions to finance measures defined by the organisations themselves. In France, the administrative courts have dealt with a series of similar cases concerning the compliance of so-called "CVO", compulsory voluntary contributions ("contributions volontaires obligatoires") with State aid rules (see Conseil d'État, 21.6.2006, Confédération paysanne, n°271450; Conseil d'État, 7.11.2008, Comité national des interprofessions à appelations d'origine et autres, N°282920; Conseil d'État, 7.5.2008, Cooperative Cooperl Hunaudaye et Société Syndigel). CJEU case law relating to parafiscal taxes (see Case C-482/99, France v. Commission ("Stardust") [2002] Rec. p.I-4397, paragraph 24; Case C-379/98, PreussenElektra [2001] Rec. p.I-7907, paragraph 35 and C-295/97, Piaggio [1999] Rec. p.I-3735, paragraph 35) was applied in those cases in order to carry out the *prima facie* assessment of the State aid nature of the measure. In order to show that the aid is derived from State resources, two cumulative conditions are required, namely that the aid constitutes (i) the use of State resources which can be translated into an additional burden on the State budget; and (ii) the public origin of the State measure (imputability to the State).

In one of these cases (Conseil d'État, 7.11.2008, Comité national des interprofessions à appelations d'origine et autres, N°282920), the Conseil d'État held that the first condition was not fulfilled as the relevant resources were private resources. The measure did not constitute State aid and should not have been notified to the Commission. The claim was therefore rejected (see a recent case cour administrative d'appel de Nantes, 28.12.2009, SAS Dijori, n°08NT00890).

3. Challenging the validity of a national recovery order

The executory act ("titre de perception" or "ordre de restitution") can be challenged before the administrative courts in the context of an opposition procedure (pursuant to the normal procedure), i.e. an "*ultra vires*" action ("excès de pouvoir") or an action for annulment. Such an action can be initiated on the grounds of the existence of an unlawful aid ("payability" ("exigibilité") or of the amount to be recovered). The recovery act adopted by the local authority can also be challenged by the addressee within two months of receipt. In principle, the introduction of an action to challenge the recovery act will automatically suspend the recovery procedure under French law.

However, in the *Scott* case (Case C-232/05, Commission v. France, [2006] ECR p.I-10071), the CJEU declared this procedural rule to be contrary to EU law, especially in relation to the principle of an effective and immediate recovery. In this case, the Commission adopted a decision stating that the preferential land price and the rate of the water treatment levy granted to Scott by France were incompatible with the Internal Market. According to Article 2 of this decision, France had to take "all measures" to recover the unlawful aid from the beneficiary. Since recovery of State aid is governed by national procedure, the General Council of Loiret and the City of Orléans issued a recovery act for the aid. In 2001, Kimberly-Clark brought actions challenging those two recovery acts before the Administrative Court of Orléans. Such actions have automatic suspensory effect in French law. As a consequence, the aid in question had not been recovered four years after the adoption of the Commission decision.

The Commission brought an action against France under Article 108(2) TFEU for the non-execution of its decision by France. The Commission stressed that the automatic suspensory effect of actions brought against demands for payment issued in order to recover aid granted does not fulfil the obligation of "immediate and effective" execution of the Commission's decision provided by Article 14(3) of Council Regulation (EC) No 659/99. The Court followed the Commission by ruling that this automatic suspensory effect is contrary to Article 14(3) of the Council Regulation (EC) No 659/99 because it prevents the recovery order from taking effect, in terms of reimbursement of State aid, before the competent national court has given its decision.

Following the judgement of the CJEU, in January 2007, the tribunal administratif d'Orléans dismissed the actions brought before it by the beneficiaries, Scott and Kimberly Clark, who, reimbursed the amount of the aid unlawfully received. On 8 March 2007, Scott and Kimberly Clark appealed against that judgment before the Cour administrative d'appel de Nantes, alleging an infringement of the formal requirements laid down in a provision of the national law. However, in December 2008, Scott and Kimberly Clark reimbursed the interest on the aid they had unlawfully received. The Cour administrative d'appel de Nantes doubts as to the compatibility of the annulment of the assessments on grounds of procedural defect with Article 14(3) of Regulation (EC) No 659/1999 and referred a new question to the Court for a preliminary ruling:

"Is a possible annulment by the French administrative court of the assessments issued for the recovery of aid declared on 12 July 2000 by the Commission of the European Communities to be incompatible with the common market, on the ground that those assessments infringe legislative provisions relating to the physical presentation of those assessments, given the ability of the competent administrative authority to remedy the vitiating defect in those decisions, such as to hinder the immediate and effective implementation of [Decision 2002/14], contrary to Article 14(3) of Regulation [No. 659/1999]?"

In a judgement of 20 May 2010, the CJEU, however, confirmed its strict approach concerning the use national procedures to justify any derogation to the recovery obligation and replied that *"Article 14(3) of Council Regulation (EC) No 659/1999 (...) is to be interpreted as not precluding, in circumstances in which amounts corresponding to the aid in question have already been recovered, annulment by the national court of assessments issued in order to recover the unlawful State aid on grounds of there being a procedural defect, where it is possible to rectify that procedural defect under national law. That provision does, however, preclude those amounts being paid once again, even provisionally, to the beneficiary of that aid".*

The procedure for the recovery of unlawful State aid can be initiated by the State issuing an act for recovery ("acte exécutoire"), which can then be subject to specific performance. This act can only be contested by the addressee, by way of an opposition action in the form of an "*ultra vires*" action ("excès de pouvoir") (See the *Boussac* case, Administrative Court of Paris,

16 February 1994). In the absence of such an act, see Commercial Court of Paris, 21.1.2003, SA Sojerca v. Jaunet). This action has suspensory effect.

4. Action contesting the validity of the Commission decision

National courts have no jurisdiction under EU law to declare acts of the Community institutions void (Case C-314/85, Foto-Frost v. Hauptzollamt Lübeck-Ost [1987] ECR I-4199). Even if the national courts consider a negative Commission decision to be illegal, they cannot prevent the parties from initiating a national recovery procedure. However a preliminary reference concerning its validity can be made to the CJEU pursuant to Article 267 TFEU.

References for a preliminary ruling concerning the validity of the Commission decision can be used when the claimant is not directly and individually concerned by the decision and therefore not able to lodge an appeal before the Community courts pursuant to Article 263 TFEU (Administrative court of Lyon (Administrative appeal court), Cour administrative d'appel de Lyon, 12.7.2007, Société Régie Networks N°06LY01447).

Moreover, the national courts should take appropriate interim measures while awaiting judgment by the CJEU (Case C-39/94, SFEI o.a. v. La Poste o.a. [1996] ECR I-3547, paragraph 53). This has not yet been put into effect by the administrative courts.

5. Damages for failure to implement a recovery decision and infringement of EU law

Actions introduced against the State for failure to implement a recovery decision are rare. Failure to implement a recovery decision is an infringement of EU law and a breach of the principles of direct effect and primacy. In such situations, the CJEU ruled that the State's liability could be engaged and damages granted, provided that the conditions in the *Francovich* and *Brasserie du Pêcheur* cases were fulfilled. Therefore a claimant can directly rely on the Commission decision to claim that it suffered from the lack of or bad recovery of the unlawful aid.

The Administration is likely to face different types of difficulties when dealing with recovery proceedings. In order to implement negative Commission decisions ordering recovery of unlawful aid, the authorities need to identify the beneficiaries, as well as the amount of aid to be recovered. In principle, this type of information is included in the Commission decision. However, national authorities may encounter practical difficulties in the situation where several undertakings have received aid (tax scheme), in cases where the benefit of the aid is indirect (for example, tax breaks) or where the amount granted varies considerably between beneficiaries. Moreover, if national authorities are responsible for determining the amount of State aid, disagreements with the Commission could arise as to the method of calculating the aid to be recovered.

The length and cost of the proceedings are two factors which could explain why complainants are deterred from challenging the recovery of State aid. A procedure before the administrative courts takes, on average, between two and six years and therefore may not be a useful solution for competitors of the beneficiary in remedying distortions of competition. This may be a reason for them to choose a proceeding by the complainant instead (i.e. challenging the act granting aid rather than, where possible, directly requesting recovery).

In *Commission v. France*, the Court ruled that the suspensory effect of actions brought against demands for payment issued for the recovery of aid granted is an important obstacle to the efficiency of recovery procedures and condemned France for its application of this rule. This kind of suspensory effect results from different types of procedures and makes the implementation of Article 14(3) of the Council Regulation (EC) No 659/99 difficult. An action by the beneficiary contesting the recovery order or any executory measures has suspensory effect. Until the national court hands down its judgment, the State cannot recover the aid, even by applying for interim measures before the administrative judge. This suspensory effect is limited to the case where the beneficiary contests the recovery order. In all other cases, the judge can order interim measures, provisional or forced execution of a judgment, as well as conservatory measures.

The problem of suspensory effect may also arise in the context of insolvency proceedings. Under French law, where the court decides to open an observation procedure (in order to decide whether the company should be sold, put into liquidation or allowed to continue its activities), all creditor claims and payments are suspended. The authorities therefore cannot seek recovery of the aid until the court has taken a final decision on the future of the company. In general, where there are a large number of beneficiaries who all contest the relevant recovery orders before the competent courts, the State authorities will not recover the total amount of the aid and may choose not to proceed with the recovery process until these actions have been decided, especially if a national court requests a preliminary ruling from the CJEU.

V. Standing of third parties before national court

In principle, national rules cannot limit legal standing to the competitor of the beneficiary (Case C-174/02, Streekgewest [2005] ECR I-85, paragraphs 14 to 21) because third parties will have *locus standi* before national courts, as soon as they have a legal interest to act.

The civil court of appeal of Basse-Terre dealt with this issue (Civil court of Appeal of Basse-Terre, 18.6.2008, Administration des douanes et des droits indirects de la Guyane and Société civile immobilière et de services Boëtie "SISB" v. SA Primistères Reynoird, N°05/00673) and held that third parties cannot request a national court to rule on the alleged incompatibility of a measure, but confirmed the national courts' jurisdiction in relation to claims for damages.

The assessment of aid measures and State aid control is an exclusive competence of the European Commission. State aid control is subject to specific procedure, initiated by the Commission and subject to the control of Community courts (Civil court of Appeal of Basse-Terre, 18.6.2008, Administration des douanes et des droits indirects de la Guyane and Société civile immobilière et de services Boëtie "SISB" v. SA Primistères Reynoird, N°05/00673).

In cases relating to the provisions of the French Code de la Santé Publique (Public Health Code) that define the public service obligation of pharmaceutical wholesalers, civil courts declared admissible the actions of the wholesalers' competitors in application of the *Boiron* case (Case C-526/04, Laboratoire Boiron v. ACOSS, [2006] ECR I-7529) (Civil court of Appeal of Versailles – 5th chamber A, 13.5.2006, Laboratoires Bristol Myers Squibb v. Agence centrale des affaires sanitaires et sociales de Paris, N°05/05183; civil Supreme Court – Commercial chamber, 26.6.2007, Société Laboratoires Boiron v. Union de recouvrement des cotisations de sécurité sociales et d'allocations familiales (URSSAF) de Lyon, venant aux droits de l'Agence centrale des organismes de sécurité sociale (ACOSS), N°Z-02-31.241).

The "public policy" ground ("moyen d'ordre public") and the determination of the beneficiaries are two examples of obstacles against interested parties (beneficiaries and competitors) obtaining enforcement of the notification obligations by national courts.

1. The public policy ground

Where the parties have not explicitly raised a violation of Article 108(3) TFEU but have claimed that a State measure constitutes State aid, there is an issue as to whether the Court should examine the State measure under Article 108(3) TFEU anyway.

Under French administrative law, the Court is under an obligation to raise any grounds of public policy of its own accord. Most of these grounds have been determined by case law according to the importance attached to censuring certain behaviors. Examples of public policy grounds include the incompetence of the administrative authority which has signed a decision or contract and the "misapplication of the scope of application of the law" ("méconnaissance du champ d'application de la loi"). The latter covers legislative texts, but also administrative regulations and case law. It has to be raised where the legality of an administrative act or decision is based on a legislative text, a regulation or case law which cannot be applied to the individuals or the situations concerned. The Conseil d'État does not recognize this ground in terms of the incompatibility between national law and EU law as a matter of public policy.

In the *Peterbroeck* case, the CJEU held that *"the impossibility for national courts or tribunals to raise points of Community law of their own motion does not appear to be reasonably justifiable by principles such as the requirement of legal certainty or the proper conduct of procedure"*. By analogy with Article 101 TFEU, which has been qualified by the CJEU as a public policy ground which should be raised of the judge's own accord, Article 108(3) TFEU could be regarded as a provision of public policy which the national court should raise of its own motion. Taking this into consideration, the interpretation given by the Conseil d'État may be questioned in light of the TFEU and the principle of primacy of EU law.

VI. Cooperation with EU authorities

1. Cooperation with the CJEU

The mechanism set out in Article 267 TFEU is often used by French judges to refer questions concerning State aid issues to the CJEU, as is shown by the number of questions referred to the CJEU during the period 2006–2009. The *CELF* and *Boiron* cases are good examples of this formal dialogue between the national and EU courts. Therefore, national court cases are often the direct application of the findings of CJEU cases. However, the second *CELF* case shows that a strict implementation of CJEU rulings can, in some cases, raise some difficulties. In that case, the Commission decision, on which the findings of a first preliminary ruling were based, was annuled by the CFI. The French Conseil d'État stayed proceedings to refer the question back to the CJEU and to ask whether, in such exceptional circumstances, it could limit the action to recover the aid. Here, it is questionable whether the national judge can use such a mechanism to hamper the recovery obligation.

2. Cooperation with the Commission

There have been no cases in which the national courts have asked the Commission for support.

VII. Trends – reforms – recommendations

The following best practices and remedies for immediate and effective recovery can be identified:

Ideal recovery cases are those where the beneficiary has been informed of a negative Commission decision and reimburses the aid to the State as soon as possible.

Therefore, it is of primary importance to inform competitors and the French legal community of all available national actions, and of the EU law principles applicable to the recovery of unlawful aid. Competitors, for example, should be aware of the ability, in some cases, to request recovery of unlawful aid before the commercial courts, without first having to obtain a decision from the administrative courts annulling the act that granted the unlawful aid. Judges, for example, should be aware of EU law principles according to which the suspensory effect resulting from certain types of procedures should be set aside.

To increase the level of information available to all parties concerned and to improve recovery procedures, it is suggested that a national, independent surveillance authority be created, which would be in charge of controlling the grant and recovery of State aid in France. This authority could, be responsible for advising beneficiaries on State aid issues, determining what constitutes State aid and questioning the French authorities on notification to the Commission. It could also review notifications in order to ensure that all the necessary information has been provided. It could further monitor all actions by the French government, the French parliament and local authorities that are likely to contain elements of State aid and alert them, if necessary, to the existence of State aid, whilst also informing the Commission and the public. As a result, the French government or the French parliament would be encouraged to comply more strictly with EU State aid law (notably with its procedural aspects), thereby avoiding unlawful State aid. In addition to this preventative approach, the surveillance authority could create a State aid database which judges could then consult when deciding State aid issues. Once certain instances of aid have been declared unlawful, the surveillance authority could advise on the most suitable way to recover the aid and help monitor the recovery process.

The difficulty with this type of authority is that it would have close ties with the authorities granting the aid and with the State, which would make it difficult to guarantee its independence from the State. In order to be credible to all parties concerned, i.e. beneficiaries, competitors, national judges, national authorities and the Commission, the surveillance authority would have to have the status of an independent regulatory authority with all corresponding privileges and organisational characteristics.

Furthermore, it is important to notice that this type of recovery takes place exclusively via administrative channels, without any court intervention. In the *EDF* case (see above), it is interesting to note that the beneficiary repaid the aid before challenging the Commission decision before the General Court (Case T-156/04, Électricité de France (EDF) and France v. Commission, not yet published). Following the EDF decision by the Commission of 16 december 2003 (OJ [2005] L 49/9), the State ordered recovery of the old from the beneficiary EDF. EDF sought reimbursement of part of the aid from RTE, EDF's department network, which led to a dispute at national nevel before the French Energy Regulation Commision. This solution is in compliance with EU law: the beneficiary used the legal means at its disposal whilst avoiding a pending recovery situation. The risk that there is no State aid or, if so, that it is compatible with the Internal Market is therefore transferred to the Commission. The Commission should encourage this type of behaviour.

Germany

Rainer Wessely, Alix Müller-Rappard*

* Hogan Lovells, Brussels.

I. General principles of member state's state aid law

1. National authorities that are competent to grant aid and to be involved in the notification procedure

In order to identify the competent authority for granting State aid in Germany, it is important to distinguish between State aid that is granted on a federal level ("**Bundesebene**") and aid that is granted by one of the Federal States ("**Bundesländer**").

The granting of State aid in Germany is decentralised and does not depend on the approval of one central authority. At federal level, the Federal government or any of the public bodies controlled by it can take the decision to grant aid. Similarly, at Federal State level one of the sixteen States ("Bundesländer") or a region or municipality (or an entity controlled by one or more Federal States or a region or municipality) can grant State aid.

As a general rule, it is the public authority who takes the decision to grant State aid that is responsible for the notification of such aid under Article 108(3) TFEU. At federal level, the Federal Ministry of Finance of the Federal German government is ultimately responsible for all State aid issues (including the assessment of aid projects and the preparation of draft notifications). Similarly at Federal State level, the officials of the Federal States are responsible for all State aid issues. In the past, the exchange between the Federal Ministry of Finance and the competent officials of the Federal States regarding the granting of State aid appears to have functioned well.

A further particularity of German law is that State aid can be granted by way of an administrative act ("Verwaltungsakt") under public law or through a civil law transaction. The respective form depends mainly on what form the State aid is to take and the formal requirements of the underlying legal act. Examples of State aid granted under civil law contracts are capital injections, loans, and guarantees, as well as contracts for the purchase or sale of real estate, supply contracts and other transactions. The Federal government, the Federal States' governments and other public entities can enter into civil law contracts and transactions where this is necessary to carry out their duties.

2. National authorities competent for recovery and an overview of the recovery procedure

In Germany, the ultimate responsibility for the implementation of negative Commission decisions with recovery obligations lies with the Federal Ministry of Finance. However, according to the German Constitution and due to the German federal system, the Federal government can only implement a recovery decision in cases in which the aid was granted by the Federal government or one of the public bodies controlled by it. In cases in which the aid was granted by one of the Federal States or a municipality, the Federal government can not take the necessary steps for recovery itself and must instead liaise with those officials at Federal State level who are responsible for State aid matters.

These officials are generally employed by the Federal Ministry of Finance of the respective Federal State. If a negative decision concerns State aid granted by different Federal States, the Federal government will consult with the responsible officials from the respective states.

The correct form of recovery has not been decided, mainly due to recent divergences in case law. The general view in the past was that unlawful State aid that had been granted by way of an administrative act under public law had to be recovered with public law means. This was normally done by the issuance of a "negative administrative act" ("**belastender Verwaltungsakt**") withdrawing the administrative act that granted the unlawful aid. There are corresponding rules to issue a "negative administrative act" at Federal level as well as at Federal state level. Similar rules were applied in cases in which the aid was granted in the form of tax benefits.

Similarly, where the State aid to be recovered was granted through a civil law transaction (for example in form of a guarantee), recovery was generally sought through civil law means. Normally in these cases, the authority that had granted the unlawful State aid had to bring a claim in front of the Civil Courts, based on the civil law provisions of unjust enrichment ("ungerechtfertigte Bereicherung") (sections 812 et seq. of the BGB). These provisions require that the transaction underlying the grant of the aid be declared null and void.

Contrary to this general principle, the Higher Administrative Court of Berlin ("**Oberverwaltungsgericht**") held in a preliminary ruling of 8 November 2005 that the "effet utile" of a negative Commission decision required that the competent national authority be allowed to recover the aid that was granted through a civil law transaction by way of an administrative act. The Court found that the Member State's recovery obligation stemming from the negative Commission decision was a sufficient legal basis for such an administrative act. According to the view of the Higher Administrative Court, the public party recovering the aid is not necessarily bound to recover it in the same manner in which it was granted.

In the aforementioned case, the General Court annulled the negative Commission decision that had led to the original recovery order. Consequently, it is unlikely that the Higher Administrative Court of Berlin will hand down a final ruling in this case.

Therefore, it is likely that in future recovery cases – based either on a negative Commission decision or on the basis of failure to notify pursuant to Article 108(3) TFEU – a reference to the "*effet utile*" will justify recovery orders using administrative procedures, even if the State aid had originally been granted through a civil law transaction.

In the event that the preliminary ruling of the Higher Administrative Court of Berlin is confirmed in another case, it can be expected that recovery of aid in Germany will only be sought using administrative proceedings in the future, as recovery in this manner has proved to be far more efficient than recovery using civil law means.

II. Identification of State aid issues at national level

1. State aid compliance by the national legislator and/or the executive power

In Germany there is no general *ex ante* control organised at executive or legislative level with a view to avoiding the granting of State aid by legislative act in violation of Article 108(3) TFEU. Similarly there is no *ex post* control of this type in Germany.

2. State aid compliance by national judges and/or the national competition authority (NCA)

In Germany there is no centralised administration competent to identify State aid issues. In particular, the national competition authority (the "**Bundeskartellamt**") is not competent to deal with State aid cases.

Similarly there are no specialised State aid courts dealing specifically with State aid cases (in contrast with special chambers at the civil courts that deal solely with antitrust cases). The question of competence depends in the first instance on the form in which the aid has or will be granted and, secondly, the authority responsible for granting the aid.

As most State aid is granted by public authorities, the administrative courts will normally be competent, all the more so if the preliminary ruling of the Higher Administrative Court of Berlin should be confirmed by other courts, stating that national authorities are allowed to recover aid by way of an administrative act even if the aid was granted through civil law means (see section I.2 above). Decisions by the administrative courts can be appealed to the Courts of Appeal ("Oberverwaltungsgerichte"), and may be further appealed to the Federal Administrative Court ("Bundesverwaltungsgericht"). However, depending on the type of aid in question, the dispute may also fall within the competence of the tax courts ("Finanzgerichte") or social courts ("Sozialgerichte").

In cases were State aid is recovered through civil law means (normally in cases in which the aid was granted through a civil law transaction) the competent court will depend on the value of the claim and the regional competency. Depending on these factors, the claim will be dealt by the competent Regional Court ("Landgericht") or Higher Regional Court ("Oberlandesgericht").

III. Unlawful aid and judicial review

1. General powers of the national courts concerning the direct effect of Article 108(3) TFEU

The powers of the German courts – both civil and administrative – to take into account the direct effect of Article 108(3) TFEU have been constantly growing in recent years.

Whilst the direct effect of Article 108(3) TFEU can be raised as an issue in civil law disputes ("**zivilrechtliche Streitigkeit**") involving two or more private persons, it is also frequently relied upon in disputes where at least one of the parties involved is a public authority.

The most frequent types of litigation are:

a. Public law disputes

In a public law dispute, the proceedings can be directed against a legislative or an administrative act ("**Verwaltungsakt**"). As a general rule, any action in Germany will be brought primarily against the administrative act, as it is not usually possible to challenge legislative acts directly. However, whilst assessing the legality of the administrative act, any court will also assess the legality of the underlying legislative act. Should the court find that the underlying legislative act infringes Article 108(3) TFEU and is therefore unlawful, it will automatically find that the administrative measure was adopted without a valid legal basis ("**Ermächtigungsgrundlage**"). This means that the administrative act based on the legislative act is unlawful and unenforceable.

There are two typical scenarios in which a violation of Article 108(3) TFEU is claimed:
In public law disputes, a company or an individual will challenge a legislative or administrative act by which allegedly unlawful State aid is granted to a third party. In these cases the claimant, which will regularly be a competitor of the beneficiary, either aims to prevent the grant of the aid, or, if the aid has already been granted, to oblige the public authority to recover it.

According to the general administrative rules the claimant inteding to challenge the grant of State aid (or to require its recovery) has to lodge a complaint ("Widerspruch", "Einspruch") with the authority that has granted or will grant the aid. Only if this formal complaint is rejected, a court action can be brought.

As explained above, the appropriate action to be brought depends on the aim of the action and on which legal basis the State aid was granted. According to the circumstances, German administrative law provides for a wide range of possible actions, such as bringing a "Anfechtungsklage"; "Verpflichtungsklage"; "Feststellungsklage"; "Allgemeine Leistungsklage" or a "Folgenbeseitigungsanspruch".

In most cases the third party will try to challenge the administrative act, for example the decision to grant State aid, by means of an action for rescission ("Anfechtungsklage").

Another typical form of public law dispute will be a situation in which a company or an individual tries to challenge a legislative or administrative act which is directly addressed to the company or the individual. These actions are consequently not targeted at the benefits granted to competitors.

In most of these cases, the claimant, a company or an individual, has to pay a tax or another national contribution. In order to avoid payment of the tax or contribution, the claimant will try to contest the legislative or administrative measure imposing the obligation to pay. Regularly, the company or individual will argue that either the request for payment itself (i.e. the administrative act), or the underlying legislative act, is unlawful.

In this context a frequent argument put forward by the claimant is that the tax or contribution (or the interpretation of the relevant provisions which were adopted by the public authority) amounts to unlawful State aid that has not been notified to the Commission and consequently infringes Article 108(3) TFEU. The court would have to rule, in cases in which it finds that the claim is well-founded, that the tax claim or the contribution order is not enforceable.

Again, the addressee of any administrative measure is usually required to first lodge a complaint ("Widerspruch", "Einspruch") with the authority that adopted the measure. A court action can be brought only once that complaint has been rejected.

In accordance with the CJEU's case law, the court, if it accepts this claim, must suspend the application of the legislative or administrative act that imposes the tax or other contribution.

A variation on this is an action by a company or an individual claiming a subjective right to receive a tax benefit or any other contribution. In these cases, the company or individual will normally make a request to the competent administrative authority, asking for a tax reduction, exemption or any other contribution. This request will often be rejected by a decision, stating that the requesting company or individual does not have the right to receive this kind of aid.

An argument often raised by the requesting company or individual is that the refusal to grant the tax benefit or contribution benefits the claimant's competitors. This could, in turn, constitute unlawful State aid. An infringement of Article 108(3) TFEU, therefore, requires an interpretation of the relevant legislative or administrative act establishing the tax exemption or contribution of which the claimant wishes to be the beneficiary.

A further variation can be found in those cases in which the authority that has granted (or agreed to grant) State aid refuses to implement the State aid decision. In certain cases, the authority will argue that the implementation of the State aid decision would violate the notification obligation, Article 108(3) TFEU.

In these cases, the (potential) beneficiary could claim that the aid does not constitute State aid or that for other reasons the obligation pursuant Article 108(3) TFEU was not applicable (e.g. because it is covered by a block exemption). The claimant would ask the court to confirm that the authority is obliged to (continue to) grant the aid.

b. Private law disputes

The consideration of Article 108(3) TFEU in private law disputes has seen a major evolution since a landmark judgment by the Federal Court of Justice ("**Bundesgerichtshof**"), the highest German court in civil law matters, in 2003.

In its judgment, the Federal Court of Justice established clearly, for the first time, that a violation of the notification obligation under Article 108(3) TFEU results in the nullity of the entire underlying transaction under German civil law. Prior to this judgment, it had been claimed that any contract granting State aid in violation of Article 108(3) TFEU should be null and void according to section 134 of the BGB. Section 134 reflects the general principle that any transaction that infringes a legal prohibition is null and void. Until the ruling of the Federal Court of Justice, it was disputed that Article 108(3) TFEU would constitute a legal prohibition within the meaning of section 134 of the German BGB and that its violation would lead to the nullity of the underlying transaction.

As a result of the ruling, any German court that is competent to hear a private law dispute will now have to reject a claim if it finds that the right claimed constitutes State aid that was not notified to the Commission pursuant to Article 108(3) TFEU.

Private law disputes can also be divided into two further categories:

(i) disputes where a company or individual challenges the grant of State aid to a third party ("**private law disputes directly targeted at competitors**"). As explained in further detail below (section 7 c) the German courts have recently ruled that a competitor does not have a right stemming from Article 108(3) TFEU to challenge the award of State aid granted to a beneficiary and to claim recovery of it. The courts found that although a breach of Article 108(3) TFEU leads to any underlying contractual agreement being null and void, these provisions are not aimed at the protection of competitors ("Schutzgesetz") pursuant to section 823(2) of the BGB; and
(ii) disputes where a company or individual challenges a payment obligation, or an obligation to provide specific services, by arguing that the legal basis of the obligation infringes Article 108(3) TFEU and that the obligation is therefore unenforceable ("private law disputes targeted at specific performance").

2. Prevention of the granting of unlawful aid

There have been no German cases in which the claimants have successfully applied for interim relief to stop the grant of unlawful State aid to a competitor, in neither public nor private disputes. As in other member states, the German legal systems appears to require that, for a claimant to apply for interim relief, it must show: (i) a *prima facie* case, i.e. an obvious breach of the law, (ii) urgency; and (iii) an irreparable harm that will be caused to it in the event that the measures being challenged are put into effect.

The company or individual intending to challenge the grant of aid under German administration law must lodge a complaint ("Widerspruch", "Einspruch") with the authority that intends to adopt the measure prior to any court action.

Apart from public law complaints, which are aimed at preventing a public authority from granting State aid to a third party, it is conceivable that a company or individual may bring a complaint directly against the potential beneficiary of the State aid, arguing that the aid is unlawful and infringes Article 108(3) TFEU. However, it is not entirely clear whether there is a legal basis for such complaints under German law.

On one hand, such a complaint could be based on Article 3 of the Act Against Unfair Competition ("Gesetz gegen den unlauteren Wettbewerb", "UWG"), which provides for "cease and desist orders". This would require that the German courts accept that Article 108(3) TFEU is aimed at protecting the fairness of competition, as the UWG is only applicable if a rule with such a scope is infringed.

Furthermore, it is possible to apply for a "cease and desist" order on the basis of section 823(2) of the BGB. Section 823(2) BGB provides for "cease and desist" orders in the case of an infringement of a statute whose object is the protection of other persons ("Schutzgesetz"). However, as discussed in section 3.1(b)(i), the German courts have recently ruled that a competitor does not have a right stemming from Article 108(3) TFEU to challenge the award of State aid granted to a competitor and to claim recovery of it. The courts found that Article 108(3) TFEU does not have the object of protecting other persons pursuant to section 823(2) of the BGB.

3. Recovery of unlawful aid and interest

When examining the recovery of State aid in Germany, a distinction must be made between recovery under administrative law and recovery under civil law.

Where aid has been granted under administrative law measures, such as State aid granted under a public law contract, the aid must be recovered pursuant to German administrative law. This is normally done in the form of a negative administrative act, which anuls the administrative act that granted the State aid and orders the repayment of the unlawful aid and interest. Any litigation regarding such recovery claims has to be brought before the administrative courts.

In cases where the unlawful aid was granted by way of a civil law transaction, for example an injection of capital into a privately owned company or the issuance of a guarantee, the State aid should in principle be recovered pursuant to the provisions of the BGB. Hence, a court action regarding a recovery claim of this type should be brought before the civil courts. Equally, if the beneficiary refuses to repay the received aid, the authority recovering the aid should bring a claim in the same courts.

However, as mentioned above, the Higher Administrative Court of Berlin has found in a preliminary ruling that the "*effet utile*" of a negative Commission decision would require that the competent national authority also be allowed to recover the aid that was granted through a civil law transaction by way of an administrative act. It is not yet clear whether this principle will be applied successfully by the German courts – either only in cases of negative Commission decisions or also in cases of failure of notification pursuant to Article 108(3) TFEU.

The recovery order generally extends to the payment of illegality interest for the unlawfully given State aid.

There have been cases in which a negative decision has been challenged in the European courts at the same time as national court proceedings (administrative proceedings as well as at civil law proceedings) and the national courts have decided to suspend the national enforcement proceedings in order to wait for the final decision at the European courts.

4. Damages claims by competitors/third parties against the granting authority before the national courts

A claim for damages will normally have to be brought against the public authority that granted the unlawful State aid. Under German law, public authorities that have breached their official duties are obliged to indemnify those private persons who have suffered damages. The obligation to notify State aid pursuant to Article 108(3) TFEU is an official duty intended to protect third parties, i.e. competitors of the beneficiary. Consequently, a damages claim could be brought in German civil proceedings, for example under section 839 of the BGB.

To date, there have been no cases concerning actions for damages brought by competitors/third parties in Germany and consequently there are no cases in which competitors were actually awarded monetary damages.

Actions for damages against the public authority may not be seen as an effective means of enforcing State aid law, as it is generally difficult to make successful damages claims against public authorities. A further problem appears to be satisfying the requirement to prove causation between the breach of Article 108(3) TFEU and the economic loss sustained by the claimant.

5. Damages claims by the beneficiary against the granting authority before the national courts

There are no reported cases concerning actions for damages by the beneficiary against the granting authority.

As in the case of damages claims brought by competitors against the granting authority, a claim for damages by the beneficiary would have to be brought against the public authority that granted the unlawful State aid. As explained above, public authorities that breach their official duties, for example their obligation to notify State aid, are obliged to indemnify private persons who have suffered a loss as a result.

However, the German courts have ruled that taking into account the principle of "*effet utile*", recipients of State aid can not generally claim that they had no knowledge of the obligation to notify the State aid as this would prevent effective recovery. Consequently, any damages claim brought by the beneficiary could not be based on the public authority's failure to notify, as long as the authority did not mislead the beneficiary about the requirement of notification. It is rather unlikely therefore that the German courts would, in a standard recovery case, grant the beneficiary compensation for the recovery, as this would lead to a factual circumvention of the recovery obligation and ultimately to the granting of State aid.

In a recent judgment, the Federal Court of Justice has recognized a right for damages of a third party giving a guarantee for the repayment of the State aid to be recognised in the case that the authority has failed to notify the State aid pursuant Article 108(3) TFEU. In this case, the guarantor was found to have a valid damages claim equalling the amount of the recovery order as he was not the beneficiary of the State aid.

6. Damages claims by competitors/third parties against the beneficiary before the national courts

Actions for damages against the beneficiary do not seem to be an effective means of enforcing State aid law in Germany. There are no cases to date concerning actions for damages against the beneficiary and consequently no cases in which competitors were actually awarded monetary damages.

The main reason for this could be that it is not clear what the appropriate legal basis for such damages claims would be.

In theory, an action for damages against the beneficiary of unlawful State aid could be based, similarly to the method described at section III.2, on section 3 UWG or section 823(2) BGB. However, as explained above, it is not yet generally accepted that an infringement of Article 108(3) TFEU leads to the applicability of section 3 UWG or section 823(2) BGB, as some courts have ruled that Article 108(3) TFEU is not a law protecting the subjective rights of third parties.

In addition, the claimant would have to show a causal link between the economic loss sustained by the claimant and the failure to notify the State aid. It is likely to be very difficult, in most cases, to show the existence of such a causal link.

7. Interim measures taken by national judges

There are different means of interim protection provided for within the German judicial system. The appropriate interim measure depends mainly on the legal basis of the State aid and the kind of action taken in the main proceedings. Action could be taken in front of the administrative or civil courts.

According to section 80(1) of the German Administrative Court Act ("VWGO") any claim against an administrative act has suspensory effect. However, it lies in the hands of the administrative body issuing the act to decide that an appeal should not have such an effect. This is normally the case where the authority finds that the immediate execution of the act is in the "public interest".

In cases of State aid recovery pursuant to a negative Commission decision, the recovering authority will normally find that an immediate recovery of the State aid is in the public interest. Consequently, it is relatively easy to ensure immediate enforcement of the national recovery decision where such recovery is based on administrative law.

The appropriate action to be brought against an immediate recovery depends, again, on the aim of the action and the way in which State aid was granted. Interlocutory proceedings are available if the relevant conditions (for example, urgency) are satisfied.

The situation is different where recovery and interim measures are sought pursuant to civil law. The German rules on Civil Procedure provide certain means such as a "freezing injunction" or "Arrest" (the claimant can freeze the assets of the defendant against whom a payment action is brought). In order to bring a successful "freezing injunction" or "Arrest" claim, the claimant has to show that, without such an interim measure, the enforcement of the judgment might become impossible. Furthermore, the claimant has to show that the underlying claim is *prima facie* well-founded.

Another possibility for the claimant is to request an injunction. In this case, the claimant has to prove that without the injunction, irreparable harm would be caused to him.

The threshold to obtain a "freezing injunction" or an injunction in civil proceedings is quite high. Consequently, if the beneficiary refuses to repay the aid, the recovering authority has to await the outcome of the court proceedings before any monies are repaid.

This is why in certain cases it appears preferable to use administrative rather than civil proceedings in Germany, in order to ensure the swift and efficient implementation of a negative Commission decision.

IV. Control of recovery procedure

1. Rules applicable to recovery

In Germany, the Federal Ministry of Finance oversees the implementation of negative Commission decisions with recovery obligations. Overall, there has been a clear improvement in recovery discipline over recent years. Where the recipient of the aid is financially viable, recovery usually takes place within the time frame set by the Commission.

2. Action for recovery

a. Recovery by the State

Where a public authority has granted unlawful State aid by means of an administrative act, it can also order repayment by means of a (negative) administrative act. In addition, if the addressee of the repayment order does not comply with the act, the authority can sue the addressee for repayment before the competent administrative court.

For State aid granted in the form of a civil law transaction, there is long-standing jurisprudence stating that such aid would have to be recovered by civil law means in front of the civil courts. In such cases, recovery occurs pursuant to the provisions of the BGB relating to unjust enrichment.

However, as discussed, the Higher Administrative Court of Berlin has ruled that the "*effet utile*" of a negative Commission decision required that aid granted by way of a civil law transaction can also be recovered by way of an administrative act. Consequently it can be expected that if this is upheld, future recovery of aid and any subsequent court proceedings will be carried out pursuant to administrative rules.

b. *Recovery by competitors*

To date, there are no published German cases where a recovery action was successfully brought by a competitor.

The most appropriate way for a competitor (or any other third party) to proceed would be to bring a complaint against the public authority that granted the State aid, requiring it to recover the unlawful aid. The competitor (or third party) would have to show that it has sufficient standing to bring the complaint, by arguing that the public authority is under an obligation to recover the State aid and that non-recovery would violate its subjective rights.

In a recent civil case the Higher Regional Court of Schleswig-Holstein ruled that Articles 107 and 108 TFEU are not to be construed so as to support claims from competitors and that a competitor would not have a legitimate interest to bring such a claim. It concluded that a competitor does not have a right stemming from Article 108(3) TFEU to claim recovery of State aid granted to the beneficiary.

A similar decision was taken by the Higher Regional Court of Koblenz in February 2009, where it was ruled that although the breach of Articles 107 and Article 108(3) TFEU leads to any underlying contractual agreement being null and void, these provisions are not aimed at the protection of competitors ("Schutzgesetz") pursuant to section 823(2) of the BGB.

3. Challenging the validity of a national recovery order

Where a public authority has issued an administrative act in order to recover unlawful State aid, the beneficiary can lodge a complaint ("Widerspruch") with the authority requesting recovery. If the complaint is rejected, the beneficiary of the aid can bring an action before the administrative courts ("Verwaltungsgerichte").

One of the problems often encountered in proceedings concerning the repayment of unlawfully granted State aid arises from the German Act on Administrative Procedure ("Verwaltungsverfahrensgesetz"), which protects private persons against the revocation of an administrative act if certain conditions are satisfied. The CJEU decided in the *Alcan* case that this law, and especially the principle of protection of legitimate expectations, must not be interpreted in a manner that makes it impossible to recover the unlawful aid.

Other cases have shown that, in practical terms, reliance on a national legal basis for recovery creates an incentive for parties to challenge aspects that may already have been dealt with in a (negative) Commission decision whose implementation is being sought. Parties that contest elements such as the amount to be recovered, the interest and other aspects can delay recovery or can (at least partially) avoid effective recovery by the national authorities.

Therefore it would be preferable to rely directly on the negative Commission decision, effectively limiting the issues that could be addressed by the national court.

4. Action contesting the validity of the Commission decision

Beneficiaries of State aid that has been found to be unlawful in a negative Commission decision are, according to established CJEU case law, precluded from questioning the lawfulness of the Commission decision before a national court. However, a beneficiary of the unlawful State aid can challenge the Commission decision before the CJEU.

In the *Alcan* decision, the Federal Administrative Court stressed that, notwithstanding the very restrictive interpretation of the defence of legitimate expectation by the CJEU, the beneficiary can bring an action before the CJEU, against Commission decisions ordering recovery of State aid in exceptional circumstances where the existence of legitimate expectation can be established.

Competitors of a beneficiary may challenge the grant of aid according to generally applicable European rules. However, it is conceivable that there is no legal basis under German law for challenging State aid that has been authorised by the Commission.

5. Damages for failure to implement a recovery decision and infringement of EU law

The situation regarding damage claims for failure to implement a recovery decision is similar to that of competitors/third parties claiming damages against the granting authority. At the time of writing, there are no reported cases concerning this type of damages action.

A claim for damages would normally have to be brought against the public authority that has to recover the unlawful State aid, i.e. the authority that granted it. Under German law, public authorities are required to indemnify private persons who have suffered loss as a result of a breach of their official duties. The obligation to recover State aid is an official duty. It is, however, questionable as to how far this obligation is intended to protect third parties, i.e. competitors of the beneficiary. A potential damages claim could be brought under section 839 of the BGB.

A further problem is satisfying the requirement to prove a causal link between the breach of the recovery obligation and the economic loss sustained by the claimant.

V. Standing of third parties before national court

It seems to be generally accepted by the German courts that competitors and third parties may have standing to bring complaints against unlawful State aid.

The overarching rule is that a company or individual has standing to bring an action against an unlawful aid granted to a competitor if the administrative act by which the aid was granted is unlawful and, at the same time, violates the claimant's rights. In 1998, the Administrative Court of Magdeburg expressly stated for the first time that a violation of Article 108(3) TFEU confers standing on a company that is directly affected by the grant of aid to a competitor.

Consequently, a complainant requiring the public authority to recover State aid that has been declared unlawful by the Commission has to show that it has standing to bring the complaint by arguing that the public authority is under an obligation to recover the State aid, and that non-recovery would violate its rights.

VI. Cooperation with EU authorities

The Federal Ministry of Finance is responsible for dealing with the Commission on State aid matters. It also oversees the implementation of negative Commission decisions with recovery obligations.

There is no formalised cooperation between the German courts and any of the European institutions, either the Commission or the European Courts. However, and as explained above, in several cases in which a negative decision was challenged at the European courts at the same time as in national court proceedings (administrative as well as civil), the national courts decided to suspend the national enforcement proceedings in order to hear the final decision from the Community courts

VII. Trends – reforms – recommendations

1. Legitimate expectations

Legitimate expectations as a means of preventing recovery has been a long standing issue in Germany. The German Administrative Law Act specifically provides that an act by which a sum of money is granted cannot be revoked, even where the aid is unlawful, if the recipient of the money has relied on the validity of the act.

Since the decision of the Constitutional Court in February 2000 in the *Alcan* case, there have been no further cases in which the principle of the protection of legitimate expectations of the beneficiary has been relied on successfully. The application of this principle will always require the beneficiary of State aid to ascertain that the aid has been properly notified to and approved by the Commission.

It is notable that, since the final judgment in the *Alcan* case, in which the CJEU held that domestic law on recovery must not be applied in a manner that makes recovery impossible, there have been very few recovery cases before German administrative courts. Apparently, recipients of State aid and the German courts have realised that reliance on general principles of administrative law is no longer possible, unless there is a clear case of reliance in good faith.

In fact, the German Federal Administrative Court has already found in a 1993 case that, as a general rule, a recipient of State aid can reasonably be required to check whether a notification pursuant to Article 108(3) TFEU has been duly made.

2. Recovery and insolvency

In several recent cases, the German courts, including the German Federal Court of Justice ("Bundesgerichtshof") have confirmed that the German insolvency rules cannot have the practical effect of rendering recovery impossible.

In these cases, the courts mainly had to deal with the question of whether recovery claims made by public authorities, which were based on the recovery of State aid that had been granted (at least partially) in the form of a public shareholding, should be treated as subordinate claims according to the general German insolvency rules or if such claims should be treated on the same footing as other first class creditors.

The general conclusion is that State aid rules supersede German bankruptcy law and that recovery claims have to be treated in the most efficient manner, i.e. they have to be classified as claims of first class creditors.

3. Recovery claims by competitors

As mentioned above, the Higher Regional Court of Schleswig-Holstein has ruled in a recent case that Articles 107 and 108 TFEU are not to be construed so as to support claims brought by competitors and that a competitor would not have legitimate interest ("Feststellungsinteresse") to bring such a claim. It concluded that a competitor would not have a right stemming from Article 108(3) TFEU to challenge the award of State aid granted to a competitor and to claim recovery of it.

This ruling was confirmed by a judgment of the Higher Regional Court of Koblenz in February 2009, which decided that although the breach of Articles 107 and 108(3) TFEU leads to any underlying contractual agreement being null and void, these provisions are not aimed at the protection of competitors ("Schutzgesetz") pursuant to section 823(2) of the BGB. The Court further explained that Article 108(3) TFEU is not a direct basis for any claim by a competitor aimed at receiving information from the beneficiary, or for any other omission, recovery or damage claim. The court concluded that competitors are not an addressee of these provisions and therefore cannot derive any subjective rights from them.

Both cases are currently under review by the German Federal Court of Justice ("BGH").

4. Stays on proceedings

There have been several cases in which the claimant has challenged recovery resulting from the negative decision of the European Commission in front of the European courts at the same time as challenging it in the national courts. In some of these proceedings, the national courts have decided to suspend the national enforcement proceedings until the final decision was taken at Community level.

Apparently, it is not yet clear to some courts that a stay on national proceedings is not permissible on the sole ground that an action against the negative decision of the Commission is pending before the Community courts.

Greece

Dr. Ioannis Koimtzoglou*,
Antigoni Lykotrafiti**

---

* KGDI Law Firm, Athens.

** European University Institute, Florence.

Scope of this report: We have been asked to update the Greek chapter of the 2006 Report on the Application of EC State Aid Rules by National Courts by Tom Ottervanger (Allen & Overy) and Jacques Derenne (Lovells) (European Union Publications Office) with respect to the period 2006–2009. For the purposes of this update we have relied on a) p. 262–275 of the abovementioned 2006 Report (the "2006 Report") and b) The Effective Application of EU State Aid Procedures – The role of National Law and Practice", International Competition Law Series, KLUWER LAW Int., Chapter I "Basic principles and structures of Greek State Aid law and control system" by Dr. A. Metaxas and E. Sgouridou (the "2007 Report") to which we will refer in the course of answering this Questionnaire. Hence, this does not constitute a comprehensive report on the theory and practice of State aid in Greece but is limited to amendments, new case-law and practical issues that have arisen since 2006 in relation to the application of EU State aid rules in Greece.

I. General principles of member state's state aid law

1. National authorities that are competent to grant aid and to participate in the notification procedure

The national authorities which are competent to grant State aid include the central government, the local or regional authorities and any public or private body established or appointed by the State to administer aid.

The Hellenic Ministry of Economy and Finance is the Authority in charge of State aid compliance and its principal role is to supervise and coordinate granting authorities. In particular, pursuant to Article 11 of the Ministry's Organisation (presidential decree 178/2000 – State Gazette 165 A'), the Directorate for European Union Affairs in the Ministry of Economy and Finance is the competent authority to ensure the supervision of Greek granting authorities and aid providers in accordance with the law of the EU.

The Directorate for European Union Affairs has published specific guidelines addressed to State aid providers in relation to compliance with the Community system of State aid control. In practice, the said Directorate also coordinates and provides guidance to the relevant Directorates of other Ministries when dealing with State aid issues.

Moreover, it consolidates the data received from the latter, which it subsequently forwards to the European Commission for the purposes of the State aid scoreboard.

2. National authorities that are competent to recover aid and an overview of the procedure

In Greece, unlawful State aid is recovered according to the rules set out in the Code for the Collection of Public Revenue(s) ("KEDE") (see Legislative Decree 356/1974). The competent authorities are the Tax Authorities, as well as special bodies entrusted with the collection of public revenues (Article 2 of KEDE).

II. Identification of State aid issues at national level

1. State aid compliance by the national legislator and/or the executive

There is no legislative procedure for *ex ante* control at national level, and there is no independent State aid Commissioner in Greece. However, the State aid Unit of the Centre for International and European Financial Law provides guidance to the public administration in order to assist it in its understanding and implementation of the EU State aid rules. (See also I.2 above about the role of the Directorate for European Union Affairs of the Ministry of Economy and Finance).

Beyond judicial control, there is no *ex post* control at constitutional or legislative level. Any form of State aid introduced in Greece, either by laws and presidential decrees or by administrative decisions and contracts between an Authority representing the State and the beneficiary undertaking, may only be challenged judicially, either incidentally by the courts or directly by individuals/legal persons affected.

2. State aid compliance by national judges and/or the national competition authority (NCA)

The Hellenic Competition Commission is not competent in the field of State aid and therefore does not issue decisions on State aid matters. The competent authorities aside from the aforementioned public authorities are the national courts. The determination of which court has jurisdiction in each case is dependent upon (i) the nature of the dispute and, (ii) the type of judicial review requested.

National courts are not, in principle, competent to rule on whether a specific national measure constitutes prohibited State aid (see decisions 220/2002, 1093/1987 and 3905/1988 of the Hellenic Conseil d'État). This is because Article 107(1) TFEU does not have direct effect and, moreover, the Commission is exclusively competent to decide whether a particular State aid is compatible with the Internal Market or not. With regard to the application of State aid law by national judges in Greece, it should be noted that there is limited case law, especially in relation to the application of Article 107(1) TFEU.

The existing national case law demonstrates that the national courts do not apply the criteria of Article 107(1) TFEU consistently. Furthermore, they do not fully examine whether the relevant measure (i) constitutes State intervention giving rise to an economic advantage; (ii) and the ensuing economic advantage, is conferred selectively to one undertaking or a specific production sector; (iii) is granted by a Member State or through State resources; (iv) affects trade between Member States; and (v) distorts competition within the Internal Market. The lack of expertise of the national courts in State aid matters, due to the lack of sufficient opportunity so far to consider the application of the EU State aid regime, has led to an approach lacking in sophistication.

In addition, although the Greek courts may submit preliminary references in accordance with Article 267 TFEU to the CJEU this right has been rarely used, national judges appearing reluctant to take advantage of the European Courts' expertise in State aid issues. An example might be the decision of the Hellenic Supreme Court of Civil and Penal Law ("Areios Pagos") in Case 20/2006 and related Case 194/2008 of 8.1.2008. This case is concerned with the issue of whether a provision of national law, which limits the compensation due to those employed in the public sector upon retirement to a certain level, constitutes aid within the meaning of Article 107(1) TFEU.

The Supreme Court had to examine, *inter alia*, whether a preliminary question should have been addressed to the CJEU as to whether mandatory Greek law 173/1967 breaches Article 107(1) TFEU. The Supreme court upheld the lower court's finding that no such action had been necessary, since the provision at issue of Law 173/1967 raised no doubts as to its aim and scope of application. The court embarked on a comparison with Community Directives and, in particular, with the conditions under which European citizens may invoke them before national courts.

It reached the conclusion that only when doubts are raised as to the notion and scope of Community directives shall national courts, against whose decisions there is no judicial remedy under national law, bring the matter before the CJEU. The court's analysis of whether a referral of a preliminary question to the CJEU is necessary is extremely brief. Moreover, the parallel the court attempted to draw between, on the one hand, the Community Directives and their invocation by the citizens before the national courts and, on the other hand, the preliminary questions and the conditions for their referral to the CJEU is not in line with the wording and rationale of Article 107(1) TFEU.

Third parties

Competitors of the beneficiary of an unlawful aid have *locus standi* to challenge the validity of the administrative act granting the aid, so long as their legal interests are directly, individually and actually affected by the aid. By "competitors" is meant undertakings engaged in an economic activity similar to that of the beneficiary. Professional associations also have *locus standi* before the national courts in State aid cases. However, the case law of the Conseil d'État requires that the disputed administrative act does not benefit certain members of the professional association. Finally, creditors of the beneficiary of unlawful aid may also act against the administrative act implementing the aid measure, provided that their legal interests are affected.

Application of EU regulations and guidelines

There are no cases so far where the national courts have expressly applied any of the Exemption Regulations adopted by the Commission. Therefore, the rules on cumulation have not yet been applied. There have also been no cases where the national courts have referred to the Commission's communications, notices or guidelines to assess the existence of an aid.

III. Unlawful aid and judicial review

1. General powers of the national courts concerning the direct effect of Article 108(3) TFEU

National courts are obviously obliged to recognize the direct effect of the stand-still obligation enshrined in Article 108(3) TFEU. In the event that national authorities breach the obligation by implementing a State aid measure before the Commission's authorization thereof, the Greek courts are competent to uphold the rights of interested parties. Therefore, recovery of unlawful aid rests with the Greek courts in cases of complaints against recipients of unlawful aid made by their competitors.

Notification obligation

The requirement to notify aid measures is incorporated into national law by means of the tortious liability of the Public Administration, set out in Articles 105–106 of the Introductory Law of the Greek Civil Code. Under these provisions, individuals may claim damages against the State and legal persons governed by public law, including for illegal acts of State organs in the exercise of their public power.

Another way of safeguarding the notification obligation, in terms of judicial protection offered to individuals (mainly competitors of recipients of non-notified aid), lies in the provisions of Articles 914 and 904 of the Greek Civil Code on liability arising in the case of unjust enrichment. Once the notification obligation is infringed, the remedies that can be granted by the national courts depend either on the means by which the State aid was granted or on the form of judicial protection requested. In the case of a lawsuit against the Greek State, the competent court shall grant compensation if damage has been caused due to a violation of European Law.

If State aid is granted through an Administrative Act (of individual or of general regulative nature), in addition to compensation, an order may be granted for annulment of the Act. If State aid is granted directly by means of a Law, the Law's provisions may be found contrary to EU Law, but no Greek court is competent to nullify the legal provisions.

2. Recovery of unlawful aid and interest

In Case 49/2006 and the related Case 3157/2007 of 8 June 2006, the Hellenic Conseil d'État had to rule on whether Article 78(2) of the Greek Constitution had been infringed by the retroactive revocation of a tax exemption on exports by Greek undertakings, after this tax exemption was found by a Commission decision to constitute illegally granted State aid (a ruling which was subsequently confirmed by the CJEU).

The constitutional provision at issue provides that "*a tax or any other financial charge may not be imposed by a statute that has effect prior to the fiscal year preceding the imposition of the tax*". The retroactive application of taxation or financial charges could therefore make the provisions under which the exemption of the export activity of Greek undertakings from the relevant tax had been revoked, invalid.

The Court reminded Greece that recovery is the logical consequence of the finding of unlawful aid. The form that the aid takes does not impact on this.

Moreover, the Court ruled that where an aid has been granted in the form of a tax exemption, and the tax exemption has been found to be unlawful, recovery should not necessarily take the form of a retroactive tax. This would be impossible to enforce, having particular regard to the principles of Community law.

It further stated that on the basis of the Commission decision, the Greek authorities merely had to take measures ordering the undertakings which had received the aid to pay back sums corresponding to the amount of the tax exemption unlawfully granted to them.

The Hellenic Conseil d'État subsequently ordered the enforcement of the Commission decision, in line with the CJEU ruling. Although the Court did not engage in any analysis of the principle of supremacy of Community Law, arguably it implicitly accepted the prevalence of Community law over national law altogether. Specifically, by declaring the Ministerial Decision null and void from the outset as contrary to Article 107(1) TFEU and subsequently endorsing the Law ordering recovery of the aid granted, the Hellenic Conseil d'État avoided any analysis of the provision of Article 78(2) of the Greek Constitution (the prohibition of retroactive taxation).

In essence, however, the Court decided its case in the light of the principle of supremacy, directly accepting the supremacy of Community law over national law and indirectly accepting the supremacy of Community law over national constitutional law.

Principle of the protection of legitimate expectations

The principle cannot be used as a "defence" for the recipients of unlawful aid. The ambit of the principle is debatable. In the aforementioned Case 49/2006 and the related Case 3157/2007 of 8 June 2006, the Hellenic Conseil d'État also dealt with the issue of the protection of legitimate expectations. If recovery were to take the form of a retroactive financial levy, it would be contrary to the Greek Constitution (Art. 78(2)), something which, in the Greek government's view, reflects general principles that govern both the national and the Community legal order, in particular the principle of legal certainty and the principle of protection of legitimate expectations.

The Court recalled that, while a recipient of unlawfully granted aid is not precluded from relying on exceptional circumstances which may legitimately have caused it to assume the aid to be lawful, a Member State, on the other hand, whose authorities have granted the aid contrary to the procedural rules laid down in Article 108 TFEU, may not rely on the legitimate expectations of recipients in order to justify a failure to comply with the obligation to take the steps necessary to recover the aid.

In compliance with the Court's ruling, which declared that Greece, by failing to comply with the Commission's decision, had failed to fulfill its obligations under the TFEU, Greece introduced Law 2214/1994, which retroactively replaced the Ministerial Decision at issue, exempting from the tax only those profits made on exports to non-Community countries. The application of this principle, however, will always require the beneficiary of State aid to ascertain that the aid has been properly notified to and approved by the Commission.

The national courts have not yet quantified the amounts to be recovered, relying instead on the quantification made by the Commission. To the best of our knowledge, the Greek courts have not yet dealt with any case where the determination of the amount was questioned.

Enforcement of negative Commission decisions

In the case of negative Commission decisions declaring aid to be incompatible, the State is obliged to abolish, alter or refuse to grant the aid. Thus, interested third parties may challenge the lawfulness of the aid (before national courts), if the national measure has been implemented. Beneficiaries have *locus standi* to challenge the administrative act implementing the aid and claim for damages. In order to succeed, they will have to demonstrate the existence of extraordinary circumstances justifying a legitimate expectation.

Enforcement of positive Commission decisions

The highest amount of aid that has been ordered by the national Courts to be recovered at national level so far was approximately GRD 23,5 billion (Case 2156/2007 – Heracles General Cement Company S.A. v. Greece). There is no information available as to the approximate duration of a recovery procedure in Greece.

Recovery of interest

In Case 2156/2007 (Heracles General Cement Company S.A. v. Greece), the Athens Administrative Court of Appeal heard a case dealing with interest due in the case of illegal State aid that had to be recovered and with the issue of whether this interest constituted a distinct category of interest. The Court of Appeal recalled that illegally granted State aid should be recovered with interest to eliminate the financial advantages resulting from the aid. Interest may only be recovered in order to offset the financial advantages actually arising from the allocation of the aid and must be in proportion to the aid.

Therefore, the Court concluded that the interest which the appellant was called on to pay back as part of the advantage enjoyed from the granting of the illegal State aid did not have the nature of accrued interest on loans or generally on other credit, within the meaning of Article 31(1)(d) of law 2238/1994. It therefore could not be deducted.

A distinction was also drawn between interest due on illegal State aid and any other type of interest under tax law. The legal basis of the obligation to make interest payments on illegal State aid is the same as the legal basis for the obligation of recovery of unlawful aid; no distinction may be drawn for the purposes of recovery between the net amount of aid granted by a Member State and the interest payable from the date on which the aid was at the disposal of the beneficiary until the date of its recovery.

The net amount of aid granted and the interest payable are inseparable for the purposes of recovery and no provision of national law could set aside or affect the obligation to pay interest. In particular, the Court stressed that accrued interest on loans or "generally" any other form of credit is irrelevant to interest due in the case of recovery of illegal aid, regardless of how widely the term "generally" is interpreted.

The court correctly pointed out, drawing upon the case law of the European Courts, that the restoration of the situation existing prior to the granting of the illegal aid may only be achieved once the aid is recovered with interest. In conclusion, both the Administrative Court of First Instance and the Administrative Court of Appeal prevented evasion of the obligation to recover by means of employment of the national law. The courts made clear that interest due on illegally granted State subsidies constitutes an autonomous category of interest, which cannot be confused or otherwise affected by other types of interest provided for under national law. To the best of our knowledge, interim measures have not been ordered thus far by the Greek courts.

Actions concerning State aid granted without prior notification

In order to challenge an enforceable administrative act before the Hellenic Conseil d'État, the claimant has to request that the court issues a reasoned opinion by virtue of which the execution of the act will be suspended. This injunction procedure can be time consuming. In cases where an administrative agreement has already been challenged or a substantial administrative dispute is pending, a person may also initiate injunction proceedings before an administrative court.

However, filing an action before an administrative court does not, in itself, suspend the effects of an administrative act unless otherwise provided for by law. The Court will, therefore, only order the suspension of the implementation of the challenged administrative act in order to avoid irreparable material or moral damage to the claimant occurring as a result of the act's execution. An injunction may not be granted by the administrative courts in the case of negative administrative acts or omissions, or if public interest or the normal functioning of the Public Administration may be affected.

3. Damages claims by competitors/third parties against the granting authority before the national courts

There have not been any cases so far in which the national courts have had to rule on the Member State's liability for violation of Article 108(3) TFEU. Therefore, the national courts have not yet cited the relevant Community principles or the Francovich/ Brasserie du Pecheur case law.

The conditions laid down by the CJEU in the Francovich case in relation to the compensation by Member States of individuals for damages incurred as a result of the State's breach of its obligations under a Directive were: (i) that the result prescribed by the Directive should entail the grant of rights to individuals; (ii) that the provisions of the Directive should undoubtedly include the content of these rights; and (iii) that a causal link between the breach of the State's obligation and the loss and damage suffered by the injured parties should exist.

The equivalent national liability principle lies in Article 105 of the Introductory Law of the Greek Civil Code, which places an obligation on the Greek State to compensate third parties for damages suffered due to an unlawful act or omission of the State. Article 105 does not impose stricter conditions than those established in the Francovich case. The national procedural rules pertaining to State liability in cases of infringement of Article 108(3) TFEU comply with the principle of effectiveness, since they do not render the exercise of rights conferred by Community law excessively difficult or practically impossible.

The Greek State is not liable to compensate for damage caused by laws adopted by the Parliament, unless such laws contain an express provision to the contrary or are found by the courts to be in violation of the Constitution or of European Union Law. Article 105 of the Introductory Law of the Greek Civil Code gives the right to any competitor of a recipient of non-notified aid to bring an action before the courts against the agent of the State who failed to notify a specific aid scheme or individual aid measure to the European Commission.

To the best of our knowledge, national courts have not yet dealt with any cases where the claimant has been forced out of business, for example due to insolvency or bankruptcy, as a direct result of the granting of an unlawful aid.

4. Damages claims by the beneficiary against the granting authority before the national courts

To the best of our knowledge, there has been no case so far before the Greek courts where a beneficiary claimed for damages for breach of EU Law by the granting authorities.

5. Damages claims by competitors/third parties against the beneficiary before the national courts

To the best of our knowledge, there have been no cases in Greece in the period 2006–2009, where either competitors or third parties have initiated damages proceedings before the national courts against the beneficiaries of unlawful State aid.

6. Interim measures taken by national judges

To the best of our knowledge there have been no decisions so far by the Greek courts ordering interim measures to safeguard third parties' interests.

IV. Control of recovery procedure

1. Rules applicable to recovery

In relation to the procedure under national law for the recovery of illegal State aid, please refer to the last paragraph of section I.2 above. In addition, under Greek law, public authorities enjoy a preferential status for the recovery of their claims resulting from Article 61 paragraph 5 of

"KEDE". The director of the Revenue Department (Treasury Office) which is competent to collect the debt must notify the State's claims to the other party.

Where the other party does not recognise the validity of a claim, he must initiate the judicial proceedings under Article 933 of the Code of Civil Procedure (see Article 62 of "KEDE"). To the best of our knowledge, there is no specific time frame for appeal or judicial review and the national courts have not yet found in any of their decisions the "existence of exceptional conditions justifying the non execution of a recovery order".

In addition, we are not aware of any decisions of the national courts where the latter have ordered the suspension of a recovery order under the conditions set by the case law of the CJEU for the granting of interim relief.

2. Action for recovery

Please refer to sections "Recovery of unlawful aid" above and "Rules of recovery".

NB: Beneficiaries of aid also have *locus standi* to challenge any administrative act ordering the reimbursement of unlawfully granted aid. In those cases where the legitimate expectations of the beneficiaries in relation to the legality of the act awarding them the aid can be justified, they would also have *locus standi* to claim for damages.

3. Challenging the validity of a national recovery order

The validity of a national recovery order may be challenged by the beneficiary before the competent national administrative courts. The beneficiary may ask for annulment of the relevant individual administrative act ordering the recovery of the aid.

4. Action contesting the validity of the Commission decision

The beneficiaries of the aid, their competitors and any natural or legal person that can prove that a particular Commission Decision addressed to the beneficiary is of their direct and individual concern may invoke the provisions of Article 263 TFEU (in cases of approval of State aid) to contest the validity of the particular Commission Decision before the European Courts. The validity of a Commission Decision may be also challenged in the national courts by means of the preliminary ruling procedure provided for in Article 267 TFEU. In cases where the beneficiaries are resisting recovery of aid that has been declared by the Commission to be illegal, their competitors may address the issue to the competent national administrative authorities.

5. Damages for failure to implement a recovery decision and infringement of law

Please refer to section "Recovery of unlawful aid" above.

V. Standing of third parties before national court

Any administrative act which grants State aid and that has a direct, individual and present effect on the legal interests of a competitor of the recipient (i.e. anyone who proves that he is engaged in an activity similar to that of the recipient) may be challenged before the competent national administrative courts by that competitor.

VI. Cooperation with EU authorities

The Greek Courts appear reluctant to submit preliminary references to the CJEU in accordance with Article 267 TFEU in relation to State aid matters and to take advantage of the European Courts' expertise in State aid issues.

VII. Trends – reforms – recommendations

The Greek courts have had very few opportunities in the course of the past three years to apply the rules and principles of the EU State aid rules in the context of relevant cases.

As a result of this lack of expertise, the national courts in most cases: (i) do not consider the criteria of Article 107(1) TFEU, as defined by the case law of the European Courts, when assessing a certain measure and whether it qualifies as an aid or not; (ii) have not considered any Commission communications, notices, guidelines or other legislative instruments on specific State aid issues; and (iii) have not applied properly European law principles, such as the principle of supremacy.

In addition, most of the relevant "State aid" decisions have been issued by the administrative courts. There have not been any cases where the civil courts have had the opportunity to rule on claims for damages against the State, for failure to notify an aid, under the legal basis of Article 105 of the Introductory Law of the Greek Civil Code; nor have they had the opportunity to rule upon actions for damages brought under Articles 914 and 904 of the Greek Civil Code for unjust enrichment (by undertakings against their competitors, who have been granted non-notified, i.e. unlawful State aid).

Furthermore, there have not been any cases so far where the Greek courts have ordered interim measures to safeguard third parties' interests in the context of pending actions concerning State aid granted without prior notification. The cooperation between the national courts and the European Courts with regard to State aid issues is still very limited and the national judges rarely address relevant preliminary questions under Article 267 TFEU to the CJEU – in some cases without proper justification for their decision (see the Hellenic Supreme Court of Civil and Penal Law ("Areios Pagos") in Case 20/2006 and related Case 194/2008 of 8.1.2008). Finally, there has been scarce application of the provisions on recovery of illegal aid by the Greek courts.

It should however be stressed that it is an encouraging development that the Athens Administrative Court of Appeal, in its examination of whether accrued interest on loans or "generally" any other form of credit bears any relevance to the interest due in the case of recovery of illegal aid, ruled that interest due on State subsidies unlawfully handed out constitutes an autonomous category of interest, which cannot be confused with or affected by any other type of interest provided for under national law.

HUNGARY

Christopher Noblet*

---

* Partos & Noblet – associated office with Hogan Lovells, Budapest.

I. General principles of Member State's State aid law

1. National authorities that are competent to grant aid and to participate in the notification procedure

In general, State aid may be granted by the decision of government bodies, municipalities or institutions or companies owned/controlled by the State. In Hungary, the notification procedure depends on the nature of the aid.

The Minister of Agriculture has competence to notify the Commission of State aid granted for the purpose of primary production, processing and marketing of agricultural products, or in relation to fishery, forestry or the development of rural areas, as specified in Annex I TFEU. The Minister shall investigate the conditions of the proposed aid within 30 days from receipt of the notification thereof. If the Minister considers that the application is in compliance with the applicable EU and Hungarian rules (especially with Article 107(1) TFEU), he should notify the Commission of the aid measure. If State aid is granted without the prior notification of the Minister and the Commission, the Minister is entitled to order the grantor to suspend the aid until the Commission adopts its final decision on the matter.

In all other cases, the Minister of Finance has competence to investigate the aid plan and forward notification to the Commission. The notification should be made by the grantor of the aid. The Minister shall issue a prior opinion as to whether the proposed aid is in compliance with the applicable rules, before forwarding it to the Commission. The Minister shall notify the grantor of the decision of the Commission.

The coordination of the notification procedure between the Minister of Finance, the grantor and the Commission is supported by the assistance of an independent department called the Subsidy Supervising Office ("Támogatásokat Vizsgáló Iroda"), which is an office of the Ministry of Finance.

2. National authorities that are competent to recover aid and an overview of the procedure

Where the Commission orders the recovery of State aid on the basis of Council Regulation (EC) No 659/1999, the competent Minister can order the authority granting the State aid to take steps in order to recover the aid from the beneficiary.

If the beneficiary does not return the aid by the deadline fixed in the order of the Minister or in the State aid agreement, then the grantor of State aid shall be entitled to the following:

- first, it shall promptly issue a collection order to the bank of the beneficiary to collect the amount granted;
- secondly, if the aforementioned form of recovery is not efficient, it shall enforce the securities established over the assets of the beneficiary pursuant to the agreement on State aid;
- thirdly, if recovery is still not achieved it shall order the Hungarian Tax Authority to collect the relevant amount of money as taxes;

– finally, it can initiate a liquidation procedure (if the beneficiary is a business organisation) or debt consolidation procedure (in the case of municipalities).

II. Identification of State aid issues at national level

1. State aid compliance by the national legislator and/or the executive power

In Hungary, no specific procedure or control is excercised by any judicial authority in relation to State aid matters. Only the State Audit Office of Hungary has competence over the legislature and State expenditures, which is an *ex post,* non-judicial control. The State Audit Office investigates the operation of institutions financed from the State budget and the utilisation of State aid granted to municipalities, foundations or business entities. The president of the State Audit Office must notify the head of the investigated organisation of their findings and he also has a reporting obligation to the Hungarian Parliament. The president has no real effective tools in relation to unlawful State aid.

The Government, as the executive power, has wide competence in State aid matters and is itself entitled to grant State aid at its own discretion.

2. State aid compliance by national judges and/or the national competition authority (NCA)

a. State aid compliance by national competition authority

In Hungary the NCA has no competence in relation to unlawful State aid.

b. State aid compliance by national judges

Where State aid has been granted by the decision of an administrative authority, any interested party (with regard to provisions expressly pertaining to such person), may request that the competent court reviews the decision of the authority within 30 days from receipt of the decision. If the decision breaches the law such party shall be entitled to submit its claim against the relevant authority.

If State aid has been granted pursuant to an agreement concluded between the beneficiary and an organization owned by the State (e.g. a development bank) and the parties failed to notify the competent Minister (and therefore the Commission), the agreement shall be deemed as null and void. Under Hungarian law, any person is entitled to plead the invalidity of an annulled contract without any period of limitation. If an agreement is found to be invalid, the situation existing prior to the execution of the agreement shall be reinstated.

In most cases, the court is not entitled to make *ex officio* investigations. In general, the court has to decide on the basis of evidence provided by the parties in the given procedure.

As there have not yet been any cases before the Hungarian courts in relation to unlawful State aid, it cannot be estimated what difficulties could arise were the court to apply the State aid criteria in order to assess the existence of a State aid.

c. *Third party rights*

Under Hungarian provisions, if a third party has an interest in a procedure between others, it shall be entitled to enter into the procedure. Such a request must be submitted in writing or orally at the hearing and the third party shall indicate on whose side it intends to intervene (the supported party) and the advantages it may gain from such intervention. The intervening party has almost equal rights in the procedure to the supported party. The actions of the intervening party will be taken into account so far as they are not contrary to the actions of the supported party, or if the supported party has omitted to take such action. The intervening party shall also be notified of all decisions and documents relating to the procedure.

In Hungary, there have not yet been any cases before the national courts in relation to unlawful State aid, therefore we do not have any example of cases in which the court has applied any of the exemption Regulations adopted by the Commission, or where it has referred to the Commission's communications or notices/guidelines-frameworks to assess the existence of State aid.

III. Unlawful aid and judicial review

1. General powers of the national courts concerning the direct effect of Article 108(3) TFEU

At the request of the plaintiff or an intervening party, the court may suspend the enforcement of the decision of the administrative authority granting the State aid, or it may require the defendant to comply with an interim measure.

If a breach of Article 108(3) TFEU is established by the court, it shall:

- repeal the relevant infringing decision and order the respective authority to initiate a new procedure; and
- reinstate the situation that existed prior to the conclusion of the agreement in the case of an invalid contract.

2. Prevention of the granting of unlawful aid

According to the Hungarian State aid regime, there is no material legal difference should an unlawful act be of private or public law. However, a minor difference exists in that if an unlawful State aid has been granted by the decision of an administrative authority, the decision may be challenged by a party concerning provisions expressly affecting within 30 days following the receipt of the decision.

If unlawful State aid has been granted under private law (by means of a contract) then any interested party shall be entitled to challenge the contract without any period of limitation. If the State aid has been granted without prior notification to the Commission, the relevant Minister can order the grantor of aid to suspend the payment of such aid. Third parties or competitors are entitled to challenge the validity of a contract or the decision of an administrative authority granting State aid, in a court procedure and are entitled to request that the court suspend the payment of the aid in question.

Under Hungarian law, the notification procedure of State aid measures towards the Commission is governed by the following government decrees:

(a) Government Decree No. 4/2009 (I.10.) – in cases where the State aid is granted for the purpose of primary production, processing and marketing of agricultural products, or in relation to fishery, forestry or the development of rural areas, as specified in the Annex I EC; and

(b) Government Decree No. 85/2004 (IV.19.) – in cases where the State aid is granted for a purpose other than those set out above.

3. Recovery of unlawful aid and interest

Unlawful aid can be recovered in one of two ways. According to Hungarian law, vertical litigation can be used if the Commission establishes that the aid to be granted is not in compliance with the applicable EU regulations and orders the recovery of such aid, and the relevant authority or other institution orders the provider of the aid to recover such subsidy.

Horizontal litigation is appropriate when a competitor or third party is entitled to request that the competent court to order the beneficiary to repay unlawful State aid. In the event of a court procedure, the plaintiff is obliged to identify the beneficiary of the aid or the court may oblige the defendant to nominate the beneficiary. In the case of unlawful State aid, the beneficiary must return the whole amount of aid granted up to the date of recovery, plus any interest established by Commission Regulation (EC) No 794/2004.

There is no difference between those recovery procedures in which State aid has been granted prior to the final decision of the Commission (approving that aid) or in which there has been a negative decision from the Commission. The court is not entitled to propose alternative remedies because it is bound by the claims of the plaintiff, although the plaintiff may claim compensation from the beneficiary.

4. Damages claims by competitors/third parties against the granting authority before the national courts

Under Hungarian law, a person causing damage to another in violation of law shall be liable for such damage. Such person shall be relieved of liability if he proves that he acted in a reasonable manner in the given situation.

In cases where the damage has been caused by a government body, liability shall be established only if the damage cannot be remedied by common legal remedies, or if the injured person resorts to the ordinary legal remedies (other than judicial review of the decision of the authority).

In both of the above situations, the injured party must prove:

- the occurrence of damage and the amount thereof;
- the liability of the party causing the damage; and
- a connection between the occurrence of the damage and the conduct of the party causing the damage.

The injured person can be indemnified for both material and immaterial damages. On the grounds of indemnification, compensation must be made for any decrease in value of the assets of the injured person and any loss of profit due to the damage. If the extent of damage cannot be precisely calculated, even if only in part, the person or authority responsible for causing the damage can be ordered to pay a general indemnification that would be sufficient to provide the injured person with full financial compensation.

In Hungary, there is no difference in terms of liability the unlawful aid is granted by an administrative body or by the Government.

5. Damages claims by the beneficiary against the granting authority before the national courts

The injured person shall be indemnified both for material and immaterial damages. In Hungary, there have been no cases in which the State has been held liable in damages for loss caused to the beneficiary by the granting of unlawful aid. In cases of shared liability between the State and the beneficiary, the liability is joint and several towards the injured person, whilst their liability towards one another is divided in proportion to their responsibility. Liability shall be divided in equal measure between the State and the beneficiary if the degree of their responsibility cannot be established. (See second paragraph of section III.4)

6. Damages claims by competitors/third parties against the beneficiary before the national courts

As the CJEU established in its judgment in *SFEI* (C-39/94, SFEI e.a. [1996] Rec. p.I-3547), a recipient of aid who does not verify that the aid has been notified to the Commission in accordance with Article 108(3) TFEU cannot be held liable solely on the basis of Community law. However, this does not prejudice the possible application of national law concerning non-contractual liability.

Under Hungarian provisions, generally a person who causes damage to another in violation of the law shall be liable for such damage. He shall be relieved of that liability if he is able to prove that he acted in a reasonable manner in the given situation. Furthermore, in the event of special and equitable circumstances, the court is entitled to grant a partial exemption from liability to a person liable for damages.

In both of the above situations, the injured person must prove:

- the occurrence of damage and the amount thereof;
- the liability of the party causing the damage;
- a connection between the occurrence of the damage and the conduct of the party causing the damage.

To avoid liability, the party causing the damage must prove that it acted in a manner that can generally be expected in that given situation. The injured person can be compensated both for material and immaterial damages. In cases where the beneficiary delays or opposes the process of recovery then neither a third party, nor a competitor is entitled to sue the beneficiary. In such cases, the authority granting the aid can enforce the recovery. A third party (e.g. a competitor) can also be compensated for any damage caused by the beneficiary of the aid due to its malicious conduct. Any delay or opposition to the recovery also increases the amount of interest payable.

7. Interim measures taken by national judges

Under Hungarian procedural law, a national judge can take interim measures. The court, on the request of either party, may order an interim measure if it is necessary in order to:

- avoid imminent damage; or
- maintain the original state of affairs; or
- protect the interests of the plaintiff deserving special consideration.

The disadvantages caused by the interim measure may not exceed the advantages thereof. The request for an interim measure may not be submitted prior to the submission of the claim. The order of the court establishing the interim measure may be appealed.

IV. Control of recovery procedure

1. Rules applicable to recovery

The rules applicable to the recovery of unlawful aid are set out in Government Decree No. 4/2009 (I.10.); No. 85/2004 (IV.19.) and No. 55/2005 (III.26.).

The competent Minister can order the grantor of State aid to take steps in order to compel the beneficiary to return the aid.

If the beneficiary does not return the aid by the deadline fixed in the order of the Minister or in the State aid agreement, the provider of the State aid shall be entitled to do the following:

- issue "prompt collection order" to the bank of the beneficiary to collect the amount of State aid granted;
- if the aforementioned form of recovery is not effective, it can enforce the securities established over the assets of the beneficiary pursuant to the agreement on State aid;
- if recovery is still not successful, it can order the Hungarian Tax Authority to collect the relevant amount of money as taxes; and
- finally, it can initiate a liquidation procedure against the beneficiary.

If the beneficiary of the aid is of the opinion that the order of the competent minister in relation to the recovery of the aid violates the law, it is entitled to challenge the order before the court. The beneficiary must submit its claim to the relevant ministry within 30 days from receipt of the decree, and the ministry shall forward the claim within 15 days to the competent court. The plaintiff may request the suspension of the execution procedure. In such cases, the court must reach a decision within eight days. The decision of the court may also be appealed. In cases where the evidencial stage is unnecessary, or if the plaintiff so requests, the court may decide on the suspension without a hearing.

The court may in its decision

- amend the decree of the authority;
- repeal the decree; or
- order the relevant authority to conduct a new procedure.

2. Action for recovery

a. By the State

If the Commission decides that the State aid can be recovered, the competent authority (the Ministry of Finance or the Ministry of Agriculture) should require the beneficiary to return such aid, plus any interest established under Commission Regulation (EC) No 794/2004.

If the beneficiary does not return the aid, it can be collected as described under section IV.1 above.

b. *By competitors*

If the competent authority fails to require the beneficiary to return the aid, a third party (e.g. competitors) is entitled to challenge the decision of the authority before a court.

c. *By beneficiaries*

If the beneficiary challenges the result of the recovery procedure established by the competent authority in its decree, it is entitled to submit an action to the competent court. The steps of the procedure are set out in section IV.1 above.

3. Challenging the validity of a national recovery order

In Hungary, a judicial review process lasts approximately eight to twelve months. The decision of the court may be appealed. The second instance procedure usually takes an additional year. (Please see fourth paragraph of section IV.1 above.)

4. Action contesting the validity of a Commission decision

Actions submitted to national courts cannot challenge the validity of a decision of the Commission if the plaintiff could have challenged this decision directly before the European courts. This also means that, if a challenge under Article 263 TFEU would have been possible, the national court may not suspend the execution of the recovery decision on the basis of the validity of the decision of the Commission.

If it is unclear whether the plaintiff is entitled to bring an action to annul under Article 263 TFEU, the national court must, in principle, offer him legal protection. However, even in these circumstances, the national court should request a preliminary ruling if the action concerns the validity and lawfulness of a Commission decision.

5. Damages for failure to implement a recovery decision and infringement of EU law

Liability for damages caused by an administrative body (e.g. if it fails to implement the decision of the Commission in relation to recovery of State aid) shall only be established if the damage cannot be remedied by common legal remedies or if the injured party has applied for all of the ordinary legal remedies (other than judicial review of the decision).

The State does not need to initiate a court procedure in order to recover State aid. If the beneficiary does not comply with the decision of the authority in relation to the recovery procedure, the authority can:

- issue a "prompt collection order" to the accounting/deposit bank of the beneficiary;
- enforce the securities granted by the beneficiary over its assets in the State aid contract;
- notify the tax authority to collect the amount as taxes; or
- initiate a liquidation procedure against the beneficiary.

Competitors may sue the administrative body or the beneficiary for damages that they have suffered.

V. Standing of third parties before national court

Under Hungarian law, if a third party has an interest in a procedure between others, it is entitled to join such procedure. To do so, the third party must:

- request to join the procedure;
- indicate in its request the party for whom it intends to intervene; and
- indicate the advantages it may gain from the intervention.

The intervening party has almost equal rights in the procedure to the supported party. The actions of the intervening party will be taken into account insofar as they are not contrary to the actions of the supported party or if the supported party has omitted to take such action. The intervening party shall also be notified of all decisions and documents relating to the procedure.

The decision of the Court accepting the intervention may not be appealed.

VI. Cooperation with EU authorities

1. Cooperation with the CJEU

On the basis of Hungarian procedural law, the national court is entitled to refer questions to the CJEU for a preliminary ruling in accordance with the provisions of the TFEU.

The national court must suspend the domestic procedure until the CJEU adopts its decision. The national court, in its application to the CJEU, must:

- set out the question referred to the CJEU;
- notify the CJEU of the facts of the case; and
- notify the CJEU of the applicable Hungarian provisions.

2. Cooperation with the Commission

Generally, the court may not conduct an evidentiary procedure *ex officio*. Hence, in most of cases, the court is bound by the evidence provided by the parties. Either of the parties is entitled to refer to case law, decisions of the Commission, general texts on State aid published by the Commission, etc. The court can examine such documents, but it is not bound by them.

Otherwise, the cooperation between the Commission and the national courts is not governed by Hungarian provisions.

VII. Trends – Reforms – Recommendations

As there have not yet been any cases in relation to unlawful State aid before the courts in Hungary, there are no substantive examples of their approach to the application of relevant EU and national provisions.

We are not aware of any anticipated reform in relation to unlawful State aid.

Ireland

Damian Collins*,
Katharine Wilson**

* McCann FitzGerald Solicitors, Brussels.

** Hogan Lovells, Brussels.

I. General principles of Irish State aid law

1. National authorities that are competent to grant aid and to be involved in the notification procedure

In Ireland, State aid issues may arise in respect of measures adopted by a number of Government Departments and state controlled entities. In general, each Department or entity will have primary responsibility for ensuring that the measures it adopts comply with the Treaty's rules on State aid. This responsibility extends to notification of the aid and interaction with the Commission. Where the measure involves the use of public funds or relates to taxation, the Department of Finance tends to exercise a supervisory role in respect of the granting of the aid and its notification, even if the measure falls mainly within the remit of another Department.

2. National authorities that are competent to recover aid and an overview of the procedure

In circumstances where aid is to be recovered, the Department or entity which granted the aid will be responsible, in principle, for its recovery. If judicial proceedings are necessary and the claim is for a liquidated amount, summary proceedings may be issued. This procedure is governed by Orders 2 and 37 of the Rules of the Superior Courts ("RSC"). Where the claim is not for a liquidated amount, it may be necessary to initiate proceedings in plenary form in the High Court. Aid that is granted by means of a tax measure (for example, a tax exemption or relief) may be recovered by way of amended assessments to the taxpayers.

II. Identification of State aid issues at national level

1. State aid compliance by the national legislator and/or the executive

In Ireland there is no obligation to identify funding as State aid when it is made available. There are no formal procedures to ensure compliance with State aid rules; however, in practice, the Department of Finance (and other Departments) will seek to ensure compliance with State aid rules within their respective areas of responsibility.

2. State aid compliance by national judges and/or the national competition authority (NCA)

In the Irish judicial system, the High Court, as a court of first instance with full jurisdiction, is competent to hear all claims relating to State aid law, including actions challenging the granting of aid, seeking the recovery of aid or seeking damages for loss arising as a result of an aid. Decisions of the High Court can be appealed to the Supreme Court. There have been very few Irish cases on State aid issues. Accordingly, it is difficult to make any general assessment of the extent to which the Irish courts comply their obligations in respect of the State aid rules. As far as the Competition Authority in Ireland is concerned, it does not have any specific duties or powers in relation to State aid. However, the legislation that establishes the Authority identifies the promotion of competition within Ireland as one of its duties. In fulfilment of this objective, the Competition Authority could advise the government about the competition implications of State aid measures. In practice, the Competition Authority has not yet played any public role in State aid compliance issues.

III. Unlawful aid and judicial review

1. General powers of the national courts concerning the direct effect of Article 108(3) TFEU

There are no special remedies under Irish law for breach of the State aid rules. The High Court has a general power to review decisions by the Irish State and public bodies. These decisions could include decisions relating to State aid and, specifically, any failure by the State to observe the provisions of Article 108(3) TFEU. Judicial review is governed by Order 84 of the RSC. An applicant for judicial review can seek any of the following remedies: an order for certiorari (a quashing order); an order of prohibition (restricting a public authority from acting); an order of mandamus (a mandatory order forcing a public authority to act); a declaration (clarifying the legal position); an injunction; and/or damages. Where aid has been granted in disregard of Article 108(3) TFEU, an order of certiorari (quashing the decision to grant the aid unlawfully) is likely to be the most appropriate remedy. It may also be possible simply to seek a declaration as to the unlawfulness of the aid. In judicial review cases, leave must be sought to bring an action (Order 84, rule 20 RSC); in order to obtain leave, an applicant must bring an *ex parte* motion (that is, without notice to the other party) based on an affidavit, which is a sworn statement confirming the facts relied on. An application for judicial review must be made promptly, and in any case within three months from the date when the grounds for the application first arose (or six months where the relief sought is certiorari) unless the Court considers that there is a good reason for extending the period within which the application can be made. To be granted leave for judicial review, the applicant must show that it has sufficient interest in the matter and must satisfy the court that it has an arguable case to be entitled to the remedies sought.

2. Prevention of the granting of unlawful aid

The High Court can issue an injunction or an order of prohibition to restrain a public authority from granting unlawful aid. The Court is also entitled to grant interim relief under Order 84, rule 20(7) RSC where leave to apply for judicial review has been granted.

3. Recovery of unlawful aid and illegality interest

There are no specific rules on the recovery of unlawful State aid and interest; however, action can be taken in the High Court to obtain orders for its recovery. Where the unlawful State aid is a liquidated amount, the most likely procedure for recovery is by summary proceedings under Orders 2 and 37 RSC. Relying on this procedure, the Department or other State entity seeking recovery of the aid would constitute itself as plaintiff in the proceedings by the issuing of a summary summons for service on the beneficiary. The next stage is the service of a notice of motion (supported by a grounding affidavit) seeking judgment for the liquidated amount before the Master of the High Court. If the beneficiary cannot show that it has a defence to the claim, then judgment will be entered immediately in favour of the plaintiff. If, on the other hand, the beneficiary can show a defence, the matter will proceed for hearing in the High Court. To date, there are no decided cases regarding the recovery of unlawful aid in Ireland. However there have been reports of one case in which recovery was sought; this was a case in which the Kingdom of Belgium, as plaintiff, instituted proceedings in the Irish High Court against Ryanair for the recovery of certain grants that had been advanced to Ryanair in connection with its operations at Charleroi Airport, which the European Commission had subsequently found to be incompatible aid. Ryanair challenged the Commission decision before the General Court and, although it had failed to request the interim suspension of the Commission decision from the General Court pending the outcome of the action, it nevertheless sought a stay of the Irish recovery proceedings pending the outcome of the General Court action. In its judgment of 30 June 2006, the High Court refused this request. After Ryanair had appealed the High Court judgment to the Supreme Court, the General Court annulled the Commission's decision, thereby rendering the recovery proceedings unnecesary and Ryanair's appeal redundant.

4. Damages claims by competitors/third parties against the granting authority before the national courts

Any competitor or third party who suffers loss as a result of the grant of unlawful State aid may bring an action to recover damages in respect of that loss. There have not been any reported examples of competitors or third parties bringing such claims, but it is likely that a damages action would be taken in tort against the State (or the specific State department or entity responsible for the aid measure), that the High Court would be the forum given its general monetary jurisdiction and that proceedings would be commenced by Plenary Summons. Interim relief might be claimed in appropriate cases prior to the trial.

5. Damages claims by the beneficiary against the granting authority before the national courts

No cases have been brought before Irish courts dealing with a claim by a beneficiary against the granting authority. It might be possible for a beneficiary to bring an action in tort against the State on the basis that the State's failure to fulfil its EU law obligations (by granting aid unlawfully) had caused it loss. Alternatively, a beneficiary could counterclaim for damages during an action for recovery brought by the State.

6. Damages claims by competitors/third parties against the beneficiary before the national courts

No claims have been brought by competitors or third parties against a beneficiary before the Irish courts. It is unclear whether an action of the type contemplated by the CJEU in the judgment in the SFEI case would be possible under Irish law.

7. Interim measures taken by national judges

Judges hearing State aid cases in Ireland may choose from a wide range of interim measures, which often mirror on an interim basis the relief sought by the plaintiff. In a situation where, for example, the plaintiff argues that its competitor is in receipt of unlawful aid, the judge might order the interim suspension or recovery of the aid.

IV. Control of recovery procedure

1. Challenging the validity of a national recovery order

There is no specific procedure for challenging the validity of a national recovery order and no such cases have been heard in the Irish courts. It is possible for a beneficiary to bring a judicial review action against a State decision to recover unlawful aid. However, in practice, it is likely to be more attractive to a beneficiary to resist recovery and raise its arguments against the validity of the national recovery order during the judicial proceedings that follow.

2. Damages for failure to implement a recovery decision and infringement of law

No cases concerning this have been decided in the Irish courts. If a competitor of the beneficiary could show that it had suffered loss through the State's failure to implement a recovery decision, it might bring an action in tort against the State (or the specific department or State entity concerned) for damages to compensate that loss. Also, it could bring an action for judicial review seeking a mandatory order to force the State to recover unlawful aid; and damages could be claimed as part of that action.

V. Standing of third parties before national court

The standing of any party, whether beneficiary or third party (competitor or other), to bring judicial review proceedings is determined by whether that party has sufficient interest in the outcome of the proceedings. The burden is on the party seeking to take action to show that its interest in the outcome is sufficient to give it standing.

VI. Cooperation with EU authorities

1. Cooperation with the CJEU

There are no examples of cooperation between the Irish courts and the CJEU on matters of State aid.

2. Cooperation with the Commission

There are no examples of cooperation between the Irish courts and the European Commission on matters of State aid.

ITALY

Gianluca Belotti*

* Hogan Lovells, Rome.

I. General principles of members state's State aid law

Under Italian law, State aid may be granted by national and local authorities (namely: Regions, Provinces, Chambers of Commerce), as well as by private entities directly or indirectly controlled/financed by these public entities, without any legal obligation for independent monitoring of their compliance with State aid rules at national level.

Even the Court of Auditors, which could be entitled to carry out such an *a priori* legality assessment at least, on those decisions which lack force of law and by which State aid is granted (Articles: 100(2) of the Constitution and 3(1)c of the law 14 January 1994, No. 20) – has adopted a very low profile role in this area.

1. National authorities that are competent to grant aid and to be involved in the notification procedure

In Italy, all public authorities (central and local) may grant State aid to undertakings; the same is true of private bodies managing public resources, for example, Consorzi Fidi who has used state resources, granted to them by the Regions and the Chambers of Commerce, to support the guarantees they provide to SMEs. It is worth noting that under Italian law the latter are regarded as public bodies.

Concerning the notification procedure, a distinction must be made between national/regional State aid projects, where the grant of aid is generally governed by public law and filing is dealt with by the competent ministry/Region, and those cases where State resources are handled by private bodies, where the final grant to undertakings is generally governed by civil law and the notification procedure requirements appear to be interpreted in a more lenient manner.

2. National authorities that are competent for recovery and an overview of the procedure

The authority responsible for enforcing negative Commission decisions ordering the recovery of unlawful State aid is generally the same entity which granted the State aid.

The recovery process is usually carried out under the supervision of an Office directly attached to the Prime Minister's cabinet ("Presidenza del Consiglio dei Ministri. Dipartimento per il Coordinamento delle Politiche Comunitarie, Struttura di Missione per le Procedure di infrazione").

This office on one hand centralises and coordinates all the information necessary to comply with the recovery obligations (defining the amount granted, identifying the beneficiaries) and, on the other hand, informs the Commission about the progress of the recovery procedure.

In cases where the unlawful State aid has been granted by local bodies, the office must liaise with the local authorities in order for them to issue an act requesting the recovery of the aid. The local authorities may be Regions, Provinces, Chambers of Commerce, regional social security units or others, depending on which local authority has granted the aid.

However, if aid is not recovered, the Office does not benefit from any powers enabling them to force the local authorities to act promptly in securing recovery.

II. Identification of State aid issues at national level

Under Italian law, there is no specific authority charged with ensuring *a priori* compliance with State aid rules. It is worth noting that the vast majority of recent State aid has been granted by local public entities, namely Regions, who enjoy significant autonomy from the central authorities. During recent months, local bodies have awarded State aid to companies largely on the basis of the General Block exemption Regulation ("GBER") of 6 August 2008 (EC Regulation No 800/2008), which to some extent has made it even easier to grant State aid, since there are no monitoring requirements and, until now, aid granted under the GBER has never been challenged before the national courts.

Through the Block exemption Regulations, a Member State can grant whole categories of aid without first notifying them to the European Commission. GBER provides for a simpler and more coordinated text that makes State aid compliance quicker and easier for the local authorities.

Furthermore, unlike some other EU Member States, there is no central entity within Italy tasked with coordinating aid projects before their implementation in order to verify that State aid rules are complied with.

The sole control is a central body in charge of EU infringement proceedings, which also covers the monitoring of the recovery of unlawful State aid, and which is directly attached to the Prime Minister's cabinet ("Presidenza del Consiglio dei Ministri, Dipartimento per il Coordinamento delle Politiche Comunitarie, Struttura di Missione per le Procedure d'infrazione).

1. State aid compliance by national legislator and/or the executive

As with every EU policy, the State (central State) is responsible for implementing State aid rules at national level. The State is in charge of notifying all aid measures to the Commission, namely aid schemes and individual aid and every modification thereof, including projects designed by local authorities.

However, the notification procedure is not always centralised: usually, local entities send details of their State aid project to the Italian Permanent Representation in Brussels in order for it to be forwarded to the Commission.

When elaborating State aid projects, local authorities are only subject to those general principles enabling State aid rules to be respected at Community level. State aid that will be granted under the Block exemptions Regulations are adopted by local entities without being subject to any compliance checks before their implementation.

Despite several efforts made in the recent past by the central authorities, there is currently no reliable system to verify whether the threshold relating to the cumulating principle has been met or exceeded.

2. State aid compliance by national judges and/or the national competition authority (NCA)

Only national courts are allowed to carry out an *ex post* identification of State aid and compliance, when formally requested to do so by an applicant. Actions may be brought by an individual before the administrative and/or civil (including commercial and labour) courts, depending on the form of the act which is challenged.

The administrative courts have jurisdiction at first and last resort for actions concerning the validity of decrees by which State aid was granted (see, for example, Administrative Supreme Court, IV Division, 30.9.2008, N.° 4692, Federchimica v. Ministero delle Politiche Agricole e Forestali; Administrative Supreme Court, VI Division, 25.6.2007, N.° 2588, Aviolamp Giannelli G. di Schito Lucia & C. s.a.a. v. Ministero dello Sviluppo Economico). Civil courts have jurisdiction when State aid is granted via a special agreement or other private act (sale of land, capital increase, State guarantee and marketing promotion). Actions before the Courts are generally dealt with within two to three years; however, for suspension requests, decisions are usually taken within three to four weeks.

It is worth noting that under Italian law, in order to obtain a suspension decision, the applicant must give strong evidence to the court that both (i) the State aid is unlawful, (ii) it would suffer an irreparable damage should the suspension request be rejected.

The Italian Competition Authority ("Autorità Garante della Concorrenza e del Mercato") is not competent to apply Article 107 and 108 TFEU.

III. Unlawful aid and judicial review

Any individual who can demonstrate a sufficient interest is entitled to commence court proceedings, before the Constitutional, Civil, Administrative and Auditors courts and the Tax Commission, claiming that the challenged aid should be regarded as unlawful and must be recovered according to Article 108(3) TFEU.

In the context of actions lodged before the civil and administrative courts, an individual may also ask for an interim decision on the suspension of the unlawfull aid, as well as applying for damages when they can prove that they have suffered an economic prejudice attributable to the contested aid (Court of First Instance of Roma, 27.1.2006, injunction 27.1.2006, Air One v. Alitalia).

The competent jurisdiction is mainly dependent on the nature of the act enabling the aid to be granted.

1. General powers of the national courts concerning the direct effect of Article 108(3) TFEU

a. Actions brought before the administrative courts

Most actions are brought before the administrative courts because State aid measures are usually granted through acts governed by public law. This entails applicants bringing an action to annul a State decision or measure involving State aid.

The complainant must lodge a submission before a regional administrative court ("TAR – Tribunale Amministrativo Regionale") demanding that the decision be annulled, proving that either the aid was given to a competitor without being previously authorised or that it does not comply with relevant GBER criteria (see for example regional Administrative Court of Lazio, III Division, 17.5.2007, N.°5138, Società Aeroporti Catania v. Ministero dei Trasporti e dell'Economia e delle Finanze, Alitalia Linee Aeree). Should the TAR reject the application, then the claimant can appeal to the Administrative Supreme Court ("Consiglio di Stato").

Before the administrative courts in Italy, it is quite common for a request for suspension to be lodged by the applicant, aimed at obtaining a stay of execution against the administrative act pending final judgment. The interim application is generally filed together with the petition and the court will discuss whether to grant a stay of execution in a single hearing ("Camera di Consiglio") with the possibility for the other parties involved (i.e. the defendant or other third parties) to file a defence (or other documents). The ensuing court order is subject to appeal before the Administrative Supreme Court.

Orders granting interim relief are only issued when certain criteria are satisfied:

(a) there is a *prima facie* case ("*fumus boni juris*"); and
(b) the applicant proves that there is an imminent risk of material damage resulting from the execution of the contested decision (*periculumin mora*) (see Regional Administrative Court of Lombardia (Brescia Division), 21.3.2006, N.°577, Sacbo Società per l'Aeroporto civile di Bergamo SpA v. Ministero Infrastrutture e Trasporti, ENAC, Alitalia SpA).

The claimant could also bring an action before the same administration who granted the aid, within a two month period running from the date of publication or notification of the contested decision, asking the body to withdraw the previous decision as it has breached the standstill clause under Article 108(3) TFEU. If the Administration refuses to withdraw its decision, the claimant can challenge this refusal before the competent administrative court. This action should be brought within two months of the notification of the refusal.

Under Italian law, there is no specific regime for cases of State liability. If the claimant challenges the State's liability, it has to do that within five years from the date on which the alleged damage occurred.

b. *Actions are brought before the civil courts*

In some cases the civil courts can decide about State aid. Civil court proceedings are governed by the Italian Code of Civil procedure and by the Italian Civil Code. The civil courts have jurisdiction when a private party claims against another private party or a public body, especially regarding the compatibility of a recovery action brought by competitors against the beneficiary of State aid (Court of first Instance of Sassari, 26.1.2009, N.°3863/08 (Order), AirOne SpA v. Ryanair Ltd e Sogeal SpA).

2. Prevention of the granting of unlawful aid

Under Italian rules, there is no *a priori* control to prevent the grant of unlawful State aid. There is no specific national authority obliged to ensure that Article 108(3) TFEU and Article 14 of Regulation (EC) No 659/1999 are complied with.

Once an aid measure is found to be unlawful, prevention of the grant can only be sought before the national courts through actions for annulment of the act (e.g.: formal decree, private agreement) on which the aid measure is based.

3. Recovery of unlawful aid and interest

The national authorities which have granted the aid are bound to recover the nominal amount of unlawful aid granted, together with the financial advantages resulting from the premature implementation of that aid. The purpose of recovery is, according to the Court, to restore the situation existing prior to the grant of the unlawful and incompatible State aid; as a matter of fact, by repaying the State aid the beneficiary forfeits the advantage that it had enjoyed over its competitors on the market and the situation prior to payment of the measures is restored. In order to effectively restore the situation existing before the payment of the unlawful State aid, all the financial advantages resulting from the granted measures have to be recovered. These recovery orders are often challenged by the beneficiary before the administrative or civil chambers (including labour) of the national courts, depending on the form of the recovery order and national rules on jurisdiction.

For example: illegal aid in the area of social security is usually recovered by INPS ("Istituto Nazionale della Previdenza Sociale"); the beneficiary can challenge the INPS recovery order before the Labour court, which enjoys exclusive jurisdiction on INPS related issues (see for example Court of First Instance of Reggio Calabria, Labour Division, 11.2.2008, M.C.T. SpA v. INPS, SCCI SpA and Equitalia Etr SpA, or Court of First Instance of Brescia, Labour Division, 8.7.2008, N.°212/08, Brandt Italia SpA v. INPS, ESATRI SpA, and Court of First Instance of Rome, Labour Division, 21.12.2007, Ericsson Telecomunicazioni SpA v. INPS and SCCI SpA).

Unless the recovery procedure follows a negative decision from the Commission, the national courts can ask, at the request of a party, for a preliminary ruling from the CJEU on whether or not the contested measure should be considered as a State aid in the light of established jurisprudence. However, national courts appear to be reluctant to act on such requests.

4. Damages claims by competitors/third parties against the granting authority before the national courts

Any individual (mainly competitors) is entitled to claim for damages as long as they can prove and quantify the amount of economic prejudice they suffered as a result of the illegal granting of a State aid to a competitor. The action for damages may be directed against the State (rectius: the central or local public body who gave the aid) as well as against the beneficiary company for unfair competition, provided that it can be proved that the contested commercial behaviour qualified as unfair competition is directly linked to the aid (see again Court of First Instance of Sassari, 26.1.2009, N.°3863/08 (Order), AirOne SpA v. Ryanair Ltd e Sogeal SpA).

The possibility for a competitor/third party to obtain compensation due to the liability of the granting authority is closely related to the existence of: (i) a real and quantifiable damage to the claimant; (ii) the injustice of the damage; (iii) the negligent or intentional behaviour of the granting authority and (iv) a causal link between the damage suffered by the competitor/third party and the unlawful behaviour of the authority.

Under Italian rules, the claimant is free to commence legal action without being obliged to first introduce an administrative request to be compensated for the loss. Before the administrative court, such an action is ancillary to the main action by which the annulment of the contested act is requested: while the latter must be commenced within two months of the adoption of the contested act on which the unlawful aid is based, the former may be commenced within the ordinary limitation period for compensation of damages, that is to say, within five years from the granting of the aid.

To date there is no case in which the State has been ordered to pay damages to competitors/third parties as a result of its liability for the granting of unlawful State aid.

5. Damages claims by the beneficiary against the granting authority before the national courts

To date, no beneficiary has claimed damages from the State for the unlawful granting of State aid which the company has been obliged to repay. However, legally speaking, nothing prevents the beneficiary from acting against the granting authority and claiming compensation, as long as the company can evidence the damages which were suffered due to the implementation of the unlawful aid.

6. Damages claims by competitors/third parties against the beneficiary before the national courts

Under Italian rules actions engaging the extra contractual liability of the beneficiary of unlawful aid can only be brought before the civil courts.

In line with Court of Justice jurisprudence, the liability of the beneficiary cannot be derived from the mere infringement of Article 108(3) TFEU, but will necessarily have to be based upon unfair competition under Article 2598 of the Italian Civil Code.

This means that, unlike for actions for damages brought against the granting authority/ public administration, actions against the beneficiary of the unlawful aid are feasible as long as it can be proved that, thanks to the unlawful aid, the beneficiary company implemented unfair competition practices pursuant to Article 2598 of the Italian Civil Code, which caused damage to competitors. In other words, in order for a competitor to win a case before the civil courts and to be awarded compensation, it will not be sufficient to prove that the beneficiary company had received an unlawful State aid.

The civil court determines: (i) whether the beneficiary benefited from the unlawful State aid; (ii) whether the beneficiary acted in a way that is contrary to the fair competition rules under the Italian Civil Code and jurisprudence; and (iii) evaluates the amount of damages to be granted to its competitors if they can prove and quantify their loss.

Until now, claims for unfair competition have rarely been invoked in the context of public procurement cases, despite the fact that the beneficiary of unlawful aid could be excluded from the tender procedure, as well as being sued for damages for unfair competition by unsuccessful bidders, arguing that the selected bidder had been able to make the best offer because of aid previously granted.

7. Interim measures taken by national judges

Any individual showing sufficient interest is allowed, in addition to the main action contesting the merit of the aid, to request interim measures with the aim of preventing the granting of alleged unlawful State aid to competitors.

Nevertheless, the unlawfulness of the aid in itself is not enough to obtain an interim measure; two further conditions must be satisfied: (i) the risk of an imminent damage (urgency) in respect of the contested right (*periculum in mora*); and (ii) a *prima facie* case (*fumus boni iuris*) (see again Court of First Instance of Rome, 27.1.2006, injunction 27.1.2006, Air One v. Alitalia).

IV. Control of recovery procedure

1. Rules applicable to recovery

Once an aid is found to be unlawful and incompatible with the Internal Market, the Commission must order the Member State concerned to recover the aid unduly granted.

Improving the enforcement of State aid decisions is a shared responsibility between the Commission and the Member States. The Commission has a duty to order Member States to recover State aid (their main challenge is to ensure that recovery decisions are complete and clear), while the Member States are responsible for the implementation of the decision; they must adopt all necessary measures to recover the aid without delay.

On 26 October 2007, the Commission adopted a notice on the implementation of decisions ordering Member States to recover unlawful and incompatible State aid (OJ 2007 C272/4). The notice provides guidance to Member States on how to achieve a more immediate and effective execution of recovery decisions. Effective and prompt recovery is essential to eliminate distortions of competition resulting from illegal and incompatible aid.

According to the consolidated jurisprudence of the CJEU, the Member State to which a decision requiring recovery of unlawful aid is addressed is obliged under Article 289 TFEU to take all measures necessary to ensure implementation of that decision. They are free to decide the best way to satisfy this obligation.

Specific legislation regarding the procedure by which public entities may enforce negative Commission decisions and recovery obligation does not exist under the Italian legal system. It is generally the duty of the authorities granting the unlawful State aid to take necessary and appropriate actions provided for under national law in order to achieve immediate and effective enforcement of the Commission decision (see for example Provincial Tax Commission of Modena, sezione VI, 10.3.2008).

National judges might be requested to examine either an appeal for the annulment of the national order to recover the unlawful measures (following the Commission's decision) or a third party appeal for compensation of the loss suffered as a result of the failure to implement the recovery decision.

In principle, when an aid is declared unlawful following a negative Commission decision, the Administration will first ask the beneficiary of the obligation to reimburse the aid. When an aid is declared unlawful following the judgment of a national court, the granting authorities are enjoined by the courts to recover the aid from the beneficiary.

a. Recovery by the State

In Italy, the applicable recovery procedure is normally determined by the nature of the measure underlying the granting of the aid. Thus, several procedures can be used to pursue the recovery of unlawful and incompatible aid: legislation should be adopted if the effects of the State aid are general and widespread, or when a measure has been granted through a legislative measure.

On the contrary, if the aid has not had a general effect, the State can use *ad hoc* measures and administrative acts. In order to implement a Commission recovery decision the State can also employ: (i) payment orders or executory acts; (ii) formal communications to the beneficiaries; and (iii) notices.

In Italy, as in any Member State, there are few traditionally recognized limits to the obligation to recover unlawful State aid: (i) the existence of exceptional circumstances that would make it absolutely impossible for the State concerned to execute the decision properly; (ii) if the recovery would be contrary to a general principle of Community law (e.g. the protection of legitimate expectation, proportionality and legal certainty which are, however, interpreted very strictly by the Court[171]); (iii) the opportunity to recover the aid is subject to a limitation period of 10 years. This period runs from the time of the award of the aid to the beneficiary.

If the undertaking concerned does not reimburse the aid, the State can seize the company's assets in the same way as other creditors under ordinary debt procedures. In the case of the insolvency or bankruptcy of the beneficiary, under Italian law State credits (unlawful State aid have to regarded as state credits) have a priority right, meaning that they have to be repaid first, before repaying other creditors.

The Administration is likely to face different types of difficulties when dealing with recovery proceedings. In order to implement negative Commission decisions ordering recovery of unlawful aid, the authorities need to identify the beneficiaries, as well as the amount of aid to be recovered. In principle, this type of information is included in the Commission decision. However, national authorities may encounter practical difficulties in the situation where several undertakings have received aid (tax scheme) or in cases where the benefit of the aid is indirect (for example, tax breaks) or where the amount granted varies considerably between beneficiaries. Moreover, if national authorities are responsible for determining the amount of State aid, disagreements with the Commission could arise as to the method of calculating the aid to be recovered.

b. Recovery by local authorities

Whenever unlawful aid has been granted by local authorities, the State does not have any power to act directly to recover it; the State generally requests and pushes local administrations to secure recovery.

However, unlike other EU Member States, there are no specific provisions stating the principle of local authority liability vis-à-vis the central State for not recovering State aid declared unlawful following a Commission decision or a court judgment, and the State can not replace local authorities in doing this.

2. Action for recovery

a. By the State

As mentioned above, the procedure for recovery of unlawful aid is quite different if the aid measure results from an administrative act or in the context of a civil law transaction.

At first instance, the State may adopt a measure similar in the form, but opposite in substance, to that granting the unlawful aid, which is then revoked; this new administrative act could be challenged by the beneficiaries before the administrative courts.

171 This exception has rarely been used. As far as the principle of "legitimate expectation" is concerned, for instance, the Court has usually considered that aid recipients normally may not have any legitimate expectations when aid is granted in breach of Article 108(3) TFEU.

Usually, the State issues a formal payment request on the basis of which it demands reimbursement of the unlawful State aid. In general, beneficiary companies resisting recovery put forward the argument that reimbursing the aid would give rise to financial difficulties and possibly bankruptcy. The principle of legitimate expectations is also sometimes referred to, i.e. that they would have expected that the public administration would have duly notified the aid measure to the Commission before implementing it.

Alternatively, in order to recover the unlawful aid, the State may be requested to bring a civil action before the national court for the annulment of the contract under which aid was granted in that it was either contrary to imperative rules, (such as Article 108(3) TFEU), or because the cause was unlawful.

b. By competitors

If the State does not promptly order recovery of the aid from the beneficiary, following either a negative Commission decision or national court judgment declaring the measure at issue as illegal, competitors can bring an action for annulment of the State's decision by which the unlawful aid was granted and apply for an injunction to order the Administration to recover the aid, or alternatively can apply directly for mandatory measures under Italian law.

Should the Administration not comply with the injunction order, issued by the administrative court, the applicant can also obtain from the administrative court a ruling that expressly requests the Administration to recover the unlawful aid ("giudizio di ottemperanza"), with the appointment of a person charged with complying with the judgment under the court's supervision ("commissario ad acta").

An action before a civil court, requesting the beneficiary to reimburse the aid to the relevant administration, can also be brought by competitors. However, unlike in the administrative courts, such an action would also be based on unfair competition. Applicants can also request the judge to order interim measures. These measures would be based upon the principle of the primacy of TFEU law over national law, so that the judge would have to set aside any national legislation or regulatory act that is contrary to Article 107 TFEU (when there is a negative Commission decision) or to Article 108(3) TFEU.

c. By beneficiaries

In Italy, the recovery of an unlawful State aid has rarely been claimed in the context of tax litigation. This is mainly due to the fact that in Italy tax is usually levied on a general basis, with no link to its final destination. Taxpayers have sometimes tried to contest the validity of a tax measure, claiming that it constituted unlawful State aid, however such claims are often dismissed by the courts.

3. Challenging the validity of national recovery order

This recovery decision/act can only be challenged before the national courts (usually the administrative chamber, but also the labour chamber) (see for example Regional Administrative Court of Sardinia, I Division, 8.6.2007, N°1204, Sardegna Lines SpA v. regione Autonoma della Sardegna) within two months of its receipt in the context of an opposition procedure (pursuant to the normal procedure). The introduction by the beneficiary of such a challenge does not usually suspend the recovery procedure under Italian law. If requested to do so, by an additional request for suspension, under new rules the court will either have to dismiss such a request, or accept it, but only in very extraordinary cases and for a limited period of time (Italian law no. 101/2008).

4. Action contesting the validity of the Commission decision

National courts – either if requested by parties or of their own volition – are always prevented from contesting the validity of the Commission decision declaring an aid as unlawful and incompatible (see again Regional Administrative Court of Sardinia, I Division, 8.6.2007, N°1204, Sardegna Lines SpA v. regione Autonoma della Sardegna).

5. Damages for failure to implement a recovery decision and infringement of TFEU law

Leaving aside actions that the Commission can take against the Member State for not complying with its order to recover unlawful State aid, competitors and third parties with sufficient interest, who can prove a loss can sue the State for failure to implement a recovery decision and for infringement of EU law under the *Francovich* and *Brasserie du Pêcheur* principles, as long as all criteria set out by the Court of Justice are fulfilled.

6. Standing of third parties before the national courts

National rules do not limit legal standing to a competitor of the beneficiary; third parties may have *locus standi* before the Italian national courts as long as they show a real and specific interest in acting. In assessing such an interest, the Italian courts usually adopt a very strict approach.

Like competitors, third parties affected by the grant of unlawful State aid have several courses of action open to them before the national courts: (i) seek the annulment of the decision by which the act is/would be granted, (ii) seek an injunction, (iii) ask for the recovery of the unlawful aid, or (iv) ask for damages, as long as they can prove they suffered such loss.

V. Cooperation with EU authorities

1. Cooperation with the CJEU

The principal instrument of cooperation between a Member State and the CJEU in proceedings concerning State aid is represented by the possibility for a national court to raise a preliminary question pursuant to Article 267 TFEU. In Italy, any court or tribunal, including the administrative and civil courts, are entitled to make a reference to the Court of Justice concerning the validity of a Commission decision declaring existing aid compatible with the Internal Market or questioning if the disputed measure or act constitutes State aid (see Constitutional Court, 15.4.2008, N.°103 and 102/08, Presidenza del Consiglio dei Ministri v. Regione Sardegna, case C-169/08; Court of First Instance of Nocera Inferiore, 20.7.2007, Socoetà Lodato Gennaro & C. v. Istituto Nazionale Previdenza Sociale/SCC, Court of First Instance of Genova, 16.6.2007, RAI v. PTV Programmazioni Televisive, N.°35 State aid project; Court of First Instance of Genova, 9.1.2007, Autostarda dei Fiori SpA e AISCAT v. Governo della Repubblica Italiana/ Ministero delle Infrastrutture – Ministero dell'Economia e delle Finanze, aid project and Court of First Instance of Roma, 14.6.2006, Nuova Agricast Srl v. Ministero delle Attività produttive). The Supreme Court (Corte di Cassazione) is quite familiar with requests for a preliminary ruling (for example see Supreme Court, Fiscal Division, 8.2.2008, N.° 3033, Ministero delle Finanze v. F.M. and Order of 17.2.2006, N.° 3525, Ministero delle Finanze v. F.M, Case C- 80/08 and C-79/08).

This was the setting for the CJEU's landmark decision in the Lucchini case (CJEU 18 July 2007 in Case C-119/05), where the CJEU ruled that Community law precludes the application even of a provision of national law, such as Article 2909 of the Italian Civil Code, which seeks to lay down the principle of *res judicata*, in so far as the application of that provision prevents the recovery of State aid granted in breach of Community law which has been found to be incompatible with the Internal Market in a final decision of the Commission.

2. Cooperation with the Commission

Italy, as with any Member State, must respect the principle underlying Article 4 TEU, which imposes a duty of genuine cooperation between EU Member States and Community institutions, with a view to overcoming difficulties whilst fully observing the Community Law provisions, particularly those provisions on State aid.

In this regard, it is strongly recommended that when a Member State encounters difficulties in the effective implementation of the Commission decision, it must actively cooperate with the Commission to resolve such issues, and to avoid a sentence condemning the inefficiency of its behaviour. It is also strongly recommended that the Commission react quickly to such requests. This, it seems, has not been the case for some requests coming from the Supreme Court ("Corte di Cassazione") in recent years.

VI. Trends – Reforms – Recommendations

A recent important legislative innovation is set out in Law of 6 June 2008, no. 101, which converts into law, with modifications, the legislative decree of 8 April 2008. It contains important provisions for the implementation of EU obligations and the execution of judgments of the CJEU designed to speed up recovery proceedings. Under this law, a request for suspension submitted to the Court by the company requested to pay back unlawful State aid is made subject to much more stringent rules than in ordinary cases.

It goes without saying that, in order to improve the entire State aid legal system at national level, as well as to improve the functioning and effectiveness of recovery procedures, a national, independent surveillance authority would be strongly welcomed; one which would be charged with monitoring both the granting and the recovery of State aid; and also empowered with strong injunction powers vis-à-vis those national authorities granting State aid and acting for its recovery.

Latvia

Andris Vitols*,
Martinš Tarlaps, Sandija Novicka**

---

* Lawyer – linguist at the European Parliament, Brussels.

** Raidla Lejins & Norcous, Riga.

I. General principles of Latvia's State aid law

The architecture of the Latvian State aid management system is compact and transparent. It is based on a framework law – Law On Control of Aid for Commercial Activity (the "Aid Control Law").

The provisions of the regulations in the State aid field have been implemented into Latvian law through this Aid Control Law.

A number of regulations arising from the Aid Control Law and dealing with specific procedural and technical aspects of it (e.g. declaration of small and medium size enterprises, granting and gathering data on *de minimis* aid, declaration of aid to the Commission, and the provision of information to the Ministry of Finance about activities carried out by aid providers in the domain of public services) have been passed by the Cabinet of Ministers.

1. National authorities competent to grant aid and to be involved in the notification procedure

According to the Aid Control Law, the central role in the granting of aid and in its notification to the Commission is allocated to the Latvian Ministry of Finance. In addition, the Permanent Representation of the Republic of Latvia to the EU is involved in the notification process to the Commission as an intermediary.

According to the Aid Control Law, the Ministry of Finance:

- performs the initial assessment of the planned aid programme or individual aid project submitted by the public authorities; this assessment also applies to planned amendments in existing aid programmes or individual aid projects;
- sends notifications to the Commission, through Latvia's Permanent Representation to the EU, regarding information associated with aid programmes or individual aid projects;
- sends summary information to the Commission via Latvia's Permanent Representation to the EU, regarding aid which has been provided in accordance with the conditions in Commission Regulation (EC) No 68/2001, No 70/2001, No 2204/2002, No 363/2004, No 364/2004 and No 1628/2006, and other Commission regulations issued on the basis of Council Regulation No 994/98; and
- prepares an annual report regarding aid provided for commercial activities.

2. National authorities competent to recover aid and an overview of the procedure

Recovery of unlawful aid is initiated by the public authority that granted the respective aid to the beneficiary. However, according to the Aid Control Law, the public authority is only entitled to initiate recovery upon receipt of the Commission's decision ordering such recovery.

If unlawful aid has been granted to the beneficiary by an administrative decision of a public authority, recovery shall be exercised in accordance with the procedures specified in the Administrative Procedure Law. A dispute or appeal of the Commission decision shall not suspend the operation thereof, except in the case where, in accordance with Article 273(4) TFEU, the decision taken by the Commission is appealed to the CJEU and it has satisfied a submitted claim regarding the suspension of the implementation of that decision in accordance with Article 278 TFEU.

If the aid has been granted to the beneficiary in accordance with a contract governed by civil law, the recovery of unlawful aid and other disputes associated with such contract shall be resolved according to the procedures specified in the Civil Procedure Law and other regulatory enactments.

Practically, the beneficiary of unlawful aid should appeal to the CJEU against the Commission's recovery decision under Articles 263(4) and (5) TFEU. The Commission's recovery decision cannot be contested before the national court if the person concerned has failed to observe the two-month limitation period for instituting proceedings against the recovery decision passed by the Commission specified in Article 263(5) TFEU.

As no recovery procedures have been initiated in Latvia so far, one can only presume that recovery would in any case be exercised in accordance with the Administrative Procedure Law. Such a presumption seems feasible, as any recovery action by national authorities may be exercised on the basis of a decision by the respective public authority based on the Commission's recovery decision, irrespective of whether the unlawful aid has been granted through an administrative act or a contract governed by civil law.

II. Identification of State aid issues at national level

1. State aid compliance by the national legislator and/or the executive power

There is no specific legislative *ex ante* control procedure by which national authorities could try to avoid granting unlawful State aid. However, prior to submitting draft legislation to the parliament, the Cabinet of Ministers ensures that the respective draft has passed a "round of conciliation" between the relevant ministries and State bodies. In particular, the Ministry of Finance is obliged to give its opinion on every single draft received in the area of its competence. As State aid issues fall within its exclusive competence, it has the right and the duty to examine legal drafts originating from other public authorities on their compatibility with the State aid provisions effective in Latvia (these include national regulatory enactments as well as regulatory enactments of the EU). Within the parliament, Legal Counsel for the Saeima (Latvian parliament) performs an *ex ante* control of the draft legislation to some extent.

Similarly, there is no *ex post* non-judicial control for dealing specifically with State aid issues.

2. State aid compliance by national judges and/or the national competition authority (NCA)

The Latvian Competition Board only deals with the application of Articles 101 and 102 TFEU. Thus, it has no competence in respect of State aid.

Since there are no court cases dealing with the application of State aid law, one can only theoretically assess the eventual procedures that could come before the court. It is most likely that the administrative courts would deal with cases concerning State aid – in most cases State aid is awarded by an administrative act issued by a public authority, and even in cases where State aid is awarded by a contract governed by civil law, the conclusion of such a contract on behalf of a public body, in most cases, would be based on an administrative act.

It is possible that third parties could bring a claim before the civil courts in Latvia, by seeking the annulment of an agreement by which State aid has been awarded to their competitors. Another option would be to claim indemnification for losses incurred due to the granting of an unlawful State aid to a competitor. However, it is not clear how the civil courts will perceive such claims. Proceedings on those grounds would be complicated and the outcome difficult to predict.

It should be noted that there is a significant difference between the way in which the burden of proof is distributed between the parties in administrative and in civil proceedings. Administrative proceedings are based on the principle of an objective investigation – the court takes an active position in order to achieve a just outcome in the case (e.g. the court is entitled to give instructions and guidance to the parties involved, and to collect evidence of its own volition). In civil proceedings, on the contrary, the determining principle is one of competition between the parties – the court takes a passive position and bases its judgment on the law and evidence provided by the parties during the hearing of the case.

Thus, from a claimant's perspective, administrative proceedings are much more favourable compared to civil proceedings, as, in the latter proceedings, the burden of proof lies exclusively with the claimant.

Latvian courts have proved reluctant to make preliminary references to the CJEU under Article 267 TFEU. Therefore, it is impossible to foresee whether the Latvian courts will make use of Article 267 TFEU in cases concerning State aid.

III. Unlawful aid and judicial review

1. General powers of the national courts concerning the application of Article 108(3) TFEU

If a public authority acts in breach of Article 108(3) TFEU, the court may, upon submission of an appropriate application by the Commission or a third party, adopt an interim measure in the form of a court decision replacing the administrative act in issue, or obliging or prohibiting performance of a certain action by the respective public authority, within a period prescribed by the court.

2. Prevention of the granting of unlawful aid

Under Latvian law, it is important to distinguish whether aid has been awarded by an administrative act or by contract governed by civil law, as different procedural regulations would apply for contesting the different awards.

In the case of an aid scheme, there is a substantial difference between the act on which the State aid regime is based and the act by which aid under that scheme is awarded to a beneficiary. The former usually takes the form of a law or regulation by the Cabinet of Ministers and, as such, would be of general application. The latter usually would take the form of an individually applicable administrative act. Regulatory measures of general application cannot be contested directly before the administrative or civil courts as they fall within the exclusive competence of the Constitutional Court ("Satversmes tiesa").

The granting or payment of an unlawful aid is avoided by obliging all granting authorities to notify the Ministry of Finance of their intention to grant aid, in accordance with the procedure set out in the Aid Control Law.

When contesting an unlawful aid before the national courts on the grounds of a procedural breach, individuals may rely on provisions of the Aid Control Law, according to which, the authority granting the aid is obliged to inform the Ministry of Finance of its intention to grant the aid to the individual(s), and the Ministry of Finance is obliged to notify the aid in issue to the Commission. However, reference to the applicable Community provisions, in addition to those of the Aid Control Law, would be useful in supporting a claim.

3. Recovery of unlawful aid and interest

Recovery of unlawful aid by a public authority would, presumably, be in the form of an administrative act obliging the beneficiary to repay the unlawful aid and interest, if any. Such an administrative act would, most probably, lead to administrative proceedings before the administrative court.

In the case of a public authority's reluctance to recover unlawful aid, competitors and/or third parties could institute "horizontal proceedings". However, such proceedings would presumably also be in the form of an administrative procedure – the respective competitor or third party would ask the granting authority to pass a decision by which the unlawful aid is recovered from the beneficiary, and a negative decision by the relevant public authority in respect of such a request would be contested before the administrative courts.

4. Damages claims by competitors/third parties against the granting authority before the national courts

Damages claims against the granting authority would have to be brought in accordance with the Law on Indemnification of Losses Caused by Public Authorities. However, there is no substantial case-law relating to the application of this law.

5. Damages claims by the beneficiary against the granting authority before the national courts

Damages claims against the granting authority would have to be brought in accordance with the Law on Indemnification of Losses Caused by Public Authorities. However, there is no substantial case-law relating to the application of this law.

6. Damages claims by competitors/third parties against the beneficiary before the national courts

To date, as there is no case law concerning damages claims against the beneficiary of an unlawful aid. It is impossible to predict, therefore, the court's attitude to such claims. Presumably, damages claims would have to be based on the non-contractual liability provisions of Latvian law.

Civil proceedings in Latvia may last for several years if a case is heard by all instances of the judiciary.

7. Interim measures taken by national judges

There is no case-law relating to interim measures developed by the courts in State aid related cases.

IV. Control of recovery procedure

1. Challenging the validity of national recovery order

A national recovery order would usually be challenged in accordance with the procedure described in the Administrative Procedure Law.

An administrative act may be contested by its addressee or by a third party, whose rights or legal interests are restricted by the relevant administrative act and who has not been invited to participate in the proceedings as a third party. Thus a failure to act, or improper action (both of which are subject to the Administrative Procedure Law), can also be challenged, *inter alia*, by third parties.

It would take approximately three to four years for a case to be heard by all the instances of administrative court and, therefore, to obtain a final and undisputable decision, it would take approximately three to four years.

If an unlawful aid has not been recovered effectively from the beneficiary, third parties may also rely on the administrative procedure in order to ensure that the relevant public authority complies fully with its obligation to recover unlawful aid effectively.

The usual time frame for an appeal for judicial review is within one month of the date of the court's decision in the relevant case.

2. Damages for failure to implement a recovery decision and infringement of EU law

Assuming that the State fails to implement a decision of the Commission on unlawful aid, a third party could use the same procedure as described above to challenge the Member State's failure to act.

V. Standing of third parties before national courts

Regarding the *locus standi* of a competitor or third party, the Administrative Procedure Law contains only one condition to be fulfilled in order to obtain standing before the national courts – that the rights or legal interests of that competitor or third party have been restricted. It is for the court to decide in each individual case whether this condition has been met.

VI. Cooperation with EU authorities

There is no case-law concerning cooperation with the CJEU and with the Commission.

VII. Trends – reforms – recommendations

It is a common impression in Latvia that the public authorities and individuals are insufficiently informed in relation to the notion of State aid and its legal regulation on both a national and Community level.

Application of the Aid Control Law is relatively rare. It is possible that regulatory enactments and many public authority decisions contain provisions which, under the Community regulations, could be regarded as granting State aid, or even unlawful State aid, to certain persons or groups of persons. However, since competitors and third parties are not aware of their legal right to institute proceedings contesting such regulatory provisions and administrative acts, no case law concerning State aid issues has developed in Latvia so far.

Having said that, it would be useful for the Commission to initiate an information campaign in Latvia by which public authorities and individuals are informed of State aid rules at

Community and national level. It would certainly improve the awareness of the general public of State aid related issues and would help to obviate distortion of competition through the inaccurate application, or even deliberate breach, of State aid rules and regulations.

LITHUANIA

Irmantas Norkus, Ilona Janciauskaite*

* Raidla Lejins & Norcous, Vilnius.

I. General principles of member state's state aid law

1. National authorities competent to grant aid and to be involved in the notification procedure

In the Republic of Lithuania the following national authorities are competent to grant State aid and to be involved in the notification procedure:

- the Ministry of Economy, which pursues strategic national economic development objectives and is focused on the promotion of innovations, improved administration of the EU structural funds, the development of small and medium-sized business and ensured energy safety;
- the Ministry of Agriculture, which is responsible for the administration of land, food, agriculture and rural development; and
- the municipalities.

The Competition Council (the "Competition Council") is also involved in the notification procedure. As of 1 May 2004, pursuant to Article 48 of the Law on Competition of the Republic of Lithuania (the "Law on Competition"), the Competition Council is a coordinating institution for State aid matters when EU State aid rules are applicable. The Competition Council gathers and stores State aid related information, and consults State aid recipients and providers on the completion of notifications and on other State aid questions. Furthermore, the Competition Council performs an analysis of State aid projects, and coordinates the submission of State aid notifications and other State aid related information and yearly reports to the Commission.

2. National authorities competent to recover aid and an overview of the procedure

Decisions of national authorities granting State aid may be appealed to the Vilnius County Administrative Court. The decisions of the Vilnius County Administrative Court may be further appealed to the Supreme Administrative Court. The decisions of the Supreme Administrative Court are final and are not subject to appeal.

Any undertakings whose interests have been violated by a breach of State aid rules can apply to the civil courts for compensation of loss and for restitution. As a general rule, competition law related damages actions may be brought to the Vilnius County Court as a court of first instance. The decisions of the Vilnius County Court may be appealed to the Lithuanian Court of Appeal. The decisions of the Supreme Court of the Republic of Lithuania are final and not subject to appeal.

II. Identification of State aid issues at national level

1. State aid compliance by the national legislator and/or the executive

Prior to the accession of the Republic of Lithuania to the EU on 1 May 2004, State aid control was enforced under the Law on Monitoring of State aid to Undertakings of the Republic of Lithuania.

As of 1 May 2004, EU State aid principles have been fully applied in the Republic of Lithuania and pursuant to Article 48 of the Law on Competition, the Competition Council is a coordinating institution for State aid matters when EU State aid rules are applicable.

Projects of national State aid are discussed with the representatives of the Competition Council prior to submission to the Government of the Republic of Lithuania. The Competition Council examines national laws, provides recommendatory conclusions and proposals with reference to compliance with EU State aid rules.

National rules on notification of State aid are established in the ruling of the Government of the Republic of Lithuania No. 1136 "Concerning Approval of Rules on Performance of Expertise of State aid Projects, Provision of Conclusions and Recommendations to Providers of State aid, Submission of State aid Notifications And Other State aid Related Information to the Commission And Other Interested Institutions" dated 6 September 2004.

Overall, national legislation on State aid rules is very limited in scope. As mentioned above, despite one article and a few procedural rulings, Lithuanian practices are based on the application of EU State aid rules.

It is noteworthy that the entire territory of the Republic of Lithuania is attributed to those regions to be supported pursuant to Article 107(3)(a) TFEU. The territory of the Republic of Lithuania is considered to be one of those regions where the standard of living is uncommonly low or the rate of unemployment is high, and therefore, significant amounts of State aid can be assigned in order to promote investment and the development of the region.

2. State aid compliance by national judges and/or the national competition authority (NCA)

The Competition Council is competent to assess applications for State aid. Pursuant to requests presented by State aid providers, and prior to submission of the notification to the Commission, the Competition Council conducts an analysis of the State aid project. The Competition Council prepares conclusions and recommendations for the State aid provider on the compliance of the proposed State aid with the EU law requirements within a period not exceeding two months. Following the completion of the evaluation, the Competition Council submits notification to the Commission within ten working days.

The Competition Council may perform an analysis of the State aid project when it has reasonable doubts that the project complies with the requirements of EU State aid principles, even though the provider has not requested additional analysis. In such cases, provided the authority competent for granting State aid does not object, notification is filed upon completion of that evaluation.

Conclusions and recommendations of the Competition Council on the compliance of the project with EU State aid rules are not binding on the provider of State aid. In addition, the State aid provider has the right to request that the Competition Council files notification with the Commission at any stage of the evaluation process.

Even though the national courts are authorized to evaluate whether a certain measure should be considered State aid under Article 107(1) TFEU, the analysis of court practice reveals that there is still a long way to go for State aid cases to be examined in the courts of the Republic of Lithuania. It should be noted that parties refer to State aid rules in their claims; however, the courts usually consider the State aid rules to be inapplicable and examine the case by applying other laws. Therefore, upon review of the application of State aid rules by the courts of the Republic of Lithuania, it may be concluded that there are only a few cases in which the concept of State aid is touched upon by applicants, defendants or interested third parties, and that this is not examined by the courts, who refuse to address the concept.

It is noteworthy that there has only been one case examined by the Constitutional Court of the Republic of Lithuania and a few very recent cases on restructuring aid where the courts, as one of the arguments under consideration, analyse the concept of State aid. As a result, at this stage it is still very difficult to draw conclusions about the awareness of State aid rules within the national courts.

III. Unlawful aid and judicial review

1. General powers of the national courts concerning the direct effect of Article 108(3) TFEU

There is no case-law in which the national courts of the Republic of Lithuania have adopted any measures to cease the infringement of Article 108(3) TFEU.

2. Prevention of the granting of unlawful aid

Providers of State aid are obliged to inform the Competition Council in advance about all intentions to grant State aid by filling out the forms established by the relevant EU regulations. The Competition Council examines whether the notification has been properly completed and all necessary documents attached. Within 10 working days of receipt, eligible notifications are passed to the European Commission through the office of the Lithuanian Permanent Representation. If the Competition Council determines that the notification is ineligible, it informs the State aid provider that the notification should be amended and indicates particular flaws.

Since 1 October 2005, the Register of Granted State aid has been in operation and is administered by the Competition Council. Information about granted *de minimis* aid, and State aid pursuant to other regulations, is gathered and stored in this register. The administration of the register contributes to ensuring that the requirements established in the *de minimis* regulations are adhered to. National authorities that are competent to grant State aid are under an obligation to check in the register that the allowed threshold for *de minimis* State aid has not been exceeded prior to granting *de minimis* State aid to a particular undertaking. National authorities competent for granting State aid have the obligation to enter data about granted *de minimis* State aid in the database of the register.

When, according to relevant regulations, the Member States are obliged to inform the Commission of aid, pursuant to Lithuanian Law, national authorities have to submit the same form to the Competition Council prior to adopting their decisions. When, pursuant to EU rules the Member States are under an obligation to submit reports to the Commission concerning the implementation of certain decisions, the national authorities are obliged to provide the Competition Council with sufficient information to assess whether the aid is compatible with relevant provisions (even though there may be no obligation to inform the Commission about the decision to grant State aid).

In the case of the Constitutional Court of the Republic of Lithuania concerning Constitutionality of the Law on Lithuanian National Radio and Television (21 December 2006, Case no. 30/03), the Constitutional Court examined, amongst other issues, the compliance of analysed provisions with State aid rules. The Constitutional Court successfully distinguished the application of Article 106 and Article 107 TFEU with reference to aid granted to providers of public services. The Constitutional Court defined the public broadcaster as a provider of public services and applied the *Altmark* test (Case C-280/00, Altmark Trans GmbH, Regierungspräsidium Magdeburg v. Nahverkehrsgesellschaft Altmark GmbH [2003] ECR I-7747). The Constitutional Court concluded that the public broadcaster fulfilled all necessary conditions; therefore, aid for the services provided by the public broadcaster should not be assessed as State aid under Article 107 TFEU.

The Constitutional Court's analysis of the second issue, i.e. whether the public broadcaster received an economic advantage which it would not have obtained under normal market conditions, reveals the level of certainty the court have tried to achieve by referring to the case-law of General Court with similar factual background, i.e. on financial aid to the Portuguese radio and television (T-46/97, SIC – Sociedade Independente de Comunicação SA v. Commission [2000] ECR II-2125).

The Constitutional Court concluded that, following the case-law of General Court, aid granted to the provider of public services is legal, as long as it ensures the provision of public functions. To conclude, the decision of the Constitutional Court is significant as being the first case where the judicial authority has examined compliance with State aid rules. Overall, the national courts refer to national and EU State aid rules in their case-law, however the courts still tend to examine cases under national laws without revealing their view on State aid arguments raised by the parties. The decision at issue indicates the first signs of application of State aid rules by the constitutional court of the Republic of Lithuania.

In the case of the Supreme Administrative Court of the Republic of Lithuania: The Representative of the Government of the Republic of Lithuania in Kaunas County v. Kedainiai District Municipality Council (7 November 2008, Case no. A525-1823/2008), where the municipality council's decision provided for granting of interest-free credits to natural persons, undertakings, cooperatives, village communities, and credit unions, neither the court of first instance, i.e. Vilnius County Administrative Court, nor the Supreme Administrative Court, referred to the concept of State aid. However, the municipality council considered the provision of interest-free credits for producers of agriculture products to be one of the forms of State aid. The municipality council stated that the provision of preferential credits is a feasible form by which to promote business in rural areas, as the list of State aid measures provided in the law is not exhaustive. Furthermore, the municipality council argued that the aid was lawful, stating that all market players were granted equal rights and access to receive support, therefore, competition was not distorted in the market. Nevertheless, the Supreme Administrative Court failed to comment on the arguments submitted by the municipality council concerning State aid. The Supreme Court concentrated instead on the scope of the rights of the municipality to offer credits and examined whether the decision providing for granting of interest-free credits complied with relevant national laws. The Supreme Administrative Court concluded that the municipality council went beyond the scope of its competence when adopting the decision to grant interest-free credits. The scope of examination by the national administrative courts is not limited to the contents of the submission, therefore the court's decision to ignore the arguments of the municipality council presupposes the conclusion that the court did not consider the State aid related arguments to be relevant or requiring of interpretation in the case at hand.

In the case of the Lithuanian court of appeal: The Vilnius County State Tax Inspectorate v. Ranga IV UAB (22 December 2009, Case no. 2-1383/2009), where the State Tax Inspectorate claimed that suspension of payment facilities to an undertaking in the process restructuring constituted State aid. The Lithuanian Court of Appeal referred to the case-law of CJEU (C-256/97, Déménagements-Mantention Transport SA [1999] ECR I-3913) and stated that the application of the private creditor's criteria proved that a state measure did not constitute State aid for the purpose of Article 107(1) TFEU.

3. Recovery of unlawful aid and interest

Decisions of national authorities granting State aid may be appealed to the Vilnius County Administrative Court. The decisions of this court may be appealed to the Supreme Administrative Court. The decisions of the Supreme Administrative Court are final and are not subject to appeal.

The case-law of the courts of the Republic of Lithuania does not establish any economic models for the calculation of damages. Damages may be calculated by comparing situations prior to and following the infringement. The value of damaged or destroyed property may be calculated as well. The courts of the Republic of Lithuania use both methods for calculation of damages.

4. Damages claims by competitors/third parties against the granting authority before the national courts

The limitation period for damages claims is three years from the moment when respective undertakings had knowledge of the injury. Usually, proceedings in the court of first instance may take from three to six months. As a general rule, proceedings in the court of appeal and in the Supreme Court may take approximately six to ten months.

5. Damages claims by the beneficiary against the granting authority before the national courts

In the case of the Supreme Administrative Court of the Republic of Lithuania: Tieskelis AB v. the State Tax Inspectorate (28 October 2005, Case no. A5-1627/2005), where in 2001 considering the economic situation, the Lithuanian Parliament approved the possibility of granting State aid to undertakings that had concluded tax loan agreements by releasing them from payment of delay charges, the undertaking Tieskelis AB applied to the local tax administrator and requested to be released from charges to the amount of approximately €295,000.

The undertaking insisted on applying relevant provisions of the Law on Tax Administration of the Republic of Lithuania providing that tax payers shall be released from payment on the condition that they have proved that they are not responsible for the infringement of the law. Neither the court of first instance, i.e. the Vilnius County Administrative Court, nor the Supreme Administrative Court referred to the rules on State aid in the case at issue. The courts analysed applicable national laws, as well as qualifications for release from payment of the delay charges, and closed the case under national tax administration laws.

Even though the scope of judicial analysis is not limited to arguments submitted by the parties, it is noteworthy that the parties did not make any references to State aid in their submissions either. The judicial argumentation presupposes the conclusion that the courts did not consider State aid rules to be relevant to the judgment.

In the case of the Supreme Administrative Court of the Republic of Lithuania: Arvi Cukrus UAB v. the Ministry of Agriculture (18 April 2008, Case no. A502-659/2008), where sugar manufacturers received mandatory export quotas of white sugar and according to the applicant, the export price of this compulsory quota was significantly lower than the sugar price in the internal market, the applicant suffered loss when complying with this order and applied for compensation.

According to the applicant, the Ministry of Agriculture erroneously explained the concept of State aid when refusing to satisfy the application for compensation. The claimant suffered loss due to the unlawful actions of the Ministry of Agriculture and claimed compensation pursuant to the rules of civil liability. According to the claimant, the compensation of loss restores the situation to that which existed before the violation, however, it does not provide for any benefit, whereas State aid leads to enrichment at somebody's expense, which would not have happened should the undertaking be operating on its own. Moreover, the applicant stated that recovery may not distort competition or affect trade between Member States despite the fact that losses are compensated from the State budget.

In this case, neither the Vilnius County Administrative Court, nor the Supreme Administrative Court, examined the concept of State aid. Even though the Ministry of Agriculture, i.e. one of the national authorities competent for granting State aid, referred to a general prohibition of State aid when refusing the applicant's claim for compensation of damages. It is noteworthy that the applicant's complaint also placed its main emphasis on the non-existence of State aid in the case under consideration. Subsequently, the applicant's submission presupposes the concentration of the courts' examination on the concept of State aid, despite the fact that the scope of examination by national administrative courts is not limited to the contents of the submission.

Nevertheless, the national courts failed to examine the understanding of State aid in this case. The courts did not consider the applicant's argument relevant and concentrated on an analysis of the legality of the actions of the Ministry of Agriculture and the concept of civil liability.

6. Damages claims by competitors/third parties against the beneficiary before the national courts

Any undertakings whose interests have been violated by a breach of the State aid rules can apply to the civil courts for compensation of loss. According to Article 6.249(1) of the Civil Code, undertakings may claim for compensation of direct damage or losses, as well as indirect damage or lost profits, but not for punitive damages. Pursuant to Article 178 of the Code of Civil Procedure, the claimant for damages must prove the infringement of State aid rules, actual loss and a causal link between the unlawful act and that loss.

As a general rule, competition law-related damages actions may be brought to the Vilnius County Court at first instance. The decisions of the Vilnius County Court may be appealed to the Lithuanian Court of Appeal. The decisions of the Supreme Court are final and not subject to appeal.

7. Interim measures taken by national judges

Due to the fact that there is no case-law in which the primary issue is related to State aid, the question of the application of interim measures has not been dealt with so far.

Overall, interim measures are available in competition law cases. The courts apply interim measures when a failure to do so would make the implementation of a prospective decision of the court impossible or significantly more difficult. Usually, the courts apply interim measures following a request submitted by one of the parties to the proceedings. Should it be necessary to defend a public interest, the courts may apply interim measures of their own initiative.

IV. Control of recovery procedure

1. Rules applicable to recovery

Decisions of the national authorities may be appealed to the Vilnius County Administrative Court. The decisions of the Court may be appealed to the Supreme Administrative Court, whose decisions are final and not subject to appeal.

2. Action for recovery

In the case of the Supreme Administrative Court of the Republic of Lithuania: TEO LT AB, Omnitel UAB, and Bite Lietuva UAB v. the Competition Council (5 April 2007, Case no. A11-381/2007), where pursuant to an order of the Minister of Internal Affairs, the public undertaking Infostruktura was authorised to act as an exclusive operator of the secure data transmission network, the providers of similar electronic communication services filed a claim with the Competition Council stating that the public undertaking was granted a competitive advantage infringing Article 4 of the Law on Competition.

Neither the Vilnius County Administrative Court, nor the Supreme Administrative Court, examined the rules on State aid. Nevertheless, the court of first instance made a reference to the national rules on notification of State aid, as well as Article 107(1) TFEU.

The court of first instance examined the case by considering the ruling adopted in the Government of the Republic of Lithuania No. 1136 "*Concerning Approval of Rules on Performance of Expertise of State aid Projects, Provision of Conclusions and Recommendations to Providers of State aid, Submission of State aid Notifications And Other State aid Related Information to the European Commission And Other Interested Institutions*" dated 6 September 2004. However, the Vilnius County Administrative Court did not elaborate on the application of national State aid provisions and Article 107(1) TFEU in light of the circumstances of the case under consideration.

Therefore, one can only presume that the court considered the authorisation of the public undertaking Infostruktura to act as an exclusive operator of the secure data transmission network to be one of the forms of State aid. It is noteworthy that the Supreme Administrative Court upheld the decision of the lower court, and yet did not refer to any provisions on State aid.

3. Challenging the validity of a national recovery order

Decisions of the national authorities may be appealed to the Vilnius County Administrative Court. The decisions of the Vilnius County Administrative Court may be further appealed to the Supreme Administrative Court, whose decisions are final and are not subject to appeal.

V. Standing of third parties before national court

In the case of the Supreme Administrative Court: Selos Parkas VsI v. the Ministry of Finance (22 January 2007, Case no. A4-581/2007), where on 10 June 2004 the Minister of Economy adopted Order No. 4-222 establishing "*Guidelines for applicants to receive financial support from the structural funds of the European Union according to the Lithuanian general programme document for 2004–2006*" (the "Guidelines") and the applicant filed a submission to the agency responsible for admission and assessment of applications for financial support from the structural funds of the EU, i.e. Verslo paramos agentura VsI (the "Agency") which was refused. Subsequently, the applicant approached the court of first instance, i.e. the Vilnius County Administrative Court, and requested that they find the decision of the Ministry of Finance to be unfounded, as well as to oblige the Ministry of Finance (the controlling institution) to recommend to the Ministry of Economy (the intermediary institution) and the Agency (the implementing institution) to re-assess their application for financial aid.

Neither the court of first instance, nor the Supreme Administrative Court, referred to arguments concerning State aid issues. The interested third party, i.e. the Agency, explained that the aid could not be granted to the applicant due to their engagement in economic activity.

Even though the third interested party, as one of the main reasons for dismissing the application for financial support from the structural funds of the EU, indicated the necessity to assess the submission under Article 107(1) TFEU, the courts did not consider it relevant to refer to State aid rules. The Supreme Administrative Court examined qualifications for the application, as well as actions of competent national authorities, and closed the case under provisions of national laws.

To conclude, the national courts have failed to elaborate on State aid arguments and to express their opinion regarding State aid in the case at issue. Overall, it is common for the courts to provide at least marginal comments on the arguments which they do not consider relevant in that particular case. However, it is noteworthy that the courts tend to artificially ignore any references to State aid made by the parties and usually concentrate on application of national laws.

VI. Cooperation with EU authorities

1. Cooperation with the CJEU

There is no precedent for the national courts referring to the CJEU for a preliminary ruling in questions raising doubts over the interpretation of State aid related EU law.

2. Cooperation with the Commission

Due to the fact that there have only been a few cases in which the concept of State aid has been touched upon by applicants, defendants or interested third parties, and that these have not been examined by the courts, there is no information as to whether the national courts ask for information from the Commission regarding factual data, statistics, market studies or economic analysis and to what extent.

As mentioned above, there has only been one case before the Constitutional Court of the Republic of Lithuania and a few very recent cases on restructuring aid, where the courts, as one of the arguments under consideration, also analysed the concept of State aid. The courts referred to the case-law of the CJEU and the General Court as well as Communication from the Commission – Community guidelines on State aid for rescuing and restructuring forms in diffuculty (OJ C 244, 1.10.2004, p. 2) but did not mention using other Commission decisions, general texts on State aid published by the Commission, the Commission's annual report on Competition policy or the monthly bulletin of the EU.

The Competition Council cooperates with the officials of the Commission. Prior to the accession of the Republic of Lithuania into the EU on 1 May 2004, the Competition Council performed the function of State aid control under the Law on Monitoring of State aid to Undertakings of the Republic of Lithuania. As of 1 May 2004, the Competition Council represents the position of the Republic of Lithuania with reference to State aid matters and participates in work shops and meetings organised by the Commission. The Competition Council coordinates the submission of State aid notifications, other State aid related information and yearly reports to the Commission.

VII. Trends – reforms – recommendations

The enforcement of State aid is evolving at national level, however, the development is still very slow. It is noteworthy that the decisions of the authorities competent for granting State aid are usually of an individual and private nature; therefore, decisions are not published or only aggregated data is made available. This lack of publicly available information on State aid granted to certain beneficiaries limits the possibilities of competitors, as well as third parties to challenge the validity of relevant acts and submit claims for damages.

The current economic recession introduced a number of cases on aid granted through state resources to undertakings under restructuring procedures. The national courts tend to follow the interpretation of State aid in the case-law of the EU courts.

Luxembourg

Emmanuelle Ragot*

* Philippe & Partners, Luxembourg.

I. General principles of Member State's State aid law

1. National authorities competent to grant aid and to be involved in the notification procedure

Different Ministries are competent to grant State aid. For example, the Ministry of Middle-class, Tourism and Housing is competent for grants to small and medium-sized companies under the Framework Act dated 30 June 2004.

The Ministry of Economy, Industry and Technology and Competition is the single point of communication for State aid with the Commission. The Ministry of Economy reports on the implementation of EU rules and takes part in international meetings and conferences about State aid.

With regard to the notification to the Commission under Article 108(3) TFEU, the Luxembourg Permanent Representation in the European Union carries out this obligation.

2. National authorities competent to recovery aid and an overview of the procedure

The procedure in cases of recovery of unlawful State aid is governed by the general administrative and civil rules. In order to recover unlawful State aid from the beneficiary, the public authority is entitled to bring a civil procedure before the civil courts.

An alternative remedy to recover unlawful aid and interest is an action in summary proceedings before the President of the District Court. Article 932(2) of the New Luxembourg Code of Civil Proceedings allows the President to grant a provisional amount with interest if the claimant meets the following requirements: the absence of a serious dispute; and the existence of urgency.

There is a serious dispute when the defendant invokes arguments that could not be rejected by the judge without hesitation. The case is urgent if the regular proceedings do not allow the recovery of this amount in due time.

The decision of the President of the District Court in summary proceedings is provisional and is not binding on the Civil Court. Any party can introduce an action before the civil court in order to obtain a definitive settlement of the litigation.

To the best of our knowledge, no case-law exists with regard to this hypothesis.

II. Identification of State aid issues at national level

1. State aid compliance by the national legislator and/or the executive

No specific *ex ante* control exists with regard to the compliance of State aid with Article 108(3) TFEU. Nevertheless, the act that grants State aid is submitted to an analysis by the State Council before adoption and promulgation.

The State Council examines the compliance of the act with the law, the Constitution and international law and gives a written opinion. A judicial control intervenes *ex post* if a claimant files an administrative or civil action with regard to State law.

It must be noted that the Ministry of Economy is the single point of communication with the Commission regarding State aid.

2. State aid compliance by national judges and/or the national competition authority (NCA)

On the basis of the 17 May 2004 Competition Act, the Competition Council is not competent to assess State aid compliance. Litigation with a State aid element must be submitted to the administrative and civil courts. No specific court or proceedings exist in Luxembourg with regard to State aid.

This report describes therefore how the general administrative and civil rules apply to State aid issues.

III. Unlawful aid and judicial review

1. General powers of the national courts concerning the direct effect of Article 108(3) TFEU

Under Article 108 TFEU the Commission examines whether State aid is compatible with the Internal Market. When Member States intend to create or to modify State aid, they must inform the Commission.

Article 108 TFEU is self-executing[172] and prohibits the implementation of State aid before the completion of preliminary examination proceedings and a final decision by the Commission.

In this hypothesis, on the basis of Article 108(3) TFEU, national courts are competent to declare a State aid unlawful if it has been granted before the conclusion of the Commission's preliminary examination proceedings.

It must be pointed out that a favourable final decision from the Commission following the preliminary examination proceedings does not regularise invalid acts of implementation by the Member State prior to the publication of that decision[173].

In the Grand-Duchy of Luxembourg, there are no specific proceedings by which to contest infringements of Article 108(3) TFEU. Actions under this provision are therefore based on

172 Except Article 108(3) TFEU, the other Articles are not self-executing: Case C-120/73, Gebrüder Lorenz GmbH v. Federal Republic of Germany and Land Rheinland/Pfalz [1973] ECR-I-1483, para. 8 ; Case C-354/90, Fédération Nationale du Commerce Extérieur des Produits Alimentaires and Syndicat National des Négociants et Transformateurs de Saumon v. French Republic [1991] ECR I-5505, para. 11.

173 Case C-354/90, Fédération Nationale du Commerce Extérieur des Produits Alimentaires and Syndicat National des Négociants et Transformateurs de Saumon v. French Republic [1991] ECR I-5505, para. 16.

the general civil liability and administrative principles and can be filed before both administrative and civil court.

a. Proceedings before the administrative courts

State aid is granted by public bodies' individual decisions on the basis of statutes and regulations. Every interested party is entitled to seek the annulment of the contested decision before the Administrative Courts ("Tribunal administratif" and "Cour administrative").

The claimant (a competitor or any interested party) may file a lawsuit against the regulation or decision awarding State aid before the Administrative Courts within a period of three months. This limitation period runs from the notification of the decision or, for a third party, from the date on which he has knowledge of the decision. For administrative regulations, the three month period runs from: i) the day of publication or; ii) if the regulation is not published, from the day of notification to the claimant; or iii) from the day on which the claimant has knowledge of the decision.

The claimant must have a personal, direct, actual and certain interest in the contested act, or must fulfil the conditions required by the law for a legal person. The scope of administrative action, in order to challenge a decision or regulation, is limited. A limited number of circumstances justify cancelling a decision or regulation: incompetence, excess or abuse of power, infringement of the law or of formalities established in order to protect private interests. The Administrative Court does not examine all elements of the litigation. The Court decides if the decision or regulation challenged in the aforementioned complaint falls into one of these categories, as invoked by the claimant.

In the Grand-Duchy of Luxembourg, if the claimant succeeds in his action, he will obtain the annulment of the decision or regulation. The public authority remains free to enact a new regulation, or to take a new decision, and the Administrative Court may not award damages for an infringement of the law, i.e. of Article 108 TFEU.

A specific administrative action to suspend an act does not exist in Luxembourg. The only possibility for the claimant to obtain suspension of the aggrieved decision is through provisory measures taken by the President of the Administrative Court during the examination of the complaint. In order to obtain such a suspension, the claimant must demonstrate a serious case and prove that the challenged decision puts the claimant at risk of serious and irreparable harm.

b. Administrative Courts cases with regard to State aid

State Council, 11 April 1989, commercial company Moulins de Kleinbettingen v. Ministry of Agriculture

In the 2006 Commission Study on State aid enforcement at national level, with with regard to Luxembourg[174], this decision was summarised as follows:

> *"The commercial company Moulins de Kleinbettingen filed for a subsidy with the Ministry of Agriculture, in accordance with the Act dated 18 December 1986, promoting agricultural development.*
> *The application was refused by the Ministry on the grounds that the claimant did not fall within the scope of application of Article 39 paragraph 1 of the act, which lists the potential beneficiaries of such subsidy, stating that such beneficiaries may, inter alia, be those undertakings whose main purpose is to increase the income of farmers in general.*
> *The claimant instituted an administrative action against this decision before the Sate Council by arguing, firstly, that the act had not been correctly applied by the Ministry and, secondly, that, by such incorrect application of the act, Article [107 TFEU] had been infringed in the sense that anti-competitive structures had been created.*
> *As far as the first argument is concerned, the State Council held that the aim of the act was to enable the Ministry of Agriculture to promote the agricultural sector. Hence, the potential beneficiaries of the subsidies were to be found amongst the agricultural population and the rural establishments. The subsidies foreseen by the act were paid by the budget of the Ministry of Agriculture. As public expenditures must not be diverted from the purpose given to them by the legislator, it was held that the Minister of Agriculture must restrict the granting of subsidies to those entities for which his Ministry is in charge. This was not the case of the company Moulins de Kleinbettingen, a private company which falls under the competence of the Department of Industry and Middle Class affairs. Accordingly, the decision of the Minister of Agriculture was upheld by the State Council.*
> *As far as the claimant's second argument is concerned, the State Council simply considered, without any further comments or explanations, that the aid granted under the act, just like the aid benefiting to the industrial sector as provided by an act dated 14 May 1986, was compatible with the exceptions set out under Articles [107(2) and (3) TFEU]. The State Council also stated that the claimant could not reasonably assert that there was a risk of the balance of the Common Market being disturbed by the mere fact that Luxembourg granted structural aid to the agricultural sector by means of the act".*

Two more recent cases illustrate the competence of the administrative court examining the legality of a decision that grants State aid and to pronounce its annulment. In these cases, the

174 T. Jestaedt, J. Derenne et T. Otteranger (Coord.), Study on the enforcement of State aid at national level, Part I, pp. 349–358, Part II, pp. 663–664.

claimant did not claim an infringement of Articles 107 to 109 TFEU, but only an infringement of national State aid law.

Trib. Adm., 17 September 2008, n°23632
An association of communes challenged two decisions, dated 26 March 2007 and 4 July 2007 of the Ministry of Home Affairs and Regional Development that refused funds for the building of a rain basin. The Administrative Court ruled that it was not competent to substitute or replace the decision but only to annul it. After examination of the arguments with regard to the compliance of the decision with the law, the Administrative Court rejected the claimant's application for annulment.

Trib. Adm., 10 December 2008, n°24181
A public limited company filed an action for annulment of a decision, dated 30 October 2007, of the Ministry of Middle-class, Tourism and Housing that refused the granting of funds. The claimant's arguments included the lack of motivation of the decision and the infringement of the law. The Administrative Court rejected that there was a lack of motivation but accepted that the decision was an infringement of the Framework Act, dated 30 June 2004, and accordingly annulled the decision.

c. *Civil proceedings*

A victim who wishes to obtain damages has to sue the public authority in tort before the civil courts. Competitors, third parties and beneficiaries can file a judicial action before the civil courts in order to claim for damages. The granting authorities will take the beneficiary to court in order to recover a State aid that has been granted unlawfully.

No specific civil rules apply to the regulation of State aid. Nevertheless, some legal provisions, which may have a significant impact in terms of efficiency, are detailed further below.

2. Prevention of the granting of unlawful aid

Preventing the grant of unlawful aid implies an action that intervenes before the implementation and grant of State aid. As discussed there is no specific administrative action by which to achieve suspension. The claimant may file an administrative action in annulment against specific regulations, or against the decision, before implementation. During the administrative proceedings, the claimant is entitled to ask the President of the Administrative Court to take provisional measures in order to suspend the contested decision[175].

It is also possible for a claimant to file an action in summary proceedings before the President of the District Court in order to prevent the granting of unlawful aid.

Under Article 933(1) of the Code of Civil Proceedings, the President of the District Court may order conservatory measures in order to prevent imminent damage.

---

175 Conditions mentioned supra.

Assuming the tribunal use this legal basis, a competitor or third party who suffers loss could invoke Article 933(1) in order to request the freezing of the aid as a supplementary measure to prevent the State from granting an unlawful State aid. However, to our knowledge, no case-law exists with regard to this hypothesis.

The other judicial remedies available are actions *a posteriori* e.g. actions based on civil liability and the recovery of unlawful aid.

3. Recovery of unlawful aid and interest

a. Civil proceedings

The Commission can declare a State aid unlawful and order the cessation of the aid, as well as recovery of the funds from the beneficiary.

Consequently, the granting authority will have to withdraw the decision granting that particular State aid. In Luxembourg, the retroactive withdrawal of a State aid decision is governed by Article 8 of the grand-ducal decree dated 8 June 1979. A public authority is only entitled to withdraw a decision with retroactive effect during the period in which an administrative action may be introduced or, if this is the case, during the period of the administrative proceedings. The grounds for this withdrawal must be the infringement of a principle that permits the annulment of the decision by the Administrative Court. (See section III.1)

If State aid has been granted on the basis of a contract, this contract may be declared void due to the infringement of Article 108(3) TFEU.

In order to recover unlawful State aid from the beneficiary, the public authority is entitled to commence a procedure before the civil court. No specific rules or proceedings are required for this recovery.

b. Summary proceedings

An alternative method by which to recover unlawful aid and interest is to bring summary proceedings before the President of the District Court.

Article 932(2) of the New Luxembourg Code of Civil Proceedings allows the President to order recovery of a provisional amount with interest if the claimant meets the following requirements: an absence of a serious dispute, and the existence of urgency.

There is a serious dispute when the defendant invokes arguments that could not be rejected by the judge without hesitation[176]. The case is urgent if the regular proceedings would not allow

176 Luxembourg Court of Appeal, 20 January 1986, Micheley et Bidasio v. Englaro, n°8349; Luxembourg Court of Appeal, 30 January 1989, Keipes v. Sicolus, n°11069.

recovery of this amount in due time[177]. The decision of the President of the District Court in summary proceedings is provisional and is not binding on the Civil Court[178].

Any party can introduce an action before the civil courts in order to obtain a definitive settlement of the litigation.

4. Damages claims by competitors/third parties against the granting authority before the national courts

If the Administrative Court is permitted by law to annul an illegal decision of the granting authorities, no damages are granted by administrative courts[179].

The competitors or third parties who consider themselves victims of an illegal decision must therefore file an action in tort before the civil courts against that granting authority in order to obtain damages[180].

Two legal bases may be invoked in this hypothesis. The general civil liability principles as set out in Article 1382 et seq. of the Civil Code and in the State and Other Public Bodies Act dated 1 September 1988, which implements civil liability principles into the relationship between the State or public authorities and private individuals.

Indeed, the State or public authorities assume responsibility for any damage caused by the defective actions of their services or agents. The claimant must prove the fault of the granting public authority, loss and a causal link between the fault of the public authority and the loss suffered.

The majority of the case-law in Luxembourg demonstrates the annulment of a decision by the administrative court due to a fault committed by the public authority[181]. It remains uncertain whether the claimant must first file an administrative action in order to obtain an annulment of the administrative decision, before bringing a civil action for damages.

Indeed, previous case-law has established that the civil courts are not competent to examine the legality of individual administrative decisions, or the liability of public authorities for their illegal decisions[182].

177 Luxembourg Court of Appeal, 1 July 1970, Pas.21, p. 378; Luxembourg Court of Appeal, 13 March 1989, Krancher v. Bodson et consorts, n°11106.

178 Luxembourg Court of Appeal, 18 February 1992, Anciens Etablissements Cloos et Kraus v. BatiConcept, n°13564.

179 Cour Lux, 25 February 1964, Pas., 19, p. 414 ; Trib. Lux., 8 May 1957, Pas., 17, p. 234 ; Trib. Lux., 6 January 1960, Pas., 18, p. 175 ; Conseil d'Etat Lux, 22 October 1980, Pas., 25, p. 90.

180 Trib. Lux, 28 May 1924, Pas., 12, p. 360.

181 Luxembourg Court of Appeal, 13 December 1983, Etat v. Nilles; Luxembourg Court of Appeal, 30 October 1986, Pas. 27, p. 266; Luxembourg Court of Appeal, 20 April 1989, n°10271; Luxembourg Court of Appeal, 10 July 1991, n°12508; Luxembourg District Court, 3 July 1986, n°408/86; Luxembourg District Court, 19 December 1984, Pas. 26, p. 285.

182 Luxembourg Court of Appeal, 13 December 1983, Etat v. Nilles ; Luxembourg Court of Appeal, 21 November 1985, Editpress; Lux. v. Etat; Court of Appeal, 22 May 1996, n°17096.

Since the mid-nineties[183], various judgments of the District Court and the Court of Appeal have accepted civil actions for damages against the state on the basis of an illegal decision without a preceding annulment of this decision by the Administrative Court. In these cases, the civil courts examined the legality of the decision or the regulation of the public authority and granted damages where they found the public authority to be liable[184].

The CJEU case "Brasserie du pêcheur"[185], as well as the direct effect of Article 108(3) TFEU, continue to engage the State's liability for infringement of EU Law[186].

As no specific proceedings or laws exist in Luxembourg with regard to unlawful State aid, competitors or third parties would have to base their action on the Civil Liability principles set out in the State and Public Bodies' Act.

5. Damages claims by the beneficiary (against the granting authority) before the national courts

In order to succeed in his action, the claimant must provide the Court with evidence that he suffered loss and that the granting public authority is responsible for that loss[187].

The legal basis for such actions is Article 1382 et seq. of the Civil Code, and the State and Other Public Bodies Act dated 1 September 1988.

The major arguments in this hypothesis would usually be, on one hand, that the beneficiary of State aid had a legitimate expectation[188] in the compliance of this State aid with the Treaty or, on the other hand, that the State is seeking recovery of unlawful State aid after an inappropriate delay. Most of the time, the beneficiary has already used the funds, made investments and would face difficulties if forced to refund the unlawful state aid. The beneficiary has relied on the State's information and advice. This could be considered as damage *per se*.

To the best of our knowledge, no case-law exists with regard to this hypothesis.

---

183 G. Ravarani, La responsabilité civile des personnes privées et publiques, 2ème édition, Pasicrisie Luxembourgeoise, 2006, p. 171, n°184.

184 Luxembourg District Court, 16 November 1994, n°924/94, confirmed by Luxembourg Court of Appeal, 9 July 1996, n°17751; Luxembourg Court of Appeal, 22 November 1995, n°16525.

185 CJCE, 05/03/1996, Cases C-46/93 and C-48/93, Brasserie du Pêcheur SA/Bundesrepublik Deutschland, The Queen/Secretary of State for Transport, ex parte:Factortame Ltd e.a.

186 F. Schockweiler, "Le dommage causé par suite d'une violation du droit communautaire par l'autorité publique et sa réparation en droit Luxembourgeois", Pas. 28, p. 38.

187 G. Ravarani, La responsabilité civile des personnes privées et publiques, 2ème édition, Pasicrisie Luxembourgeoise, 2006, p. 99 et seq.

188 Case C-5/89, Commission v. Federal Republic of Germany [1990] ECR I-3437, para. 14 and 17.

6. Damages claims by competitors/third parties (against the beneficiary) before the national courts

a. Civil proceedings

If a competitor or third party has a personal interest in suing the beneficiary of an aid, he may ask the civil courts for damages due to the infringement of Article 108(3) TFEU.

Pursuant to Article 1382 of the Civil Code, this action in liability requires a fault of the beneficiary, a loss suffered by the claimant and a causal link between the fault and that loss. The alleged loss must be a direct loss of the claimant.

To the best of our knowledge, no case-law exists with regard to this hypothesis.

b. Action for discontinuance

Another possible action against the beneficiary of State aid is an action for discontinuance before the President of the District Court, in the Commercial Chamber. The procedure is the same as in summary proceedings.

This action is based on Article 14 of the Act dated 30 July 2002, regulating certain commercial practices and sanctioning unfair competition. The unfair competition can be defined as an action contrary to honest commercial, industrial or liberal practices, or the diversion or an attempt to divert a competitor's clients or competitive power. The acceptance by a beneficiary of an unlawful State aid when he was aware of its irregularity could be, under certain circumstances, regarded as unfair competition.

The claimant must show evidence of a personal interest and of a competitive situation. The President of the District Court can order the discontinuance of any act of unfair competition. If the claimant so requests, the President's order could be accompanied by a restriction order for each day of non compliance with his decision ("astreinte").

As an additional sanction, the order could be advertised or published in relevant newspapers. The action for discontinuance does not allow an award of damages. If the competitor intends to recover damages, he must file a civil action before the civil courts.

7. Interim measures taken by national judges

In Luxembourg, the President of the District court is competent to grant interim measures. Among all of the possibilities infra, two types of actions must be highlighted:

- for competitors, an action for discontinuance in case of infringement of Article 14 of the Act dated 30 July 2002, regulating certain commercial practices and sanctioning unfair competition; and
- for the granting institution, an action in recovery of unlawful aid based on Article 932(2), of the New Luxembourg Code of Civil Proceedings in order to recover a provisional amount with interests.

The New Luxembourg Code of Civil Proceedings also establishes the possibility for a claimant to file an action in summary proceedings before the President of the District Court under Article 933(1) of the Code of Civil Proceedings. In this situation, the President of the District Court may order conservatory measures in order to prevent imminent damage.

To the best of our knowledge, no case-law exists in this regard. Nevertheless, a competitor or third party who suffers damage could invoke this action in order to ask for the freezing of the State aid, as a supplementary measure by which to prevent the State from granting the unlawful aid.

IV. Control of recovery proceedings

1. Rules applicable to recovery

The recovery of unlawful State aid is subject to the New Luxembourg Code of Civil Proceedings. These rules apply to summary proceedings as well as to civil actions before the civil courts. In order to recover State aid, the granting authority withdraws the granting decision and asks for a refund of the aid. The summary proceedings will only be successful if the defendant does not invoke serious arguments against the action.

2. Action for recovery

a. By the State

(i) Civil proceedings

The Commission can declare a particular State aid unlawful and order the end of that unlawful aid, as well as the recovery of the funds from the beneficiary.

Consequently, the granting authority has to withdraw the decision granting this particular aid. In Luxembourg, the retroactive withdrawal of a State aid decision is governed by Article 8 of the grand-ducal decree dated 8 June 1979. A public authority is only allowed to withdraw a decision with retroactive effect during the period in which an administrative action may be introduced or, if this is the case, during ongoing administrative proceedings. The basis of this withdrawal must be the infringement of a principle that permits the annulment of the decision by the Administrative Court.

If the aid has been granted on the basis of a contract, this contract may be declared void in light of an infringement of Article 108(3) TFEU.

In order to recover unlawful State aid from the beneficiary, the public authority is entitled to introduce a civil procedure before the civil court. No specific rules or proceedings are required for this recovery.

(ii) Summary proceedings

An alternative method by which to recover unlawful aid and interest is an action in summary proceedings before the President of the District Court.

Article 932(2) of the New Luxembourg Code of Civil Proceedings allows the President to order recovery of a provisional amount with interest if the claimant meets the following requirements: the absence of a serious dispute and the existence of urgency.

There is a serious dispute when the defendant invokes arguments that could not be rejected by the judge without hesitation. The case is urgent if the regular proceedings would not allow the authorities to recover this amount in due time.

The decision of the President of the District Court in summary proceedings is provisional and is not binding on the Civil Court. Any party can introduce an action before the civil court in order to obtain a definitive settlement of the litigation.

b. By competitors

Actions introduced by competitors' do not usually lead to the recovery of the aid but are based on the civil liability or on the prohibition of unfair competition (cf. infra).

c. By beneficiaries

Actions introduced by beneficiaries' do not tend to recover aid but are based on the civil liability principles (cf. infra).

3. Challenging the validity of a national recovery order

Different defences could be invoked against the recovery action or order. One argument arises from Article 8 of the grand-ducal decree dated 8 June 1979, which deals with the retroactive withdrawal of an administrative decision.

A public authority is only allowed to withdraw a decision with retroactive effect during the period in which an administrative action may be introduced, or during the length of ongoing administrative proceedings. The basis for this withdrawal must be the infringement of a principle that permits the annulment of the decision by the Administrative Court.

The beneficiary could also argue that the civil court is not competent to examine whether an administrative decision is valid or not. In summary proceedings, every serious contestation prevents the President of the District Court from ruling on the case.

4. Action contesting the validity of the Commission decision

Some parties can argue that the Commission has erred in its decision and may ask the judge to refer the relevant question to the CJEU on basis of Article 267 TFEU.

In this hypothesis, a civil or administrative action must be introduced before the national judge, who is then competent to refer a prejudicial question to the CJEU.

5. Damages for failure to implement a recovery decision and infringement of EU law

To the best of our knowledge, no case-law exists with regard to this hypothesis.

V. Standing of third parties before the national courts

Third parties must show that they have a personal interest in the resolution of the litigation. If they apply for damages, they must provide evidence of the loss that they have suffered, as well as a causal link between the defendant's fault and the damage.

VI. Cooperation with EU authorities

1. Cooperation with the CJEU

CJEU case-law is used as a non binding guide in order to interpret Articles of the TFEU and European regulations.

During national proceedings, at one party's request or of his own volition, the judge has the ability to refer to the Court of Justice a prejudicial question in order to interpret a legal question relation to European Law (Article 267 TFEU).

2. Cooperation with the Commission

The Ministry of Economy is the single point of communication with the Commission regarding State aid.

State aid for the protection of the environment illustrates some cooperation with EU authorities; Article 7 of the Development and Economic Diversification Act dated 27 July 1993 was contrary to the Community guidelines on State aid for environmental protection (JO 2001/C37/03). The Commission ordered, therefore, the end of this State aid scheme by 31 December 2003 and future compliance with Community guidelines on State aid for environmental protection.

On 13 February 2003, the Ministry introduced Bill 5099 at the Chambers of Members. After notification, the Commission found the bill to be in compliance with Community guidelines. The Luxembourg Conseil d'État gave its opinion on 7 October 2003. After examination by the Commission of Economy, Energy and Transport, the bill was adopted by the Chambers on 27 January 2004 and the Environment Protection, Rational Use of Energy and Production of Renewable Energy Act of 22 February 2004 was published in the Memorial A 2004 vol. 24 on 4 March 2004.

VII. Trends – reforms – recommendations

To the best of our knowledge, no reform is currently being contemplated with regard to the control of State aid, the implementation of Commission decisions or the procedure for recovery of unlawful state aid.

The Law of 28 May 2009 has modified the law of 30 June 2004 creating a general framework for State aid schemes for the small firms and traders sector. The new law has increased the aid rate and/or amount that may be perceived by Luxembourg companies.

A new law was introduced on 18 February 2010 that foresees aid schemes for the protection of the environment and the rational use of natural resources. The aid may take the form of capital subsidies or interest allowances.

Similarly to other fields of competition law, the State aid sector would benefit from being organised as a governmental department with guidelines for the notification proceedings on a national level, the recovery of unlawful aid and a database listing all decisions. This would help to create a coherent State aid administration.

MALTA

Franco Vassallo*

* Mamo TCV Advocates, Valletta.

I. General principles of Member State's State aid law

Malta's infrastructure regarding State aid law is still in its infancy and the implementation of a complex legal framework addressing State aid issues remains at a developmental stage. Legal tools have been enacted to facilitate the adoption of the European legal framework and to render possible the importation of European principles on State aid into Maltese legal practice.

1. National authorities competent to grant aid and to be involved in the notification procedure

Legal Notice 210 of 2004 introduced the State aid Monitoring Regulations (the "Regulations") into the Maltese legal system in order to provide a mechanism whereby the grant and exercise of State aid could be scrutinised, so as to ensure compliance with EU Law.

State aid is granted subject to an examination by a State aid Monitoring Board, (the "Board") established under The Business Promotion Act (the BPA – Chapter 325 of Laws of Malta). This Board has been equipped with a number of statutory functions which *inter alia*, empowers it to "*establish and implement appropriate rules of procedure and methodological systems which lead to an effective state aid monitoring and reporting system*"[189].

The Board plays a central role in the monitoring and reporting procedure. Regulation 6 of the aforementioned Regulations obliges any provider of "new aid" to notify the Board without delay of any proposals to grant such aid[190].

Once a proposal has been submitted to the Board, it shall conduct a formal examination of the proposed aid, whereupon within 40 days it shall issue a preliminary opinion regarding the notified aid. Only once the Board is fully satisfied, having reviewed all the submitted information which it deems to be central to its decision, that the proposed aid is in full compliance with and does not operate counter to the Regulations, shall it issue a final opinion.

Notifying the Board about any proposed aid is mandatory. Certain penalties are prescribed by law in the event of non-notified aid. Whenever the Board is made aware, or becomes aware through its own initiative, of any non-notified aid, it has the power to suspend such aid pending a full examination and opinion, to be compiled and issued by the Board[191].

2. National authorities competent to recover aid and an overview of the procedure

There is no specific mechanism or authority tasked with recovering unlawful aid, although Article 9 of the Regulations states that recovery shall be in line with Article 14 of the Council Regulation (EC) No 659/1999 of 22 March 1999.

---

189 Article 58 (1C) BPA.

190 The term "new aid" is assigned the same meaning by Article 1 of Council Regulation (EC) No 659/1999.

191 Regulation 8 of the Regulations.

In such a situation, the remaining available remedies would have to be based on existing procedures based on general principles of civil law (e.g. procedures before the Civil Courts for damages or for recovery of "payments which were not due").

We note that, so far, no judgments have been given by the local courts following a claim regarding State aid. Our observations regarding judicial remedies will therefore be based on a reading and interpretation of the applicable laws, rather than on judicial pronouncements in this regard.

II. Identification of State and issues at national level

As has been indicated, the BPA established "the Board", which is the main authority overseeing the award of State aid. Article 58 of the BPA establishes the functions of the Board which are very wide but, at the same time, not very clearly defined. The Board's functions are the following:

- to establish and update a comprehensive State aid inventory;
- to review and assess existing and new State aid, and provide advice about their compatibility with the principles contained in the relative present and future acts of the EU;
- to establish and implement appropriate rules of procedure and methodological systems which lead to an effective State aid monitoring and reporting system;
- to provide expert opinions, positions and proposals for the formulation and implementation of State aid policy;
- to prepare an annual report on State aid in Malta, on the basis of the established methodology used in the EU;
- to assist in the identification and implementation of appropriate capacity building concerning State aid measures;
- to act as the pertinent body concerning State aid in Malta; and
- to exercise such other functions and duties as may be prescribed.

1. State aid compliance by the national legislator and/or the executive

The Regulations prohibit the grant of any State aid which would directly or indirectly distort or prevent competition within the market by awarding advantages to certain undertakings, to the detriment of others, and which would adversely affect trade between Member States. Such grant would be declared as being incompatible with the Internal Market.[192]

The only competent authority tasked with the responsibility of ensuring compliance with this principle, as well as other requirements, both at the municipal and European level, is the Board.

192 Regulation 3, The Regulations.

2. State aid compliance by national judges and/or the national competition authority (NCA)

The Commission for Fair Trading (NCA) set up by Chapter 379 of the Laws of Malta (The Competition Act)[193] does not have a direct competence to adjudicate on State aid compliance as the law stands. However, Article 30 of the Competition Act specifically states that applies to Government departments and to any body corporate, established by law, or to any company or other partnership in which the Government, directly or indirectly, holds a controlling interest or to which the Government has granted special or exclusive rights in any field[194].

Therefore if such State aid does infringe the Competition Rules it is mooted that the Commission for Fair Trading would, on the face of it have jurisdictional competence;

III. Unlawful aid and judicial review

1. General powers of the national courts concerning the direct effect of Article 108(3) TFEU

As a general rule the Civil Court of Malta has jurisdiction over all civil and commercial matters[195].

2. Prevention of the granting of unlawful aid

The Board acts as a "watchdog" ensuring that no unlawful aid is granted to any undertaking or group of undertakings. Through a series of notifications and reviews, the Board prevents the granting of unlawful aid.

3. Recovery of unlawful aid and interest

As regards the procedure to recover unlawful aid, there is yet to be a Maltese precedent of the procedure embodied in Article 14 of the Council Regulation. As stated, the Maltese provisions merely state that unlawful aid shall be recovered by the provider of aid, in line with Article 14 of the Council Regulation.

---

193 Article 4, The Competition Act.

194 Article 30[2] insofar as the application of such rules does not obstruct the performance, in law or in fact, of the particular tasks assigned to them.

195 Chapter 12 of the Laws of Malta "The Code of Organisation and Civil Procedure" ("COCP"): The Civil Court shall take cognisance of all causes of a civil and commercial nature, and of all causes which are expressly assigned by law to the said Civil Court.

4. Damages claims by competitors/third parties against the granting authority before the national courts

Any person suffering damages may seek redress by filing procedures before the First Hall of the Civil Court. An action against the Government can only be filed, at risk of nullity, following 10 days from the service of an official letter or judicial protest clearly stating the facts of the matter[196].

5. Damages claims by the beneficiary against the granting authority before the national courts

See 4 of section III above.

6. Damages claims by competitors/third parties against the beneficiary before the national courts

See 4 of section III above.

7. Interim measures taken by national judges

Any person who has a claim against another person or authority is entitled to file a precautionary warrant asking the court for an interim remedy pending proceedings on the merits of their claim[197]. There are several types of precautionary warrant, but those which are most relevant to this scenario would be:

a. A garnishee order: This warrant is described as follows in Chapter 12 of the Laws of Malta: (sometimes referred to as the COCP)

> *"Where a creditor ... in order to obtain the payment of a debt owing to him, desires to attach in the hands of a third party moneys or movable property due or belonging to his debtor, he may do so by means of a garnishee order[198]."*

Any moneys or movable property seized under a garnishee order would be deposited with the Court pending proceedings and may be withdrawn by the claimant in the event of a successful outcome. The applicant is bound to bring the action in respect of the right stated in the warrant within twenty days from the issue of the warrant.

---

196 Article 460 of Chapter 12 of the Laws of Malta.

197 Articles 829 to 877 of Chapter 12 of the Laws of Malta.

198 Article 375 of Chapter 12 of the Laws of Malta.

b. A warrant of propitiatory injunction

The object of a warrant of propitiatory injunction is to restrain a person from doing anything whatsoever which might be prejudicial to the person suing out the warrant[199]. The Court will hear the parties and must decide, within one month from the filing of the application, whether the claimant, *prima facie*, has the right which he is claiming, and whether the issuing of the warrant is necessary to protect the claimant from an "irremediable prejudice". Should the Court uphold the application for the issuing of the warrant, the claimant would then have to file proceedings regarding the merits of the claim within 20 days.

Pursuant to Article 15 of the Competition Act[200], the Commission for Fair Trading may, at the request of the Director of the Office of Fair Trading, or of an undertaking, or of a complainant, through the Director, take interim measures intended to suspend any restrictive practice under investigation if it is urgently necessary to avoid a situation that is likely to cause serious, immediate and irreparable prejudice to the interests of any undertaking or to harm the general economic interest. Such a request should be accompanied by a "reasoned report" prepared by the Director, stating the measures deemed to be necessary. The Commission may subsequently issue an order, based on a "reasoned decision", which shall have immediate effect and shall remain in force for a period of three months unless revoked. The Commission for Fair Trading may issue the same order for further three-month periods.

IV. Control of recovery procedure

1. Rules applicable to recovery

In the absence of a dedicated procedure for the recovery of damages in relation to State aid, the claimant (whether that claimant is the State, competitors or the beneficiary) would have to rely on general principles of civil law and procedure. Hence, all procedures for the recovery of damages to be awarded by a court of law are carried out under the jurisdiction of such courts and subject to the general principles of civil procedural law. The court seized in such proceedings would be the Court of Magistrates (where the claim is for an amount not exceeding €11,646.87) or the First Hall of the Civil Court (for larger claims). In both cases, an appeal can be made to the Court of Appeal (in its inferior jurisdiction in the case of appeals from a decision of the Court of Magistrates; in its superior jurisdiction in the case of appeals from the First Hall of the Civil Court).

2. Action for recovery

See 3 of section III above.

199 Article 873 of Chapter 12 of the Laws of Malta.

200 The Competition Act.

3. Challenging the validity of a national recovery order

No specific procedure is in place by which the validity of a national recovery order can be challenged. The complainant would have recourse to the ordinary courts through ad hoc proceedings, which might take the form of an action for judicial review of administrative actions pursuant to Article 469A of Chapter 12 of the Laws of Malta.

4. Action contesting the validity of a Commission decision

Any person who feels aggrieved by a Commission decision regarding State aid may complain directly to the Commission using the apposite form issued by the Commission, namely the "Form for the submission of complaints concerning alleged unlawful State aid" (2003/C 116/03). There is no particular procedure to follow at a national level.

5. Damages for failure to implement a recovery decision and infringement of EU Law

General principles of civil and procedural law would apply (see above).

V. Standing of third parties before national courts

Again, one should refer to the general principles of civil procedural law. Chapter 12 of the Laws of Malta states that any person who shows, to the satisfaction of the court, that he is interested in any suit already pending between other parties, may, on an application, be admitted as a party to that suit at any stage thereof, whether in first or in second instance[201]. Case law has established that the interest shown should not merely be a vague or academic one, but that the applicant should be in a position to show that the outcome of the ongoing suit would have a real and direct effect on its rights and/or obligations.

Should an applicant be admitted as party to the suit, that applicant would have the same procedural rights and duties as any of the other parties, including the possibility to present evidence and to make submissions.

VI. Cooperation with EU authorities

In terms of the BPA (Chapter 325 of the Law of Malta), the State aid Monitoring Board has various powers and duties of a policy-making and regulatory nature. Amongst its functions is the preparation of an annual report on State aid in Malta, based on EU methodology. The Board is, therefore, the entity which is in the best position to co-operate with the EU Authorities, particularly in the implementation of Community rules on State aid and the provision of

201 Article 960 of Chapter 12 of the Laws of Malta.

information regarding State aid in Malta. Apart from these general powers and duties however the law does not stipulate or impose specific ways in which the Board should co-operate with the EU authorities.

As regards the national courts, it should be observed that there have been no cases heard relating to the grant of State aid. We therefore are not in a position to state what the national courts would do, were they to be faced with doubts over the interpretation of EU law regarding State aid, as such a circumstance has so far never arisen.

1. Cooperation with the CJEU

There are no examples of cases in Malta in which a national court has referred a question for preliminary ruling in the field of State aid.

2. Cooperation with the Commission

There are no examples of cases in which the national authorities have asked the for Commission's support.

VII. Trends – reforms – recommendations

Maltese law regarding the provision of State aid remains procedurally primitive, in the sense that an over-reliance on provisions of EU regulations is evident. The absence of a structural framework to address concerns arising out of State aid cases remains Malta's greatest disadvantage in this respect and more often than not, aggrieved parties are confused as to how best to proceed with their claim or grievance. In the absence of specific procedures, claimants would have to rely on general rules of civil and procedural law. These remedies are only adequate up to a point, since better results would be achieved with the establishment of specific procedures (and possibly a dedicated court or judicial/quasi-judicial authority) to determine such matters. Aside from the establishment of the Board, whose discretionary powers are wide but not clearly defined, it is fair to say that Maltese legal development in the field of State aid remains strictly based on the frameworks established by European Law, which have been grafted onto pre-existing principles and procedures of national civil law.

In light of the lack of adequate mechanisms for State aid claims and related disputes, it would be opportune to have the functions and competences of the Board extended, and at the same time, clarified. More specifically, the Board, which has already been granted quasi-judicial competence to decide on the award of aid, might be granted the added faculty of hearing claims pertaining to the grant of unlawful aid and reciprocal claims for damages.

Aside from powers of suspension, a series of interim measures should be clearly defined and made available for the Board to apply, in order for the provision of temporary remedies to be made.

Finally, in the event of a non-compliant provider, rather than refer the matter back to the Minister responsible for the provision of the aid, the Board should be granted the authority to proceed against the particular Ministry responsible for providing the aid, in the event that the opinion of the Board is not respected and complied with.

The Netherlands

Mariëtte Swart, Anton Louwinger, Selma ter Kuile*
Paul Adriaanse**

* Hogan Lovells, Amsterdam.

** Leiden University.

I. General principles of Member State's State aid law

1. National authorities competent to grant aid and to be involved in the notification procedure

In the Netherlands, the federal Government (*rijksoverheid*) as well as the regional Governments (*provincies*) and local Governments (*gemeenten*) are, within their own powers and responsibilities, allowed to grant State aid. Each of these Governments is responsible for the correct notification of the State aid with the Commission, it being understood that the federal Government will ultimately be held responsible for any failures in relation to the notification.

The State aid could be granted both by way of an administrative act (*besluit*) under public law or by way of a private law transaction. Subsidies and fiscal benefits will normally be granted on the basis of an administrative act, whereas capital injections, loans and guarantees will typically be granted on the basis of a private law transaction.

An administrative act is defined under Article 1:3 of the General Administrative Law Act (*Algemene wet bestuursrecht* – "**GALA**") as a written decision of a public authority intending to cause legal effect under public law. Article 1:1 of the said Act defines public authority (*bestuursorgaan*) as (i) a body of a legal entity which has been established under public law (i.e. the federal, regional and/or local Government) or (ii) another person or body which is vested with any public authority. To the extent that these public authorities qualify as legal entities pursuant to Article 2:1 of the Dutch Civil Code (*Burgerlijk Wetboek* – "**DCC**"), they could also act as a party in private law transactions.

2. National authorities competent for recovery and brief description of the procedure

Depending on the form of the State aid, three types of procedures could be distinguished for recovery of unlawful State aid in the Netherlands (i.e. administrative law procedure, civil law procedure and tax law procedure). These procedures should be initiated by the public authority that granted the unlawful State aid against the recipient of the aid.

In recent years, it has been established that the administrative law procedure, civil law procedure as well as the tax law procedure do not yet contain balanced provisions enabling in all situations the obligatory recovery of unlawful State aid. For this reason, a legislative proposal has been prepared aiming to create appropriate tools in order to comply with the requirements imposed by European law in respect to recovery of State aid.[202] The object and effect to each of the recovery procedures are set out below.

Administrative law procedure

Where State aid has been granted by way of an administrative act (*besluit*), the unlawful aid must be recovered pursuant to the administrative law procedure, which provides for several

---

202 Lower House of the States General, nr. 31418.

decisions of the relevant public authority: (i) to repeal the administrative act granting the State aid and (ii) to issue a decision for payment in order to recover the money unduly paid.

Special procedural rules apply in relation to the repeal and recovery of subsidies, which have been laid down in Article 4:48 of the GALA and following Articles. In all other situations, where administrative law does not provide for a legal basis to take a decision to repeal and recover State aid, the power to take such a decision could, according to established case law of the Conseil d'État (*Raad van State*), be derived from general principles of administrative law. An exemption is made in relation to the recovery of interest which, according to established case law of the Conseil d'État, cannot be ordered without a legal basis in administrative law.

The legislative proposal provides for an amendment of GALA, pursuant to which the procedural rules relating to the repeal and recovery will apply to all forms of State aid within the meaning of Article 107(1) of the TFEU Treaty (and not only to subsidies). Public authorities, granting State aid, will be given the discretionary power to recover such aid from the respective beneficiary for the purpose of implementing a recovery decision rendered by the Commission or a court decision that is no longer subject to appeal. This includes the power to recover interest in accordance with the relevant provisions of Regulation (EC) No 659/1999.

In addition, the legislative proposal provides that any rules and provisions of Dutch law relating to statutory interest, limitation and recovery periods that are not in line with requirements imposed by European law, shall not be applicable in the context of the recovery of State aid.

Civil law procedure

If the unlawful State aid was granted by way of a private law transaction, the aid must be recovered pursuant to a civil law procedure on the basis of either Article 6:203 of the DCC (undue payment) or Article 6:212 of the DCC (unjustified enrichment). Such a procedure should be initiated before the civil courts.

The legislative proposal provides for a separate legal basis under civil law for the recovery of State aid as the existing procedures based on undue payment and unjustified enrichment proved to be ineffective. Any defences that the beneficiary may have by virtue of these procedures can no longer be invoked under the new recovery procedure.

The civil law provisions relating to the recovery of interest will also be brought in line with the requirements imposed by European law.

Tax law procedure

Special procedural rules apply to the recovery of taxes (tax State aid) under the General Tax Act (*Algemene Wet inzake Rijksbelastingen* – "**AWR**").

In order to determine whether tax State aid can be recovered under the AWR, it first needs to be established in what form the tax State aid was granted. Tax State aid can be granted in the form of (general) legislative measures or an individual decision concerning an individual taxpayer or group of taxpayers. This distinction is relevant since if tax State aid has been granted on the basis of an (individual) decision the beneficiary of such aid can in principle invoke the provisions of GALA and the non-codified general principles of sound administration, including, for example, the principle of legitimate expectations in case a recovery procedure is initiated. With respect to taxes, other than self-assessed taxes, this will generally not be possible if tax State aid was granted in the form of legislative measures. Below we will only describe the possibility of recovering State aid which has been granted by way of a relief of taxes to which the AWR applies (i.e. taxes levied at the national level).

The most likely option for recovering unlawful State aid involving taxes for companies should be by issuing an additional tax assessment within the meaning of Article 16 AWR (applicable to taxes levied through assessment) or Article 20 of the AWR (applicable to self-assessed taxes).

An additional assessment can only be issued on the basis of Article 16 of the AWR if:

- erroneously no tax assessment has been issued or if a Dutch taxable profit has been determined at too low an amount;
- there is either a new fact to consider (not taken into account initially) or the taxpayer acted in bad faith; and
- the additional assessment can be issued within a period of five years starting after the taxable fact occurred (i.e. the granting of State aid).

Generally, if tax State aid is ruled to contradict Article 107 TFEU this will not result in the recognition of a new fact. After all, this would be a development in law not so much the tax authorities identifying a factual matter concerning the individual taxpayer, which they were not aware of at the time the initial assessment, was issued.

The existence of a new fact is not needed for the Dutch tax authorities to successfully invoke Article 16 of the AWR, if it can be proven that a taxpayer acted in bad faith when accepting the tax State aid. No case law exists in this respect; however it may be difficult to argue for the Dutch tax authorities that a taxpayer acted in bad faith when relying on Dutch legislation. This may be different if such reliance took place at a moment in time that it could reasonably be assumed that the relevant Dutch rules contradict Article 107 TFEU.

From case law it also follows that no new fact is required in cases where it is clear that the tax authorities made a mistake when issuing the initial tax assessment. No new fact is needed (i) in the case of obvious typing or writing errors and (ii) when it is clear (e.g. from correspondence between the taxpayer and the authorities) that they would assess in a certain manner but did not. Generally, this exception does not seem to be relevant with respect to tax State aid granted.

Finally, it is also important for the Dutch tax authorities to be able to invoke Article 16 AWR, that the Dutch tax authorities can only issue an additional assessment within 5 years after the end of the relevant tax year. This period is extended with the period during which extension for filing of the relevant tax returns was granted. After this 5 year period has elapsed, generally no possibility exists to issue additional assessments.

The tax authorities can issue an additional assessment on the basis of Article 20 of the AWR if:

- the tax amount paid is too low because an exemption, reduction or refund has been granted by mistake;
- the additional assessment can be issued within a period of five years following the year in which the taxable fact occurred; and
- the issuance of an additional assessment does not violate the general principles of sound administration (*beginselen van behoorlijk bestuur*).

For issuing an additional assessment pursuant to Article 20 of the AWR – which only applies to self-assessed taxes like wage tax and VAT – the existence of a new fact is not required. However, the absence of a new fact will most likely play an important role in deciding whether the issuance of an additional assessment violates the general principles of sound administration (*beginselen van behoorlijk bestuur*).

Dutch tax law does not provide for other means of collecting tax in respect of previous periods. It has been argued that some of the conditions applicable to the issue of additional assessments, on the basis of either Article 16 or Article 20, may have to be disregarded (to the taxpayer's disadvantage) on the basis of the direct effect of Article 108 TFEU. However, it is unclear whether such position will be upheld by the Dutch courts.

Since the tax-specific possibilities for Dutch tax authorities to issue additional assessments may currently be limited, it is fair to say that in most cases tax State aid can only be recovered based on the possibilities offered by Dutch civil law.

The legislative proposal introduces a new paragraph to Article 16 of the AWR pursuant to which an additional assessment may be issued in case (unlawful) tax State aid has been granted to a tax payer without the need for a new fact or bad faith of the taxpayer. In addition, it is proposed that there will no longer be a statute of limitation with respect to such additional assessments (in case of tax State aid). Similar changes are proposed with respect to Article 20 AWR, as a result of which it should also be possible to recover (unlawful) tax State aid based on this Article.

With respect to Article 20, the possibilities for taxpayers to invoke the general principles of sound administration (i.e. the principle of legitimate expectations) will also be limited as a result of the (proposed) introduction of the (explicit) possibility to revise or redraw assessments (including self-assessed taxes) on the basis of tax State aid having been ruled unlawful.

Finally, the proposed changes would also concern the possibility to levy interest calculated over the amount of (unlawful) tax State aid.

II. Identification of State aid issues at national level

1. State aid compliance by the national legislator and/or the executive

In the Netherlands, there is no *ex ante* control organised at constitutional level or at legislative level with a view to avoiding the granting of State aid by legislative act in violation of Article 108(3) TFEU.

However, given the obligation for Member States under Article 21 of Regulation (EC) No 659/1999 to provide the Commission annually with an overview of all aid granted within the said period, the Dutch Government has introduced a scheme by which State aid co-ordinators within the different ministries are requested to keep a list of all aid granted within the Netherlands. Regional and local Governments are also requested to keep such a list. All information from these Governments is collected by the State aid department (*Coördinatiepunt Staatssteun*) within the Dutch Ministry of Interior and Kingdom Relations (*Ministerie van Binnenlandse Zaken en Koninkrijkrelaties*), after which it is sent to the Commission.

2. State aid compliance by national judges and/or the national competition authority (NCA)

In the Netherlands, there is no authority which has the specific task of ensuring the compatibility of public measures with State aid, nor are there specialised State aid courts dealing only with State aid cases. The jurisdiction of a court in relation to such cases will mainly depend on the form of the State aid and on the public authority granting the aid.

The Netherlands Competition Authority (*Nederlandse Mededingingsautoriteit* – "**NMa**") has no jurisdiction in the field of State aid.

III. Unlawful aid and judicial review

1. General powers of national courts concerning the direct effect of Article 108(3) TFEU

Although it is possible for a national court to adopt a preliminary decision on the compatibility of a State aid with the Internal Market – the final decision lies, in this respect, with the Commission. Instead, a national court is bound to safeguard the rights that individuals derive from the direct effect of Article 108(3) TFEU in anticipation of the final decision of the Commission and to make sure that the standstill obligation is respected by the public authorities.

The direct effect of Article 108(3) TFEU has been acknowledged by the Dutch courts in several cases in which the court was requested to decide upon the validity of the administrative act giving effect to the State aid, the suspension of the aid and/or the restitution of the aid already granted. Such request can be made by (i) summary proceedings (*kort geding*) with a civil court in order to obtain an interim injunction (*onmiddelijke voorziening bij voorraad*) or (ii) initiate proceedings with an administrative court in order to obtain preliminary relief (*voorlopige voorziening*), (please refer to paragraph III.2). Alternatively, a claimant could ask for judicial review by a civil court which is always competent, provided that the procedural requirements (i.e. admissibility conditions and limitation periods) have been taken into account.

Relevant in this respect is the *Baby Dan* case[203] in which the court of appeal appears to suggest that the decision to order interim measures on the basis of Article 108(3) TFEU is provisional. The court of appeal acknowledged in this particular case that, once the State aid has been notified, it is up to the Commission to decide whether the aid is compatible with the Internal Market. Although it is possible for a national court to adopt a preliminary decision, a national court could not adopt a final decision on the compatibility of the State aid with the Internal Market. However, such a preliminary decision was according to the court of appeal not relevant in this particular case as Baby Dan's claim related to the compensation of damages rather than (i) the suspension of the State aid or (ii) the reimbursement of the State aid which are the only legal consequences that can be derived from such decision.

2. Prevention of the granting of unlawful aid

In the Netherlands, there are two distinct ways to prevent public authorities from granting unlawful State aid. Parties can either initiate (i) summary proceedings (*kort geding*) with a civil court in order to obtain an interim injunction (*onmiddelijke voorziening bij voorraad*) or (ii) initiate proceedings with an administrative court in order to obtain preliminary relief (*voorlopige voorziening*).

Interim injunction

Article 254 of the Code of Civil Procedure ("**CCP**") provides that in urgent cases which require an immediate decision, a party may request a provisionally enforceable judgment by means of summary proceedings. The procedure is relatively simple. It is initiated by a writ of summons (*dagvaarding*), followed by oral pleadings and a decision of the President of the Court. Although in theory, the decision of the President in summary proceedings is provisional, in practice it is often considered to be binding by the parties concerned.

Initiating summary proceedings can be an effective remedy to suspend the execution of the private law agreement, until the procedure of Article 108 TFEU has led to a final decision by the Commission. However, the *UPC* case[204] demonstrates that this is not always the case. In this particular case, the Court of Appeal refused to order the Municipality of Amsterdam to suspend an investment which was liable to constitute State aid, although the Commission had initiated an Article 108(2) TFEU procedure. The Court of Appeal held that the standstill

203 Court of Appeal Amsterdam, 29 June 2006 (LJN AZ 1425).

204 Court of Appeal Amsterdam, 18 January 2007 (LJN AZ 6508).

obligation of Article 108(3) TFEU only applies where the measure under consideration does constitute State aid. It does not apply where the Commission is merely asked to confirm that the measure does not constitute State aid.

Preliminary relief
Alternatively, a party may request an administrative court for preliminary relief on the basis of Article 8:81 of the GALA. Such a request can only be made by an interested party (*belanghebbende*) within the meaning of Article 1:2 of the GALA (i.e. a party whose interests are directly affected by the administrative act)[205]. When doing so, the interested party shall need to prove that the following conditions are met:

- an administrative act granting the State aid is involved;
- a notice of objection (*bezwaar*) or an appeal (*beroep*) regarding the same administrative act (*besluit*) is pending; and
- it has an urgent interest (*spoedeisend belang*).

3. Recovery of unlawful aid and interest

For a description of the recovery procedures under Dutch law for unlawful State aid and interest, please refer to section I.2.

4. Damages claims by competitors/third parties before national courts against the granting authority

Civil courts have jurisdiction over actions for damages related to the unlawful implementation of aid. Competitors who have suffered loss as a result of unlawful aid can bring actions for damages before a civil court against the public authority that granted the aid and against the beneficiary. The court has to interpret and apply the concept of State aid contained in Article 107 TFEU, to determine whether aid given, without observance of the preliminary examination procedure laid down by Article 108(3) TFEU should be subject to the procedure of Article 108(3) TFEU.

An action for damages for a breach of Article 108(3) TFEU can be initiated by a competitor on the basis of Article 6:162 DCC (unlawful act). For Article 6:162 of the DCC to be applicable, the claimant (i.e. the competitor) must prove, amongst other things, (i) that there is an unlawful act, (ii) damage and (iii) causation, in the sense that the damage must still be (iv) attributable to the infringement by the defendant (i.e. the public authority). In practice, it appears to be very difficult to for a competitor to prove the latter two conditions.

205 The Conseil d'État (*Raad van State*) held in Cases ABRvS 17 May 2001 (AB 2002, 58), ABRvS 6 November 2002 (AB 2003, 115), ABRvS 17 December 2003 (AB 2004, 262) and ABRvS 14 February 2007 (AB 2008, 76) that a competitor can be regarded as an interested party within the meaning of Article 1:2 GALA.

5. Damages claims by the beneficiary before national courts against the granting authority

A beneficiary, who has suffered loss as a result of unlawful aid, can also claim damages from the public authority that granted the aid on the basis of Article 6:162 of the DCC (unlawful act). Such a procedure should, again, be initiated before the civil courts.

Relevant in this respect is the *Residex* case[206], in which Residex claimed damages from the Municipality of Rotterdam for granting unlawful State aid by way of a guarantee that had not been properly authorised. The Court of Appeal held that the guarantees qualify as State aid that should have been notified with the European Commission. Since such notification had not taken place, the guarantees were to be considered as unlawful aid. Unlawful State aid is null and void. According to the Court of Appeal, Residex should have taken greater care in verifying whether the State aid rules had been complied with when the guarantees were issued by the Municipality, especially given that these guarantees were issued for a very large amount (i.e. €100 million).

6. Damages claims by competitors/third parties before national courts against the beneficiary

Competitors who have suffered loss as a result of unlawful aid can initiate an action for damages before a civil court against the beneficiary of such aid. The procedure is similar to the procedure set out in paragraph III.4 where it will, again, be difficult for the competitor to prove the causal link between the unlawful act and the damage suffered.

The *Baby Dan* case is one of the few State aid cases that has been initiated by a competitor, claiming damages. In this particular case, the question was raised what legal consequences should be drawn from the failure to notify a State aid with the Commission in accordance with Article 108(3) TFEU. According to the court of appeal, such failure could not result in an unlawful act of the beneficiary of the State aid, as it is not the obligation of the beneficiary to arrange for the State aid to be notified. Instead, this obligation lies with the public authority that granted the State aid. Moreover, the Court of Appeal held that no causal relationship could be established between the alleged damage and the failure to notify the aid.

7. Interim measures taken by national judges

The judicial system in the Netherlands provides for different types of interim measures. The appropriate interim measure mainly depends upon (i) the nature of the State aid (i.e. by way of an administrative act under public law or by way of a private law transaction) and/or (ii) the legal actions taken by the claimant, which could comprise of a legal action either before the administrative courts or before the civil courts (reference is made to paragraph III.2).

---

206 Court of Appeal The Hague, 10 July 2007 (LJN BD 6981). See also District Court Rotterdam 24 January 2007 (LJN AZ 6902) and District Court Rotterdam, 24 January 2007 (LJN AZ 6904).

Administrative law provides for different types of interim measures, such as the suspension of the aid decision and/or the restitution of the aid already granted, provided that the conditions of Article 8:81 of the GALA are met. Damages could even be asked for on the basis of Article 8:73 of the GALA.

Similar measures could be asked for before the civil courts.

IV. Control of recovery procedure

1. Rules applicable to recovery

Different types of procedures could be distinguished for recovery of State aid in the Netherlands (i.e. administrative law procedure, civil law procedure and tax law procedure).

2. Action for recovery

a. By the State

When a public authority has granted unlawful State aid by way of an administrative act (besluit), it can repeal the administrative act granting the State aid and issue an administrative act for repayment from the beneficiary of the aid that has already been granted. If the beneficiary refuses to repay the unlawful State aid, an order of a civil court should be asked for in order to be entitled to execution, since, under current Dutch law, an administrative recovery act from a public authority is considered not to give such a right. Such judicial authorisation shall no longer be required once the legislative proposal (as described in paragraph I.2) comes into effect. On the basis of this legislative proposal, public authorities, granting State aid, will be given the discretionary power to recover such aid from the respective beneficiary for the purpose of implementing a recovery decision rendered by the Commission or a court decision that is no longer subject to appeal.

If the unlawful State aid was granted by way of a private law transaction, Dutch law currently provides that the aid must be recovered pursuant to a civil law procedure on the basis of either Article 6:203 of the DCC (undue payment) or Article 6:212 of the DCC (unjustified enrichment). These procedures leave room for the beneficiary to invoke certain defences in relation to these Articles (i.e. *eigen schuld-verweer*). This will, however, no longer be possible once the legislative proposal comes into effect. The legislative proposal will provide for a separate legal basis under civil law for the recovery of State aid.

b. By competitors

Public authorities have – in accordance with established case law of the CJEU – an obligation to order recovery of unlawful State aid unless this would be contrary to a general principle of law. It remains to be seen to what extent this obligation aims to protect third parties (i.e. competitors). To date, there are no reported cases in which a competitor initiated an action against a public authority enforcing a recovery decision of the Commission which has not (yet) been timely and/or correctly put into effect by that public authority.

3. Challenging the validity of a national recovery order

An administrative order by a public authority to recover unlawful State aid from the beneficiary of such aid can be appealed by that beneficiary before the administrative chamber of the district court. The Administrative Chamber of the Conseil d'État (Afdeling bestuursrechtspraak van de Raad van State) has jurisdiction in an appeal against the decision of the district court. However, district courts are only competent where no other administrative court is designated by the relevant legislation. In legislation on subsidies, for example, the Court of Appeal for Trade and Industry (*College van Beroep voor het Bedrijfsleven*) is often the relevant appeal court.

Appeals are only admissible after an internal review procedure (*bezwaar*) within the administration has been completed. A request for such a review should be directed to the public authority which took the decision. Parties may also agree to skip the administrative review and immediately address the court if they think administrative review will lead to no result. Re-examination may also be carried out by a higher administrative body (*administratief beroep*). Subsequent judgments of the district court can be appealed to the Administrative Chamber of the Conseil d'État or the Court of Appeal for Trade and Industry.

Difficulties arise when – even after the recovery order has become final and conclusive – the beneficiary refuses to repay the received aid. The fourth tranche of GALA, which came into effect on 1 July 2009, provides provisions dealing with public debt in this respect. It is provided that a public authority can issue an administrative act (reference is made to paragraph IV.2) on the basis of which the aid may be reclaimed. This administrative act can be contested by the beneficiary.

In case of non-payment by the beneficiary, an order of execution (providing the necessary entitlement to enforce payment) shall need to be obtained by the public authority that has granted the aid. GALA does not currently provide public authorities with a legal basis on which to issue such an order of execution. This will change once the legislative proposal comes into effect (reference is made to section IV.2).

4. Action contesting the validity of the Commission decision

Beneficiaries of State aid that was found unlawful by the Commission are – according to established case law of the CJEU – precluded from questioning the unlawfulness of the Commission decision before a national court.

5. Damages for failure to implement a recovery decision and infringement of EU law

Public authorities have – in accordance with established case law of the CJEU – an obligation to order recovery of unlawful State aid unless this would be contrary to a general principle of law. It remains to be seen to what extent this obligation aims to protect third parties (i.e. competitors). To date, there are no reported cases in which a competitor initiated an action against a public authority claiming damages from the public authority for failure to implement a recovery decision of the Commission.

In theory, it would be possible for a competitor to claim damages from the public authority on the basis of Article 6:162 of the DCC (unlawful act), (reference is made to paragraph III.4). It would, however, be very difficult for the competitor to prove causation between the breach of the recovery obligation and the loss sustained by the competitor.

V. Standing of third parties before the national court

Dutch civil courts do generally allow claimants (being both competitors and third parties) to claim damages for the loss suffered as a result of unlawful aid.

VI. Cooperation with EU authorities

1. Cooperation with the CJEU

In recent years, Dutch courts have cooperated on some occasions with the CJEU in relation to State aid issues. The *X B.V.* case[207] appears to be one of these occasions. In this particular case, the Supreme Court decided to stay proceedings in order to await the outcome of a preliminary ruling that had been requested by the Supreme Court to the CJEU in a similar procedure, taking the view that the outcome of this preliminary ruling could be of relevance in the *X B.V.* case. Both X B.V. (i.e. the claimant) and the State Secretary of Finance (i.e. the defendant) were given the opportunity to comment on the outcome of this ruling.

2. Cooperation with the Commission

Dutch courts do, in their own decisions, regularly refer to decisions of the Commission. It is not known to what extent these courts rely on information from the Commission such as factual data, statistics, market studies and economic analysis.

---

207 Supreme Court, 21 April 2005 (LJN AU 3125).

VII. Trends – reforms – recommendations

Over the last few years, there has been a steady increase in the number of State aid cases handled by the Dutch courts, which is mainly caused by a remarkable increase in the number of cases brought by competitors.

In these cases, competitors tend to claim interim measures (such as the suspension of the aid and/or the restitution of the aid already granted), rather than damages. There is no clear explanation for this tendency, as Dutch law does provide adequate opportunities for competitors to claim damages. Possibly, competitors are discouraged by the length of the judicial proceedings before the Dutch courts. Summary proceedings with a civil court to obtain an interim injunction or proceedings with an administrative court in order to obtain preliminary relief tend to be shorter and provide a quick remedy.

Also, it appears to be very difficult for a competitor, in order to validly claim damages, to prove that the damage that it suffered is caused by an immediate infringement by the defendant (i.e. the public authority and/or the beneficiary).

Another development that was established during recent years is that the State aid rules are more frequently used to challenge zoning plans underlying large projects. Such projects require substantial investments, which are often partly borne by the Dutch Government. Interested parties (*belanghebbenden*) have challenged the approval given for the underlying zoning plans as well as the investments made by the Dutch Government in such projects on several occasions (e.g. *Vestia* case[208], *Evelop* case[209] and *Eelde* case[210]), by stating that such investments constitute a form of State aid within the meaning of Article 107(1) TFEU that should have been notified with the Commission. On almost every occasion, the competent courts ruled that there was no need to establish whether the investments made by the Dutch Government constitute a form of State aid. All of these projects would still be executed – even without the financial support of the Dutch Government – as the execution of neither of these projects was depending upon the financial support of the Government. Article 107 TFEU can therefore, according to the competent courts, not prevent a project from being executed. One exception thereto was made in the *Eelde* case, in which the Conseil d'État (*Raad van State*) ruled that the investments made by the Dutch Government should have been notified with the Commission.

Dutch law does not yet contain balanced provisions enabling in all situations the obligatory recovery of unlawful State aid. Problems have been encountered in the administrative law procedure, the civil law procedure as well as the tax law procedure. Currently, a legislative proposal is pending which aims to create appropriate tools in order to comply with the requirements imposed by European law in respect of recovery of State aid. It is not yet clear when this legislative proposal will become effective.

---

208 Conseil d'État, 26 June 2006 (LJN AY 5061).

209 Conseil d'État, 22 October 2008 (LJN BG 1152).

210 Conseil d'État, 11 June 2008 (LJN BD 3598).

POLAND

Robert Gago*

* Hogan Lovells, Warsaw.

I. General principles of member state's state aid law

The regulation of State aid in Poland has changed significantly since the country's accession to the EU State aid procedure is regulated under the Act on proceedings in cases concerning State aid (Ustawa o postępowaniu w sprawach dotyczących pomocy publicznej, Journal of Laws from 2007 no. 59 item 404 as amended).

The statute regulates State aid issues at national level. The main authorities competent in the field of State aid are the President of the Office of Competition and Consumer Protection (the "OCCP"). In relation to issues concerning the grant of State aid in the agriculture and fisheries sectors, the minister of agriculture is the competent authority. The authorities mentioned above are responsible for preparing opinions on the legality of State aid presented in aid schemes and individual aid, notifying aid to the Commission and for monitoring State aid. They are also obliged to prepare annual reports on the results of their monitoring, including the assessment of effects which any aid granted has on the state of competition. Both the President of the OCCP and the minister of agriculture (in their relevant fields of competence) have the power to bring an action in law and represent Poland in cases concerning State aid before the CJEU and General Court (with the consent of the Council of Ministers).

The Council of Ministers also play an important role in Polish State aid procedure, since the notification of an aid scheme must be approved by the Council (except notification of aid schemes established under local laws). In addition, the Council of Ministers draws up the map of regional aid and determines the methods by which to calculate the value of aid granted. The Council also has the power to issue several executory acts concerning the technical aspects of granting State aid.

II. Identification of state aid issues at national level

1. State aid compliance by the national legislator and/or by the executive power

Polish law introduced a control mechanism relevant to specific aid schemes before their notification to the Commission. The act on proceedings concerning State aid provides a general obligation to obtain an opinion on aid in the form of aid schemes, individual aid and individual aid for restructuring (defined as activities aimed at restoring an undertaking's ability to compete). A motion to issue an opinion concerning the compatibility of State aid with the Internal Market must be submitted by the authority initiating the project or by the authority granting the individual aid, save in the case of a motion regarding individual aid for restructuring which must be submitted by the beneficiary. Such an opinion shall be issued within 60 days in the case of individual aid, or within 21 days in the case of an aid scheme.

Apart from the aforementioned opinion, there are certain other formal requirements which must be fulfilled.

Firstly, if the aid is an aid scheme, notification requires approval by the Council of Ministers. If the aid scheme does not require notification, it will not need to be approved by the

Council. This relates to aid schemes which fall within block exemptions if they obtained a positive opinion for *de minimis* aid (where *de minimis* aid is notified, the President of OCCP/ the minister of agriculture may express reservations regarding transparency within 14 days). If the Council approves the notification, the President of the OCCP or the minister of agriculture (where appropriate) is obliged to notify the aid to the Commission through the Polish Permanent Representation to the EU.

If the aid is an individual aid and the opinion issued finds it incompatible with the Internal Market, the applicant may within 14 days, press for notification. However, in relation to individual aid for restructuring, the authority granting the aid may change its opinion concerning the grant of aid. In that case, the notification will not be submitted.

As set out above, Polish regulation provides for broad *ex ante* control. Such a model helps to avoid the rejection of notifications by the Commission but on the other hand, it is thought that it makes the process too complicated because the aid must also be assessed by the Commission.

Polish law also provides for *ex post* control. The act on proceedings concerning State aid requires the President of the OCCP (or the minister of agriculture in his field of competence) to monitor State aid by gathering, processing and transferring information, notably on the type, form and size of the aid granted. The authorities granting the aid are obliged to prepare such reports and submit them to a relevant authority. They are also under an obligation to inform the President of the OCCP, the minister of agriculture or the minister of public finance where required. The authorities preparing projects granting State aid within the scope of Block exemption Regulations must inform the President of the OCCP (or the minister of agriculture in appropriate scope) about the future grant of aid within an aid scheme. Authorities which are to grant individual aid must inform about the grant of such aid. If State aid is granted by law the reporting obligation is imposed on the bodies which obtain the declaration or other documents concerning the amount of decreased obligations from the beneficiaries. Failure to fulfil reporting obligations may lead to a fine of up to €10.000 being imposed on the beneficiary.

The President of the OOCP is also required to record local laws regarding the grant of State aid under the conditions specified in the regulations. Arrears in respect of public finance are also subject to reporting obligations (reports should be submitted to the minister of public finance). This procedure helps in respect of monitoring tax reliefs.

The President of the OCCP and the minister of agriculture (in their respective fields of competence) prepare annual reports on the results of the monitoring process for the preceding year. The Council of Ministers presents the report to the Polish parliament.

Ex post reporting obligations are quite broad. This fact may be assessed as a positive aspect as it minimizes the risk of granted aid not being used in conformity with its description.

2. State aid compliance by national judges and/or the national competition authority (NCA)

The Polish Competition Authority has relatively broad powers in the field of State aid. The Polish legislator made the assumption that a competition authority with general responsibilities for protecting competition and consumers would be the most appropriate as regards State aid issues, particularly since the President of the OCCP monitored State aid before Poland joined the EU. Both *ex ante* and *ex post* control fall within the field of competence of the OCCP. The President of the OCCP is responsible for cooperating with the authorities granting the aid, contacting European institutions (*inter alia:* making notifications to the Commission), representing Poland before European courts as well as monitoring State aid. The President of the OCCP may also impose a fine for failure to fulfil reporting duties.

When it comes to litigation issues, it should be underlined that in Poland both civil and administrative courts may be competent in State aid matters. The respective competence depends on the nature of the decision or agreement on the basis of which the aid is granted. For instance, if the aid is granted on the basis of an administrative decision, the case shall fall within the competence of the administrative court, whereas in a case when the aid is granted on the basis of a contract, the case shall fall within the competence of the civil court. According to the Act on proceedings in cases concerning State aid, the authority should demand the recovery of the aid where the Commission orders the aid recovery. No special court or department exists for State aid matters.

Regarding the rules of evidence and the courts' powers of investigation it should be noted that Polish civil law places the burden of proof on the party which asserts a given fact. This rule is subject to some exceptions. In civil litigation all facts that are essential in order to decide the case are subject to evidence. There is no closed catalogue of evidence. The court can adduce different types of evidence. A party which submits a request to the court to adduce evidence is obliged to determine the facts that are to be proven by this evidence. There are no rules of disclosure under Polish law. The law obliges any person to present to the court upon request any document which is in his possession (there are certain exceptions to this rule). However, the requested document must be identified.

As regards the administrative courts, they examine the case on the basis of the legality of the decision. The court therefore relies on the material gathered during the administrative proceedings by the authority.

The fact that there have so far been no preliminary references to the CJEU concerning State aid does not imply any reluctance to do so. Rather this has been caused by a lack of cases which would require taking such step.

It is difficult to assess at this stage in the development of litigation concerning State aid whether third party interests should be taken into account by the court when it examines the existence of an aid. According to Polish rules on civil proceeding, a third party may join proceedings when it has a legal interest in that decision. Legal interest exists when the judgment may have an effect on the legal not merely factual sphere of the intervener's interest.

The Polish courts are applying some exemption regulations adopted by the Commission, in particular Commission Regulation (EC) No 1998/2006 of 15 December 2006 on the application of Articles 107 and 108 TFEU to *de minimis* aid.

III. Unlawful aid and judicial review

1. General powers of national courts concerning the application of Article 108(3) TFEU

Polish proceedings do not provide for any means by which the court may order the termination of an infringement of Article 108(3) TFEU. If the subject of the litigation is a contract on the basis of which the aid was granted, the court may state that the contract is void because it was concluded contrary to binding law provisions. If the unlawful aid was granted on the basis of an administrative decision, the court has no power to overrule such decision. It may only inform the relevant granting authority, which in this case would be obliged to change or annul such decision. It is possible that in such a case the court may apply some interim measures (e.g. order to place a specific amount on deposit at the court).

2. Prevention of the granting of unlawful aid

There is a slight difference between a private and a public act if there are doubts as to its lawfulness.

If the aid was granted by way of an administrative decision, the granting authority may suspend the performance of the decision *ex officio* on the grounds that the decision in question may be void (because it may be contrary to the law). Whereas if the aid is granted on the basis of the contract, the granting authority may suspend the execution of the agreement de facto and eventually bring an action before the civil court in order to establish the non-existence of any legal relationship (according to the Polish Civil Code, legal action contrary to the binding law is void).

3. Recovery of unlawful aid and interest

Procedures which enable the recovery of unlawful aid are dependent upon the character of the contract or decision on the basis of which the aid was granted. The act on proceeding concerning State aid expressly states that a beneficiary is obliged to return an amount representing the equivalent public aid for which the Commission ordered obligatory recovery.

The President of the OCCP or the minister of agriculture (in their respective fields of competence) must immediately pass a copy of the Commission decision on obligatory aid recovery to the granting authority in the case of an aid scheme (the authority then passes the decision to a beneficiary). In the case of individual aid the copy of the Commission's decision shall be passed to both the granting authority and to the beneficiary.

According to the Act on proceedings in cases concerning State aid, the authority which has issued the decision or the granting authority which has entered into an agreement must demand recovery where a decision on obligatory aid recovery has been issued by the Commission. If the aid is granted on the basis of an administrative decision, the authority which issued the decision may change or annul that decision or it may order reimbursement of the aid granted.

If the aid is granted on the basis of the contract, the authority granting the aid has the right to file a lawsuit asking the court to terminate the agreement or to order the beneficiary to reimburse the aid. The legal basis for the recovery would be civil code provisions on undue performance (i.e. performance without valid legal grounds).

The President of the OCCP, or the minister of agriculture where appropriate, has the same powers as the prosecutor in civil, administrative proceedings or proceedings before the administrative court, i.e. it may *inter alia*: bring a lawsuit and take part in the proceedings.

Compulsory collection of an amount equivalent to the granted aid together with interest is carried out in accordance with regulations regarding the administrative enforcement procedure or with regulations on judicial enforcement procedure.

Under Polish law there is no direct possibility of recovering unlawful aid in litigation between a beneficiary and a third party. A third party may only petition the granting authority to initiate a recovery procedure. The authority shall inform the third party about the manner in which it dealt with the petition but the third party cannot force the authority to recover the aid directly.

It may be assumed that the court will use the EU guidance when quantifying the amount to be recovered. However, it may also refer to the Polish regulation of the Council of Ministers on detailed methods of calculating the value of State aid granted in different forms from 11 August 2004 (Journal of Laws from 2004, no. 194 position 1983).

It is possible that the court will refrain from adjudicating on a case concerning State aid if the case is under examination by the Commission. Under provisions of Polish civil proceedings and proceedings before administrative courts, the court may suspend the proceedings *ex officio* if the judicial decision depends upon the effect of other proceedings – this solution seems to be reasonable.

The recovery of illegality interests is subject to the general procedure on claims. In the event the interests are not returned voluntarily, the action that should be undertaken depends on the nature of the legal relationship. If the aid was granted on the basis of an administrative decision, rules of enforcement in administrative proceedings will be applied. Where the aid was granted on the basis of a contract, the granting authority must bring a lawsuit before the court.

In one of the cases[211], the civil court ordered the recovery of part of the aid with the interests scalculated in a similar way to tax arrears according to the agreement between the parties (the aid was granted on the basis of the contract).

The Polish courts' experience in State aid cases is not developed. Therefore it is difficult to assume at this stage how courts will apply the method set by the Commission in the Implementing Regulation to define the interest rate to be applied.

211 Case I ACa 1059/08 Agency for Restructuring and Modernization of Agriculture against M.L. (individual).

4. Damages claims by competitors/third parties before national courts against the granting authority

Liability of the State is regulated by the Polish Civil Code. There is a difference between liability with respect to liability for damage caused by an authority exercising its administrative powers and liability for damage caused by actions concerning regular business activities outside the imperium. It may be assumed that granting public aid should be qualified as exercising authority. The Polish Civil Code states that the State Treasury, territorial self-government unit or another legal person acting as a public authority is liable for damage caused by unlawful activity or cessation which occurred in exercise of such authority. The conditions for liability under national law are: unlawful activity in exercising authority, damage and the existence of causal nexus between them. Where the performance of public authority tasks is mandated, under agreement, to a territorial self-government unit or another legal person, joint and several liability for damage inflicted is borne by the contractor and by the territorial self-government unit mandating such tasks or by the State Treasury.

Therefore, it may be stated that the conditions are less difficult to fulfil than those presented in the *Francovich* case. Polish law does not require the breaches to be "sufficiently serious".

If damage was caused by the issuance of a legislative instrument, redress may be demanded provided that the instrument does not comply with the Constitution, a ratified international agreement or another act, when assessed in the course of appropriate proceedings. Where damage was caused by the issue of a legally valid judgment or final decision, redress may be demanded following non-compliance of such judgment or decision with the law stated in the course of appropriate proceedings. This also refers to a case in which a valid judgment or final decision was issued under a legislative instrument stated to be non-compliant with the Constitution, ratified international agreement or act.

Although no such case has been identified so far in Poland, there are no obstacles to enforcing liability for violation of Article 107(3) TFEU in parallel to a violation of Article 108(3) TFEU.

Concerning the assessment of the damage caused in situations where the breach caused the claimant to lose an asset, the court would probably make a comparison between the state before and after the infringement. Proving that the breach prevented the claimant from improving its asset position would be far more difficult and would require evidence as to the probability of improvement and existence of a causal nexus with the infringement.

5. Damages claims by the beneficiary before national courts against the granting authority

There are no available cases where the State has been declared liable for damages caused to the beneficiary by the granting of unlawful (and incompatible) aid.

It is difficult to assess how damages would be split in the case of shared liability between the State and the beneficiary. General rules provide that if the injured person contributed to the emergence or increase of the damage, the duty to compensate for it shall be reduced according to the circumstances, and in particular the degree of fault of both parties.

6. Damages claims by competitors/third parties before national courts against the beneficiary

Direct damage actions

Although no such case has been identified in Poland so far, it seems possible that a third party could base its damage action on non-contractual liability or on unfair competition regulation. Non contractual liability (in the form of liability *ex delicto*) requires proof of the existence of: damage, a fact which has caused the damage and the causal nexus between the damage and the fact. The person who suffered the damage may demand redress for it.

The Act on unfair competition dated 16 April 1993 (Ustawa z dnia 16 kwietnia 1993 o zwalczaniu nieuczciwej konkurencji, Journal of Laws 1993 no. 47 item 211 with further amendments) provides for wider range of possible claims. According to Polish regulation, an act of unfair competition is an act contrary to law or good customs which threatens or infringes the interests of competitor or client (the Act on unfair competition does not provide for a closed catalogue of unfair competition acts). In case of the performance of such act, the entrepreneur whose interests was threatened or infringed may request for example: cessation of the unlawful acts, removal of the effects of the infringement, compensation for damage on a general basis.

There are no obstacles to using such methods in the event that the beneficiary opposes and delays the process of recovery.

In practice the estimated average duration of complex civil law proceedings where both parties are business undertakings can vary from 1 year to 2 years (first and second instance). Where the cassation is admissible it would take additional year to have a judgment of the Supreme Court. There are significant differences between different regions.

Recovery of undue advantages enjoyed by the beneficiary

It is not possible for the court to order the recovery of undue benefits, resulting from the unlawful aid, in litigation between the beneficiary and a third party. The third party may include undue benefits in the estimation of the amount of damages claimed, and then general provisions shall be applied. (i.e. damage action, action on the basis of unfair competition act).

7. Interim measures taken by national judges

Under Polish Civil Proceedings, the claimant can file a motion for an interim measure before the proceedings have been started or during the proceedings in order to secure his claims. The main rule is that the interim measure, if granted by the court, cannot lead to the direct satisfaction of the claim that the applicant is seeking in the main proceedings. To be granted an interim measure the applicant needs to prove to the existence of the claim and the existence of his or her legal interest in being granted an interim measure. The applicant must also specify the type of measure sought.

Depending on the type of the claim, the court has different types of interim measures available. In the case of a pecuniary claim (e.g. damage action on the basis of non contractual liability), the Polish civil proceedings code provides a closed catalogue of interim measures, including seizing movable assets, establishing a mortgage. In the event of a non-pecuniary claim (e.g. cession of unlawful act), the court may provide any interim measure which it finds appropriate in the given circumstances.

IV. Control of recovery procedure

1. Challenging the validity of a national recovery order

Polish law does not provide for any special procedures under which the validity of national recovery orders can be challenged.

In cases where the recovery is ordered by an administrative decision, a party may bring an appeal against a decision to the second instance authority. If the decision was issued by a minister, an unsatisfied party may only ask the minister to review the case. Bringing an appeal action has a suspensive effect unless the decision is enforceable by law immediately or when it is granted immediate execution (e.g. for reasons of public interest).

After exhaustion of available appeal means before the authorities, there is also the possibility to appeal to the administrative court, and in specific circumstances administrative court decisions can be appealed to the Supreme Administrative Court. Bringing an action before the administrative court does not suspend the application of the decision. However the authority may suspend the performance *ex officio* or the court may order the suspension of the performance of the decision on the claimant's request.

In the event that recovery was ordered by civil court (e.g. by termination of the contract granting the aid), the regular appeal procedure is applied (court of second instance or in some cases also an extraordinary means of appeal – the appeal for cassation of the second instance judgment by the Supreme Court – is available). An appeal has a suspensive effect except in relation to an appeal for cassation. However, if an appeal for cassation is brought, the court of second instance may suspend the performance of the judgment if there is a risk that irreparable damage will occur.

In practice the estimated average duration of complex civil law proceedings where both parties are business undertakings can vary from 1 year to 2 years (first and second instance). Where cassation is admissible it would take an additional year to obtain a judgment from the Supreme Court. There are significant differences between different regions.

2. Damages for failure to implement a recovery decision and infringement of EU law

There are no special means of engaging State liability for failure to implement a Commission recovery decision.

The Polish Civil Code states that if damage was inflicted by the failure to issue a judgment or decision, where the obligation is provided for in legal provisions, redress for such damage may be demanded after the illegality of such failure to issue a judgment or decision is assessed in the course of appropriate proceedings.

It seems to be possible to bring an action demanding action by the authority. If a person lodges a complaint against the negligent or inappropriate performance of duty by the proper authority and the complaint is not dealt with within the deadline (one month), the claimant has the right to make an objection to the higher public administration authority. If the higher authority accepts the validity of the complaint, it shall set an additional deadline for dealing with the case and clarify the reasons for the delay and the identity of the parties responsible for the failure to deal with the case within the deadline. Where necessary, the higher authority takes steps to ensure that future deadlines for dealing with the case are respected.

In the event that no proper steps are taken by the administration, there is also the ability to bring an action against the lack of activity before the administrative court. If the court finds unlawful inactivity, it would oblige the authority to take appropriate steps. Such a judgment would enable a damage action to be brought in the civil court providing that the plaintiff proved the existence of a causal link between the inactivity of the authority and the damage.

If the beneficiary resists recovery action, the authority which issued the recovery decision may initiate administrative enforcement according to the enforcement procedure in administration (Ustawa z dnia 17 czerwca 1966 r. o postępowaniu egzekucyjnym w administracji, Journal of Laws 2005, no. 229, item 1954 with further amendments). In a case where the recovery is based on a judgment of the civil court, compulsory recovery is performed after obtaining the final judgment (Ustawa z dnia 17 listopada 1964 r. kodeks postępowania cywilnego, Journal of Laws 1964 no. 43 item 296 with further amendments).

V. Standing of third parties before national courts

Under Polish regulations, there is no direct provision of law granting a third party or a competitor the right to claim termination of the granting or recovery of aid. It may only bring damage actions against Member States or the beneficiary based upon general rules of civil non-contractual liability. Such an action requires the fulfilment of the prerequisites for a damages action. Alternatively, a competitor may bring an action against the beneficiary on the basis of an unfair competition act as presented above.

It is doubtful whether a third party would be able to prove legitimate legal interest in order to gain *locus standi* either in administrative proceedings which aim to annul a decision granting aid or in civil law proceedings before the civil court aimed at obtaining a declaration of invalidity where unlawful aid has been granted on the basis of a civil contract. There is no case law by the Polish courts on this issue. Taking experience from other fields of law we must say that the courts tend to narrow the concept of legitimate legal interest. Very often the parties whose factual interests were endangered were denied legal protection. We can only guess that any party seeking to prove legitimate interest would invoke Article 108(3) TFEU as a provision having direct effect and support its position with references to the Commission notice on enforcement of State aid law by national courts (OJ (2009) C85/1).

Under Polish civil proceedings, the burden of proof is placed, in principle, on the party that asserts a given fact.

VI. Cooperation with EU authorities

1. Cooperation with the CJEU

We have found no cases concerning State aid where the court cooperated with the CJEU.

2. Cooperation with the Commission

Although no such case concerning State aid issues is available, it seems, from general observation of the Polish judiciary, that national courts show a greater tendency to use available case-law and general texts published by the Commission rather than asking for an opinion of the Commission.

VII. Trends – reforms – recommendations

Development of State aid enforcement at national level has been relevantly slow. There are a small number of cases where State aid issues are an element. Most of the cases deal with small procedural issues based on Polish procedural law provisions.

It seems necessary to regulate the issue of the recovery of unlawful aid not granted by a contract or an administrative decision (for example granted automatically *ex lege* or in a case where the aid is granted in the form of contribution in-kind). There is some legal uncertainty on that matter. In view of the doctrine on this point, this may cause certain practical obstacles in relation to vindicating unlawfully granted aid.

One of the main barriers to the enforcement of State aid rules before the Polish courts is the lack of any clear legal basis under domestic law that could be used to justify the existence of legal interest and consequently for bringing legal actions by competitors or a third party before the administrative or civil courts.

Another drawback is the lack of specific "injunctions" that would enable the civil court to order the recovery of unlawful aid or to suspend granting of aid. The claimant may only request interim measures to secure its claims for damages (e.g. through a mandatory mortgage over the plaintiff's real estate). Current interim measures do not secure the prevention of damage to a competitor's business as a consequence of unlawful aid (e.g. aid granted in breach of the suspension obligation resulting from Article 108(3) TFEU.

Although existence of clear law is crucial, it should be kept in mind that it is only one of the elements of effective law enforcement. Success of State aid on a national level also depends on other factors like increased legal awareness and the knowledge and experience of the national authorities responsible for applying that law. An improvement could be the issuance of a specific set of guidelines on enforcement of State aid on the basis of Polish law provisions which would provide potential claimants with practical advice on the means by which they could assert their claims.

Portugal

Manuel Porto, João Nogueira de Almeida*

* Coimbra University.

I. General principles of member state's state aid law

1. National authorities competent to grant aid and to be involved in the notification procedure

State aid in Portugal may be provided by private or public means.

Private intervention can be made, for example through participation in the capital of companies, subscription of bonds, granting of guarantees or loans by State-owned or State-controlled institutions (for example the participation in the capital and guarantees given to TAP (European Commission, SG (2000) D/107766, of 21.10.2000, and C (2002) 1328 fin., of 9.4.2002), or the guarantee given to EPAC).

Granting State aid by private means of intervention may have the following consequences, as compared with public intervention:

- where private law is the legal basis for intervention, transparency may be undermined due to publicity obligations which could not be repected;
- though the intervention is private, the rules infringed are of a public nature. As a result of dual jurisdictions in Portugal (judicial and administrative), remedies against civil or commercial acts should, in principle, be resolved by judicial courts. However, once the rules infringed are of public nature, these courts will find themselves incompetent to judge the actions brought before them.

In this situation it is arguable that the infringement of public law provisions by private law means should be resolved by the administrative courts, not only to prevent a negative conflict of jurisdictions, but also because prior to the private law intervention an administrative act or decision must have been taken (that allowed, for instance, the definition of the terms of the participation in a company or the conclusion of another civil or commercial law contract). An administrative jurisdictional action would take place in reference to that administrative decision or to any contract whose invalidity derived from it (see (b) of number 1 of Article 4 of the Statute of the Administrative and Tax Courts, Estatuto dos Tribunais Administrativos e Fiscais, approved by Law 13/2002, of 19 February and modified by Law 107-D/2003, of 31 December).

State aid provided by public means of intervention may be structured in a number of different ways under the Portuguese legal system.

Tax exemptions

It is questionable whether tax exemptions really constitute State aid as they are of general application, whereas a State aid is usually granted to an individual entity. Nevertheless, tax exemption (or reductions in a tax rate) is of financial benefit to undertakings to which it applies.

Portugal has always had a complicated system of tax exemptions, although the Portuguese government is now seeking to reduce and rationalize the system.

One important step was taken after the tax reform of 1988-9, with the Statute of Tax Benefits (Estatuto dos Benefícios Fiscais, Decreto-Lei 215/89, of the 1st July, amended by Decreto-Lei 198/2001, of 3 July). Following other initiatives, a working group report was published in 2005 which included a new proposal to reduce the benefits and rationalize the system (Luís Máximo dos Santos (Editor), Reavaliação dos Benefícios Fiscais, Cadernos de Ciência e Técnica Fiscal, n. 198, Lisboa, 2005).

Compensatory indemnities

These are given each year to both public and private firms. Compensatory indemnities are one of the main reasons for economic distortions and inequities in the Portuguese economy, tending to favour, in particular, urban public transport in two cities, and public broadcasting over private broadcasting (Manuel Porto and João Nogueira de Almeida, State aid in Portugal, Chapter 19, in The Effective Application of EU State aid Procedures, edited by Paul F. Nemitz, Kluwer Law International, 2007).

Legislation was approved (Decreto-Lei 167/2008, of the 26 August 2008), establishing the legal framework for public subsidies, and addressing, in particular, compensatory indemnities.

This legislation follows the principles of transparency and EU competition rules, in particular in relation to the Community framework for State aid in the form of public service compensation (2005/C 297/04, published in the Official Journal of 29 November 2005) and the Communication from the Commission on the application of State aid rules to public service broadcasting (published in the Official Journal of 15 November 2001) as well as the Community rules on the services of passenger railways and road transport.

Other methods of providing public State aid that are particularly relevant in Portugal are the administrative contracts (whether international or not) to provide companies with land or property under normal market conditions. In these cases, the justification for public aid is usually the promotion of regional cohesion.

2. National authorities competent for recovery and brief description of the procedure

In Portugal there is no single authority with general competence to procure the recovery of unlawfully granted aid.

However, in some specific cases the law which allows aid to be granted also establishes mechanisms for its recovery. This is the case in the above mentioned Decreto-Lei 167/2008. According to Article 10, n. 1 and n. 2, the payments made in breach of the rules should be returned within 30 days of the period set out in the agreement. If the amount of unlawful aid is less than 10 % of the total amount of aid, and if the agreement remains in effect for the following period, it can be held to be an advance of the payment for the following period.

Article 10 n. 5 provides that the amounts given in breach should be returned via the public tax law enforcement, based on the document issued by the Directorate General of the Ministry of Finance.

II. Identification of State aid issues at national level

1. State aid compliance by the national legislator and/or the executive power

In Portugal there is no system of organized control for the concession of unlawful aid, in violation of Article 108(3) TFEU. The Government and the Portuguese Parliament (Assembleia da República) may however seek the advice of the Advisory Council (Conselho Consultivo) of the Portuguese Attorney General (Procurador Geral da República). The Advisory Council may provide an analysis on the compliance of an Act or agreement with Article 108(3) TFEU.

The Government can also ask the National Competition Authority ("**NCA**") to intervene. According to Article 13(1) of the Portuguese law of competition (lei 18/2003, of 11 June 2003), aid granted to undertakings by the State or by any public entity should not significantly restrict or harm competition in the whole or in part of the market. The Government or any other person (including public corporations and individuals) can ask the NCA to analyse any aid or proposal of aid, and to recommend the measures required to prevent the aid having a negative effect.

2. State aid compliance by national judges and/or the national competition authority (NCA)

In the *Antrop* case, the Supreme Administrative Court (Supremo Tribunal Administrativo) asked the CJEU about the possibility of Articles 107 and 108 TFEU having direct effect, in relation to imposing public service obligations on a public company.

The reference was submitted in the course of proceedings between, on the one hand, the Associação Nacional de Transportadores Rodoviários de Pesados de Passageiros (Antrop) and a number of other undertakings ("Antrop and Others"), and, on the other hand, the Conselho de Ministros (Council of Ministers), the Companhia de Carris de Ferro de Lisboa SA ("Carris") and the Sociedade de Transportes Colectivos do Porto SA ("the STCP") regarding compensation payments of €40 916 478 and €12 376 201 respectively, awarded to the latter bodies in respect of 2003 by Resolution No. 52/2003 of 27 March 2003 of the Conselho de Ministros.

In 2003, the NCA gave advice on the provision of services by higher education schools in competition with private initiatives, the law on installation/changes for commercial firms, State measurement control (IPQ) and the use of public infrastructures to stock and dry cereals (INGA). In 2004 advice was given on purchasing of communication services by the State Central Administration and measures used to dynamise/reinforce competition in the market of liquid fuels.

III. Unlawful aid and judicial review

1. General powers of national courts concerning the direct effect of Article 108(3) TFEU

According to EU law, the Portuguese authorities must order the repayment of non-notified aid, of notified aid granted in breach of the standstill obligation, and of unlawful State aid declared incompatible by the Commission.

The beneficiaries may agree to repay the aid unlawfully received. The chance of this is higher if the beneficiaries are public or private firms subject to close public intervention. But, in many cases, aid is not returned and a legal procedure must be followed. The type of legal procedure depends on the characteristics of the act through which the aid was granted.

Aid is often granted by a public procedure. One way of attributing the aid is by law (in the Portuguese case, lei, decreto-lei or a regional decreto legislativo).

It is possible to use a law to give a concrete benefit, it being acknowledged nowadays that laws are not always of general application. For example, it is clear that, according to the Portuguese Constitution, a law may be used to give a tax benefit, an exemption or a reduction of the rate. As mentioned above, this is State aid and thus must fulfill the requirements of Articles 107 and 108 TFEU.

Bearing in mind the acceptance of EU law by Portuguese law, in relation to determining Portuguese legislative procedures it could be argued that to evaluate the conformity of a national law with Articles 107 and 108 TFEU a claim should be made to the Constitutional Court (together with the capacities of intervention of the common judicial and administrative courts, in relation to laws which are reported, in a specific case, as not in conformity with the Constitution and/or other rules, like EU law).

In most cases State aid is granted through administrative procedures, regulations ("regulamentos"), administrative acts ("actos administrativos") or administrative agreements ("contratos administrativos").

In these cases, administrative courts are competent, by way of special jurisdiction in relation to authority acts and contractual agreements entered into under administrative requirements. Alternatively, Portuguese administrative law allows the annulment of administrative acts, subject to any administrative or judicial decision within a year. It is likely that, because Member States cannot rely on judicial restrictions in their internal law to prevent or limit the recovery of State aid, that delay would be considered inapplicable, due to the primacy of EU law.

There are other factors which render judicial actions in State aid cases difficult: (i) the discretionary power of public entities, and (ii) the lack of transparency of the aid.

Although the capacity for intervention seems lower when State aid is granted through private mechanisms, it is likely that the administrative jurisdiction reform encompasses and will resolve this problem, as described above. Nevertheless, no case law is available yet to confirm this.

IV. Recovery of unlawful aid

1. Recovery of unlawful aid and interest

Following reforms made in 2003 by both the Statute of the Administrative and Tax Courts, and the Code of Procedure in Administrative Courts (Código do Processo dos Tribunais Administrativos, approved by Law 15/2002, of the 22 February 2002 and modified by Law 4-A/2003, of the 19 February 2003), the capacity of these courts is no longer limited to the traditional "action for annulment"; they can also compel the entity which has granted the unlawful aid to take a decision which is legally due, and leads to the recovery of damages arising from an administrative act or from a failure to act.

A particular difficulty arises in Portugal when a Commission decision concerns aid granted by a non-State public entity, either at the local level (municipalities) or at regional level (the autonomous regions of Azores and Madeira).

The Portuguese Government has limited means by which it can recover aid granted in violation of Articles 107 and 108 TFEU on these local and regional entities. The Governmental supervisory powers over municipalities are restricted to inspections. This can only lead, with the intervention of the administrative courts, to the dissolution of the organ and to the loss of the mandate of its members (Law 27/96, of 1 August). But this will only happen in limited situations, strictly defined by law, none of which is likely to be relevant to Article 108 TFEU. The autonomous regions are not subject to administrative control by the central Government.

2. Damages claims by competitors/third parties before national courts against the granting authority

There is no case in Portugal concerning damages claims by competitors/third parties against the State. However, as such, competitors demonstrating a direct and individual interest in the annulment of an administrative decision that grants State aid are recognized as legitimate parties. As regards administrative agreements, there is a possibility for judicial enquiry of actions brought about by non contractual parties.

ROMANIA

Dragos Dumitru*

* Fruth Oprisan Si Asociatii, Bucharest.

I. General principles of Romania's State aid law

1. National authorities competent for granting aid and involved in the notification procedure

In Romania, the law governing the principles of grant and recovery of State aid are provided by the Government Emergency Ordinance 117/2006 on the National Procedures in the Area of State Aid ("Ordonanta de urgenta no. 117/2006 privind procedurile nationale in domeniul ajutorului de stat") published with the Official Gazette no. 1042 of 28 December 2006 as amended and approved by Law 137/2007 for the Approval of Emergency Ordinance no. 117/2006 on the National Procedures in the Area of State aid ("Legea 117/2007 pentru aprobarea ordonantei de urgenta 117/2007 privind procedurile nationale in domeniul ajutorului de stat") published with the Official Gazette no. 354 on 24 May 2007.

In the light of the above legislation, State aid can be granted only after being authorised by the Commission with the exception of State aid not subject to notification which can be granted with the observance of the laws in force. The notifications on State aid by the granting authorities are submitted to the Competition Council, which issues a note on the compliance with the obligations under the EU legislation regarding the drawing up of the State aid schemes.

The Competition Council represents Romania before the Commission in proceedings regarding State aid. In this capacity the Competition Council informs the requesting parties about the decisions adopted by the Commission.

The Competition Council is also the monitoring authority of State aid. In this respect, the authorities granting State aid are obliged to check the way in which granted State aid is utilized, in order to decide upon the steps to be taken and to submit to the Competition Council in the requested format all data and information necessary to monitor State aid at national level.

State aid beneficiaries are obliged to submit to the granting authorities periodical reports on the State aid granted in accordance with their request. The Competition Council organises the registry of State aid and draws up the annual report of the State aid granted in Romania which is submitted to the Government published with the Official Gazette and transmitted to the Commission. The Competition Council and the State aid granting authorities appoint representatives authorised to assist the Commission to conduct on site inquiries.

2. National authorities competent for recovery and brief description of the procedure

If the Commission decides that a State aid measure must be recovered, the beneficiary of such aid is obliged to reimburse the amount representing the equivalent of the aid to be reimbursed, except for cases in which the Commission decision has been suspended.

A copy of the decision of restitution issued by the Commission is sent by the Competition Council to the granting authority. The granting authority must immediately send the same to the beneficiary.

If the aid beneficiary fails to reimburse the State aid, the granting authority, based upon the Commission decision, shall file a legal claim for the annulment of the State aid and the recovery of the relevant amount with Bucharest Court of Appeal.

II. Identification of State aid issues at national level

1. State aid compliance by the national legislator and/or the executive power

There is neither an *ex ante* nor an *ex post* control organised at constitutional or legislative level. There no *ex ante* control organised by the executive power. The executive power is involved in the *ex post* control in the sense that the State aid providers are obliged to monitor the way in which the State aid is used by the beneficiaries and to provide the Competition Council with the information necessary to monitor the State aid measures at national level. The State aid providers may order the termination or recovery of the State aid already granted.

2. State aid compliance by national judges and/or the national competition authority (NCA)

The centralised administration in charge of State aid compliance is the Competition Council ("Consiliul Concurentei") which plays the role of the single contact with the Commission and provides specialised assistance to the authorities granting State aid and to the beneficiaries in order to ensure compliance with the obligations undertaken by Romania as member of the EU including in the process of drafting of the official documents establishing State aid measures.

The Competition Council ensures the briefing of the granting authorities of the beneficiaries and the public on the relevant European legislation. The Competition Council briefs the Government on its State aid activity every six months.

In keeping with its authority in the field of State aid, the Competition Council is mainly involved in the following activities:

- it provides opinions both on the notifications submitted by the granting authorities to the Commission and on the modifications of such notifications;
- it represents Romania before the Commission in procedures regarding State aid;
- it monitors the grants of State aid at a national level and keeps the record of the State aid granted; and
- it cooperates with the representatives of the Commission in the process of on site verification.

Two other elements should be mentioned:

(a) The national court competent in disputes generated by grants of State aid is the Bucharest Court of Appeal .
(b) The above court is not called to assess the existence of aid within the meaning of Article 107(1) TFEU.

III. Unlawful aid and judicial review

1. Prevention of the granting of unlawful aid

The procedure offered by Romanian law to prevent the granting of unlawful aid is strictly administrative and consists of the approval of State aid by the Commission or the issuance of an opinion by the Competition Council in case of block exempted State aid.

There are no national provisions on which individuals can rely to ensure the obligation of notification.

2. Recovery of unlawful aid and interest

Under Romanian law the procedure enabling the recovery of unlawful aid from the beneficiary who does not voluntarily pay back the State aid consists of an administrative claim filed by the granting authority with the Bucharest Court of Appeal ("Curtea de Apel Bucuresti"), having as its object the annulment of the document which authorised the grant of the aid and the recovery of the aid and the relevant interest.

The decision of the court is subject to appeal in front of the High Court of Cassation and Justice of Romania ("Inalta Curte de Csatie si Justitie a Romaniei"). The court is not competent to identify the beneficiary of an aid nor to quantify the amount to be recovered with the exception of the interest which must be calculated in relation with the interest rate indicated in Regulation (EC) No 659/1999.

The above procedure presupposes the existence of a Commission decision declaring the aid unlawful. The procedure is the same in case the Commission has decided the provisional recovery of the State aid. The court is not competent to propose alternative remedies. It is difficult to asses how long does a recovery procedure will last. Generally, the procedures last for a few months.

3. Damages claims by competitors/third parties before national courts against the granting authority

There are no cases in Romania in this respect.

4. Damages claims by the beneficiary before national courts against the granting authority

There are no cases in Romania in this respect.

5. Damages claims by competitors/third parties before national courts against the beneficiary

There are no cases in Romania in this respect. We assume that the procedure used would be non contractual liability.

6. Interim measures taken by national judges

There are no cases in Romania in this respect.

IV. Control of recovery procedure

1. Rules applicable to recovery

To challenge the validity of national recovery order, the applicant must claim (in front of an administrative section of a court) that his interests have been affected by the unlawful act issued by the granting authority consisting in the recovery order. However, it would be difficult to support such a claim, given the circumstances in which the recovery order is based upon a decision of the Commission.

However, to the best of our knowledge, there are no cases in Romania in this respect.

2. Action for recovery

There are no cases in Romania in this respect.

Slovakia

Erika Csekes, Andrea Oršulová, Juraj Corba*

* Ružička Csekes s.r.o., Bratislava.

I. General principles of member state's state aid law

1. National authorities competent for granting aid and involved in the notification procedure

According to the State Aid Act (*zákon o štátnej pomoci*) no. 231/1999 Coll. as amended (hereinafter referred to only as "State Aid Act"), the following entities are considered to be granting authorities: (i) State authorities; (ii) regional self-governing authorities; (iii) municipalities; and (iv) other legal entities which grant State aid on the basis of a specific statute.

The Slovak Ministry of Finance co-ordinates affairs related to State aid (not only in relation to granting authorities but also in relation to the institutions of the EU). The Slovak Ministry of Finance is also exclusively involved in the notification procedure (it acts as an intermediary between granting authorities and the Commission). There is one exception to this general rule, which is contained in the Investment Aid Act (*zákon o investičnej pomoci*), no. 561/2007 Coll. as amended. If the so-called investment aid is subject to notification to the Commission, the notification is done directly by the Slovak Ministry of Economy.

2. National authorities competent for recovery and brief description of the procedure

The State Aid Act contains a general obligation on the granting authority to initiate recovery of the granted aid (including interest) once the aid has been declared unlawful by the Commission in its decision. In other words, the authority which granted the unlawful State aid bears the responsibility for its recovery following the relevant negative decision of the Commission.

Given the relatively narrow definition of granting authorities contained in the State Aid Act it is unclear, once a negative Commission decision is adopted, which public authority is responsible for recovery in a case where the State aid was granted by an entity not included in the list of granting authorities, e. g. by a public entity or private intermediary which has granted aid without proper national legal basis (in accordance with the Community law and case-law of the Commission and the CJEU/General Court such a situation cannot, in practice, be excluded *a priori*).

Recovery of unlawful State aid before the adoption of a final decision by the Commission would necessarily be handled by the relevant national court dealing with the action filed to that end by a competitor.

The procedure for recovery is not explicitly stated (neither the specific type of recovery order nor the single specific type of procedure is provided for). Therefore, in principle, the procedure depends on the means by which the State aid was granted – be it an administrative decision, a contract, or any other act of the relevant authority. It is up to the granting authority to find the appropriate procedure available under national law for recovery and to use it, or even to choose among those available, in conformity with requirements of EU law.

II. Identification of State aid issues at national level

1. State aid compliance by the national legislator and/or the executive power

There is no specific *ex ante* control of legislature provided for in order to avoid the granting of State aid by legislative act in violation of Article 108(3) TFEU. Theoretically, *ex post* control of legislature can be exercised by the Slovak Constitutional Court, which reviews conformity of national legislation with international treaties and the national Constitution (the national Constitution itself provides for primacy of EU acts over national legislation). However, this type of procedure has never been used for these purposes and cannot be initiated by undertakings or individuals. Moreover, it is not clear whether the Slovak Constitutional Court would be willing to undertake such a review and to abolish a legislative act on these grounds. *In concreto*, it is not clear whether the Slovak Constitutional Court would abolish such legislative act or would simply only refer to the general obligation of national authorities not to apply national legislation if that contravenes Community Acts in the field of State aid.

With respect to sub-statutory (regulatory) legislative acts or local legislation passed by regional self-governing authorities and municipalities, the State Attorney (*prokurátor*) may intervene and request the abolition of relevant legislative acts in the form of the so-called "protest pursuant to State Attorney Act" (*zákon o prokuratúre*), no. 153/2001 Coll. as amended.

As far as *ex ante* control of executive power is concerned, prior to notifying the Commission of aid proposed by the relevant granting authority, the Slovak Ministry of Finance checks the conformity of the granting authority's proposal with EU State aid rules (including the completeness of data). In order to be able to fulfil that task, the State Aid Act empowers the Slovak Ministry of Finance to request relevant and necessary information from public authorities or enterprises. This mechanism, however, does not apply to the so-called investment aid, which is administered and (if necessary) notified to the Commission by the Slovak Ministry of Economy.

As far as *ex post* control of executive power is concerned, the State Aid Act empowers the Slovak Ministry of Finance to undertake a governmental audit of the granting authority which granted State aid. If it is found that the aid was unlawfully granted, the granting authority is obliged to discontinue the granting of the aid. There is also the possibility that the State Attorney (*prokurátor*) may intervene and request the abolition of the relevant act or measure by means of issuing the so-called "protest pursuant to State Attorney Act" (*zákon o prokuratúre*), no. 153/2001 Coll. as amended.

In addition to the above, the State Aid Act contains various obligations of the granting authorities to report all relevant aid-related information to the Slovak Ministry of Finance (including *de minimis* aid). This enables the Slovak Ministry of Finance to fulfil its reporting obligations towards the Commission and the Slovak government.

The Ministry of Finance is empowered to impose financial sanctions on legal entities or individuals which breach their statutory duties and refuse to co-operate or report relevant information to it.

2. State aid compliance by national judges and/or the national competition authority (NCA)

a. State aid and NCA

The Slovak NCA (the Slovak Anti-Monopoly Office) is not competent as such in the field of State aid. However, it should be noted that the Competition Act (*zákon o ochrane hospodárskej súťaže*), no. 136/2001 Coll. as amended, contains section 39 titled "*Other forms of forbidden restrictions of competition*". This section forbids State, regional and local (municipal) administrative authorities, in the exercise of their administrative powers, to restrict competition, for instance by means of obvious support which gives advantages to a particular undertaking. The NCA is empowered to impose financial sanctions on administrative authorities if they act in breach of the above ban.

Section 39 of the Competition Act is worded relatively broadly. It has also been applied by the NCA to a financing of the Slovak Press Agency by the Slovak Ministry of Culture through State financial resources in budgetary years 2005 and 2006. The NCA found that the Ministry of Culture has distorted competition, because it enabled the Slovak Press Agency to finance from the State resources services, which are provided on the market under competitive conditions, in competition with a private press agency (see decisions of the Council of Slovak Anti-Monopoly Office (Rada Protimonopolného úradu Slovenskej republiky), no. 2006/39/R/2/023 and of 24 March 2006 and no. 2007/39/R/2/012 of 23 February 2007). Both decisions of the NCA were subsequently quashed by the Bratislava Regional Court (acting as administrative court, see decisions of the Bratislava Regional Court (Krajský súd v. Bratislave), *Ministerstvo kultúry Slovenskej republiky v. Protimonopolný úrad Slovenskej republiky*, no. 2 S 218/06-42 of 24 October 2007 and *Ministerstvo kultúry Slovenskej republiky v. Protimonopolný úrad Slovenskej republiky,* no. 2 S 113/07-145 of 7 May 2008). According to the information available, appeals against these decisions filed by the NCA are still pending before the Slovak Supreme Court.

The Slovak Ministry of Culture has not objected in the above proceedings on the basis of lack of competence of the NCA on the ground that the issue of financing of the Slovak Press Agency can only raise questions regarding the provision of State aid, in which only the Commission has exclusive competence. It seems that the issue of (potential) State aid has not been addressed in the proceedings before the NCA nor has it been discussed in the subsequent judicial review proceedings.

b. State aid and national courts

Practice of national courts in the area of State aid has not developed yet. Aside from those few judgments reported in the Case Summaries there were no other judgments of national courts related to State aid issues identified. In particular, no practice in the area of private enforcement of State aid rules has developed yet.

Therefore, all conclusions and remarks related to the practice of national courts contained in this report (see section III–VI of this report) are only brief and hypothetical, not confirmed by the decisional practice of the national courts.

III. Unlawful aid and judicial review

1. General powers of national courts concerning the direct effect of Article 108(3) TFEU

In general, there are two types of courts which have jurisdiction to apply Article 108(3) TFEU: standard civil courts and the so-called administrative courts (this distinction is purely functional; from the organisational point of view the administrative courts form an integral part of the civil courts).

The powers and procedures before these courts differ: while the civil courts handle disputes between private parties (including public authorities acting in contractual relationships, not exercising their public powers), the administrative courts only review acts and measures taken by public administration authorities.

The types of actions against public administration authorities exercising their public powers and *locus standi* of persons entitled to file such actions are strictly defined by law in the proceedings before administrative courts. On the other hand, civil courts may, in principle, hear any type of action by any person whose rights or protected interests were breached or jeopardised.

As far as the civil courts are concerned, the Act on Court Seats and Districts (*zákon o sídlach a obvodoch súdov Slovenskej republiky*), act no. 371/2004 Coll. as amended, stipulates that the Bratislava II District Court (*Okresný súd Bratislava II*) shall have exclusive (specialised) jurisdiction to deal at first instance with all disputes concerning "*protection of rights arising from competition*", and appeals against its decisions should be handled by Bratislava Regional Court (*Krajský súd v Bratislave*). Due to the lack of established practice is has not been authoritatively settled, whether this exclusive competence (which in any event concerns only private law disputes) also covers disputes which have their basis in State aid rules, or whether it only covers disputes based on competition law in narrower sense.

2. Prevention of the granting of unlawful aid

Unlike the civil courts, the administrative courts do not have the power to issue an interim measure or other kind of preventative decision. Therefore, if the State aid is about to be granted by a public authority in the course of exercising of its public powers (for instance by means of individual administrative decision), effective judicial prevention of granting of unlawful aid may be problematic.

It is of course questionable, whether this restriction imposed on administrative courts by the Civil Procedure Act (*Občiansky súdny poriadok*), no. 99/1963 Coll. as amended, is acceptable from the point of view of the *Factortame – Siples – Unibet* line of cases, heard in the

CJEU, which require that a court seized of a dispute governed by Community law must be in position to grant interim relief in order to ensure the full effectiveness of the judgment to be given on the existence of the rights claimed under Community law. On the other hand, it is also possible that this lack of power of administrative courts to issue interim measure or other types of preventative decisions can be overcome simply by reference to provisions contained in national law, namely section 244 subsection 6 of the Civil Procedure Act, which stipulates that the provisions on administrative judiciary apply (only) proportionally to situations, when the obligation to review acts and measures of administrative authorities stems from international treaties, by which the State is bound.

3. Recovery of unlawful aid and interest

As already mentioned above, the procedure for recovery is not explicitly stated in the State Aid act nor does it appear in other national legislation. Neither the specific types of recovery order nor single specific types of procedure is provided for.

If a negative decision of the Commission has already been issued, it is up to the granting authority to find the appropriate procedure available under national law for recovery and to use it, or even to choose among those available. In principle, recovery by means of civil judicial proceedings should always be possible, as the State Aid Act contains a general duty on those entities/persons in receipt of aid which had been declared incompatible/unlawful by the Commission to refund it (including the relevant interests). This general statutory duty can be invoked before a court.

4. Damages claims by competitors/third parties before national courts against the granting authority

Because of undeveloped judicial practice no relevant information can be provided. No single case involving public authority liability on the basis of Community law has been identified (even outside the State aid field). Also any conclusions regarding the relationship between Community liability principles and (non-contractual) national liability principles would be speculative and premature.

5. Damages claims by the beneficiary before national courts against the granting authority

See answers in section III.4, which apply *mutatis mutandis.*

6. Damages claims by competitors/third parties before national courts against the beneficiary

See answers in section III.4, which apply *mutatis mutandis* also in relation to the private liability of beneficiary. In addition to that it has been noted that should these types of disputes arise in the future, one can anticipate controversy surrounding what should actually be the relevant legal regime applicable to damage claims against a beneficiary. Due to the unclear wording of legislation a question will most likely arise as to whether these types of claims should be governed by damage liability provisions of the Commercial Code (*Obchodný zákonník*), no. 513/1991 Coll. as amended or by damage liability provisions of the Civil Code (*Občiansky zákonník*) no. 40/1964 Coll. as amended. These regimes contain different rules and conditions of damage liability (for instance they differ as regards limitation periods for submitting damage claims to a court). This important question of the applicable legal regime can only be authoritatively settled only by future judicial practice.

7. Interim measures taken by national judges

Because of undeveloped judicial practice no relevant information can be provided. For a general note regarding interim measures see answers in section III.2.

IV. Control of recovery procedure

1. Rules applicable to recovery

See answers to section I.2 and III.3.

2. Action for recovery

a. By the State

As the *FRUCONA Košice* (The Regional Court Košice, 21.4.2008, n° 2Cob/155/2007, Tax Office v. FRUCONA Košice a.s.), there has already been one case in which the granting authority (tax office) requested recovery by means of a civil action. The substance of the action was based on the general statutory duty of the recipient of aid to return that aid (including interests) once it had been declared unlawful by negative decision of the Commission. As already mentioned above, this general duty is contained in the State Aid Act. The action failed before the first instance and the appellate court. For more detailed information see the case summary.

In connection with this case, the Commission has filed an action against the Slovak Republic on the basis of Article 108(2) TFEU (C-507/08, *Commission of the European Communities v. Slovak Republic*, pending) for failure to immediately and effectively enforce the Commission's negative decision. Proceedings are still pending.

The case is a good illustration of the possible weaknesses and hurdles experienced by the granting authority in the recovery of unlawful aid through civil judicial proceedings.

b. By competitors

We have not identified any cases in which a competitor has filed an action requesting recovery.

c. By beneficiaries

We have not identified any cases in which a competitor has filed an action requesting recovery.

3. Challenging the validity of national recovery order

In general, the national law does not provide for a single specific type of recovery order. It also does not contain rules which would "automatically" transform a negative decision issued by the Commission into a national enforcement title enabling immediate enforcement (execution) of the Commission's decision against the beneficiary.

Therefore, there is no one specific way of challenging the validity of a national recovery order. The possible means of defence available to the beneficiary necessarily depend on how the granting authority proceeds with recovery against it. Given the general statutory duty of recipients of unlawful aid to return it (including interests), recovery by means of judicial proceedings (civil action) should in principle always be open to granting authorities. In such judicial proceedings the beneficiary enjoys the standard rights of defence. It also enjoys the right to use all available means to have the court's decision (the actual recovery order) reviewed by appellate bodies (i. e. to use all standard ordinary or extraordinary remedies available under national law, possibly including a constitutional complaint to the Slovak Constitutional Court).

As illustrated in the *FRUCONA Košice* case, which is the single case of recovery so far indentified, national courts have accepted various beneficiaries' arguments (for more details see the case summary). One of those arguments (although not couched specifically in these terms) resembles application of principle of legitimate expectation. The court of first instance (as well as the appellate court) came to a conclusion that no State aid has been granted due to lack of knowledge on the side of the beneficiary that the measure in question (tax debt write-off) did actually constitute State aid. The courts did not deal with the relevant case-law of the CJEU related to application of legitimate expectations in recovery proceedings.

4. Action contesting the validity of the Commission decision

One action of a beneficiary has been identified in which the validity of the Commission decision was contested before the General Court. This relates to the *FRUCONA Košice* case. The beneficiary sought the annulment of the Commission's negative decision of 7 June 2006 on State aid implemented by the Slovak Republic for the applicant (Decision C 25/2005), insofar as it treats the applicant as a recipient of incompatible State aid and compels it to repay to the Slovak Republic the entirety of the tax write-off with interest (Case T-11/07, *Frucona Košice, a. s. v. Commission*).

In support of its action, the beneficiary (the applicant) relied on the following ten pleas in law: By its first plea, the applicant claimed that the Commission made a manifest error when determining the amount of the alleged State aid. By its second plea, the applicant submitted that the contested decision violates an essential procedural requirement and fails to have regard to Article 39 TFEU (Common Agricultural Policy). In fact, the applicant claimed that DG Agriculture (and not DG Competition) was the competent directorate to carry out the investigation and take the procedural and formal steps that led to the contested decision. By its third plea, the applicant further submitted that the contested decision violated Section 3, Annex IV of the Treaty of Accession, Article 296 TFEU, Article 108 TFEU and Regulation (EC) No 659/1999 because the Commission lacked jurisdiction to issue the contested decision. By its fourth plea, the applicant contended that the Commission had erred in fact and in law in applying Article 107(1) TFEU when it found bankruptcy proceedings to be more favourable than the tax settlement. By its fifth plea, the applicant alleged that the Commission was in error by finding the tax execution procedure to be more beneficial than the tax settlement. By its sixth plea, the applicant submitted that the Commission had made a manifest error in law and in fact by failing to discharge the burden of proof thereby violating Article 107(1) TFEU and Article 296 TFEU. In addition, the applicant submitted that the Commission disregarded the legal standards set forth by the Court on the application of the private creditor test. By its seventh plea, the applicant claimed that the Commission had made an error in law and fact by failing to adequately assess and have regard to the evidence at its disposal. By its eighth plea, the applicant alleged that the Commission had made an error in law and in fact by taking into account irrelevant evidence such as internal differences within the tax administration. By its ninth plea, the applicant further submitted that the decision violated Article 296 TFEU by lacking sufficient reasoning to justify its conclusions. Lastly, by its tenth plea, the applicant alleged that the Commission erred by not exempting the tax settlement as restructuring aid and by retroactively applying the 2004 Restructuring Guidelines (Community guidelines on State aid for rescuing and restructuring firms in difficulty, OJ (2004) C 244/2).

According to publicly available information, it seems that the beneficiary has not requested that the General Court issue an interim measure suspending the effectiveness of the Commission decision. The proceedings are still pending.

5. Damages for failure to implement a recovery decision and infringement of EU law

No case of filing an action claiming damage for failure to implement a recovery decision and infringement of EU law has been identified.

V. Standing of third parties before national court

No case of competitor or third party filing a Stateaid related action before a national court has been identified. The issue of *locus standi* of these persons has not been addressed or clarified and settled by the judicial practice.

VI. Cooperation with EU authorities

1. Cooperation with the CJEU

As documented by the reported *FRUCONA Košice* case, no cooperation between the CJEU and a national court has been initiated by the national court(s) handling the case concerning recovery of unlawful aid.

Neither any other national court has submitted a request to the CJEU for a preliminary ruling related to State aid issues.

2. Cooperation with the Commission

No case of cooperation of national court with the Commission has been identified.

VII. Trends – reforms – recommendations

As a result of the widely publicised action initiated by the Commission against the Slovak Republic before the CJEU for non-recovery of unlawful aid from the beneficiary Frucona Košice a. s., local lawyers and public authorities have generally become much more aware of the issue of EU regulations on granting of State aid and of the powers of the Commission which it enjoys in this area.

Despite the problems and hurdles that the granting authority has experienced in this case when trying to recover the aid trough national judicial proceedings, no information is available about any kind of envisaged reform of State aid rules on the national level. However, if the Slovak Republic loses its case before the CJEU, this may well result in major re-consideration of national legislation applicable in the field of State aid (especially recovery procedure).

Besides that, one could recommend that the national legislation (especially the State Aid Act) should be reviewed in such a way that it does not duplicate or attempt to "summarise" the EU State aid rules, if not really necessary. As the EU State aid law is constantly evolving and is by nature case-bound, national legislation attempting to codify or "mirror" the EU State aid rules may well create a false impression on the scope of applicability of the EU rules, to the detriment of legal certainty.

One might also recommend that the national legislation clarify more precisely which competent civil courts have jurisdiction to hear actions in the field of private enforcement of State aid rules, and the applicable legal regime for damages (Commercial Code or Civil Code).

Last but not least, a better access to national courts' judgments in the field of State aid would help to spread general knowledge on applicable rules and standards. It seems that currently there is no real guarantee that all these judgments are easily accessible to the public, including lawyers.

SLOVENIA

Lea Lekočevič*

* Head of the State aid Monitoring Department, Ljubljana.

I. General principles of Member State's State aid law

State aid entails intervention by the State in relationships between entities that act on the market. The recipient of State aid is thus in a better position in comparison to its competitors. By distorting competition, State aid can cause a general lowering of the efficiency of the economy as a whole which, in turn, has a similar detrimental effect on social welfare. The central criterion for distinguishing between State aid that is compatible with the principles of market economics and measures that represent prohibited State aid is that of effective competition. Therefore, all State aid is prohibited with the exception of that granted in accordance with the specific rules and procedures defined in the provisions of the European Agreement relating to competition. The essential reason for legal regulation of the issue of State aid is thus to observe the principle of protection against the possible distortion of competition and alteration of market structure.

A short historical review (for a better understanding of the current settlement)

By signing the European Agreement, Slovenia committed itself to adapting the area of State aid to the *acquis communautaire*. Three elements were important for the fulfilment of the commitments: the legal basis, administrative competence, and implementation.

The State Aid Control Act (Ur. l. RS, 1/00 and 30/01) was adopted in 2000 and regulates the procedure and control of the granting and utilisation of State aid. The act's basic objective is to enforce market economics and to preserve competition. Secondary legislation has also been adopted to ensure the implementation of the act, viz.:

- the Decree on the content and procedure of supplying data for preliminary and subsequent State aid control (Ur. l. RS, 36/00), which regulates the content and procedure for the notification of State aid;
- the Decree on the purposes and conditions for the granting of State aid and on the appointment of the ministries responsible for the management of State aid schemes (Ur. l. RS, 59/00 and 38/03), which lays down the purposes for which, and conditions under which, State aid may be granted and the ministries responsible for managing individual aid schemes; and
- the Rules on the preparation of the annual survey of State aid (Ur. l. RS, 19/00), which regulates the content and form of the annual survey of State aid for the previous year.

In order to ensure administrative competence in the implementation of the system of State aid control, the Commission for State Aid Control (hereinafter referred to as the Commission) was established by virtue of a government resolution made under the State Aid Control Act. The State Aid Control Section was established to carry out specialist, administrative and technical tasks for the Commission, and was an internal organisational unit at the Ministry of Finance.

In accordance with the law, the Commission conducted *ex ante* and *ex post* control of the granting of State aid; proposed the annual survey to the Slovenian government for adoption;

adopted the annual report on its work, forwarding it to the government for adoption; and worked with international bodies in this area. A system of records of State aid granted, organised according to the recipient and the party granting the aid, and according to the category and instruments and a review of State aid granted under the *de minimis* rule was established to ensure transparency. With the establishment of the legal basis and the competent authorities, the conditions for implementing the rules in the area of State aid were put in place.

On the day Slovenia joined the EU (1 May 2004) the area of State aid control and the regulation of State aid changed. Control of the granting of State aid in a Member State became the responsibility of the Commission. On the same day, the existing Slovenian legislation governing the area of State aid ceased to be valid, and in its place the European legislation in this area applied directly. The law and all the aforementioned secondary legislation ceased to be valid.

In order to continue to ensure the right level of administrative competence to implement the legal system in the area of State aid, it was necessary for a special department at the Ministry of Finance to continue its work to ensure that State aid was granted in compliance with the *acquis communautaire*, to perform an advisory role for all agents of State aid and to provide a thorough overview in the area of State aid by administering a central database, and reporting on this to the Government and the National Assembly.

1. National authorities competent for granting aid and involved in the notification procedure

The National Assembly of the Republic of Slovenia adopted a new Law, the Monitoring of State Aid Act published in the Official Gazette of the Republic of Slovenia, no. 37/2004 (hereinafter referred to as the Law). Through the Law, Slovenia aimed to retain the existing monitoring system. Specifically, the Law's objective is to define the procedures for notifying and granting State aid. Integral support in connection with State aid continues to be available through a special department at the Ministry of Finance (hereinafter: the Ministry).

Among the main principles of the existing system of State aid upon which the Law also aims to focus are the transparency of notification and granting of State aid; *ex ante* verification of compatibility with the rules by the competent authority for all types of State aid; the forwarding of notification to the Commission and the responsibility for national control in the case of block exemptions; the provision of centralised records of all State aid and compulsory periodic reporting; and advice for the parties granting public funds and the recipients.

In this manner the possibility of State aid being granted, (particularly in the case of block exemptions and aid granted under the *de minimis* rule, that is prohibited because of incompatibility with EU rules), and the funds received thus being returned with interest on arrears, are reduced.

The Law lays down the entire procedure in connection with the granting of State aid, viz.: notification and *ex ante* verification of compatibility with the rules by the competent department; the issue of an opinion by the competent department and the forwarding of notification to the Commission; the procedure for communication between the Commission and the competent authority with regard to any additions to specific notifications; and everything until the notifying party is informed by the competent authority of whether the State aid has been approved or rejected.

2. National authorities competent for recovery and brief description of the procedure

If the Commission decides that the State aid must be recovered, the Ministry will send the decision to the granting authority. The granting authority has to request the recovery of incompatible State aid from the beneficiary.

II. Identification of State aid issues at national level

1. State aid compliance by the national legislator and/or the executive power

The Law charges the Ministry with the duty of monitoring the granting and utilisation of State aid and administering records on State aid. All institutional units within the state sector must forward information in connection with schemes and individual State aid to the Ministry.

The precise procedure and the content of the information forwarded are set out in secondary legislation.

The Ministry maintains a database of State aid that has been granted, and also collects information on the effectiveness and efficiency of State aid expenditure. On the basis of the information forwarded it draws up a report once a year on State aid that has been granted, and submits it to the Government. The Government then submits it to the National Assembly for discussion. In the annual report the Ministry also includes an assessment of the effectiveness and efficiency of the State aid that has been granted.

The Ministry carries out the following tasks pursuant to the Law:

- handling and assessment of the notification of State aid and forwarding it to the Commission;
- handling, assessment and provision of an opinion on State aid that entails a block exemption and aid under the *de minimis* rule;
- collection, processing and monitoring of information on State aid and on aid granted under the *de minimis* rule, and administration of records of such information;
- drawing up of an annual report;
- provision of advice to recipients of State aid.

A body that draws up a specific scheme of State aid or intends to grant individual State aid must first notify the State aid to the Ministry. The same procedure applies in the case of a supplement to or changes in existing State aid and in the granting of State aid under the *de minimis* rule.

The Ministry of Finance is charged with the duty of handling and assessing notified State aid. Within 45 days it forwards the notification to the Commission and informs the notifying party of this. If during the *ex ante* verification of compatibility with the rules, the Ministry assesses that the notified aid is incompatible, it informs the notifying party of this and calls on the notifying party to bring the aid into line with the rules. A notifying party that persists in retaining the content of the State aid as notified must make a declaration to the competent authority that it consents to the forwarding of notification with the aforementioned content to the Commission. As soon as the Ministry receives a decision from the Commission regarding the State aid, it informs the notifying party of this. Until that time the implementation of the State aid to which the notification relates is withheld and prohibited.

Pursuant to this, the Ministry is responsible for all correspondence, additional questions, explanations and supplements to notifications of State aid between the Commission and the notifying party.

In the area of block exemptions and the *de minimis* rule, a control role has been assigned to the Ministry, as it is not necessary to notify such State aid with the Commission, but merely necessary to inform the Commission within 20 days of the aid being granted. For this State aid, it is the Ministry that issues the opinion on compatibility with the rules, not the Commission. The opinion on compliance with block exemptions must be issued within 45 days of the aid being received, and the opinion for aid under the *de minimis* rule must be issued within 15 days. In the event of non-compliance, the Ministry calls on the recipient of the State aid to rectify it, setting a deadline for bringing it into line with the rules. Implementation is prohibited until a positive opinion has been issued. The Ministry informs the Commission of the granting of State aid under the Block exemption Regulations.

One of the competent authority's other important tasks is to advise notifying parties on the correct application and interpretation of the rules in the area of State aid; to help in drawing up the legal basis; and to propose measures for rectifying any irregularities or discrepancies in the granting of State aid.

In order to ensure transparency in the area of State aid, the Ministry administers records of:

- all notifications;
- notifications forwarded to the Commission;
- State aid granted; and
- aid granted under the *de minimis* rule.

2. State aid compliance by national judges and/or the national competition authority (NCA)

Generally, in administrative disputes, decisions are made by the administrative court and by the Supreme Court. First instance decisions are made by the administrative court, unless otherwise stipulated by law. Moreover, the decisions on complaints against a decision of the first instance courts, i. e. decisions on extraordinary legal remedies, are made by the Supreme Court.

In the field of State aid, the administrative court is competent for adjudication on actions concerning administrative decisions applicable in Slovenia. As stated above, the administrative court has ruled only once on this, in the case discussed. The case concerned the application of the *de minimis* rule (Sodba U 3/2005). The claimant in the case challenged the State's decision to refuse to make an application for State aid, since, according to the *de minimis* rule, a company engaged in transport activity is excluded from more favourable treatment. The claimant's main argument was that the relevant undertaking was not solely engaged in transport. However, the administrative court overruled the disputed decision, stating that the exception (due to the fact that damage was caused by natural disaster) should be considered as well. The court consequently annulled the disputed decision and sent the matter to the competent body for a reconsideration.

According to Administrative Dispute Act (ADA-1), which came into force on 1 January 2007, and was published in Official Gazette of the Republic of Slovenia, no. 133/06, national courts have no special investigation powers in cases concerning State aid.

So far, Slovenia has not commenced any preliminary reference procedures (in any field). It has to be restated that the Supreme Court has not yet dealt with any cases concerning EU State aid law. Every case has to be decided by the administrative authority first. Then the administrative court has to review the disputed decision. Therefore, it normally takes about five years for disputed decisions to reach and to be adjudicated by the Supreme Court. Since Slovenia's rather late accession to the EU (2004), the lack of Supreme Court jurisprudence in the field of State aid is not surprising.

Spain

Casto González-Páramo, Sonia Pérez*

* Hogan Lovells, Madrid.

I. General principles of Member State's State aid law

1. National authorities competent for granting aid and involved in the notification procedure

Competence for granting aid

In order to understand the Spanish procedure for granting State aid, it is important to bear in mind that Spain is organised into a semi-federal structure in which the powers of the central administration are shared with its seventeen autonomous territorial communities ("Autonomous Communities"), each one with its own independent regional administrative body. According to its semi-federal structure, regional administrations[212] are also competent for granting State aid and setting State aid schemes circumscribed to their respective territory whereas the central administration would predominantly carry out such activity at national level.

National Authorities involved in the notification procedure

a. *Notification by the Member State to the Commission*

Despite the capacity of regional administrations to set and grant State aid, the competence to notify the granting of State aid to the Commission remains exclusively within the central administration's scope of powers. In this regard, Royal Decree 1755/1987, of 23 December, on the notification procedure to the Commission of projects aimed at setting, granting or modifying internal aid by public administrations (hereinafter "Royal Decree 1755/1987") sets forth the procedure to be followed by public administrations when a State aid project is to be notified to the Commission.

Before the implementation by regional administrations or by the central government of a project regarding State aid, the project must be submitted to the Comisión Interministerial para Asuntos de la Unión Europea[213] ("Comisión Interministerial"). This administrative body is in charge of coordinating the notification of projects of both national (to be implemented by any of the Ministries of the central government) and regional (by regional administrations) scope. State aid projects shall be submitted to the Comisión Interministerial at least three months before their implementation. The submissions shall include as many precedents, studies and reports as necessary to determine the purpose, scope, recipients and amount of the State aid scheme. Within one month from the reception of the project, the Comisión Interministerial shall submit it to the Commission.

212 In this report, regional administrations means local and regional (Autonomous Community) administrative bodies.

213 This administrative body was created by Royal Decree 1567/1985 of 2 September.

b. *Notification by the Autonomous Communities to the Comisión Interministerial*

Apart from the provisions set by Royal Decree 1755/1987 regarding notification of State aid, the central administration has entered into individual agreements with the Autonomous Communities in order to coordinate the mechanisms of notification of State aid projects to the Comisión Interministerial. In particular, on 29 November 1990 the central administration and the Autonomous Communities entered into a cooperation agreement regarding notification of State aid measures[214] whereby a procedure of notification to the Comisión Interministerial through a "coordinating organ designed to this effect" in each Autonomous Community was established. In addition, some Autonomous Communities have passed specific regulations establishing internal procedures for the notification of State aid[215], or have designated specific departments within the regional administration in charge of the notification of State aid to the Comisión Interministerial[216].

c. *Supplementary regime of notification*

The Spanish Law on Administrative Procedure 30/1992 of 26 November (Ley de Régimen Jurídico de las Administraciones Públicas y del Procedimiento Administrativo Común, "Law on Administrative Procedure") establishes a supplementary notification regime to the one explained above. In particular, the Law on Administrative Procedure provides that when a resolution or a provision must be notified to the EU institutions, public administrations[217] shall submit it to the body of the central administration in charge of making notifications to the European institutions[218] (that is to say, the Comisión Interministerial). If a term to fulfil this obligation is not specifically determined in the relevant EU provision, the Comisión Interministerial shall submit the project within 15 days from its reception or in any case with enough time for the fulfilment of such obligation.

2. National authorities competent for recovery and brief description of the procedure

National authorities competent for recovery

In Spain, the implementation of the recovery procedure of unlawful State aid is carried out by the same administration which set the scheme of aid or granted the unlawful State aid concerned.

The recovery procedure is initiated by a decision ordering the recovery. This decision may be issued by:

---

214 See Spanish official journal 216 of 8.9.1992.

215 In particular, the Canary Islands, Cantabria, Castilla y Leon and the Basque Country.

216 In particular, Madrid.

217 In this report public administrations means local, regional and national administrations.

218 See Article 10 Law on Administrative Procedure.

a. *The administrative body of superior hierarchy to the granting administration*

Both competitors of the company receiving the aid and public administrations may challenge the validity of the administrative act formally granting the aid before the administrative body of superior hierarchy to the granting administration (recurso de alzada) through an administrative procedure. The decision taken by the superior administrative body may be appealed under judicial proceedings before a Contentious-Administrative Court[219] both by (i) competitors of the beneficiary or by (ii) a public administration (if the appeal is rejected by the administrative body of superior hierarchy) or by (iii) the beneficiary (opposing the recovery).

b. *The granting entity*

The same public administration which was competent to set a scheme of aid or grant a particular aid may, of its own initiative, initiate recovery proceedings under the so-called "procedure of revision of its own acts" ("revision de actos de oficio")[220].

The problems of State aid recovery under this procedure derive from the fact it requires the enactment by the granting entity of an administrative act formally annulling the prior granting administrative act. A second decision stating the need of recovery by such administration is then needed. This procedure requires a positive opinion by the Conseil d'État ("Consejo de Estado"), a consultive administrative body within the central administration. It is to be noted that the procedure of revision of its own acts by public administrations is only possible with respect to acts which are *ipso iure* void[221] and the administrative act granting an unlawful State aid is not specifically included within the acts qualifying as *ipso iure* void under Spanish Law.

c. *A decision by the Commission or a declarative judgment by the CJEU*

Recovery proceedings may be initiated by (i) either a decision of the Commission or (ii) a declarative judgment by the CJEU addressed to the granting administration.

If the granting administration does not start recovery proceedings, any other public administration or competitor of the beneficiary may bring a claim before a Contentious-Administrative Court to obtain the mandatory enforcement of the Commission's decision or the CJEU judgment.

---

219 The Administrative judicial proceeding deals with claims against the various branches of the public administration and is governed by the Spanish Act on judicial administrative proceedings.

220 See Article 102 Law on Administrative Procedure.

221 Under Spanish Law, acts enacted in breach of the Law may be (i) ipso iure void or (ii) voidable. An ipso iure void act is an act void in itself, i.e. it does not need a formal declaration by a Court providing for its annulment. On the contrary, voidable acts are valid and have legal effects unless and until they are declared null and void by a Court.

Brief description of the recovery procedure

There is not a specific recovery procedure regarding State aid under Spanish law. In the absence of specific regulation, public administrations apply the general provisions on administrative proceedings set by the Law on Administrative Procedure[222], which shall be applied in conjunction with the rules contained in the Spanish General Law on Subventions 38/2003 of 17 November (Ley General de Subvenciones, "General Law on Subventions"). The General Law on Subventions provides that recovery proceedings shall be initiated as a consequence of a declaration by the Commission on the need to recover a State aid considered as illegal or incompatible with the Internal Market[223].

It must be noted that the General Law on Subventions has a limited scope of application regarding State aid as it only covers those State aid which are granted in the form of a "subvention"[224] which is a stricter concept than that of State aid (as defined by the CJEU). In particular, a subvention is any monetary payment made by a public administration in favour of public or private entities which fulfils three requirements:

(a) There is no direct consideration in exchange of the State aid by the beneficiaries;
(b) The granting of the State aid is conditional to the implementation of a specific objective, project, activity or conduct by the beneficiary or to the existence of a particular and special situation; and
(c) The purpose of the specific project, action, conduct or situation is to foster an activity of public interest, or to promote compliance of a public objective.

II. Identification of State Aid Issues at National Level

1. State aid compliance by the national legislator and/or the executive power

Ex ante control of the State aid

a. Control by the Comisión Interministerial

The powers of the Comisión Interministerial include both (i) the coordination of the acts of the central administration in economic matters in connection to the EU and (ii) the right to be informed about the decisions relating to the EU approved by the Ministries of the central government in their respective areas of competence (see above section I.1.a).

Hence, the Comisión Interministerial carries out an *ex ante* control to verify that the State aid granted by public administrations fulfil the EU requirements. In this regard, Royal Decree

222 See Title VI Law on Administrative Procedure.

223 See Article 37.1.h) General Law on Subventions.

224 See Article 2 General Law Subventions.

1755/1987 establishes the obligation on any public administration intending to set, grant or modify internal aid measures to submit the project concerning a State aid scheme or an individual State aid to the Comisión Interministerial at least three months before its entry into force. The project shall include as many precedents, studies and reports as necessary in relation to the aim, scope, addressees and amount of the State aid scheme or individual State aid.

When the State aid scheme relates to regional incentives, the Comisión Interministerial shall request the opinion of the Advisory Council[225]. After its review, the Comisión Interministerial shall submit the projects to the Commission for approval according to Article 108(3) TFEU.

The General Law on Subventions (of supplementary application to the Law on Administrative Procedure) provides that in those cases where, according to Articles 107 to 108 TFEU, projects for the setting, granting of modification of a subvention shall be communicated to the Commission, public administrations shall communicate such projects in accordance with the Law on Administrative Procedure[226] and any other regulations in this regard, in order to declare their compatibility with EU Law[227]. In these cases, a subvention may not be made effective until a declaration of compatibility is issued.

b. *Publication of the terms and conditions to benefit from a subvention*

Prior to the granting of subventions, the official terms and conditions of their granting shall be approved by order of the respective Ministry and published in the National Official Journal. With the purpose of avoiding the granting of several State aid to the same beneficiary (and its incompatibility with the Internal Market), the terms and conditions for granting a subvention shall determine the compatibility or incompatibility with other subventions, aid, income or resources with the same purpose granted by any other national or European public administrations, private entities or international organisations[228].

c. *Control by the Intervención General de la Administración del Estado*[229]

The General Law on Subventions describes the requirements for the granting of a subvention[230]. These specifically include the *ex ante* control of the administrative acts granting the aid by the Intervención General de la Administración del Estado.

---

225 The Advisory Council (Consejo Rector) was created by Royal Decree 50/1985 of 27 December, on regional incentives for the correction of economic geographic inequalities.

226 See Section 1.1.c) "Supplementary regime" of this report.

227 See Article 9 General Law on Subventions.

228 See Article 17.3.m) General Law on Subventions.

229 Articles 44 and 45 General Law on Subventions grant the competence for the financial control of subventions to the Intervención General del Estado.

230 Article 9 General Law on Subventions.

Other requirements are (i) the competence of the public administration for granting the subsidy, (ii) the existence of appropriated and sufficient credit to fulfil the economic obligations derived from the granting of a subvention, (iii) compliance with the granting procedure of the legislation in force and (iv) the approval of the expenditures by the competent administration.

Ex post control of State aid measures

Self control by the granting administration

A public administration which has granted a State aid may, of its own initiative, control the legality of its granting administrative act. According to the Law on Administrative Procedure[231], public administrations may carry out a revision of their own administrative acts ("revision de actos de oficio"), which requires a previous positive opinion of the Conseil d'État. Under this procedure the granting administration may declare the granting act as null and void, and enact a new decision ordering the recovery of the unlawful aid. It is to be noted that this procedure is only applicable if the granting act is *ipso iure* void[232], otherwise the validity of the act has to be challenged before an Administrative Court. To palliate the drawbacks that appearance before a Contentious-Administrative Court may cause, especially as regards time and expenses, the General Law on Subventions has enabled a procedure whereby the Spanish administrations may issue a decision of recovery based on Articles 107 and 108 TFEU, which shall be enforceable in spite of the granting administrative act not being declared as null and void by a Contentious-Administrative Court.

National database of subventions and public aid[233]

Another means of *ex post* control of State aid is provided by the national database of subventions and public aid granted in Spain[234]. This national database contains information on the subventions and public aid which have been granted in Spain in accordance with the Law on Administrative Procedure. In particular, public administrations shall provide the Intervención General de la Administración del Estado with information on the subventions and public aid managed by them, including the terms and conditions of the subventions, calls for applications, identification of the beneficiaries, recovery decisions and sanctions imposed. This database has been implemented in order to fulfil the requirement imposed by the EU to implement a better efficacy and control of the subsidies granted. The national database of subventions and public aid has a confidential character and may only be communicated to other public administrations.

231 See Article 102 Law on Administrative Procedure.

232 See footnote 10 on the difference between ipso iure void and voidable acts.

233 The national database on subventions and public aid was created by ministerial order of 13.1.2000.

234 See Article 20 General Law on Subventions.

2. State aid compliance by national judges and/or the national competition authority (NCA)

State aid compliance by the national competition authority

The Spanish Competition Act 15/2007 of 3 July ("Ley de Defensa de la Competencia", "LDC") grants the Spanish Competition Commission ("Comisión Nacional de la Competencia", "CNC") powers for the maintenance of effective competition in relation to the potential effects of State aid[235]. In particular, the CNC shall analyse the competition implications of State aid criteria and policies applied by the public administrations. It shall also:

- elaborate on general or specific reports in relation to State aid regimes and individual aid measures and their impact on effective competition in the Spanish markets. These reports shall be made public after their notification to the public administrations concerned; and
- submit recommendations and proposals to public administrations for the preservation of effective competition in Spanish markets.

The CNC shall draft an annual report on the State aid schemes and individual aid granted in Spain, which shall be made public after its submission to the Ministry of Economy and to the Commission of Economy and Treasury of the Parliament ("Congreso de los Diputados"). The competition authorities of the Autonomous Communities may submit their reports on public aid granted within their respective geographical scope to the CNC in order for them to be included in its annual report. The CNC published in July 2009 its first annual report on Public Aid measure granted in Spain 2008. This report may be consulted at www.cncompetencia.es.

Within the context of its jurisdiction on State aid control, the Comisión Interministerial (see sections I.1 and II.1 above) shall communicate to the CNC:

- the submission to the Commission of projects on State aid measures included in the scope of application of Articles 107 and 108 TFEU at the time of their notification for approval;
- the State aid granted in Spain by virtue of Exemption Regulations of the EU legal framework; and
- the submission of the Spanish annual report on State aid to the European Commission[236].

---

235 See Articles 11, 26.d) and 27 LDC.

236 Article 21 Council Regulation (EC) No 659/1999 of 22 March 1999 laying down detailed rules for the application of Article 93 of the TFEU Treaty provides that "Member States shall submit to the Commission annual reports on all existing aid schemes with regard to which no specific reporting obligations have been imposed in a conditional decision".

The CNC is also entrusted with the responsibility of making the information on State aid available to the competition authorities of the Autonomous Communities. It also coordinates the activity of these authorities in this field[237].

State aid compliance by national judges

As a cons of the EU legal framework equence of the semi-federal structure of Spain, under Spanish law the territorial jurisdiction of Spanish judges depends on the administrative body granting the aid. Hence, if the State aid has been granted by:

- local administration: any controversy shall be dealt by the Contentious-Administrative Courts of the relevant province;
- an Administrative body of an Autonomous Community: the Contentious-Administrative division of the Superior Court of Justice of that Autonomous Community; or
- the central administration: the Central Contentious-Administrative Courts.

As regards the assessment of aid within the meaning of Article 107(1) TFEU by Spanish courts, the following aspects may be pointed out:

a. Analysis of State aid criteria

State aid law is still developing in Spain and hence, in general, national courts do not analyse in depth compliance with State aid criteria (i.e. State resources, selective advantage, restriction of competition and effect on trade, etc.) in their judgments. Commonly, Spanish courts tend to consider that public funded aid constitute selective competitive advantages and also assume that they may have an effect on trade.

Notwithstanding the above, Spanish courts have carried out a detailed analysis of State aid criteria in the so-called "Basque Country tax cases", where they found difficulties in determining whether a tax scheme fell into the scope of Article 107 TFEU or not. One of the latest cases in which the Superior Court of Justice of the Basque Country provided in-depth analysis of the State aid criteria is Appeal 890/2008, where a regional tax law of Vizcaya was appealed by the region of Castilla y León on the grounds that it set a tax regime which qualified as a State aid and had not been notified to the Commission.

237 See Law 1/2002 of 21 February on coordination of the State competences with the autonomous communities in Competition Law issues. This law establishes mechanisms of allocation of jurisdiction between the national competition authority and the regional competition authorities regarding Competition Law and sets reciprocal information mechanisms on this matter.

b. Powers of investigation

There are no special powers of investigation with regards to State aid. When verifying the existence of State aid, Spanish courts have the standard powers of investigation that the Law grants them. These powers include the capacity to order the necessary measures of inquiry, in particular the production by one of the parties or a third party of a particular document providing specific information.

c. Article 267 TFEU

In general, Spanish courts seem reluctant to request preliminary rulings from the CJEU in all areas of EU Law. In this regard, it is significant that in 2008 only one preliminary ruling concerning State aid was submitted to the CJEU, namely appeal 104/2004 Unión de Televisiones Comerciales Asociadas v. Federación de Asociaciones de Productores Audiovisuales, which was answered by the CJEU on 5 March 2009.

d. Third parties

The Spanish Act on judicial administrative proceedings 29/1998 of 13 July ("Ley reguladora de la jurisdicción contencioso-administrativa", "Act on Judicial Administrative Proceedings") allows the active intervention in the contentious-administrative proceedings of third parties holding a right or having a legitimate interest in the object of the proceedings[238]. The burden of proof of the legitimate interests is on the third party alleging them.

e. Application of EU regulations and guidelines

Spanish courts are increasingly demonstrating in depth knowledge of the EU regulations and guidelines applicable to State aid cases. Recently, Spanish courts have applied Exemption Regulations (in Appeal 77/2006 of 31.1.2007 and Appeal 7075/2004 of 13.2.2008) as well as decisions of the Commission (in Appeal 4139/2001 of 7.7.2008), have decided on the application of different EU regulations to a specific national scheme of aid (in Appeal 372/2005 of 5.5.2008) and have confirmed the refusal of State aid on the basis of the EU guidelines (in Appeal 328/2004, of 20.9.2006, Appeal 734/2003 of 14.3.2006 and Appeal 496/2004, of 13.4.2007).

A recent example of good application of an EU regulation to a Spanish case, in which the Court analysed in depth the EU legislation, is Appeal 372/2005 of 5.5.2008 Association Taula D' Entitats del Tercer Sector Social de Catalunya ("ATDETSS") v. Regional Administration of Catalonia. In this appeal the Superior Court of Justice of Catalonia decided on the potential

---

238 See Article 19 Act on Judicial Administrative Proceedings.

application of Regulation 2204/2002[239] to a scheme of aid set by a regional Decree of Catalonia, which had been declared to be subject to Regulation (EC) No 69/2001 by the Administration of Catalonia. The Superior Court of Justice of Catalonia concluded that taking into account the scope and purpose of the scheme of aid concerned, it had been correctly subject to Regulation (EC) No 69/2001 and that the Commission had expressly stated that this Regulation applied to the Regional Decree 81/2005.

Despite the improvement in compliance with EU law by Spanish courts, Spain is still only halfway to complete application of the EU State aid regime since there are also cases where Spanish courts have given preference to national legislation in breach of the principle of primacy of EU Law. An example of such cases is Appeal 95/2008 of 10.7.2008 where the Administrative Legal Organ of Alava[240] ("ALOA") annulled a decision denying the deferment and break up of a recovery payment and submitted the case to the competent administrative organ to decide again on the case. ALOA based its decision on the existence of regional legislation allowing for the deferment and break up of tax debts despite the request of effective and immediate recovery of certain unlawful State aid by a decision of the Commission.

III. Unlawful aid and judicial review

1. General powers of national courts concerning the direct effect of Article 108(3) TFEU

Contentious-Administrative Courts may declare administrative acts approved in breach of Article 108(3) TFEU as null and void if a competitor of the beneficiary of a State aid or a public administration file an action for annulment or contesting its legality. The Contentious-Administrative Court's decision may be appealed in a second judicial instance before the Contentious-Administrative division of the Superior Court of Justice of the Autonomous Community (in case of decisions of regional administrations) and in an ulterior instance before the administrative division of the Supreme Court.

2. Prevention of the granting of unlawful aid

Under Spanish Law, national courts do not have specific powers regarding the prevention of the granting of unlawful State aid, since they may only review the legality of a State aid as a consequence of the filing of a claim by a third party.

---

239 Regulation (EC) No 2204/2002 on the application of Articles 87 and 88 of the EC Treaty to State aid for employment.

240 The Economic-Administrative Court of Alava is denominated Administrative Legal Organ of Alava (Organismo jurídico administrativo de Alava) in this region.

Within the administration, the CNC has been entrusted with supervisory powers to analyse the criteria set by the Spanish administrations for granting State aid. In particular, the CNC shall consider the potential anticompetitive effects on the market of the proposed State aid scheme and request information in relation to the projects and State aid granted by local, regional and national administrations[241]. In addition, the CNC has the duty of issuing general or specific reports on the impact of State aid measures on effective competition in the markets[242].

3. Recovery of unlawful aid and interest

Procedure

Two situations may occur when an unlawful aid has to be recovered by the granting administration:

- Voluntary recovery by the granting administration: the administration which granted the unlawful State aid starts recovery proceedings of its own initiative by approving a so-called administrative act of recovery. If the beneficiary refuses to return the granted aid, the grantor may file a request of recovery before a Contentious-Administrative Court in order to obtain a mandatory execution of the administrative act of recovery.
- Refusal to initiate recovery proceedings by the granting administration: a competitor or a public administration may file a request before a Contentious-Administrative Court to obtain a judicial declaration on the necessity for recovery or, if such declaration is not executed by the granting administration, to obtain the mandatory execution of the recovery.

Identification of the beneficiaries

In case of an aid scheme declared unlawful by a Contentious-Administrative Court, the granting authority is responsible for the identification of the beneficiaries.

Quantification of the amount to be recovered

Regarding the quantification of the recovery, the General Law on Subventions provides that after the enactment of a recovery decision, public administrations shall initiate the recovery procedure for the amount of the State aid received and interest for late payment accrued as from the date of payment of the subsidy until the date when the recovery was decided[243].

---

241 See Article 11.1 and 4 LDC.

242 See Article 26.1.d LDC.

243 See Article 37.1.h) General Law on Subventions.

4. Damages claims by competitors/third parties before national courts against the granting authority

General regime

Competitors of the beneficiary and third parties may claim damages under the general administrative procedure if an administrative act whereby a State aid was granted is declared null and void by a public administration or by a Contentious-Administrative Court.

The Law on Administrative Procedure[244] sets a liability regime for public administrations, whereby individuals have the right to be compensated by public administrations for any damage to their goods or rights, provided that the damage:

- results from the normal or abnormal functioning of the public services; and
- is effective, economically appreciable and individualised regarding one person or a group of persons.

Depending on the case, the right to be compensated may be claimed before (i) the relevant Ministry, (ii) the Council of Ministries or (iii) the competent body of the regional administrations. The claim may be filed up to one year after the damaging event (or its manifestation). The decision issued by one of the bodies mentioned above concludes the administrative procedure and may only be appealed before a Contentious-Administrative Court.

Special regime

Apart from the general regime of liability of public administrations, the General Law on Subsidies sets forth a special liability regime of public administrations or their managing bodies or entities which carry out actions of management and control of aid financed by the European Agricultural Guidance and Guarantee Fund, the European Regional Development Fund, the European Social Fund and any other European funds[245].

The financial responsibilities of public administrations shall be determined by the administrative bodies in charge of the proposal or the coordination of the payments of each European fund. Prior to the enactment of the decision on its financial responsibility, the relevant administration shall be given audience. The decision shall be submitted to the Ministry of Economy for the relevant liquidations or compensations to be implemented with the public administration.

---

244 See Article 139 and subsequent.

245 See Article 7 General Law on Subsidies.

5. Damages claimed by the beneficiary before national courts against the granting authority

The beneficiary of a State aid may claim damages against the granting administration resulting from the annulment of the granting administrative act under the general liability regime of public administrations (see above).

6. Damages claims by competitors/third parties before national courts against the beneficiary

Competitors of the beneficiaries may bring an action before a Commercial Court in order to obtain compensation for those damages suffered as a consequence of the granting of a State aid. In this regard, the Unfair Trade Act 3/1991 of 10 January[246] ("Ley de Competencia Desleal", "Unfair Trade Act") considers as unfair any action by the beneficiary of the State aid in breach of Competition law resulting on damages to third parties.

The Unfair Trade Act put at the competitor's disposal an action for compensation of damages caused by the illegal act, if the beneficiary acted with bad faith or fault. This action may be exercised within the longer of the following periods:

- one year from the date the claimant knew about the disloyal conduct; or
- three years from the date when the disloyal conduct was carried out.

7. Interim measures taken by national judges

a. *Interim measures taken during the course of judicial proceedings*

The claimant may request the competent Contentious-Administrative Court which will ultimately decide on the main proceedings, to take interim measures regarding the State aid granted unlawfully. The procedure to request interim measures is regulated by the Act on Judicial Administrative Proceedings[247] that allows the claimant to request either the suspension of the administrative act or any other measures necessary to ensure the effectiveness of the judgment while judicial proceedings are taking place.

The granting of interim measures is subject to the fulfilment of two requirements:

- *fumus boni iuris*: i.e. a high probability of the existence of the right which deserves judicial protection; and
- *periculun in mora*: i.e. the possibility that the effectiveness of the final judgment may be put at risk if interim measures are not taken.

---

246 See Articles 18 to 26 Unfair Trade Act 3/1991.

247 See Articles 129 to 136.

The procedure to adopt interim measures by the Contentious-Administrative Court is carried out separately from the main proceedings. The counterparty shall be given audience within ten days from the date on which the interim measures were requested (except for urgent measures which can be taken without audience) and the decision shall be taken within the next five days. Interim measures shall remain in force until a final judgment is issued or until the end of the main procedure where they were requested, and may be modified or revoked during the course of the judicial proceedings if the circumstances which justified their adoption change.

b. Interim measures taken during the course of administrative procedures

According to the Law on Administrative Procedure, interim measures may also be adopted by the public administration, of its own initiative or by request of a party, if the effectiveness of the final resolution by the administration may be put at risk[248].

In addition, the General Law on Subventions foresees the possibility of retention of payments as an interim measure once the decision of recovery has been approved[249]. In this event, the granting administration may suspend the payments to the beneficiary of the amounts pending. It may do so (i) of its own initiative; (ii) according to a decision of the European Commission; or (iii) by proposal of the Intervención General de la Administración del Estado or the entity carrying out the payment of the State aid.

The requirements to suspend the payment of a State aid as interim measure are the following:

- the enactment of a motivated resolution, which must be notified to the beneficiary;
- the possibility that the reimbursement may be put at risk;
- proportionality of the measure in relation to the objective envisaged;
- the measures shall be maintained until the final decision is issued by the relevant administration in charge of the recovery and may not exceed such period; and
- the interim measure may be suspended if the circumstances that originated its adoption disappear or the beneficiary proposes its substitution by other guarantee.

IV. Control of recovery procedure

1. Rules applicable to recovery

There are no specific rules applicable to the recovery procedure under Spanish law. As a consequence of this absence of regulation, public administrations must apply their general rules

248 See Article 72 Law on Administrative Procedure.

249 See Article 35.1 General Law on Subventions.

contained in the Law on Administrative Procedure. The stages of the general procedure (of recovery) may be summarised as follows:

- declaration of the illegality of a State aid by (i) the granting administration of its own initiative; (ii) a decision by the Commission; (iii) a judgment of the CJEU; or (iv) a Contentious-Administrative Court by request of a third party (a competitor of the beneficiary or a public administration);
- annulment of the granting administrative act by the granting administration (only if the action for recovery is exercised by the granting administration of its own initiative);
- decision on the initiation of recovery procedure by the granting administration; and
- reimbursement by the beneficiary of the aid granted unlawfully.

2. Action for recovery

a. Exercise of the action for recovery

The action for recovery may be exercised by (i) the granting administration; (ii) the European Commission; (iii) the CJEU; (iv) a competitor of the beneficiary; or (v) a public administration.

b. Problems regarding the initiation of the recovery procedure by the granting administration of its own initiative

The problems with the initiation of the recovery procedure by the granting administration under Spanish law have already been highlighted. In particular, the procedure under which the granting administration revises its own acts requires that the administrative act qualifies as *ipso iure* void, and it is not clear whether an administrative act granting an unlawful State aid falls within this category of acts. On the contrary, if the granting act is considered as voidable it shall be deemed as valid and have legal effects until it is declared null and void by a Contentious-Administrative Court.

The problematic nature of the Spanish recovery procedure of State aid was highlighted by the Commission in Joined Cases C-485/03 to C-490/03, Commission of the European Communities v. Kingdom of Spain, where it pointed out the irrelevance of the internal administrative difficulties found by Spain in the recovery of State aid by saying that:

> *"since Spanish law does not expressly provide for a mechanism for recovery of the unlawful and incompatible aid, it was decided to resort to proceedings for review, on the initiative of the authorities themselves, of the tax measures governing the grant of aid, as laid down in the General Tax Code of each of the Historic Territories. However, the national authorities deliberately chose a procedure which makes recovery extraordinarily difficult, namely proceedings for a declaration that certain measures susceptible of annulment have an adverse effect, which renders necessary the satisfaction of a series of cumulative conditions, which it is extremely*

difficult to fulfil, above all from a temporal point of view. Domestic law provides for a number of procedures which, at first sight, are less problematical, such as review of provisions and measures which are ipso jure void, a procedure which appears to be perfectly applicable to the aid granted in breach of the procedure laid down in Article [108 of the TFEU]. Recourse to that procedure would probably be less problematical, in so far as it allows a declaration of nullity by the administration itself, without the need to fulfil the requirements laid down for the abovementioned declaration of adverse effects. The national authorities do not appear in this case to have chosen either the least problematical procedure or the most relevant procedure among those available to them within the domestic legal system."

The General Law on Subventions has partially mitigated the problems existing in the Spanish legal system regarding recovery of State aid. It has established a new regime of reimbursement of subsidies whereby proceedings for the recovery of a subvention shall be initiated if a decision adopted in accordance with Articles 107 and 108 TFEU declares the need for recovery[250]. This provision omits the need to issue a declaration of annulment of the provision (and hence the procedure of revision of its own acts by public administrations) and allows the recovery of the State aid.

c. *The decision on the initiation of the recovery*

In general, the administration which granted the unlawful State aid is responsible for its recovery. In these cases, the procedure of recovery is initiated by an administrative act issued by the granting administration requiring the beneficiary to return the aid received.

However, if the decision to recover has been issued by the Commission or the CJEU its enforcement shall be carried out by the public administration before which the recovery may be appealed[251].

If an aid granted by the Commission or any other EU entity is declared as unlawful by the national entity in charge of controlling the legality of aid granted in Spain, the decision to recover shall be issued by the national entity managing the public funding at national level ("órgano gestor nacional"). It may do so (i) of its own initiative, (ii) by proposal of other entities of the administration with powers to control public funding, (iii) by requirement of an administration of superior hierarchy to the granting entity, or (iv) by claim of a competitor of the beneficiary.

d. *Procedure of reimbursement*

The reimbursement shall be carried out according to the general administrative provisions contained in the Law on Administrative Procedure[252], and where applicable to the specific

250 Title II, Chapter I (Articles 36 to 43).

251 See Article 41.2 General Law on Subventions.

252 See Title VI Law on Administrative Procedure.

provisions of the General Law of Subventions. The procedure shall guarantee the beneficiary of the aid's right of audience. The decision and notification of the recovery of the unlawful aid must take place within twelve months from the date of the initiation of the proceeding, although this term may be suspended or extended in certain cases[253].

3. Challenging the validity of national recovery order

The decision to recover concludes the administrative procedure[254]. To oppose a recovery order granted in the administrative procedure, the beneficiary of a State aid may exercise a judicial action. In particular, the beneficiary may file an action for annulment which challenges the legality of the recovery order before a Contentious-Administrative Court.

There have also been cases where the beneficiary has filed an action based on legitimate expectations although these have normally been dismissed by the courts.

4. Action contesting the validity of the Commission decision

According to Articles 263, 264 and 266 TFEU, natural or legal persons may start proceedings before the CJEU contesting the validity of a Commission decision which, although in the form of a regulation or a decision addressed to another person, is of direct and individual concern to the claimant.

5. Damages for failure to implement a recovery decision and infringement of EU law

If a Spanish entity in charge of implementing a recovery decision fails to take any action in breach of EU Law, the affected individuals or legal entities are allowed to claim damages by virtue of the regime of liability of public administrations set by the Law on Administrative Procedure (see above section III.4)

V. Standing of Third Parties Before National Court

Article 24 of the Spanish Constitution states that the right to legal protection of individuals qualifies as a fundamental right that may be claimed by any individual or legal entity before a Spanish Court. Third parties are allowed to defend their interests in administrative procedures and in judicial proceedings:

(a) Administrative procedure: Article 31 of Law on Administrative Procedure allows the intervention in the procedure of "interested parties". To qualify as an interested party, an

---

253 See Articles 41 to 43 General Law on Subventions.

254 See Article 42 General Law on Subventions.

individual has to prove title over a right or a legitimate interest which may be affected by the result of the procedure. Interested parties may, at any time before they are given audience, make statements and submit documents or other evidence, which shall be taken into account by the resolutory body in its decision.

(b) Judicial proceedings: Article 19 of the Spanish Act on judicial administrative proceedings points out that third parties may be admitted if they have a direct and legitimate interest in the result of the proceedings. Also Law 1/2000 of 7 January on Civil Procedure, of supplementary application in judicial administrative proceedings, foresees the intervention of third parties with direct and legitimate interest before the national court where the suit was brought. It states that the court shall assess the suitability of the intervention within 10 days from the date of filing. Once the third party has been admitted into the proceedings, it shall be considered as a party and allowed to make any statements that deemed necessary in order to defend the claims and interests which could not be protected in previous stages of the procedure where the third party could not intervene for reasons of not being present.

The burden of proof of the affectation by the result of the proceedings of a direct and legitimate interest relies on the claimant. Once a third party is admitted to the proceedings, it is allowed to make any declarations that are deemed convenient for the defence of its interests that could not be protected in previous stages of the proceedings.

VI. Cooperation with EU authorities

1. Cooperation with the CJEU

Spanish courts still seem to be reluctant to refer to the CJEU for preliminary ruling when they have doubts on the interpretation of EU law. Recently, the Supreme Court has only brought prejudicial questions in relation to the cinematographic sector and to the Basque tax regulations (which still seem to cause problems after the CJEU preliminary rulings).

Two cases may be highlighted as examples of the cooperation by Spanish Courts with the CJEU. The first one is the latest preliminary ruling issued to the CJEU by the Supreme Court and the second one has a special importance because it has set a precedent for the analysis of the concept of State aid by Spanish Courts in the Basque tax cases.

In appeal 104/2004 Unión de Televisiones Comerciales Asociadas (UTCA) v. Federación de Asociaciones de Productores Audiovisuales (FAPA), the Supreme Court issued three preliminary questions regarding the interpretation of Royal Decree 1652/2004 on obligatory investments for the finance in advance of European and Spanish cinematographic and TV films. In particular, the Supreme Court asked whether a national rule requiring television operators to assign a percentage of its exploitation revenue to finance cinematographic films produced by the Spanish cinematographic industry and in Spanish language constituted a State aid.

The Court of Justice issued a preliminary ruling on 5 March 2009, Case C-222/07 where it stated that *"Article [107 TFEU] must be interpreted as meaning that a measure adopted by a Member State, such as the measure at issue in the main proceedings, requiring television operators to earmark 5 % of their operating revenue for the pre-funding of European cinematographic films and films made for the production of works of which the original language is one of the official languages of that Member State does not constitute a State aid in favour of the cinematographic industry of that Member State"*.

Another preliminary question on the cinematographic sector in Spain was issued by the CJEU in Case C-17/1992 Federación de Distribuidores Cinematográficos v. Estado Español and Unión de Productores de Cine y Televisión, where the CJEU clarified that national rules which reserve the grant of licenses for dubbing films from third countries into one of the official national languages to distributors who undertake to distribute national films are precluded by the TFEU.

The Basque tax regulations have also been (and remain) subject to several prejudicial questions brought by the Spanish Supreme Court. On 11 September 2008 the CJEU issued a judgment gathering several questions regarding Basque tax regulations (Joined Cases C-428/06 to C-434/06) Unión General de Trabajadores de La Rioja (UGT-Rioja) and others v. Juntas Generales del Territorio Histórico de Vizcaya and others. In its judgment, the CJEU stated that when a regional Government has enough institutional, procedural and economic autonomy to determine the operative framework of the companies located in its territory, the regional tax measures should not be considered as State aid (since these measures would not have the exclusive character that determines such qualification). However, the infringement of its competences by the regional Government when passing a piece of legislation would determine the assessment of the regional legislation as it if were a national one.

This judgment has been followed by the national courts in its latest judgments, such as in appeal 3672/2007 (Supreme Court) and appeal 890/2008 (Superior Court of Justice of the Basque Country), where the courts had to decide on two regional pieces of legislation of Vizcaya (a province of the Basque Country). The controversial character of the special tax regime of the Basque Country in Spain is also evidenced by the large number of resolutions issued by the national courts and the number of provisions that have been annulled by the Supreme Court prior to the enactment of substituting legislation causing confusion and a certain legal loophole.

2. Cooperation with the Commission

a. Cooperation by national courts

Cooperation with the Commission by national courts has a limited scope as a consequence of the specific configuration of the Spanish judicial system. The Spanish judicial system is based on the separation of the judicial organ and the person/entity alleging the charges. This is known under Spanish law as the principle of prosecution and involves that the judge is not competent to carry out the investigation since it could influence its outcome and put his impartiality at risk. Hence, under Spanish law it is the claimant or the Public Prosecution who are in charge of carrying out the necessary investigations in order to bring in trial evidence which demonstrates the culpability of the defendant.

b. Cooperation by competition authorities

The Spanish competition authorities cooperate with the Commission by submitting reports and information on the creation and implementation of State aid rules in Spain. This activity is coordinated by the Representación Permanente de España ante la UE, created by Royal Decree 260/1986 of 17 January.

VII. Trends – Reforms – Recommendations

In conclusion, the evolution of the enforcement of State aid in Spain is rather slow due to the fact that the role that the applicable Spanish legislation assigns to the competition authorities on State aid is quite limited. In the absence of adequate powers of investigation and/or enforcement, national courts take into account and effectively apply the different Commission guidelines, communications and EU regulations on State aid at the time of deciding on cases. As for preliminary questions, although national courts seem to be aware of the existing preliminary rulings issued by the CJEU it would be desirable, given the apparent need for it, for national courts to bring more prejudicial questions which help them with the application of EU Law to Spanish cases.

We understand that the CNC could have had a more pro-active role in monitoring State aid measures. In particular, the CNC could reinforce cooperation with the central and regional administrations. This could be achieved by strengthening the mechanisms of communication between the CNC and the Autonomous Communities.

The application of the Law on Administrative Procedure to the recovery procedure does not seem very suitable. In this regard, adequate and specific legislation that takes into account the particularities of this subject should be passed. With the purpose of systematizing the recovery procedure, the new legislation should combine both the existing provisions of the Law on Administrative Procedure and the General Law on Subventions regarding public aid recovery. It should also include a clear definition of the administrative bodies with jurisdiction for the recovery, the procedure and the system of appeals.

Sweden

Ulf Öberg, Ida Otken Eriksson, Jakob Lundström*

* Advokatfirman Öberg & Associés AB, Stockholm.

I. General principles of Member State's State aid law

1. National authorities competent to grant aid and to be involved in the notification procedure

Under Swedish law, there is no particular national authority that is competent to grant aid and to be involved in the notification procedure.

As noted in several recent reports,[255] a very large number of State entities have to observe EU State aid rules in their daily activities: beside all government authorities, 21 county administrations, 290 local municipalities, 21 regional municipalities and over 1500 public undertakings. However, there is no central authority to assist all these entities in their dealings with EU State aid rules.

The Ministry of Enterprise, Energy and Communication ("Näringsdepartementet") is responsible for handling government business relating to State aid to the business sector.[256] Thus, all communication on EU State aid issues, e.g. notifications and questions of recovery goes through this Ministry. Still, due to the Swedish Constitutional prohibition against governmental interference in particular cases ("11 kap 7 § regeringsformen") and the constitutional autonomy enjoyed by municipalities, the Ministry has only a very limited say as to the substance of the individual cases it handles.

Different governmental agencies have been appointed to administer particular areas of law and the application of certain relating block exemptions, e.g. the Agency for Economic and Regional Growth ("NUTEK" – employment, transport, certain regional development), the Agency for Innovation Systems ("VINNOVA"), the Swedish ESF Council ("ESF-rådet" – the social funds), and the state-owned ALMI group providing financing to small and medium sized enterprises. These agencies act under particular legislative provisions and will not be commented on in further detail in this report.

Within the general legal framework applicable to State aid, the rules differ depending on whether the aid is granted by the government/government authorities or by local/regional authorities.

It follows from the Swedish Act on the national budget ("Lag (1996:1059) om statsbudgeten"), that State aid granted by the government must be made transparent in the state budget, which must then be approved by the Parliament.

As for aid granted by government authorities, the Swedish Decree on State aid to the Trade and Industry ("Förordning (1988:764) om statligt stöd till näringslivet") identifies a number of conditions that should be fulfilled before aid is granted. According to this Decree (21–22 §§), the government must be informed of all State aid measures that may be reviewed by the

255 See e.g. the report drafted by Ingeborg Simonsson for the 2006 FIDE conference, and the research report drafted by Jörgen Hettne and Maria Fritz for the Swedish Competition Authority, "EU:s statsstödsregler i nationell tillämpning: Behövs effektivare tillsyn och kontroll i Sverige?", December 2008, http://www.kkv.se/upload/Filer/Trycksaker/Rapporter/uppdragsforskning/forsk_rap_statsstodsregler.pdf.

256 http://www.sweden.gov.se/sb/d/2112/a/19592.

Commission before the aid is granted. It should also be stated, as a general condition for the granting of aid, that the aid may be amended or annulled and recovered if the Commission, by a final decision, or the CJEU, should find that the aid is unlawful, within the meaning of Article 108 TFEU. The Decree also prescribes that the government will decide on the annulment or amendment of State aid measures and in each particular case, on the conditions for repayment of aid.

As to State aid granted by local and regional authorities, the Swedish Local Government Act ("kommunallagen (1991:900) 2 kap 8 §") prohibits the grant of aid to individual undertakings. According to the Act on the Implementation of the European Communities State aid Rules ("Lag (1994:1845) om tillämpningen av Europeiska gemenskapernas statsstödsregler 6 §"), local and regional municipalities are obliged to inform the government of all kinds of State aid planned which may be reviewed by the Commission. This Act also prescribes that the government may annul a decision of a local or regional municipality if the Commission in a final decision or the CJEU should find that the aid granted is unlawful, within the meaning of Article 108 TFEU. As to recovery, the Act refers to the generally applicable rules on correction of execution in the Local Government Act ("kommunallagen (1991:900) 10 kap. 15 §").

2. National authorities competent to recover aid and an overview of the procedure

There is no national authority specifically competent to recover aid. All Community communication goes through the Ministry of Entreprise, Energy and Communication ("Näringsdepartementet").

As described above, the government has a legal basis to annul decisions on unlawful State aid granted by government authorities. The government also sets the conditions of recovery in each individual case.

However, as regards aid granted by local and regional municipalities, the competence of the government to annul decisions is limited to those situations in which the Commission or the CJEU has actually declared the aid to be unlawful. It is not clear, but generally assumed within the legal doctrine that this competence would not apply in a case where the illegality of the aid is "only" stated by a national court. Moreover, the rules do not permit governmental action before a Commission decision has become final, i.e. is not appealed to the General court.

As for the recovery of aid granted by local and regional municipalities, the Act on the Implementation of the European Communities State aid rules ("Lag (1994:1845) om tillämpningen av Europeiska gemenskapernas statsstödsregler"), refers to the generally applicable rules on correction of municipality decisions that have already been effected, but are subsequently annulled by a court. According to these provisions, the municipality shall ensure that enforcement is rectified as far as this is possible. However, a recovery decision does not necessarily affect, according to national civil law principles, the validity of a contract already entered into between a municipality and an individual party, as it is generally agreed that, according to national law, a civil law contract cannot be declared invalid even though a public authority or undertaking has acted illegally or outside its scope of competence. An aid recipient could possibly, therefore, invoke civil law in order to prevent recovery, arguing that all national procedures have been complied with and that there are no other causes of action for recovery under the general principles of civil law.

In this description of the general architecture of Sweden's State aid law, we refer only to explicit legal procedures prescribed by law or recognised by the Swedish courts. Obviously, the national rules have to be interpreted in the light of the directly effective EU State aid provisions and the case-law of the CJEU. Thus, in our view, it is very doubtful whether a Swedish court would actually accept such civil law arguments presented by an aid recipient in order to resist recovery, should such a case be initiated.

II. Identification of State Aid Issues at National Level

1. State aid compliance by the national legislator and/or the executive

All proposed legislative acts normally pass before the Council on Legislation ("Lagrådet") before being adopted by the Parliament. The Council on Legislation considers the legal aspects of the proposed act, in particular issues of a constitutional character or relating to fundamental rights. The statements of the Council on Legislation are not, however, binding.

Besides the Council on Legislation, there is no specific *ex ante* control organised at constitutional or legislative level with a view to preventing the granting of State aid by legislative act in violation of Article 108(3) TFEU.

Nor is there any particular *ex post* non-judicial control to the same end. However, according to the Swedish Act on the Legal Review of Certain Governmental Decisions ("Lag (2006:304) om rättsprövning av vissa regeringsbeslut"), private and legal persons may appeal those decisions taken by the government which include a review of their civil rights or obligations (as referred to in Article 6 of the European Convention on Human Rights), directly to the Supreme Administrative Court ("Regeringsrätten"). It is not clear, but cannot be excluded, that this extraordinary legal remedy could also apply also in State aid cases, e.g. could be initiated by a competitor, or in a case where the government decides on a tax arrangement whereby certain parties are required to pay taxes which are subsequently transferred as unlawful State aid to certain beneficiaries.

There is no specific *ex ante* control or *ex post* non judicial control applicable to the other administrative, regional or local entities that may grant State aid. Still, as described above, the Ministry of Enterprise, Energy and Communication ("Näringsdepartementet") functions as a single point of communication with the Commission.

It cannot be excluded that the Ministry could, in certain situations, at least unofficially, function as an expert advisor to other entities who are unsure as to how to apply the State aid rules. As described above, the Ministry can only play a purely non-binding advisory role, due to the constitution provisions on local autonomy and the ban on governmental interference in particular cases.

2. State aid compliance by national judges and/or the national competition authority (NCA)

The Swedish competition authority is not competent in the field of State aid. State aid questions may be raised both before the civil and the administrative courts. The rules on *locus standi* are complicated and will be discussed in detail below. However, the Swedish Supreme Court has recently clarified that a competitor may, before the civil courts and with the purpose of preventing damage, seek to prohibit an authority from granting unlawful State aid.[257]

So far, State aid questions have mostly been presented to the administrative courts by interested third parties challenging decisions of municipalities to sell public assets allegedly below market price.

The impressive number of court procedures in this field during the last few years (22 cases identified) is no doubt related to the Commission intervention in the *Åre/Konsum Nord* case[258], which is currently pending before the fifth chamber of the General Court. In this case, the Commission opened a formal investigation and later decided that the municipality in Åre had granted unlawful State aid by selling a piece of land to Konsum Nord for 2 million SEK when a competitor had presented an offer to acquire the same piece of land for 6 million SEK.[259] The Commission intervention resulted in extensive media coverage, followed by a vast debate on municipality sales of public assets. Of all the cases identified at a national level, 22 out of 24 concern municipality residents who appeal decisions of municipalities to sell different public assets, allegedly below market price.

This development has been encouraged by certain public interest litigants, mainly the politically non-partisan think tank, the New Welfare Foundation ("Den Nya Välfärden"). The Foundation is devoted to influencing public and official opinion about democracy, social welfare and private enterprise. It was the New Welfare Foundation, through the Ombudsman for enterprise ("Företagarombudsmannen"), that complained about the *Åre/Konsum Nord* case to the Commission and the Foundation generally encourages litigation in this field.

Once the EU State aid rules have been invoked and the national court decides to apply these rules (a certain preference towards solving cases on the basis of national State aid law instead of on the basis of EU State aid law can be detected), the State aid criteria in themselves do not appear to pose the national courts any particular difficulties. Thus, the national courts generally accept *inter alia* that advantages may be granted in other ways than by direct cash grants.

Still, certain problems can be detected as to how to identify the actual value of the advantage (e.g. in order to establish whether the *de minimis* threshold applies) and as to which party should assume the burden of proof. Moreover, there seems to be a certain hesitation as to the exact requirements of the conditions relating to restriction of competition and effect on trade.

---

257 Decision of the Swedish Supreme Court, "Högsta domstolen", 22 October 2009, Stockholms kommun and Stockholms Stadshus AB/NDSHT Nya Destination Stockholm Hotell & Teaterpaket Aktiebolag, Case no. Ö 1261-08.

258 Case T-244/08, Konsum Nord v. Commission.

259 Commission Decision No. C 35/2006, 30 January 2008, Sale of land below market price, C(2008)311 final.

Most of the State aid procedures so far initiated under Swedish law have been administrative proceedings, where the administrative courts have the possibility to carry out different investigations. However, no use seems to have been made of these investigative powers. The ruling in Case C-526/04, *Laboratoires Boiron* has not been referred to.

Moreover, so far, no Swedish court has decided to make a preliminary reference under Article 267 TFEU to the CJEU on the notion of aid.

Given the complicated *locus standi* rules (see below) it has been difficult, or in most cases before the administrative courts impossible, for other interested third parties (competitors) to participate in the proceedings. To date, no competitors have in fact intervened in such cases.

We have no example of cases in which a national court has applied any of the Exemption Regulations adopted by the Commission. However, in the recent *Thomas Svensson* case,[260] the Administrative Court of Appeal in Stockholm referred to the possibility of an exemption.

The national courts are competent to verify whether an aid has been granted in compliance with the rules on cumulation, but so far this question has never been raised.

In the *Thomas Svensson* case, referred to above, the Administrative Court of Appeal in Stockholm made extensive references to EU State aid rules, CJEU rulings and Commission practice and guidelines. Other national rulings also refer to EU rules, guidelines, case-law and Commission practice.

III. Unlawful aid and judicial review

1. General powers of the national courts concerning the direct effect of Article 108(3) TFEU

The national courts may first and foremost annul a measure that is found to have been adopted contrary to Article 108(3) TFEU. This has been the purpose of most of the procedures identified at national level, except for some civil lawsuits which were settled or withdrawn before a final court ruling was given. However, the Swedish Supreme Court has very recently clarified that a competitor may, before the civil courts and with the purpose of preventing damage, seek to prohibit an authority from granting aid.[261]

If the unlawful aid stems from a government authority ("förvaltningsbesvär"), the administrative courts are competent not only to annul it, but also to change the substance of the decision, i.e. the administrative court has the same competence as the deciding authority.

If the aid stems from a municipality ("kommunalbesvär"), the competent administrative court has no right to change the content of the decision, only to annul it.

260 Ruling of the Administrative Court of Appeal in Stockholm, "Kammarrätten i Stockholm", 16 February 2009, Thomas Svensson v. Stockholms stad, Case no. 4514-07.

261 Decision of the Swedish Supreme Court, "Högsta domstolen", 22 October 2009, Stockholms kommun and Stockholms Stadshus AB/NDSHT Nya Destination Stockholm Hotell & Teaterpaket Aktiebolag, Case no. Ö 1261-08.

2. Prevention of the granting of unlawful aid

There are no particular procedures under national law designed to prevent the granting/payment of unlawful aid. Generally applicable procedural rules, e.g. on interim measures, apply. Nor are there any particular national provisions on which individuals can rely before the national courts in order to ensure the respect of the obligation of notification.

It is important in respect of the *locus standi* and recovery rules whether the unlawful act is of a private or public character and whether it is part of a State aid regime and thus granted by law, or granted individually by an administrative act, see below.

However, as to the substance, it should not be of importance whether the unlawful act is of private or public character. It is generally agreed in legal doctrine that organs of the Swedish State (including municipalities) are not able to avoid the applicable legislation by conferring State aid through private law agreements instead of public law acts.

Two of 24 cases identified at national level during the study concerned proceedings other than local residents appealing a decision from their municipality board. In one of these cases, a potential beneficiary appealed a decision not to consider certain costs as eligible for aid within an aid scheme.[262] The administrative courts agreed that the costs were not eligible for aid.

In the other case, a competitor, the television company "Kanal 5", appealed a decision from the National Radio and Television Agency ("Radio- och TV-verket") to reduce the concession costs of the television company "TV 4".[263] In this case, Kanal 5 was at first instance considered not to have legal standing, but the Administrative Court of Appeal reversed this decision. However, as to the substance, the Administrative Court in Stockholm did not find that the selectivity criteria was complied with and dismissed the action.

In a third case, Skyways Express AB initiated proceedings against the public airport Kristianstad Airport. Skyways argued that an agreement between the Airport and a competing airline, City Airline AB, was illegal as it constituted unlawful and non-notified State aid. In this case, Kristianstads District Court granted interim measures, prohibiting the Airport from implementing the agreement.[264] The decision on interim measures was confirmed on appeal by the Court of Appeal ("Hovrätten over Skåne och Blekinge").[265] However, the case was subsequently withdrawn.

Likewise, Norrköping District Court granted interim measures in an action initiated by Skyways Express AB against the airport in Norrköping. Skyways claimed damages and tried to obtain an injunction (by referring to the Swedish Competition Act ("Konkurrenslagen 2008:579")) against the municipality of Norrköping as regards the implementation of certain

262 Ruling of the Administrative Court of Appeal in Jönköping, "Kammarrätten i Jönköping", 20 October 2008, Länsstyrelsen i Örebro Län v. AB Göta Kanalbolag, Case no. 1036-07.

263 Ruling of the Administrative Court in Stockholm, "Länsrätten i Stockholm", 17 June 2008, Kanal 5 and TV4 v. Radio- och TV-verket.

264 Decision of the District Court in Kristianstad, "Kristianstads tingsrätt", 28 March 2007, Skyways Express AB v. Kristianstad Airport AB, Case no. T 1644-06.

265 Decision of the Court of Appeal in Skåne and Blekinge, "Hovrätten over Skåne och Blekinge", 26 April 2007, Kristianstad Airport AB v. Skyways Express AB, Case no. Ö 916-07.

agreements including certain guarantees to the competing airline company Cimber Air A/S.[266] The plea for an injunction on the basis of the Competition Act was dismissed as inadmissible (as it should have been raised as an infringement of competition law before the Swedish Competition Authority and the Market Court), but the pleas on damages were declared admissible.[267] However, following a notification of the measure to the Commission, the latter stated that the measures were not considered to constitute State aid and that the Commission had no objections.[268] Subsequently, the Court of Appeal ("Göta Hovrätt") annulled the decision of the District Court on interim measures, referring to the decision of the Commission.[269] The case before the District Court was finally withdrawn.

In another case, the Metro newspaper initiated proceedings against the Swedish State before the Stockholm District Court on account of the Swedish rules on taxation of advertisements in different newspapers ("reklamskatten"). A complaint was also launched with the Commission, who is now investigating the complaint, together with an investigation of the Swedish rules on financial support to newspapers. However, the case before the Stockholm District Court was withdrawn at an early stage.

Lastly, the Swedish Supreme Court ("Högsta domstolen") has recently confirmed that competitors may initiate proceedings before the civil courts in order to claim damages and may also seek injunctions against the granting authority before the civil courts in order to prevent damage resulting from unlawful State aid being transferred to competitors.[270]

3. Recovery of unlawful aid and interest

There are no specific procedures in Swedish law enabling the recovery of unlawful aid. Generally applicable rules must be applied and it is assumed that court action in this field would have to take place in civil courts.

However, to the best of our knowledge, there has not been an action of this kind in Sweden. It is, therefore, difficult to draw any conclusions in respect of whether the national courts would have the possibility to identify the beneficiaries in case of an aid scheme, how they would quantify the value of the aid, whether they could propose alternative remedies and how they would handle the question of legitimate expectations/sharing of responsibility. Nor has there, to the best of our knowledge, been any litigation in Sweden concerning the recovery of interest. A competitor introducing a claim for recovery of illegal interests would have to apply traditional civil procedural rules interpreted in the light of the directly applicable EU State aid rules.

---

266 Decision of the District Court in Norrköping, "Norrköpings tingsrätt", 20 April 2007, Case no. T 2522-06.

267 Decision of the District Court in Norrköping, "Norrköping tingsrätt", 25 January 2007, as confirmed on appeal by the Court of Appeal, "Göta Hovrätt", 18 March 2007, Case no. Ö 638-07.

268 COM(2007)D/3274 Final – State aid No. 791/2006 – Sweden, Business Case Norrköping.

269 Decision of the Court of Appeal, "Göta Hovrätt", 9 August 2007, Case no. Ö 1369-07 and Ö 1266-07.

270 Decision of the Swedish Supreme Court, "Högsta domstolen", 22 October 2009, Stockholms kommun and Stockholms Stadshus AB/NDSHT Nya Destination Stockholm Hotell & Teaterpaket Aktiebolag, Case no. Ö 1261-08.

So far, to the best of our knowledge, there have only been two cases of recovery of unlawful State aid in Sweden. In both cases, the amounts due were paid back on a "voluntary" basis, and all litigation was avoided (see below).

4. Damage claims by competitors/third parties against the granting authority before the national courts

To the best of our knowledge, there have been very few Swedish court procedures in which competitors/third parties have claimed damages from the granting authority, and in fact, no final court rulings. Several civil court procedures have been initiated involving claims for damages for State aid given to a competitor, but none of these procedures has so far resulted in a final court ruling.

In the course of this report, practising lawyers have expressed their frustration at the fact that it is not known to what extent such claims for damages would be admissible and how the claims would be appreciated, i.e. what requirements would be formulated as to the proof of loss. A recent ruling of the Swedish Supreme Court[271] sheds light on the admissibility question, but uncertainty remains as to the appreciation of the claim for damages.

However, a competitor/third party can initiate an action for damages against the State or another authority directly on the basis of EU law or according to the Swedish Tort Liability Act ("Skadeståndslagen" (1972:207) 3 kap 2 §). Through this procedure, a civil court may decide whether an aid granted constitutes unlawful State aid. Within the context of this procedure, the court is not competent to annul the decision, it may only state on the claim for damages. Still, the court may order that the implementation of the disputed measure be suspended.

A competitor/third party may also request that the question of damages is settled by the Office of the Chancellor of Justice ("Justitiekanslern"), pursuant to the Act on the Handling of Damage Claims against the State ("Förordning (1995:1301) om handläggning av skadeståndsanspråk mot staten"). Within both contexts, the Community conditions for liability in damages (the *Brasserie du Pêcheur* principles) can be directly invoked.

5. Damages claims by the beneficiary against the granting authority before the national courts

There have been no court procedures in Sweden in which the beneficiary has demanded damages from the granting authority due to the unlawfulness (or incompatibility) of aid. If such a claim were to be presented, it is generally assumed that it would have to be within an action for damages instituted in the civil courts and in accordance with the Swedish Tort Liability Act ("Skadeståndslagen" (1972:207) 3 kap 2 §).

As stated above in the context of the possibility for competitors/third parties to bring damage claims, the civil court would not be able to annul the measure, but only to find on the damages,

---

271 Decision of the Swedish Supreme Court, "Högsta domstolen", 22 October 2009, Stockholms kommun and Stockholms Stadshus AB/NDSHT Nya Destination Stockholm Hotell & Teaterpaket Aktiebolag, Case no. Ö 1261-08.

and the beneficiary would also have the possibility to complain to the Office of the Chancellor of Justice ("Justitiekanslern"). Within these contexts, the Community conditions for damages (the *Brasserie du Pêcheur* principles) could be directly invoked.

6. Damages claims by competitors/third parties against the beneficiary before the national courts

It is generally assumed that it is not possible, either under Swedish competition law or other acts, to hold recipients of an illegal aid liable in damages towards competitors. To our knowledge, there have been no court procedures in Sweden in which competitors or third parties have demanded damages from the beneficiary, directly or indirectly (recovery of undue advantages). Still, if such an action were to be presented, it would have to be within an action for damages against the beneficiary instituted in the civil courts.

7. Interim measures taken by national judges

To our knowledge, there are very few examples of Swedish cases in which a national court has ordered interim measures in respect of State aid measures. Still, the general procedural rules on interim relief apply. In a couple of the cases identified, applications for interim measures have been rejected.

In two cases, however, as mentioned above, interim measures were granted. Skyways Express AB initiated proceedings against the public airport in Kristianstad. Skyways argued that an agreement between the airport and a competing airline, City Airline AB, was illegal as it constituted unlawful and non-notified State aid. In this case, Kristianstads District Court granted interim measures, prohibiting the airport from implementing the agreement.[272] The decision on interim measures was confirmed on appeal by the Court of Appeal ("Hovrätten over Skåne och Blekinge").[273] However, the case was subsequently withdrawn.

Likewise, Norrköping District Court granted interim measures in an action initiated by Skyways Express AB against the airport in Norrköping, prohibiting the municipality of Norrköping from implementing certain agreements, including certain guarantees to the competing airline company Cimber Air A/S.[274] Following a notification of the measure to the Commission, the latter stated that the measure was not considered to constitute State aid and that the Commission consequently had no objections to the measure.[275] Subsequently, the Court of Appeal ("Göta Hovrätt") annulled the decision of the District Court on interim measures, referring to the decision of the Commission,[276] and the case before the District Court was with-

272 Decision of the District Court in Kristianstad, "Kristianstads tingsrätt", 28 March 2007, Skyways Express AB v. Kristianstad Airport AB, Case no. T 1644-06.

273 Decision of the Court of Appeal in Skåne and Blekinge, "Hovrätten over Skåne och Blekinge", 26 April 2007, Kristianstad Airport AB v. Skyways Express AB, Case no. Ö 916-07.

274 Decision of the District Court in Norrköping, "Norrköpings tingsrätt", 20 April 2007, Case no. T 2522-06.

275 COM(2007)D/3274 Final – State aid No. 791/2006 – Sweden, Business Case Norrköping.

276 Decision of the District Court in Norrköping, "Norrköpings tingsrätt", 20 April 2007, Case no. T 2522-06.

drawn. The Court of Appeal ("Göta Hovrätt") refused to share costs between the parties, even though the notification to the Commission was only launched after the initiation of proceedings before the District Court and in spite of the fact that the decision of the Commission was not known to Skyways at the time the appeal was launched.

In the course of this report, several practising lawyers have expressed their frustration at the difficulties in obtaining interim measures in this field.

IV. Control of recovery procedure

1. Rules applicable to recovery

No specific procedures have been enacted in Sweden for the recovery of unlawful State aid. As stated above, the rules which are applicable depend on whether the aid has been granted by government authorities or municipalities.

If the aid has been granted by government authorities, the government decides ad hoc on the conditions of recovery. If the aid has been granted by municipalities, the Local Government Act ("kommunallagen") applies. The municipality should ensure that enforcement is rectified as far as possible.

As mentioned briefly above, there is a possible conflict between, on the one hand, EU recovery rules and case-law and, on the other hand, national law on beneficiaries rights to invoke civil law principles. At least, the express rules on recovery are not in line with the EU law requirements that recovery should take place directly following a Commission decision to this effect, irrespective of whether the decision is appealed to the General Court. Furthermore, the express rules on recovery only apply in cases where the illegality of the aid has been stated in a final decision taken by the Commission or the CJEU, not "only" by a national court.

So far and to the best of our knowledge, there have only been two recovery cases in Sweden. In both, the disputed amounts were repaid voluntarily by the beneficiaries.

In the first case, the government required the Swedish National Tax Board ("Skatteverket") to execute the recovery of unlawful State aid, in the form of tax benefits granted to companies active in the electricity sector, in accordance with Council Regulation (EC) No 659/1999 of March 1999, laying down detailed rules for the application of Article 108 TFEU. The recovery was requested by way of a formal letter to the beneficiaries. The Swedish government informed the Commission, by letter of 12 July 2005, that recovery had taken place.[277]

In the Åre/Konsum Nord case, now pending before the General Court,[278] the Commission found that the municipality of Åre had sold a piece of land to Konsum Nord below market price.[279] Faced with the recovery decision of the Commission, Konsum Nord found it unclear whether the amount should be paid to the government or to the municipality that had sold the

277 N2005/5064/NL.

278 Case T-244/08, Konsum Nord v. Commission.

279 Commission Decision No. C 35/2006, 30 January 2008, Sale of land below market price, C(2008)311 final.

piece of land and who, in the opinion of Konsum Nord, would benefit doubly from the transaction if the disputed amount was repaid. Therefore, Konsum Nord deposited the sum in escrow with the County Administrative Board ("Länsstyrelsen") in accordance with the rules in the Swedish Act on the Deposit of Money in Escrow ("lag (1927:56) om nedsättning av pengar hos myndighet"). This act applies in cases where a debtor is neither aware, nor should be aware, of the identity of the creditor, as well as where there is uncertainty as to which of two or more persons is the rightful creditor, and where the debtor cannot reasonably be deemed obliged, at his own risk, to determine to which of them payment should be effected. In such a case, the debtor shall be entitled to effect payment by depositing the sum on behalf of the creditor in escrow with the County Administrative Board.

2. Action for recovery

It is not entirely clear which rules would apply should a beneficiary refuse to comply with a recovery decision, or if a competitor or beneficiary should challenge a national recovery decision.

3. Challenging the validity of national recovery order

No particular rules have been enacted in Sweden by which to challenge the validity of national recovery orders.

4. Action contesting the validity of the Commission decision

The validity of the Commission decision needs to be contested before the General Court. There is only one example of such a case in Sweden (see the pending Case T-244/08, Konsum Nord v. Commission).

5. Damages for failure to implement a recovery decision and infringement of EU law

If the government should fail to implement a Commission recovery decision, this could be invoked by competitors within the context of an action for damages initiated before the civil courts. We refer to what was stated above under section III.4 which should apply *mutatis mutandis*.

V. Standing of third parties before national court

The Swedish conditions of *locus standi* in State aid cases are complicated and unclear. Many practising lawyers express frustration in this regard. However, a recent decision from the Swedish Supreme Court has clarified the possibility for competitors to claim damages and to have illegal State aid measures suspended.

There is no specific procedure to challenge decisions or measures from state entities under Swedish administrative law. In the absence of specific provisions, the Swedish Administrative code applies ("förvaltningslagen (1986:223)"). Under this Act, concerned parties have standing to appeal decisions provided that the decision has been negative/unfavourable to the party in question. Both the requirement of a decision and of concern have traditionally been interpreted very restrictively by the Swedish Courts, and it is generally assumed among academics that competitors and other interested parties may face certain difficulties in gaining standing on a strict national law basis. Obviously, it is possible that the conditions could be interpreted more loosely in the light of the case-law of the CJEU, if this was properly invoked within the context of such a procedure. Thus, in one of the cases identified at national level, the Administrative Court of Appeal granted the television company Kanal 5 standing to challenge a decision of the National Radio and Television Agency, that allegedly involved State aid to a competing television company, TV4, by reducing the concession costs.[280]

In respect of the judicial review of decisions from local or regional municipalities and in the absence of specific provisions, the Local Government Act ("kommunallagen") applies. According to this Act, natural persons resident in the municipality and owners of land within the municipality have standing. Thus, a competitor or other interested third party will only be able to challenge a State aid decision from a municipality, if it is a landowner in the municipality, or can convince a resident of the municipality to bring proceedings.

Moreover, in the absence of specific provisions, parties challenging decisions within the Swedish administrative courts have to meet their own litigation costs. On the other hand, there is no obligation to compensate the costs of the winning party if the case is lost.

According to the Administrative Code ("förvaltningslagen (1986:223)"), normative acts cannot be subject to judicial review in the abstract (in Swedish law there is no general action for a declaration). In the Court of Justice case of *Unibet*,[281] the Court declared that *"the principle of effective judicial protection of an individual's rights under Community law must be interpreted as meaning that it does not require the national legal order of a Member State to provide for a free-standing action for an examination of whether national provisions are compatible with Article 56 TFEU, provided that other effective legal remedies, which are no less favourable than those governing similar domestic actions, make it possible for such a question of compatibility to be determined as a preliminary issue, which is a matter for the national court to establish".*[282] The Court expressly stated that it is for the national courts *"to ensure that the examination of the compatibility of the law with Community law takes place irrespective of the assessment of the merits of the case with regard to the requirements for damage and a causal link in the claim for damages".*[283]

---

280 See ruling of the Administrative Court in Stockholm, "Länsrätten i Stockholm", 17 June 2008, Kanal 5 and TV4 v. Radio- och TV-verket.

281 Case C-432/05, Unibet (London) Ltd and Unibet (International) Ltd v. Justitiekanslern [2007] ECR I-02271, paragraphs 58-65.

282 Op. cit, paragraph 65.

283 Op. cit., paragraph 59.

Thus, the conformity of certain normative measures with EU law may be tried by an interested party within the context of an action for damages. Still, it must generally be assumed that competitors and other interested parties may be hesitant about using this new procedural tool in cases where there is no clear basis for actual damages, for instance where the competitor or the interested third party has difficulties establishing a loss or causal link. As mentioned above, the airline Skyways has initiated two court procedures in this respect, but neither has led to a final ruling on the State aid issue. Instead, in one of the cases, it was clarified that competitors cannot, together with the claim for damages before the ordinary courts, obtain an injunction against an alleged State aid measure on the basis of the Swedish Competition Act ("Konkurrenslagen 2008:579"). Claims for injunctions on the basis of the Swedish Competition Act must be initiated as a competition law claim, before the Swedish Competition Authority and the Market Court.[284]

It is clear from the cases identified relating to State aid in Sweden, that in almost all the cases, the action has been initiated by a private citizen, resident in the municipality, and who has an interest in principle as a general tax payer that the municipality does not sell assets below market price. It could be asked if the scarcity of other court proceedings is quite simply due to the demanding and complicated *locus standi* rules.

However, in a recent decision, the Swedish Supreme Court has confirmed that competitors may initiate proceedings before the civil courts in order to claim damages. Furthermore, the Supreme Court clarified that a competitor may also, before the civil courts and with the purpose of preventing damage, seek to prohibit an authority from granting aid.[285] The possibility of obtaining such a prohibition must be seen as a very effective remedy against unlawful State aid and may be invoked both against governmental, local and regional entities.

Finally, as mentioned above, it is not settled, but cannot be excluded, that State aid decisions taken by the government can be challenged pursuant to the Swedish Act on Legal Review of Certain Governmental Decisions ("Lag 2006:304 om rättsprövning av vissa regeringsbeslut"). According to this Act, private and legal persons may appeal decisions taken by the government, which include a review of their civil rights or obligations (as referred to in Article 6 in the European Convention on Human Rights), directly to the Supreme Administrative Court. The Act could be applicable in certain State aid situations, e.g. could be initiated by a competitor, or in the case that the government should enforce a tax arrangement whereby certain parties are required to pay taxes which are subsequently transferred as unlawful State aid to other beneficiaries. In order to obtain *locus standi* under this legal review procedure, the notion of "party" is interpreted broadly, the main requirement being that the decision taken by the government should include a review of the appellant's civil rights and obligations as referred to in Article 6 of the Convention.

---

284 Decision of the District Court in Norrköping, "Norrköping tingsrätt", 25 January 2007, as confirmed on appeal by "Göta Hovrätt", 18 March 2007, Case no. Ö 638-07.

285 Decision of the Swedish Supreme Court, "Högsta domstolen", 22 October 2009, Stockholms kommun and Stockholms Stadshus AB/NDSHT Nya Destination Stockholm Hotell & Teaterpaket Aktiebolag, Case no. Ö 1261-08.

As to the question of the burden of proof, the Administrative Court of Appeal in Stockholm stated in the *Thomas Svensson* case,[286] that the burden of proof should be decided in accordance with national procedural law and thus, should be assumed by the claimant. However, the Court added that this did not mean that the municipality could be entirely passive in the proceedings, in particular as regards different kind of documents relating to the municipality's decisions and acts, which a private party may find it difficult to get access to.

VI. Cooperation with EU authorities

1. Cooperation with the CJEU

So far, no Swedish court has referred a preliminary question to the CJEU in cases concerning the application of Articles 107(1) TFEU or Article 108(3) TFEU.

2. Cooperation with the Commission

It does not appear that any Swedish court has so far asked the Commission for the transmission of relevant information, or asked for an opinion concerning the application of the State aid rules.

Still, the Swedish courts do not seem hesitant to use and refer to CJEU case-law, Commission decisions and different kinds of State aid rules, once EU State aid law has been invoked and is found to be applicable. However, a general preference towards resolving State aid problems according to national law, in preference to EU State aid law arguments, can be detected in certain rulings.

VII. Trends – reforms – recommendations

The Swedish State aid framework has recently been subject to heavy criticism in several national reports and academic articles.[287] A number of flaws compared to CJEU case-law have been identified. As concluding remarks in these writings, it has notably been pointed out that an independent national State aid authority is necessary in order to increase the efficiency of

---

286 Ruling of the Court of Administrative Court of Appeal in Stockholm, "Kammarrätten i Stockholm", 16 February 2009, Thomas Svensson v. Stockholms stad, Case no. 4514-07.

287 See the above mentioned report drafted by Ingeborg Simonsson for the 2006 FIDE conference, http://www.fide2006.org, and the research report drafted by Jörgen Hettne and Maria Fritz for the Swedish Competition Authority, "EU:s statsstödsregler I nationell tillämpning: Behövs effektivare tillsyn och kontroll i Sverige", December 2008, http://www.kkv.se/upload/Filer/Trycksaker/Rapporter/uppdragsforskning/forsk_rap_statsstodsregler.pdf. See also e.g. Ulf Bernitz in Europarättsligt Tidskrift (ERT) 2007, p. 505, "Statsstödsrätten och Sverige: Hög tid för lojal implementering" as well as the Green paper drafted by the Swedish Commission on business confidence ("Förtroendekommissionen").

State aid control in Sweden. Furthermore, calls have been made for less strict criteria for the *locus standi* of competitors and other third parties in State aid cases, and thus an amelioration of the conditions for private enforcement. A major step in this direction has already been taken with the recent decision of the Swedish Supreme Court ("Högsta domstolen") confirming that competitors may initiate proceedings before the civil courts in order to obtain damages and in order to prevent damage by unlawful State aid being transferred to competitors.

The lack of express recovery procedures has also been criticised, along with the uncertainty as to the legal effect of unlawful State aid decisions on civil law contracts, the general prohibition on reformation *in pejus* and the principle of legitimate expectations. In addition, in certain cases, the government is only competent to recover unlawful State aid after the Commission or the CJEU has taken a final decision in the matter, and not if the unlawfulness is "simply" stated by a national court. Moreover, the limited possibility of governmental recovery is clearly not in line with the EU law requirements that recovery should take place directly following a Commission decision to this effect, irrespective of whether the decision is appealed to the General Court.

Without a doubt, the application and enforcement of EU State aid rules faces several challenges in Swedish law. During the course of this report, we have encountered widespread frustration, not only among lawyers, but also among judges and public servants, over the many unsettled issues in respect of the Swedish implementation of the EU State aid rules. However, in February 2010, the Swedish Government appointed a Special Expert to investigate wether Swedish legislation is compatible with EU State aid rules. The Special Expert is i. a. to examine wether the rules on recovery should be amended.

Still, one important question is to what extent "first movers", without waiting for substantial and procedural reforms, may obtain full respect of the EU State aid rules by simply applying national existing or "new" procedures and by invoking before national courts and authorities the direct effect and primacy of EU law and case-law.

This study has demonstrated the importance of Community action in the field of State aid. After the Commission's decision in the Åre/Konsum Nord case which is currently pending before the General Court,[288] a large number of similar cases has been identified and proceedings initiated before the national courts by interested third parties. Thus, information and communication about the EU State aid rules is extremely important.

As to information on Swedish case-law in this field, no databases or journals systematically publish relevant court decisions. Thus, it would be useful to start publishing these decisions in a more user-friendly manner e.g. by making them searchable in a national database. Certain initiatives have already been taken in this respect, but not all courts have started to use these tools yet.

---

288 Case T-244/08, Konsum Nord v. Commission.

United Kingdom

Katharine Wilson*

* Hogan Lovells, Brussels.

I. General principles of United Kingdom's State aid law

1. National authorities competent for granting aid and involved in the notification procedure.

The TFEU Treaty provisions on State aid have not been specifically implemented into UK law[289]. The application and enforcement of State aid obligations finds its authority in the European Communities Act 1972. Council Regulation (EC) No 659/1999 laying down detailed rules for the application of Article 93 (now Article 108 TFEU) of the EC Treaty (the "Procedural Regulation") is also directly applicable in the UK.

The central government of the United Kingdom ("UK") has responsibility for the grant of State aid at the national level and must ensure compliance with EU law. However, the UK is a quasi-federal jurisdiction with extensive devolution of legislative and executive authority, including for the grant of State aid, to Scotland, Wales and Northern Ireland. The different regions of England also exercise administrative powers with regard to State aid. Therefore the initial assessment of a potential aid measure and subsequent grant of that aid will most often take place at a local or regional level.

Within central government the relevant departments for State aid purposes are the Department for Business Innovation and Skills ("BIS") (formerly known as the Department for Business, Enterprise and Regulatory Reform, and previously as the Department for Trade and Industry) which is generally responsible for State aid, the Department for Environment Food and Rural Affairs, which is responsible for agricultural aid and the Department for Transport, which is responsible for transport aid. In Scotland and Wales the devolved authority is responsible for compliance with State aid law where it is granting the aid or where it is accountable for the authority granting the aid. In Scotland the devolved authority is the Scottish Executive[290] and in Wales it is the Welsh Assembly. In Northern Ireland, the Department for Enterprise Trade and Investment is responsible for local coordination of State aid policy and granting of aid.

The State aid Branch of BIS provides advice, guidance and training on State aid rules to national, regional and local government and government agencies. It co-ordinates and advises on complaint cases, court cases and formal investigations. It is also the channel through which notifications seeking EU approval for State aid must be routed. The central government must ensure that the different regional authorities are fully informed about EU State aid procedural and substantive law and are able to apply it in practice. Formal responsibility for communication with the Commission and notification under Article 108(3) TFEU lies with the central government, via the UK Permanent Representation in Brussels.

---

289 It should be noted that whilst EU law applies throughout the UK, there are important substantive and procedural differences between the legal systems in England and Wales (which form one legal system), Scotland and Northern Ireland. References to UK law mean the legal systems applicable in each of the regions, where differences between these legal systems are pertinent they will be highlighted.

290 Within the Scottish Executive, the State aid Unit, as part of the Business, Enterprise and Energy Directorate aims to assist those involved in approving or granting public funding within State aid rules.

On 11 June 2010, BIS published a "beginner's guide" providing simple guidance on the EU State aid rules. It explains the definition of State aid, the rationale for the basic prohibition and the methods for obtaining approval. It also explains the consequences of granting illegal State aid.

2. National authorities competent for recovery and brief description of the procedure

Given that the EU State aid rules have not been specifically implemented into UK law, there are no specific provisions governing the recovery of aid by national or regional authorities. The UK Government is primarily responsible for compliance with any Commission decision finding unlawful and incompatible aid. There has only been one recovery case in the UK courts, as far as we are aware, on which to base conclusions but the practice appears to be that the UK Government will bring an action in the High Court against the recipient of illegal aid[291]. The action could be brought either under the contract by which the aid was granted or by relying on the direct applicability of the EU State aid recovery provisions. The basis of the action would be the duty of the UK to comply with the Commission decision.

Actions for recovery of fiscal or agricultural aid, grant of which may more often be based on statutory provisions rather than a civil law contract, would be based expressly on the directly applicable provisions of EU State aid law under the Procedural Regulation.

II. Identification of State aid issues at national level

1. State aid compliance by the national legislator and/or the executive power

As outlined above under section I.1, the State aid Branch of BIS pursues activities to foster adequate knowledge and understanding by all regional authorities of the State aid rules in order to ensure compliance with procedural obligations.

The UK has a long history of early and active engagement with the Commission in order to ensure any potential aid is granted within the rules concerning notification. However, given the increase in workload of the Commission this regular consultation with the relevant State aid departments (in DGs COMP, AGRI and MOVE) is no longer possible and the UK government has consequently adopted a more risk-based approach to assessment and notification. One of the main factors to consider in assessing whether a measure constitutes State aid, and subsequently whether notification is required, is the risk for the business concerned of a failure to notify as well as the risk for the granting authority (in terms of complaints, recovery and damages).

---

291 In Scotland, this action would be most likely to be brought in the Court of Session. However it is not impossible for such an action to be brought in the Sheriff Court.

The UK may also notify aid to the Commission on a conditional basis, where the government reserves its position as to whether the measure concerned constitutes State aid or not but notifies in order to obtain legal certainty.

2. State aid compliance by national judges and/or the national competition authority (NCA)

The Office of Fair Trading ("OFT") has produced advice and position papers on State aid rules and reform and has examined the risk posed to competition by subsidies. It has been active in monitoring implementation of aid, for example the OFT produced a report on Northern Rock in application of its market study powers in sections 5 to 7 of the Enterprise Act 2002. During the parliamentary debate of the Banking (Special Provisions) Bill 2008, which resulted in the temporary public ownership of Northern Rock, a commitment was made that the OFT would publish an annual report assessing any competitive implications of the public support for Northern Rock.

The competent courts for State aid cases are the High Court, for civil actions, and the Administrative Court, for judicial review of decisions by public authorities (e.g. grants, recovery orders)[292]. However, there is a relative lack of State aid cases before the courts, which makes it difficult to form conclusions concerning State aid compliance or otherwise by national judges.

It seems that the assessment of the existence of aid within the meaning of Article 107(1) TFEU can cause difficulties for the courts due to uncertainty as to the correct principles to apply. Different criteria have been suggested by the courts over the years, and it is unclear what the correct solution should be if such criteria produce conflicting results in different factual circumstances. As an example of the difficulties encountered and differing possible interpretations of the concept of State aid, in the *GIL Insurance* case[293] the European courts took a completely opposite view of the proper scope of the EU State aid provisions to that which had been adopted at each level of the English court system until the House of Lords. The English courts had classed the measure in question as a State aid because it met all the criteria laid down in the case law of the European courts, however what they had failed to do was consider the wider context and interpret the State aid rules against the constitutional background of the European treaties and the interaction with Member States' retained powers in the field of taxation. This case also highlighted the importance of preliminary rulings in the UK in the State aid field, by demonstrating the difference in reasoning between the UK courts and the European courts.

Compliance with Block exemption Regulations is ensured mainly by inter-departmental cooperation within the levels of government. Grants of aid measures covered by any Block exemption Regulations are kept on record and each private contract contains provisions which

---

292 In Scotland, the Court of session has exclusive jurisdiction for judicial review actions, see Chapter 58 of the Court of Session Rules.

293 Case C-308/01, GIL Insurance and Others v. Commissioners of Customs & Excise [2004] ECR 1-4777.

permit reduction or recovery of aid if thresholds in the overarching legislation have not been complied with.

III. Unlawful aid and judicial review

1. General powers of national courts concerning the direct effect of Article 108(3) TFEU

The main procedure available in the UK to deal with the direct effect of Article 108(3) TFEU is judicial review.

Judicial review lies against any person or body which performs public duties or public functions, such as the State and local authorities. A decision by a public authority in relation to State aid may be judicially reviewed by the High Court in England and Wales under Section 31 of the Supreme Court Act 1981 in accordance with Part 54 of the Civil Procedure Rules. In Scotland the power of judicial review of all administrative actions is held with the Court of Session. There are procedural differences with the law of England and Wales but the substantive law is the same, with this in mind the description below will focus on the procedure and terminology used in England and Wales. Decisions in each jurisdiction are regarded as persuasive in the other.

The principal remedies available in judicial review proceedings under Section 31[294] are the prerogative remedies of quashing orders, prohibiting orders and mandatory orders. Claimants may also seek, in addition to or instead of these, a declaration and/or injunctions.

As regards non-notification, a quashing order or a declaration would be the most appropriate remedy. A quashing order can be used to quash a decision already taken by a public authority to grant aid without Commission approval or before the Commission has reached a decision. However, claimants often seek a declaration that a measure adopted or proposed by a public authority is incompatible with EU law (as it has not been notified under Article 108(3) TFEU for example) as public bodies will act in accordance with such declarations without the need for a quashing order.

A claim for judicial review may only be brought with the permission of the High Court. An application for such permission must be made promptly and, in any event, within three months of the grounds for bringing the claim arising (there is no formal time limit in Scotland but delay can be raised as a defence). The application must state the remedy sought, the reasons for the claim and be accompanied by supporting evidence. If permission is granted, the matter will proceed to a substantive oral hearing, following submission of reply evidence by the defendant and any interested parties and detailed grounds by all parties.

294 See 58.4 Court of Session Rules for remedies available in Scotland.

2. Prevention of the granting of unlawful aid

Claimants can request a prohibiting order by way of judicial review which restrains a public authority from acting outside its powers, for example if it was proposing to grant aid which was incompatible or not notified. A claimant can also request an injunction to stop a public body from taking a particular action or decision.

In the proceedings in *Factortame II*, it was held that an interlocutory injunction could be granted, preventing a government minister from implementing legislation alleged to be contrary to Community law, pending final determination of the issue (by the European courts). The CJEU ruled that, where a national court is seized of a case involving issues of EU law and it is necessary to grant interim relief in order to ensure the full effectiveness of rights claimed under directly applicable EU law, any rule of national law preventing the grant of such interim relief must be set aside. The question of whether interim relief should be granted is a matter for the national courts.

There are no specific national provisions on which individuals can rely before national courts to ensure respect for the obligation of notification, but Article 108(3) TFEU is directly applicable and can be invoked by claimants as a basis for the duty to notify.

3. Recovery of unlawful aid and interest

National courts can declare that a measure constitutes State aid and that the government should recover that aid where it has not been notified on the sole basis that it has not been notified. There are no specific provisions in UK law governing the recovery of aid by national or regional authorities. If legal proceedings are undertaken in order to secure recovery of aid, this would be by action in the civil courts under the contract (if any) by which aid was granted, or alternatively (if there is no contract) by relying on the direct applicability of EU provisions on recovery of aid.

Where the Commission has issued a decision finding incompatible and illegal State aid and requiring recovery, the practice appears to be that the UK government will bring an action against the aid recipient in the High Court (if the beneficiary does not agree to repay the aid before judicial proceedings need to be launched). It would also be possible for competitors to seek a mandatory order from the courts, under the judicial review procedure outlined above, requiring the State to recover aid in accordance with a Commission decision.

We are only aware of one recovery case in the UK to date. It concerned aid granted by the UK government to British Aerospace to assist in the acquisition of Rover which exceeded the amount authorised by the Commission's decision in 1988. Proceedings were launched in the High Court by the UK to recover the excessive part of the aid following a negative Commission decision in 1990, but the proceedings were stayed pending challenge of that negative decision before the European Courts by British Aerospace and Rover[295]. Although the decision was annulled on procedural grounds, the Commission subsequently took another negative decision

---

295 Department of Trade and Industry v. British Aerospace plc and Rover Group Holding plc [1991] 1 CMLR 165.

following the correct procedure. Ultimately repayment was made (without continuance of the court action in the UK) of £44.4 million and £13.2 million in interest from 18 August 1990 to 23 May 1993. The interest was calculated at the usual rate governing State debts in the UK.

4. Damages claims by competitors/third parties before national courts against the granting authority

Competitors who consider themselves to have suffered economic damage as a result of the failure of the authorities to recover aid contrary to a decision of the Commission could bring an action for damages against the national authorities in the civil courts.

The *GIL Insurance*[296] litigation concerned a challenge to alleged aid and a claim for compensation through proceedings for the restitution of tax, where the aid consisted of a more favourable tax treatment granted to a competitor. It was argued that the remedy did not lie in retrospectively taxing the standard rate tax payers at the higher rate, but in declaring the higher rate to have been unlawful to the extent that it exceeded the standard rate and ordering repayment of the excess of the higher rate over the standard rate to competitors of the recipients of alleged aid. This question regarding the correct remedy to apply was referred to the European courts, who replied that the differential rates of tax did not actually constitute State aid and therefore no answer on remedies was given.

In *Banks v. Coal Authority*[297] the CJEU ruled in proceedings under the State aid provisions of the ECSC treaty that restitution was not an appropriate remedy. It stated that the remedy should not consist of an order exonerating the higher tax payer and effectively extending the aid, but rather should take the form of an order for recovery of the aid. In fact, the court stated that the higher rate taxpayer's remedy should lie in an action for damages against the State for having wrongfully granted the aid in accordance with the *Factortame* principles. Such an action was commenced as part of the GIL Insurance case but given the decision of the CJEU was not pursued.

5. Damages claims by the beneficiary before national courts against the granting authority

No cases have been found of this nature. However, it would be possible for a beneficiary to bring a damages claim against the State in the civil courts, in the same way as a competitor outlined above, or a beneficiary could bring a judicial review action and claim damages at the same time, if it could prove that it had suffered economic damage by the granting of unlawful aid.

---

296 GIL Insurance Ltd v. Commissioners of Customs and Excise [2001] Eu. L.R. 401 (VAT Tribunal), Case C-308/01, GIL Insurance Ltd v. Commissioners of Customs and Excise [2004] ECR I-4777.

297 Case C-390/98, [2001] ECR I-6117.

6. Damages claims by competitors/third parties before national courts against the beneficiary

At present there is no basis under UK law for a competitor to introduce a damages action against a beneficiary of unlawful aid.

In the one case of which we are aware which has dealt with this point, the claimant based its action on the existence of a Community law tort[298]. Following the *SFEI* case, the High Court rejected the view that there was a cause of action in EU law against the beneficiary and did not consider whether there could be an action for damages under UK tort law as this was outside the scope of the claim.

7. Interim measures taken by national judges

As far as we are aware, there are no examples of the courts granting interim measures to suspend the payment of aid. Under a judicial review procedure, the courts can grant either a prohibiting order or an injunction to prevent the grant/suspend the payment of alleged unlawful aid (if the action is brought in time). Injunctions can also be granted on an interlocutory basis during civil proceedings.

In the *British Aerospace and Rover* case the national court stayed recovery proceedings pending the outcome of an annulment action before the European courts.

IV. Control of recovery procedure

1. Challenging the validity of national recovery order

If a beneficiary wished to challenge a recovery order, they could resist the recovery action in the Courts (brought by the UK government) whilst bringing an annulment action against the underlying Commission decision in the European courts. The national courts would then be likely to stay the recovery proceedings pending the outcome of the annulment action (as in the *British Aerospace and Rover* case referred to above). However, a stay was not granted in the more recent case in the Republic of Ireland where an application by Ryanair for a stay of recovery proceedings brought by the Kingdom of Belgium pending challenge of the Commission decision by Ryanair was refused by the court (see the National Report for Ireland)[299] and the judge specifically declined to follow the judgment in British Aerospace and Rover.

298 Betws Anthracite Ltd v. DSK Anthrazit Ibbenburen GmbH [2003] EWHC 2403 (Comm) (G).

299 Kingdom of Belgium v. Ryanair Limited [2006] IEHC 213.

2. Damages for failure to implement a recovery decision and infringement of EU law

If competitors consider that they have suffered economic damage through the failure of national authorities to recover aid properly following a decision of the Commission, they can bring a damages action against such authorities in the civil courts. It may also be possible to request a court order (a mandatory order) via judicial review requiring the State to recover aid in accordance with the terms of the Commission decision and to include a request for damages.

V. Standing of third parties before national court

In order to bring a judicial review case (whether brought by a competitor or a beneficiary) the applicant must show that they have "sufficient interest" in the matter to which the claim relates (Section 31(3) of the Supreme Court Act 1981). In claims for judicial review the court's permission to proceed is required and therefore standing is considered by the courts at the permission stage, although it is only obvious cases that will be rejected for lack of sufficient interest at this stage, often the issue is actually considered at trial.

In the case where a right of appeal to the courts against an administrative or judicial decision is conferred by a statutory provision, the right may be confined to a "person aggrieved", or a person who claims to be or feels aggrieved, as was the case in Merger Action Group v. Secretary of State for Business Enterprise and Regulatory Reform[300], however, in that case the court held that the factors that informed the test as to standing would not be wholly different from the test of sufficient interest, despite the fact that the tests were phrased differently.

There is no specific test of standing to bring a damages claim in the High Court for competitors or beneficiaries. However, there must be a legal basis for the claim and the claimant must bring evidence to support its loss and damage (and causation) on the balance of probabilities.

VI. Cooperation with EU authorities

1. Cooperation with the CJEU

The UK courts have always been willing to seek preliminary rulings from the CJEU on points of interpretation of European law. More recently, the courts have become aware of the danger of "overburdening" the European courts with too many requests for preliminary rulings, which can delay the entire process making it less effective. However, this concern should not be taken too far as the GIL Insurance case emphasises the continued importance of such cooperation in the area of State aid.

---

300 [2008] CAT 36.

2. Cooperation with the Commission

It appears that little use has been made by the UK courts of the possibilities for cooperation with the Commission despite the fact that such assistance could be useful, particularly on the concept of State aid. It may be that the Commission is reluctant to express itself on specific cases or that in practice courts are not willing to seek help from an administrative body on issues of law.

VII. Trends – reforms – recommendations

Reviewing UK practice in State aid reveals few court cases on which to base an assessment of the understanding and treatment of the State aid rules by judges. Also, in most of the cases that have been brought in recent years, State aid principles are only employed as part of a whole range of arguments used to attack action taken by a public authority in an almost scattergun approach to achieving annulment of an administrative decision. In most of these cases, the State aid argument is not particularly strong and therefore fails to convince the court.

Likewise, there are few examples of competitors (or beneficiaries) seeking damages for loss suffered as a result of the grant of unlawful aid and there has only been one recovery action (as far as we are aware) in the UK courts to date.

One reason for the relative scarcity of cases may be the importance placed on compliance with the State aid rules by the UK government. The UK has traditionally followed non-interventionist market-orientated politics but there are many cases of aid being granted. It is simply the case that the government ensures, where necessary, that aid is notified to and approved by the Commission.

This high level of compliance evidently reduces the opportunities for direct challenge (at least on the basis of Article 108(3) TFEU) of State aid measures and perhaps discourages competitors from claiming damages and thereby necessarily implicitly challenging the Commission's approval decision. There is a high level of inter-departmental cooperation within the government at the different levels with responsibility for State aid and emphasis is placed on educating authorities about the State aid rules and updating this education as and when the rules are changed. For example, BIS produces a publication called "*The State aid Guide*", which is aimed at practitioners and is currently being updated following the swathe of regulations and guidance adopted by the Commission during the financial crisis.

The financial crisis has, so far, only produced one case raising State aid issues before national courts[301]. This was not a typical State aid case, concerning as it did a challenge to a decision not to refer a merger to the relevant national competition authority for further assessment. Interestingly, the applicants (who were third parties and not competitors) were granted standing to challenge the decision under the applicable statutory test and they claimed, *inter alia*, that the decision was tainted by an error of law in its adoption of misguided statements on

301 Merger Action Group v. Secretary of State for Business, Enterprise and Regulatory Reform [2008] CAT 36.

the effect of State aid on the competitive position of a business. Essentially, they considered that HBOS should have received State aid rather than being taken over by Lloyds TSB and therefore were trying to obstruct the merger. However, due in part to the confines of administrative law the judge rejected the appeal without needing to decide firmly on the State aid aspects.

The judicial review procedure may also be in part responsible for the lack of claims as it sets a short time limit to bring claims, requires claimants to seek permission at a preliminary stage and has a circumscribed legal remit, all of which can serve to discourage applicants. However, the courts have shown themselves to be confident and keen to deal with the specifics of State aid law when the occasion arises. We can hope that it may arise more often in the future in the interests of development of UK State aid jurisprudence.